European Integration

Athina Zervoyianni, George Argiros
and George Agiomirgianakis

First published 2006 by
PALGRAVE MACMILLAN
Houndmills, Basingstoke, Hampshire RG21 6XS and
175 Fifth Avenue, New York, N.Y. 10010
Companies and representatives throughout the world

PALGRAVE MACMILLAN is the global academic imprint of the Palgrave
Macmillan division of St. Martin's Press, LLC and of Palgrave Macmillan Ltd.
Macmillan® is a registered trademark in the United States, United Kingdom
and other countries. Palgrave is a registered trademark in the European
Union and other countries.

ISBN-13: 978–0–333–77218–8
ISBN-10: 0–333–77218–0

This book is printed on paper suitable for recycling and made from fully
managed and sustained forest sources.

A catalogue record for this book is available from the British Library.

Library of Congress Cataloging-in-Publication Data
Zervoyianni, Athina.
European integration / Athina Zervoyianni, George Argiros, and
    George Agiomirgianakis.
        p.   cm.
   Includes bibliographical references and index.
    ISBN 0–333–77218–0 (pbk.)
    1. Monetary unions–Europe.   2. Europe–Economic integration.
    3. Monetary policy–Europe.   I. Argiros, George.   II. Agiomirgianakis,
    George M.   III. Title.
    HG925.Z47 2004
    337.1′42–dc22   2003067267

10   9   8   7   6   5   4   3   2   1
15   14   13   12   11   10   09   08   07   06

Printed and bound in China

Contents

Acknowledgements

The authors and publishers are grateful to the following for permission to reproduce copyright material in this book:

Ashgate Publishing for a table from P. Raines and R. Brown, *Policy Competition and Foreign Direct Investment in Europe* (1999).

Federal Reserve Bank of St Louis for a table from P. Pollard, 'Low Wages and Foreign Investment', *Federal Reserve Bank of St Louis National Economic Trends* (October 1996).

Blackwell Publishing for a table from R. Barrell and N. Pain, 'Foreign Direct Investment, Technological Change and Economic Growth within Europe', *Economic Journal*, 107 (1997).

Elsevier for a table from R. Barrell and N. Pain, 'Domestic Institutions, Agglomerations and Foreign Direct Investment in Europe', *European Economic Review*, vol. 43 (1999), and two tables from J. Hatzins, 'FDI and Relative Unit Labour Costs (ULC): UK' and 'FDI and Relative Labour Costs: Germany', *European Economic Review*, vol. 44 (2000).

Every effort has been made to contact all the copyright-holders, but if any have been inadvertently omitted the publishers will be pleased to make the necessary arrangement at the earliest opportunity.

The European Union: Evolution, Institutional and Legislative Structure and Enlargement

George Argiros and Athina Zervoyianni

Introduction

On 1 January 2002, the euro became the common currency for the 12 EU states participating in the eurozone; and on 1 May 2004 ten more countries joined the EU increasing the number of member states from 15 to 25. Whatever the success of these developments, it is certain that European integration has entered a new era.

Indeed, although the integration of Europe was proposed as early as in the fourteenth century, it was the post-Second World War era that saw serious and comprehensive attempts to integrate Europe. The result of these attempts was the establishment of the European Coal and Steel Community (ECSC), which was to be the first stone in the foundation of a united Europe. The approach to integration was sectoral, based on the functional ideology that common problems needed common solutions. The ECSC was followed by the establishment of two other Communities, the European Economic Community and Euratom. The European Economic Community pursued general economic integration through the setting up of a common market, while Euratom was devoted to sectoral matters.

The first major amendment to the founding Treaties was the Single European Act, whose main aim was the establishment of the single European market. Later, the Treaty of Maastricht created the European Union with broad economic, political and social objectives.

However, European integration is a multi-layered and dynamic project: the most ambitious enlargement ever became a reality in April 2003 when Cyprus, the Czech Republic, Estonia, Hungary, Latvia, Lithuania, Malta, Poland, Slovakia and Slovenia signed accession agreements. The dynamic character of European integration inspires all aspects of its functioning, and at the same time creates some uncertainty regarding the future. There is no doubt that the international economic and political environment is quite different since the conclusion of the founding treaties. Until today the European Community has shown a high degree of adjustability to changes in the international environment, but the EU is growing ever more complex and its multiple functions, powers and identities are reflected in its increasingly diverse and labyrinthine institutional configuration and legislation. It would be unrealistic at the moment to argue for a comprehensive and monolithic constitutional structure to cover the whole functioning of the EU. Nevertheless, given the magnitude of its powers and tasks, it would be appropriate to accept a number of comprehensive constitutional norms enforceable at all levels and in all aspects of the EU's multiple policy-making and law-making processes. At the same time, it is questionable whether the present structure of, and approach to, European integration are sufficient to give answers to the new emerging needs. The time may be ripe to initiate a comprehensive debate about the future of European integration.

In the next section we examine the development of the Community from the early 1950s until today. We then consider its institutions and organizational structure, before focusing on its legislation and law-making processes. Finally, the enlargement of the EU to incorporate 10 more countries and the associated implications and challenges are discussed.

Historical Background: A Path of Increasing Economic Links

The European Coal and Steel Community and the European Defence Community

The first attempt towards integration in Europe took the form of the Schuman Plan. In May 1950, Robert Schuman, then Minister of Foreign Affairs in France, made a proposal for the integration of the coal and steel industries of France and Germany. This proposal, known as the 'Schuman Plan', had been elaborated by Jean Monnet, one of the most active integrationists of the time. The Schuman Plan, while conceived mainly as a French–German scheme, was open to any country wishing to participate. Indeed, the Plan was favourably received in France, Germany, Italy and the Benelux countries – that is, Belgium, the Netherlands and Luxembourg. On 18 April 1951 in Paris these six countries signed a treaty establishing the European Coal and Steel Community (ECSC) that came into force in July of the following year.[1,2]

The ECSC was founded upon a common market, common objectives and common institutions (Article 1 ECSC). Indeed, at the time, the establishment of a common market for the coal and steel industries seemed rational for both economic and political reasons. On the one hand, greater efficiency would be gained in this important part of the economy through economies of scale. On the other hand, as the member states' coal-making industries would be put under common control, war between France and Germany would be made impossible.

The 'transfer' of legislative and administrative powers in the area of coal and steel from the six member states to the ECSC differentiated the character of this Community from other traditional international organizations based on intergovernmental decision-making. In particular, the Paris Treaty established four autonomous and independent institutions for administering, controlling and supervising the development and operation of the member states' coal and steel industries. These institutions were: (a) the High Authority, (b) the Council, (c) the Assembly and (d) the Court of Justice. The High Authority (equivalent to the European Commission of today) was the leading institution for the implementation of the Treaty. It was empowered, in particular, to take legally binding decisions, and it also had the authority to procure funds, to fix minimum and maximum prices for certain products, and to fine firms when a breach of the competition rules of ECSC was discovered (Articles 14, 49, 61 and 64–5 ECSC). The Council of Ministers consisted of representatives of government of the member states. Its task was to harmonize the actions of the High Authority with those of national governments, which were responsible for the general economic policies of their countries (Article 26 ECSC). The Assembly was composed of representatives of national parliaments and was confined to having merely an advisory role in matters relating to the production and consumption of coal and steel. On the other hand, the Court of Justice had the competence to adjudicate on disputes concerning the activities of the ECSC.

As the Community approach to European integration was gaining momentum, a French initiative, known as the 'Pleven Plan', for establishing a European Defence Community was put on the table. The main goal of this plan was to put defence matters under common control and thus create a framework for German rearmament, something that had the strong support of the United States because of the Soviet threat. Negotiations progressed and a treaty establishing the European Defence Community (EDC) was signed on 27 May 1952 by France, Germany, Italy and the Benelux countries. The EDC aimed to create a unified European Army to be put under the control of the EDC institutions, which would result in putting under common control member states' foreign policies as well. However, defence matters and foreign policy were more sensitive areas for member states than coal and steel. Thus the treaty establishing the EDC failed to be ratified by the French parliament.

The EEC and Euratom

While the rejection of the European Defence Community by the French was a setback, the determination to integrate Europe was not lost. The integrationists merely became less ambitious, focusing their efforts on economic relations and relegating political integration to a more distant future.

In particular, proposals for a broadly based economic integration were advanced by the Benelux countries. The Messina Conference of 1955, which was attended by the foreign ministers of all the ECSC countries, was to be the forum for initial discussions on these matters. Indeed, two objectives were agreed: that of establishing a European common market; and that of developing atomic energy for peaceful purposes. An intergovernmental committee, chaired by the Belgian Foreign Minister P.H. Spaak, was set up and entrusted with the task of making proposals to this end. The United Kingdom failed to participate, although it was invited.[3] The Spaak Report was published in April 1956, and, in the light of its conclusions the six ECSC states started negotiations on the content of two new treaties. The treaties were finally signed in Rome on 25 March 1957, and established two further communities: the European Economic Community (EEC), and the European Atomic Energy Community (Euratom). These came into force on 1 January 1958.

The Rome treaties extended the area of joint action and increased the necessity of taking collective measures. The Euratom Treaty turned out to be of relatively small significance: many of the core activities of civilian nuclear powers failed to be passed out of the hands of the member states and into the hands of Community institutions.[4] The EEC Treaty was by far the most significant development in European integration, having much broader scope than both the Euratom and the ECSC Treaties. Indeed, the Preamble to the EEC Treaty states a determination to lay the foundations of an ever-closer union among the people of Europe and stipulates that 'The Community's task will be to promote a harmonious development of economic activities, a continuous and balanced expansion, an increase in stability and accelerated raising of the standard of living and closer relations between the states belonging to it.'

Two principal means for achieving this were proposed by the EEC Treaty: the creation of a common market; and the progressive approximation of the member states' economic policies (Article 2 EEC). The creation of a common market involved the elimination of trade barriers to the free movement of goods and services as well as the abolition of obstacles to the free movement of persons, services and capital between member states (Article 3 EEC). At the same time, the erection of a common custom-tariff regime *vis-à-vis* third countries and the creation of a system to prevent competition from being distorted were required. In addition, for the proper functioning of the common market, the laws of the member states had to be harmonized. Finally, common policy-making in the spheres of agriculture, social affairs, transport and economic relations towards third countries were envisaged.

The EEC Treaty and the Euratom Treaty also created a set of supranational institutions having legislative and administrative powers to handle their affairs. These were the Council, the Commission, the Assembly, and the Court of Justice. This institutional structure of the Rome treaties was different from that of the ECSC Treaty. In the context of the Rome treaties, the Commission principally had executive powers and was responsible only for initiating decision-making, while decision-making power was concentrated in the hands of the Council. The reason for this difference between the ECSC Treaty and the Rome treaties was that the former provided for most arrangements for the supranational governance of the coal and steel sectors in a considerably detailed fashion. By contrast, the EEC Treaty, with the exception of the provisions concerning the creation of a customs union, established only a framework for common action, leaving fundamental political and economic choices to be made by the Community institutions. It was thus inevitable that the final say on such choices would be left to the Council, the institution in which member states were directly represented.

In 1965, a treaty known as the Merger Treaty was signed, establishing a single set of institutions operating for all Communities. This came into force in July 1967. Thus, after 1967, all three European Communities were served by a single Council (Articles 145 EC, 26 ECSC, 115 Euratom), a single Commission (Articles 155 EC, 8 ECSC, 124 Euratom), a single Assembly (now European Parliament, Articles 137 EC, 20 ECSC, 107 Euratom) and a single Court of Justice (Articles 164 EC, 31 ECSC, 136 Euratom). At the same time, additional institutions were added to the original ones, including the European Council and the Court of Auditors.

The Growth of the Community

By the early 1960s the Community project seemed to be well on the way to being judged a success: the integration of product markets, together with the generally healthy global environment, had created wealth through economies of scale and improved competitiveness. This early success of the Community project posed serious questions for the elite of those states that had decided to remain outside the Community. Thus, as a response to the Rome treaties, Austria, Denmark, Norway, Sweden, Switzerland, Portugal and the United Kingdom decided to create a European Free Trade Area (EFTA) by signing the Stockholm Convention on 4 January 1960.

Soon, however, some of the EFTA countries, and in particular the United Kingdom, felt that the European Free Trade Area association was an inadequate forum for achieving their economic and political ambitions. The Community was by far a much more successful and ambitious project than the EFTA, and the governing elite of the United Kingdom decided to reconsider the merits of membership in the Community. Indeed, two consecutive governments, one Conservative headed by Macmillan and one Labour headed by Wilson, applied for membership, but their applications met the strong opposition of President de Gaulle of France and were thus forwarded together with the applications of Denmark, Ireland and Norway. These four countries had to wait until the succession of President De Gaulle by George Pompidou to the Presidency of France for negotiations to be formally opened on 30 June 1970. Finally, a Treaty of Accession was signed on 22 January 1972, which came into force on 1 January 1973, and the United Kingdom[5], Ireland and Denmark became members of the three Communities. Norway's application was withdrawn following an adverse referendum result on the issue of membership.

The 'northern enlargement' was followed by a 'southern enlargement'. Greece became the tenth member state on 1 January 1981, and, after long and difficult negotiations, Spain and Portugal joined the Communities on 1 January 1986. [6,7] The momentum was maintained and the attraction of the Community to other European states was sufficiently strong to induce them to start negotiations for membership. Austria, Sweden and Finland became full members at the start of 1995, raising the total membership to fifteen.[8] And in April 2003, 10 more countries, Cyprus, Malta, the Czech Republic, Hungary, Slovakia, Slovenia, Poland, Estonia, Latvia and Lithuania, signed accession agreements and formally became member on 1 May 2004.[9]

The Single European Act

The Single European Act (SEA) was signed on 17 February 1986 and came into force on 1 July 1987. It represented the most important revision of the treaties since they were adopted,[10] bringing about changes and reforms to the Community by adjusting its institutional structure and expanding its competence. One of the principal objectives of the SEA was to ensure the completion of the European internal market. Indeed, Article 8a of the Act inserted into the Rome Treaty a commitment 'to adopt measures with the aim of progressively establishing the internal market over a period expiring on 31 December 1992'. This placed on a formal footing the Commission's White Paper for the completion of the internal market.[1]

The internal market project required significant legislative activity by the Community. To facilitate the passage of legislation, the Act introduced into several areas qualified majority-voting by the Council instead of unanimity. In addition, a new legislative procedure, the so called 'co-operation procedure', was set up and introduced into various areas of decision-making. This procedure enhanced the powers of the European Parliament in the legislative process. Another institutional change was the creation of the Court of First Instance to assist the Court of Justice.

The Act also introduced new areas of Community competence, some of which had already been asserted by the institutions and supported by the Court but had not been expressly contained in the founding treaties. The new titles inserted into the Rome Treaty were: Economic and Social Cohesion (Article 130a–e EEC) aiming at reducing disparities between the various regions of the Community; Social Policy; Health and Safety at Work; Research and Technological Development (Article 130f–q EEC); and Environmental Policy (Article 130r-130t EEC). The Single European Act also introduced into the Rome Treaty the first formal reference to 'co-operation in economic and monetary policy' and to the European Monetary System (EMS) which had been in operation since 1979. In addition, foreign policy cooperation was brought more closely into the mainstream and given a stronger support structure, although the philosophy of the SEA was to keep it strictly separate from the institutional and decision-making system of the European Communities.

The Treaty on European Union

The momentum for negotiations generated by the Single European Act continued abate after its adoption. In June 1988, a committee chaired by the President of the Commission, Jacques Delors, was set up to examine the feasibility of establishing an Economic and Monetary Union in Europe. Following its report in 1989, the European Council decided to hold an intergovernmental conference on the subject, and to hold at the same time another intergovernmental conference on 'political union'. The necessity of holding the latter was derived from the collapse of communism in Eastern Europe and the new role that the Community was expected to play in international affairs after the cold war.

Intergovernmental conference negotiations were formally opened in Rome on 15 December 1990, and on the basis of these negotiations a draft Treaty was presented by the Luxembourg Presidency to the European Council in 1991. A revised version of the draft was agreed by the Heads of State or government at the Maastricht meeting in December 1991, and the Treaty on European Union (EU) was signed, again in Maastricht, on 7 February 1992. The EU Treaty came into force on 1 November 1993.

The Treaty on European Union comprises seven titles, with articles identified by capital letters to avoid confusion with the numbering of the founding treaties. Title I sets out various broad objectives in the so-called 'common provisions'. Titles II, III and IV list the amendments to the EEC, ECSC and Euratom Treaties respectively. These are referred to in the Maastricht Treaty as the 'first pillar'. [12] Title V contains provisions relating to a Common Foreign and Security Policy. This constitutes the 'second pillar'. Title VI covers the 'third pillar' of Justice and Home Affairs, that is police cooperation, reducing drug trafficking and fraud, regulating immigration from third countries, and so on. And Title VII contains the Treaty's 'final provisions'. In addition to these seven titles, there are 17 Protocols, which mainly develop or explain the provisions of the Treaty, and 33 Declarations.

The EU Treaty enters three distinct spheres of competence: (a) the European Communities, (b) the Common Foreign and Security Policies, and (c) cooperation in the fields of Justice and Home Affairs. The Union is thus wider than the European Community, although it is founded upon it.[13] Indeed, after Maastricht, there are four Treaties: the Treaty on European Union, the European Community Treaty, the European Coal and Steel Treaty and the European Atomic Energy Treaty.[14] Unifying factors consist of common objectives, common principles, a single institutional framework and certain common procedures.

With regard to the aims of the European Union, Article B of the EU Treaty stipulates that the Union will set itself the following objectives (see European Commission (1992)):

- To promote balanced and sustainable economic and social progress, in particular through the creation of an area without internal frontiers, through the strengthening of economic and social cohesion and through the establishment of economic and monetary union.
- To assert its identity on the international scene through the implementation of a common foreign and security policy including the

eventual forming of a common defence policy which
lead to a common defence.

- To strengthen and protect the rights and interests c
  states' nationals through the introduction of a citizenship of the
  Union.
- To develop close cooperation on justice and home affairs.
- To maintain in full the *acquis communautaire* and build on it with
  a view to considering to what extent the policies and forms of
  cooperation introduced by the Treaty may need to be revised so as
  to ensure the effectiveness of the mechanisms and the institutions
  of the Community.

Article G of the EU Treaty introduces several amendments to the EEC
Treaty. For example, it formally accepts the name of the 'European
Community' (EC). This has symbolic rather than substantive value,
but it signals the increased interest of the Community in matters
that do not belong to the economic domain. However, central to the
changes made by Article G of the EU Treaty to the EEC Treaty is the
creation of an Economic and Monetary Union. The broad purpose of
this objective is set out in Article 3A EC. According to this Article:

- The activities of the member states and the Community will
  include the adoption of an economic policy which will be based
  on the close coordination of member states' economic policies, on
  the internal market and on the definition of common objectives,
  and conducted in accordance with the principle of an open market
  economy with free competition.
- These activities will include the irrevocable fixing of exchange rates
  leading to the introduction of a single currency and conduct of a
  single monetary- and exchange-rate policy, the primary objective
  of which will be to maintain price stability and, without preju-
  dice to this objective, support the general economic policies in the
  Community.
- The activities of the member states and the Community will
  comply with the principles of: stable prices, sound public finances
  and sustainable balance of payments.

A strict timetable for the attainment of EMU in three stages with provi-
sion for a European Monetary Institute and subsequently a European
Central Bank is established by the new objectives. The EU Treaty
has also added new areas of Community competence, including:
culture, public health, consumer protection, trans-European networks,
and industry and development cooperation. At the same time, it
has expanded existing areas such as environmental protection and
economic and social cohesion. In addition, the concept of 'European

citizenship' (conferred on nationals of member states) has been introduced, a Parliamentary Ombudsman has been established, and the
principle of subsidiarity has been made formal as an attempt to
address the question of allocation of responsibility between different
levels of administration in the Community. Under the EU Treaty,
the Community's legislation procedures are also adjusted once again,
increasing Parliament's power and influence.

The Treaty of Amsterdam

The second paragraph of Article N of the EU Treaty stipulates that:

> a conference of representatives of the governments of the Member
> States shall be conveyed in 1996 to examine those provisions of
> this Treaty for which revision is provided in accordance with the
> objectives set out in Articles A and B.

Indeed, an intergovernmental conference (IGC) opened its work in
Turin[15] on 29 March 1996, with topics reserved for consideration
including:

- revision of the tripartite structure of the TEU;
- extension of the co-decision procedure;
- amendment of the common foreign and security policy and
  defence provisions; and
- extension of Community competence to energy, civil protection
  and tourism.

Serious preparations for the IGC only began at the Corfu European
Council in 1994 where a reflection group was set up. The report of the
group was submitted to the Madrid European Council in December
1995,[16] and it was accepted as the basis for the March 1996 IGC. The
report stated that the IGC should be based on three broad themes:

- making Europe more relevant to its citizens;
- enabling the Union to work better and preparing it for enlargement; and
- giving the Union greater capacity for external action.

A first draft revision of the Treaty was presented by the Irish Presidency
at the European Council Meeting in Dublin. Although the draft was to
be amended considerably during the Dutch Presidency that followed,
it provided the blueprint for the Treaty of Amsterdam that was agreed
on 17 June 1997 and finally signed on 2 October 1997.

Two significant changes were made by the Treaty of Amsterdam
to the EU Treaty. First, a new 'Title on Employment' was added to

the EU Treaty giving powers to Community institutions to coordinate national employment policies.[17] Second, a new 'Title on Visas, Immigration and other Policies' related to free movement of persons was introduced in the EC Treaty with the aim of establishing an area of freedom, security and justice. In this Title there was a shift of competencies from the third pillar to the first pillar of the European Union Treaty.

In addition to the acquisition of the new competencies, the powers of the European Parliament were enhanced by shifting a number of Community competencies to legislative procedures in which the European Parliament had increased powers. Also, the number of areas where qualified majority voting in the Council was taking place had been extended and provision were made for allowing some member states to integrate at a faster rate when others did not wish to (the so called 'flexibility provisions').

The Treaty of Nice

After the conclusion of an intergovernmental conference for revising the treaties, the Treaty of Nice was signed on 26 February 2001. However, this Treaty was received with dissatisfaction[18] because of the limited number of reforms that had been decided. The most important changes were in the areas of voting in Council, cooperation, judicial reforms and the composition of the EU Institutions. Institutional changes were considered necessary for the accession of new member states.

A declaration by the member states on the future of the EU was appended to the Treaty of Nice, according to which the European Council had to improve the democratic nature and the efficiency of the process that would produce treaty reforms in 2004. In discussing amendments to the treaties, major themes such as the division of powers, democratic legitimacy and transparency, were to be addressed.

Because of the importance of the questions raised about the future of European integration, national governments agreed to change the Treaties' reform process. Throughout the 1980s and the 1990s the reform process was dominated by national governments, with reform measures decided upon at intergovernmental conferences. In an attempt to widen the discussion about fundamental reforms in the Treaties, the EU Heads of State agreed to establish a 'Convention' consisting of representatives of national governments, representatives of the European Parliament and of national Parliaments and the Commission. Chairman of the Convention was agreed to be Valéry Giscard d' Estaing. The Convention, called *Convention on the Future of Europe*, held its inaugural plenary session on 28 February 2002 and was called to end its works in spring 2003 so that decisions would take place at the Rome Summit of December 2003. The Convention finished its works on time, in spring 2003, and presented a *Draft Constitutional Treaty*. The EU Heads of State failed to reach agreement on some of the elements of this draft Treaty at the Rome Summit of 13 December 2003. Negotiations followed and finally the *Constitutional Treaty* was signed on 29 October 2004 (see Smits (2005) for an assessment). The Treaty has to be ratified by all the member states, and it was expected to be in force from November 2006 onwards. However this may be delayed because of the negative results of the 2005 French and Dutch referenda.

EU Institutions and Organizational Structure of the European Union

According to Article 7 of the EC Treaty as amended by the Treaty of Nice, the tasks entrusted to the Community are to be carried out by five main institutions: the Council, the Commission, the European Parliament, the Court of Justice and the Court of Auditors. Besides these institutions there are two other bodies that assist the Council and the Commission by giving advisory opinions; these are the Economic and Social Committee and the Committee of the Regions. The other important body, the European Central Bank is currently playing a central role in the EMU.

The Council of Ministers (Articles 202-210 EC)

Composition. The Council consists of member states' representatives who are authorized to commit national governments to decisions. Council members must thus be persons holding political office, that is ministers and not civil servants. The ministers attending the Council vary depending on the subject matter being discussed. In particular, the various Specialist Councils are attended by ministers dealing with the matters in the agenda; for example finance ministers attend the Finance Council, transport ministers attend the Transport Council, agriculture ministers attend the Agriculture Council, health ministers the Health Council, and so forth. Above all these Councils sits the General Affairs Council, consisting of foreign ministers, which has an overarching competence considering matters not claimed as their own by one of the specialist Councils.[19]

The Council meets when convened by its President on his own initiative or at the request of one of its members or of the Commission. The presidency of the Council is held in turn by the member states for a six-month period. As for the presidency's duties, these include, besides taking the Chair at Council meetings, the arrangement of meetings and the setting of provisional agendas. Such agendas must be circulated by the President to the other members of the Council at least a fortnight in advance and must contain an indication of the items on which a vote may be taken. In general, the presidency may develop policy initiatives within fields that are of particular concern either to the Council as a whole or to the member state that currently holds the presidency. Indeed, in recent years a rivalry has developed between presidencies regarding their 'productivity record', and this has undoubtedly resulted in the adoption by the Community of many policy measures. However, the six-month session is a rather short period to ensure adequate coordination and therefore much depends on the work of the Secretary General and the staff of the General Secretariat.

Another task of the presidency is to coordinate the work of the different Specialist Councils. The President of the Council also has an important liaison role to play with the President of the European Parliament and the President of the Commission. Moreover, the presidency represents the Community externally.

The Committee of Permanent Representatives. The work of the Council is prepared by the Committee of Permanent Representatives which is known by its French acronym, COREPER, and its members are senior national officials based in Brussels. This Committee in fact operates at two levels: COREPER I and COREPER II. COREPER I comprises deputy permanent representatives and is responsible for technical matters, such as internal-market legislation, transport, environment and so on. COREPER II consists of permanent representatives of ambassadorial rank and deals with issues more political in nature, such as, for example, external relations, and economic and financial affairs.

COREPER can set up working groups made up of national officials for doing the preparatory work. These working groups examine the Commission's proposals and prepare a report which indicates the areas where agreement has been reached (Part A), and all the other areas (Part B). COREPER usually accepts all areas that have been agreed upon by the working group, focusing the debate on those issues where agreement has not been reached, that is those in Part B. Council agendas are then divided into Part A and Part B. Items listed in Part A are those that COREPER has agreed, and may be adopted by the Council without discussion unless a member state raises an objection at the Council, in which case the item is referred back to COREPER for further discussion before reappearing on the Council's agenda. Part B covers items where further discussion is needed. In this case there are also highlights of the points of disagreement in COREPER.

Voting. There are three systems of voting in the Council: simple majority, qualified majority and unanimity. In the simple majority case, each member state has one vote (Article 205(2)); however, there are only very few cases where a Council decision is taken by simple majority.

In the qualified majority case, the principle of equality of states is departed from and the more populous states are given more votes than the less populous ones (Article 205 (2)).[20] In particular, before the recent enlargement a total of 87 votes were allocated to the 15 member states in such a way so as to correspond very roughly to differences in population size.[21] The distribution of votes was as follows: Germany, France, Italy and the UK 10 votes each; Spain 8 votes; Belgium, Greece, the Netherlands and Portugal 5 votes each; Austria and Sweden 4 votes each; Denmark, Ireland and Finland 3 votes each; and Luxembourg 2 votes. A qualified majority consisted of 62 votes out of 87. It was thus taking 25 votes to form a blocking minority, a minimum of three states.[22] And it was taking a minimum of eight states to achieve the required 62 votes for a qualified majority. This meant that a measure supported by governments representing a substantial majority of the Community's population could in principle be adopted. However, where the Council was to act without a proposal from the Commission, a qualified majority decision also required the *positive* votes of at least 10 member states. Moreover, to obtain a qualified majority, 62 positive votes were needed, in the sense that any purported abstentions were considered as contributing to the minority block. This qualified-majority system has recently been extended to an increasing number of areas, including the internal market, the environment, consumers and the free movement of workers and capital, among other.

As far as unanimity is concerned, the EC Treaty required the Council to act by unanimity in the following areas:

- In a number of matters of a constitutional nature. For example: acceptance of a new member state; managing the Community's own resources; concluding association agreements with other states or agreements on a subject where any internal rule would have to be adopted by unanimity under the Treaty; amendments to the Statute of the European System of Central Banks; and agreements regarding the conversion rates at which the euro would substitute for the national currencies.
- In some politically sensitive issues. For example indirect taxation; state aids in exceptional circumstances; and taking measures necessary for attaining one of the objectives of the Community under the general power provided by Article 308 (ex Article 235 EC).

- In some procedural decisions. For example, to hold certain Council meetings in public; and to include items in the Council agenda other than those included in the provisional agenda.

Where the Treaty provided for the Council to act by unanimity, abstentions by member states did not prevent the act in question from being adopted.

The powers of the Council. The Council plays a central role in the creation of law in the internal-Community sphere. The principal manifestation of this resides in the fact that the Council will have to give its approval to any legislative initiatives that emanate from the Commission before they become laws. The Council can also present legislative proposals [23] and can trigger policy initiatives through the use of resolutions and opinion. In addition, it can delegate legislative powers to the Commission and has coordinating powers in the sphere of the general economic policies of member states. These latter powers have taken on new importance since the establishment of Economic and Monetary Union. The Council can in fact undertake unilateral surveillance of the economic policies and performances of member states; and is empowered to intervene to prevent a member state from running excessive government deficits. It also has a coordinating role in policy areas where responsibility lies with member states, such as foreign and security policy, justice and home affairs.

Another area in which the Council has important powers is that of external relations: Council authorization is required if the Commission is to open negotiations with third countries, and it is the Council that takes the decision to conclude agreements.

The European Council. The European Council was not part of the institutional structure envisaged by the EEC Treaty. It has evolved during the last 30 years following the decision taken by Community leaders at the Paris Summit of December 1974 to hold regular meetings at the highest level within a 'European Council'. The first European Council meeting was held in Dublin on 10–11 March 1975, but its position was formalized a few years later by the Single European Act. Indeed, according to Article 2 of the SEA, the European Council 'brings together the Heads of State or Government of the Member States and the Commission's President who are assisted by the Ministers of Foreign Affairs and a member of the Commission'. The meetings are chaired by the head of state or government of the member state that holds the presidency of the Council. The European Council meets at least twice a year. The strong intergovernmental nature of this institution is reflected in the preparation for the meetings that are organized jointly by the national foreign ministries and the Council Secretariat.

The role of the European Council has also evolved rather than being established formally by the Community treaties. Its role is in fact a political one, which is confirmed by Article 4 of the Treaty on European Union which states, in its first paragraph, that 'the European Council shall provide the Union with the necessary impetus for its development and shall define the general political guidelines thereof'. The type of issues that are currently considered by the European Council can be grouped into six categories:

- the development of the Community
- constitutional aspects affecting the operation of the Community
- the state of the European economy as a whole
- initiation or development of particular policy strategies
- conflict resolution, external relations and new accessions to the Community
- common foreign and security policy

The Commission (Articles 211-219 EC)

Composition. The Commission is a collegiate body. Before the May 2004 enlargement it consisted of 20 members with each member state having one Commissioner except for the larger member states – France, Germany, Italy, Spain and the United Kingdom – which had two Commissioners each. The number of Commissioners had increasingly being seen as too large and as threatening the discipline and coherence of the Commission, and there was intense discussion in the European Council to find a solution to this problem before the May 2004 enlargement.[24]

Commissioners must have general competence and ought to be persons whose independence is beyond doubt. In particular, they are charged not to take instructions from governments or any other bodies, and the member states have undertaken to respect that principle and not to seek to influence the Commissioners in the performance of their tasks. In addition, Commissioners must not find themselves in a position where a conflict of interests arises. Therefore they must not engage in any other occupation during their period of office. The EU Treaty provides for a new procedure for the appointment of Commissioners, giving the European Parliament a greater role (Article 214 EC). Under this procedure, the governments of member states, after consulting the European Parliament, nominate by common accord the person they intend to appoint as President of the Commission. In consultation with the proposed President, they then nominate those they intend to appoint as members of the Commission. After that, the President and members of the Commission are subject as a body to a vote of approval by the European Parliament. Following a debate, Parliament votes its approval or disapproval by a simple majority of votes cast.[25] If approved by Parliament, the President and members of the Commission are appointed by common accord of the member states' governments.

Commissioners are appointed for five years but this may be renewed once. As a body, the Commission is accountable to the European Parliament, which can, by a motion of censure, dismiss it. When a new Commission comes into office, the President who provides political guidance to the Commission allocates portfolios to the Commissioners giving them responsibility for one (or more) major Community policy area. There is a considerable difference in the prestige attached to the different portfolios, with the result that considerable bargaining takes place for the most prestigious portfolios. Indeed, in addition to the prospective Commissioners, member states themselves engage in considerable manoeuvring in order to have their own nationals in portfolios of importance to them.

Commissioners are assisted by personal staff (cabinet) under the chief of cabinet, and by a staff of permanent Community officials who are organized into Directorates General corresponding to the major different areas of Community policy. The President of the Commission chairs its meeting. He also has a seat by right at the European Council and attends the annual international summits of the Group of Seven (that is, the seven leading industrial countries). In addition, he presents the annual legislative programme of the Commission to the European Parliament and replies to the debate on this programme. In general the President plays an important role in shaping the overall policy of the Commission and in developing major ideas for the future direction of the Community.

The powers of the Commission. The Commission plays a complex role in the Community system, an important aspect of which is that it is nearly always required to initiate the legislative process in making a proposal.[26] The Council is usually able to exercise its legislative powers only in relation to a text that has been formulated by the Commission.[27] In this sense, although it is true that major political initiatives within the Community may also be triggered by the European Council, the right of the Commission to put forward proposals for Community Acts places it in the forefront of policy development.[28] Indeed, the European integration process is largely dependent on the activity of the Commission and the quality of its work, and the most celebrated example of this has been the Commission's White Paper on the Completion of the Internal Market.[29]

Apart from participating in the shaping of measures taken by the Council and the European Parliament, in certain areas the Commission has its own powers to pass legislation without any intervention from other institutions. The Commission also exercises legislative powers that have been delegated to it by the Council. An area in which delegated legislative powers are commonly used by the Commission is the Common Agriculture Policy. The Council has passed regulations under Article 37 EC giving the Commission these legislative powers. Competition policy is another area in which several significant regulations have been enacted by the Commission as a result of delegated powers given to it by the Council Regulation 17/65. Although much of the delegated legislative powers of the Commission are of a technical nature with little policy discretion, this is not always the case. For this reason, on 13 July 1987 the Council passed a decision establishing a catalogue of forms of procedures for the exercise of implementing power conferred on the Commission.[30] It is for the Council, when adopting an Act delegating legislative power to the Commission, to determine which procedure should be attached to the exercise of that power. This is very important because the extent of the constraints imposed on the Commission varies from one procedure to another.[31]

In addition to its legislative powers, the Commission also has executive powers in a number of areas. It is responsible for ensuring that the Community's revenue is collected and passed on by national authorities. It is also responsible for overseeing and coordinating the Community's structural funds; that is the European Social Fund, the Guidance Section of the European Agriculture and Guidance Fund, the Financial Investment for Fisheries Guidance, and the European Regional Development Fund. It is also responsible for administering Community aid to third countries and represents the Community in its external trade relations with third states and international organizations.

Finally, the Commission has the important role of 'being a guardian of Community law'. It has the right to initiate infringement proceedings against member states that act in breach of Community law. It also intervenes in all cases where the Court of Justice is asked for a preliminary ruling on the interpretation or validity of Community law. And it has been granted powers to declare illegal state aids that are provided by member states and anti-competitive practices by private undertakings.

The European Parliament (Articles 189-201 EC)

The European Parliament (EP) is the institution that has undergone much more transformations in its history than any other Community institution. Its life began as a relatively powerless Assembly in the founding treaties to become the active and considerably strengthened institution that it is today. Although the Assembly of the founding treaties was calling itself European Parliament, the name 'European Parliament' was officially recognized much later, by the Single European Act.[32]

Composition and structure. Originally, all members of the European Parliament (MEPs) were drawn from the parliaments of the member states, and they therefore all had a dual mandate. Since June 1979, however, when the first Euro-elections were held, the European Parliament has become a body of representatives elected by universal suffrage. Every citizen of the EU, who is resident of a member country, has the right to vote as well as to stand as a candidate in European Parliament elections.[33] However, the electoral procedure is not fully uniform, and this lack of uniformity has resulted in election to the European Parliament being subject to considerable anomalies.

Members of the European Parliament (MEPs) are elected as representatives of national political parties and sit in cross-national legislative European political groupings, broadly following the ideological divisions familiar in national politics. There are many political groups within the European Parliament; the largest two are the Party of European Socialists (PES) and the European Peoples Party (EPP), predominantly Christian Democrats. Up until May 2004, when the 2003 Accession Treaty come into force, there were 626 MEPs, elected for five years and divided up as shown in Table 1.1 (Article 190 EC).[34]

Table 1.1 Number of Members in Parliament before the May 2004 enlargement

Member States	Votes
Austria	21
Belgium	25
Denmark	16
Finland	16
France	87
Germany	99
Greece	25
Ireland	15
Italy	87
Luxembourg	6
Netherlands	31
Portugal	25
Spain	64
Sweden	22
United Kingdom	87

The European Parliament elects its own President, together with Vice-Presidents in a secret ballot by an absolute majority of votes cast. The President and the Vice-Presidents constitute the Bureau of Parliament.[35] Together with the chairpersons of the various political groups, they formerly constitute the enlarged Bureau of Parliament, which since 1994 is called the Conference of Presidents. The Conference of Presidents takes decisions on the organization of Parliament's work and draws up the draft agenda of Parliament's part-sessions.

The European Parliament has a large number of standing committees, with some sub-committees dealing with a wide range of subject matters and carrying out much of its legislative work through drawing up reports on relevant issues. The standing committees also make non-legislative reports resulting in many cases in Parliamentary Resolutions. The Parliament is also helped by a large secretariat that provides substantial legal and administrative assistance.

The Annual Plenary is held on the second Tuesday of March every year.[36] Plenary sessions are, however, normally held once every month except in August. Most of the sessions are held in Strasbourg but certain sessions and committee meetings are held in Brussels. The Parliament's Secretariat is hosted in Luxembourg.

The powers of the European Parliament. The formal powers of the European Parliament are broadly of three kinds: it is involved in various ways in the legislative process of the Communities; it has control over the budget of the Communities; and it exercises political supervision over the performance by the Commission of its tasks. As the legislative powers of the EP will be discussed in the next main sub-section, we will confine our discussion here to its supervisory and budgetary powers.

The supervisory role of the European Parliament. The Parliament's supervisory role can be seen in its scrutining of the activities of all the other Community institutions through questions put to them. There is an express Treaty obligation on Commissioners to reply to written and oral questions at Question Time (Article 197(3)), and although the Council is not obliged to reply to questions from the European Parliament, it does so in practice. An annual general report is also required to be submitted by the Commission to the Parliament, and in addition an annual report on the progress of the Union is required to be submitted by the European Council. Of greater significance, however, is the Parliament's debate on the annual legislative programme of the Commission presented by its President at the beginning of each year.

The European Parliament from its launch also has the supreme political weapon of passing a motion of censure on the activities of the

Commission by which it can force it to resign as a body. The motion of censure can be tabled by a two-thirds majority of the votes cast representing a majority of MEPs. However, a motion of censure has never been carried out.

Any citizen of the Union or any resident of a member state has the right to petition the European Parliament on a matter that comes within Community competence and affects him directly. An Ombudsman is appointed by the Parliament with the power to receive complaints from persons entitled to petition concerning instances of maladministration in the activities of Community institutions or bodies.[37] The Ombudsman conducts inquiries either on his/her own initiative, or in response to a complaint received directly from the person concerned or through a member of the European Parliament. The Ombudsman has no jurisdiction where the alleged facts are or have been the subject of legal proceedings.

The European Parliament also has another tool for supervising the activities of the other institutions by initiating, or intervening in legal action before the Court of Justice. In addition, it can establish committees of inquiry to investigate alleged contravention or maladministration in the implementation of Community law (Article 193).

The budgetary powers of the European Parliament. As far as the powers of the Parliament in the budgetary sphere are concerned, it is worth noting that since the adoption of the Budgetary Treaties of 1970 and 1975, the European Parliament has become an equal partner with the Council. Their respective powers in the budgetary procedure are determined by a crucial distinction in the budget between the part that relates to 'compulsory expenditure' and the part that relates to 'non-compulsory expenditure'.

Compulsory expenditures have been defined as 'such expenditure as the budgetary authority is obliged to enter the budget to enable the Community to meet its obligations both internally and externally under the Treaties and acts adopted in accordance therewith' (Article 272 EC). This part consists largely of expenditure relating to the Common Agricultural Policy in which the Council has the last word. Non-compulsory expenditures include expenditure on the structural funds, on research and on aid to third countries. Non-compulsory expenditure is confined to just under half of the budget and its annual rate of increase is determined by the Treaty.

The budgetary procedure is initiated by the Commission: the Commission puts forward to the Council the preliminary draft budget for the following financial year no later than September of the current year. The Council then prepares the draft budget on the basis of the Commission's preliminary draft budget and submits it to the European Parliament for its first reading before 5 October. The Parliament has the right to propose modifications to the compulsory expenditure parts of the budget, and to amend items classified as non-compulsory expenditure.[38] The draft budget is then passed to the Council for a second reading, where the Council may modify any of the amendments to the non-compulsory expenditure made by Parliament and may reject Parliament's proposed modifications to compulsory expenditure. Modifications proposed by Parliament that have the effect of increasing compulsory expenditure stand as rejected if they are not explicitly accepted by the Council.[39] If, within 15 days, the Council proposes no modifications to Parliament's amendments, and agrees on the Parliament's proposed modifications to compulsory expenditure, the draft budget becomes final. If this does not occur, the modified draft budget goes back to Parliament for its second reading. At its second reading Parliament no longer has the right to touch the parts of the budget related to compulsory expenditure. However, acting by a majority of its members and three-fifths of the votes cast, it can within a 15-day period amend or reject any modifications to its amendments to the non-compulsory expenditure made by the Council. Otherwise, the budget is deemed to have been adopted. However, Parliament may, by a majority of its members and two-thirds of the votes cast, reject 'for important reasons' the entire draft budget and request a new draft budget to be submitted. When this occurs, the previous year's budget continues to operate on a one-twelfth basis.

The European Court of Justice and the Court of First Instance (Articles 220–245 EC)

Composition and structure. The Court of Justice, to which the Court of First Instance is attached, is the judicial institution of the Community. It consists of Judges, one from each member state, and Advocates-General who are appointed by the common accord of the member states' governments for a renewable term of six years. The qualifications for selection as a Judge or Advocate General require 'persons whose independence is beyond doubt and who pass the qualifications required for appointment to the highest Judicial offices in their respective countries or who are juris consults of recognized competence' (Article 223(1) EC). Judges and Advocates-Generals rank equally in precedence according to their seniority in office.[40]

The Court of Justice sits in Chambers of three and five judges, as well as in plenary sessions where the quorum is seven judges. However, the Court sits in plenary session when a member state or a Community institution that is a party to the proceedings so requests.

The judicial and administrative business of the Court is directed by the President, who is elected by the Judges from among their own for a renewable period of three years. The President presides at hearings and deliberations of the Court, fixes or extends the dates and times of the Court sittings, deals with most applications for interim measures and appoints a Judge Reporter in each case. The EC Treaty defines the role of the Advocates-General as 'acting with complete impartiality and independence to make, in open Court, reasoned submissions on cases brought before the Court of Justice' (Article 222 EC). Each Advocate-General, who is assigned to a given case, presents, at the end of the oral procedure and before the Judges begin their deliberation, a fully reasoned Opinion. Although the Advocate-General's Opinion is generally very influential, it is in no way binding on the Court. In fact, the Advocate-Generals do not participate in the Court's deliberation; the Court deliberates in secret and the final decision on a case is taken by majority voting. The judgements are delivered in open court. No dissenting judgements are delivered.

The Court of First Instance. The Court of First Instance was established in 1988.[41] Under the terms of Article 168A it was inserted into the EEC Treaty by the Single European Act and began to hear cases in November 1989. It sits in Chambers of three and five Judges or in plenary session. There are no Advocates-General, but any of the Judges may be called upon to act as Advocate-General in a given case, in which case he may not then take part in the Court's deliberation and decision. The Court of First Instance elects its own President from among its members who directs the Court's judicial business and administration and presides at plenary sittings and deliberations.

The reason for the creation of the Court of First Instance was to relieve the case load of the Court of Justice. In particular, the Court of First Instance has jurisdiction to deal with staff cases, cases concerning claims against the Community for damages regarding its non-contractual liability, all the actions brought about by 'non-privileged' applicants (that is, natural or legal persons other than a Community institution or a member state), and cases concerning merger control and Community trademarks. However, it has no jurisdiction to deal with preliminary references.

It is worth mentioning that the decisions of the Court of First Instance are 'subject to a right of appeal by the Court of Justice on points of law only and in accordance with the conditions laid down by the statute' (Article 225(1) EC). Article 51 of the Statute of the Court provides that 'it shall lie on the grounds of lack of competence of the Court of First Instance, a breach of procedure before it which

adversely affects the interests of the appellant as well as the infringement of Community law by the Court of First Instance'. In principle,
an appeal to the Court of Justice does not have suspensory effect.
However, where the Court's of First Instance decision has declared a
regulation void, its decision will take effect only after the two-month
period for bringing an appeal has expired or when, if the appeal has
been brought, has been dismissed.

The jurisdiction of the Court of Justice. The European Court has
no inherent jurisdiction: it only has such jurisdiction as is conferred
on it by the treaties. According to the EC Treaty, the Court's general
task is to ensure that in the interpretation and application of the
Community treaties' provisions the law is observed. There are also a
number of specific tasks which can be classified into two categories.
The first category concerns direct actions, that is actions that begin in
the European Court of Justice, and includes:

- enforcement actions against member states when they fail to fulfil
  an obligation under the treaties
- actions for judicial review: these may be either actions to annul a
  Community measure or actions to oblige a Community institution
  to pass a measure that has previously refused to pass
- actions for damages for non-contractual liability of the Community

The second category consists of actions that begin in national courts
from which a reference for a preliminary ruling is made to the
European Court. Questions referred from the national courts to the
Court of Justice are concerned with the validity and interpretation of
the acts of Community institutions.

The Court of Auditors (Articles 246-248 EC)

The Court of Auditors was established by the second Budgetary Treaty
of 1975 and since then has been considered as the fifth Community
Institution. It is composed of representatives of member states. Its
members are appointed unanimously by the Council, after consultation with the European Parliament, for a period of six years.

The Court of Auditors is not a judicial body; its task is to scrutinize
the finances of the Community and ensure sound financial management. It examines the accounts of all revenue and expenditure of all
bodies set up by the Community and provides the Council and the
European Parliament with a statement of assurance as to the reliability of the accounts and the legality of the transactions. The Court
of Auditors also assists the Council and the European Parliament in

exercising their control power over the budget's implementation. It draws up at the end of each financial year an annual report that is sent to the other Community institutions.

The European Central Bank and the European System of Central Banks

Composition. Following the decision to proceed to the third stage of EMU, the European Central Bank (ECB) was brought into being and the European Monetary Institute went into liquidation.

The ECB has its own independent legal personality and has two decision-making bodies: the Executive Board and the Governing Council. The Executive Board is composed of a President, a Vice-President and four other members, all appointed jointly by the member-states ' governments after they have consulted the European Parliament. They serve for eight years and their posts are non-renewable. The Governing Council consists of members of the Executive Board plus the governors of those national central banks whose countries are participating in the EMU. The President of the Council and a member of the Commission may also participate in the ECB's meetings but do not have the right to vote. This is a reflection of the ECB's independence: it implies that no instructions are to be given to the ECB by any Community institution.[42]

The ECB must be placed alongside the European System of Central Banks (ESCB).The ECSB is composed of the ECB and the national Central Banks (CBs). Unlike the ECB, the ESCB has no legal personality and in fact is not an institution itself; but it provides the framework through which the monetary policy of the European Union is conducted by the ECB and the national CBs.

Regulatory powers. The primary objective of the ECB is to maintain price stability, but other tasks are (Article 105(2) EC):

- to define and implement the Community's monetary policy
- to conduct foreign exchange operations
- to hold and manage the official foreign reserves of the member states
- to promote the smooth operation of the payments system

The central power of the ECB is its exclusive right to authorize the issue of banknotes within the Community. This allows the ECB to control the money supply and gives it the power to set short-term interest rates. The ECB is also responsible for formulating monetary policy in Europe, by taking decisions relating to intermediate monetary objectives, to key interest rates and to foreign exchange reserves, and for establishing necessary guidelines. The executive board of the ECB implements monetary policy in accordance with the guidelines and decisions laid down by its governing Council.

For carrying out its tasks, the ECB can adopt *Regulations*, *Decisions* and *Recommendations*. It also has the power to impose fines or periodic penalty payments on undertakings for failing to comply with obligations contained in its Regulations and Decisions. In addition, the ECB has the power to make regulations relating to the holding by national credit institutions of minimum reserves with the ECB, and to impose sanctions in case of non-compliance.

Other Bodies

The Economic and Social Committee (Article 257 EC). This is an advisory body, with its members appointed by the Council for a four-year renewable term. The Committee consists of representatives of producers, farmers, carriers, workers, dealers, craftsmen, professional occupations and the general public. It has consultative powers in many areas of Community competence.

The Committee of the Regions (Article 263 EC). This is an advisory body established by the EU Treaty to give regional authorities greater input in the decision-making process. Its members are appointed by the Council for a four-year renewable term. The Committee of the Regions should be consulted in the fields of education, culture, public health, employment, social matters, environment and economic and social cohesion. However, its opinions carry only limited weight with the other institutions.

EU Legislation and Law-making Process

Types of Community Legislation

One of the most striking features of the Community is the power entrusted by member states to the institutional actors to enact legislation for the purpose of attaining the objectives of the Treaties. There are five main types of Community legislation:

- Regulations
- Directives
- Decisions
- Recommendations
- Opinions

Starting with *Regulations*, according to Article 249 of the EC Treaty, a Regulation has general application. That is, it applies to all member states, it is binding in its entirety, and it is regarded as directly applicable within all member states. The direct application of a Regulation means that its entry into force and its application in the legal order of a member state are independent of any national implementing measure. Thus Regulations, once made, automatically become part of the national legal systems without any intervening measure either by governments or by the legislature. They are the most powerful Community legal instruments; they are to be treated as 'law'. Regulations have to be published in the Official Journal of the Community and come into force on the date that is specified in them or, if no date is specified, on the twentieth day following their publication.[43]

Unlike Regulations, *Directives* do not necessarily have general application as they do not have to be addressed to all the member states but may be directed to any one of them. They are binding on those member states to which they are addressed as to the end to be achieved. They leave to national authorities the choice of form and method of their implementation. This allows a member state to use the legislative format it considers most appropriate for effectively achieving the aim of the Directives. It is for this reason that Directives have proved to be a very valuable legislative means for developing Community policy, given that member states have differing legal systems, especially in cases where harmonization rather than strict uniformity is needed. Indeed, the potency of this legislative means has been increased considerably by important case-law of the Court of Justice.

The Maastricht Treaty requires Directives applied to all member states also to be published in the Official Journal. The date of entry into force of Directives is either the date specified in them or, in the absent of a specific date, the twentieth day following that of publication. Failure on the part of a member state to give effect to a Directive through complete or correct implementation by the stated date, may lead to persons being unable to rely on the provisions of it in their dealings with that member state.

As far as *Decisions* are concerned, unlike Directives they are binding in their entirety upon those to whom they are addressed. Decisions must be notified to the addressees and come into effect when the requirement of notification to those to whom they are addressed is complied with. Addressees may be member states or natural and legal persons. Decisions adopted under Article 249 of the EC Treaty must be published in the Official Journal. All other Decisions need not be published.

Although Community institutions are free in many occasions to choose any form of legislation for policy-making, there are a number of areas in which the Treaty provides for the use of Decisions as the chosen method. For example, Decisions are used in Competition Policy when the Commission rules that a firm or firms have acted in breach of Articles 81 and 82 of the EC Treaty. Decisions are also used in the area of state aids when the Commission acts requiring a member state to abolish or amend measures of aid to national undertakings. The Council can also delegate power to the Commission to issue a Decision that is within its own competence.

Decisions while binding in their entirety, unlike Regulations, are not intended to have general application. They are directed at one or more member states or one or more natural or legal persons at a time. The general-application characteristic as a distinction between Regulations and Decisions is an issue of particular importance regarding the action for annulment under Article 230.[44] In particular, the natural or legal persons having limited *locus standi* can bring actions (for annulment only) against Decisions addressed to them, not against other Community acts. For this reason the standing of natural and legal persons under Article 230 is dependent on whether a Community measure takes the form of a Regulation or a Decision. The Court, however, has ruled that, in examining the question of whether a measure constitutes a Regulation or a Decision, it cannot restrict itself to considering the official title of the measure but must also take into account its object and content.[45] That is, the nature of a measure depends on its substance rather than on how it is labelled by the adopting institution. Thus, the Court of Justice can treat measures which are labelled Regulations but are not of general application as being in reality Decisions. This is permitted by reference to Article 230, which states that natural or legal persons can institute annulment proceedings against a Decision in the form of a Regulation which is of direct and individual concern to them.

Turning now to *Recommendations* and *Opinions*, Article 249 explicitly states that they have no binding force. While these measures cannot have direct effect, it is compulsory for a national court or tribunal to make a reference to the European Court concerning the validity or interpretation of such measures.[46] This is because a Recommendation or Opinion may be used as an instrument for interpreting other provisions of Community law that are binding. The Commission has general powers to make Recommendations or deliver Opinions on matters dealt with in the Treaty whenever it considers that it is necessary to do so or where the Treaty expressly so provides.

All types of Community legislation – that is, Regulations, Directives, Decisions, Recommendations and Opinions – are capable of being reviewed by the Court of Justice, and there are some substantive and procedural requirements for the legality of Community legislation. The principal substantive requirement is that the preamble to a particular provision of Community law should state clearly the legal basis on which it is made. As regards the procedural requirements, in addition to the duty to notify and publish, reasoning must also be given for any Community legislation. In particular, legislation must set out in a concise and clear manner the factual background, the purposes or aims which it is striving to attain, and the law that has led the institution in question to adopt it, so that it can be possible for the European Court to review its legality.

Types of Legislative Procedure

The making of Community legislation should not be compared with those of national or federal states in which a single body is identified as the 'legislature' and the procedure for law-making is more or less uniform. In the Community, the procedure is not uniform and the players that comprise the legislature vary according to which procedure is applied in any particular area of Community action. The distinguishing characteristic of the different procedures is that they are determined according to the extent of participation and the degree of power that the European Parliament has in each. The main types of Community's legislative procedures are:

- the consultation procedure
- the cooperation procedure
- the co-decision procedure
- the assent procedure

The *consultation procedure* was the only procedure in the original Treaty that gave the European Parliament a guaranteed role in the legislative process. This role was a consultative one: the legislative power in the original Treaty was concentrated upon the Council and the Commission. Under the consultation procedure, a measure is first proposed by the Commission. The European Parliament is consulted on the proposal, and the Council takes the decision in accordance with the voting requirement laid down in the relevant Treaty provisions. The European Parliament has only one reading in which to consider the Commission's proposal, and its views are not binding on either the Council or the Commission. The consultation of the European Parliament takes place in relation to the Commission's original proposal. In particular, the responsible committee of the European Parliament examines the validity and appropriateness of the chosen legal basis of the Commission's proposed measure; that is, whether the principle of subsidiarity and the citizens fundamental rights are respected, whether sufficient financial resources are provided, and so on.[47]

Where the EC Treaty provides for the consultation of the European Parliament, the Council cannot adopt a proposal prior to receiving the Parliament's opinion. Failure to wait for its opinion before it adopts the measure can lead to the measure being annulled[48] unless the need to adopt the legislation is urgent and the European Parliament fails to cooperate sincerely with the Council.[49] Reconsultation of Parliament is required if changes, not prompted by Parliament itself, to the substance of the text that has been the subject of the first consultation are made by the Commission or the Council. Reconsultation is not required if the changes are either technical or go in the direction of wishes expressed by the Parliament itself in its Opinion.[50,51]

It is obvious that the European Parliament remains marginalized under the consultation procedure: consultation is only a procedural requirement, with the Council not being required to take account of its view or to give reasons for rejecting it. The consultation procedure is still widely used, particularly in those areas where member states are relatively cautious about developing Community legislation, such as for example citizenship (Articles 18, 19 and 22 EC), agriculture (Article 37(2) EC), state aids (Article 89 EC), indirect taxation (Article 93 EC), industrial policy (Article 157(3) EC), certain aspects of research and development (Article 172(1) EC), environmental taxes, planning and measures significantly affecting member states, and choice of energy policy (Articles 175(2) and 308 EC).

As far as the *cooperation procedure* is concerned, this procedure was introduced by the Single European Act and was set up to be used for many of the measures that were designed to implement the single market. Today this procedure still remains in use with regard to Articles 102, 103 and 106 EC that are related to certain aspects of European economic and monetary union. The prominent feature distinguishing the cooperation procedure from the consultation procedure is the greater engagement of the European Parliament. Indeed, the cooperation procedure consists of two phases. The first phase corresponds to the consultation procedure, and is the first reading by the European Parliament. There is no time limit on Parliament to pass its Opinion to the Council at this first reading stage. After Parliament has passed its Opinion, the Council, unless it exercises its power to amend the Commission's proposal by unanimity, acting by a qualified majority adopts a common position. The common position is then forwarded to the European Parliament with a full explanation for the reasons that have led to its adoption, as well as with an explanation for the Commission's position. At this second-reading stage, the Parliament has a three-month period in which to react to the common position. The mode of Parliament's reaction determines the further course of the second-reading stage. There are three possibilities:

- Parliament does not act at all within the three-month period, or approves the common position. The Council then adopts definitively the Act in question in accordance with the common position.
- Parliament rejects the common position. The Council can then pass the measure only by unanimity within three months.
- Parliament may propose amendments to the Council's common position within the three-month period by an absolute majority of its component members.

If the third possibility happens, the proposal is referred back to the Commission. The Commission has one month to reexamine the proposal, taking into account the amendments proposed by the Parliament. If the Commission does not accept the amendments of Parliament, it is under an obligation to forward them to the Council together with the reexamined proposal and its opinion on them. The Council, within three months, can adopt the Commission's reexamined proposal by qualified majority. Unanimity is required in the Council in order to amend the proposal as reexamined by the Commission. If no decision is made within the three-month period, the Commission's proposal is deemed not to have been adopted.

The cooperation procedure clearly increases the European Parliament's influence on the Community legislative process. It puts the European Parliament in a position to be able to block a measure if it is allied with one member state. This power to reject the Council's common position and to put in danger the adoption of the measure can be used by Parliament not only to gain informal influence but also to enable it to set the agenda, particularly where the position of the other players is unclear. Thus before the signing of the Amsterdam Treaty, 54 per cent of Parliament's amendments proposed at first reading were accepted by the Commission and 41 per cent by the Council; on the second reading, the figures were 43 per cent and 21 per cent respectively.

Turning to the *co-decision procedure*, this legislative procedure was first introduced at Maastricht by the EU Treaty. The areas covered are:

- free movement of workers
- freedom of establishment

- mutual recognition of qualifications
- freedom to provide services
- provisions concerning the approximation of laws that have as their object the establishment and functioning of the internal market
- incentive measures in the field of public health and culture
- specific action supporting or supplementing national policies on consumer protection
- guidelines covering the objectives, priorities and broad lines of measures envisaged in the sphere of trans-European networks in the areas of transport, telecommunications and energy infrastructures
- multinational programmes on research and technological development
- programmes setting out priority objectives for environmental policy

The co-decision procedure further enhances the European Parliament's powers in the legislative process: the crux of it is that unless the Council and Parliament agree on the final text of the legislation, neither is given the last word and the legislation simply fails. The co-decision procedure begins in the same way as the cooperation procedure, with a first reading culminating in the adoption by the Council of a common position after obtaining the Opinion of the European Parliament, which is then communicated to the Parliament with a full explanation of the reasons that have led the Council to adopt it. There is, however, a difference compared with the cooperation procedure: in the co-decision procedure, the Commission's proposal is sent both to the Council and to the European Parliament.

If, within three months of receiving the Council's common position, the European Parliament at a second reading approves it or does not take a decision, the Council adopts the measure in accordance with its common position. If, however, the European Parliament by an absolute majority of its component members rejects the Council's common position, the proposed Act is deemed not to have been adopted.

Finally, the European Parliament can propose amendments to the Council's common position. These are forwarded to the Commission and the Council, the former being required to deliver an Opinion on the amendments. The Council then has three months to approve all Parliament's amendments, acting by qualified majority or by unanimity, in relation to those amendments on which the Commission has expressed a negative opinion and adopt the Act in question accordingly. If the Council does not approve all Parliament's amendments, a Conciliation Committee must be convened by the President of the Council in agreement with the President of the European Parliament. This committee is composed of the Council's members, or their representatives, and the European Parliament.[52] The Commission, which still has the power to amend the proposed Act if this will be helpful for the process of conciliation, participates in the Committee's work and tries to reconcile the disagreements between the Council and the European Parliament. The task of the Conciliation Committee is, within a six-week deadline, to reach agreement on a joint text by a qualified majority on the Council side and by a simple majority on Parliament's side. In fulfilling this task, the Conciliation Committee must address the common position on the basis of the amendments proposed by Parliament. If within the six-week period the Committee approves a joint text, there is a further period of six weeks in which the Council acting by a qualified majority, and the European Parliament acting by an absolute majority of the votes cast, have to approve it and adopt the Act in question accordingly. If either of the institutions or both institutions fail to do so, the proposed measure is deemed not to have been adopted. If there is no joint text approved by the Conciliation Committee within the time limit of six weeks, the proposed Act is deemed not to have been adopted.

The co-decision procedure thus increases the European Parliament's powers. In several important fields of Community competence, the European Parliament has with the co-decision procedure the power to prevent the adoption of legislative acts of which it does not approve. It can in effect exercise a negative block on such Acts.

Nevertheless, the European Parliament has no legal power to force the adoption of amendments that the Council does not want. In this sense, the EP's legislative power has its limits because its negative capability, if used very often, might create the impression that it impedes the progress of the Community. Of course, the Parliament's last word in blocking legislation is a significant bargaining power when the Council is keen to pass legislation on a particular topic governed by this procedure. This is more so when one takes into account the fact that the Council will be prevented from continuing the legislative process if Parliament rejects its common position at a second reading. Moreover, Parliamentary amendments, even when not accepted by the Council, could be used as the formal starting point for setting the agenda of the Conciliation Committee, given that this Committee, in finding out a joint text, must address the Council's common position on the basis of Parliament's proposed amendments. The European Parliament therefore strengthens its bargaining power in a very much increased conciliatory legislative process, in which both institutions, the European Parliament and the Council helped by the Commission, attempt to provide an agreed piece of legislation. Consequently, the co-decision procedure has established a greater formal equality between the Council and the Parliament in the legislative process compared with the other legislative procedures.

Finally, under the *assent procedure*, the Council, acting on a proposal made by the Commission or the ECB or even Parliament, can adopt the measure only if the European Parliament gives its assent. The Council must act unanimously in order for the measure to be adopted, while, apart from the Article 190(3) EC measure, the European Parliament will give its assent by a simple majority of votes cast.

The assent procedure was first introduced into the EEC Treaty by the Single European Act only in relation to the accession of new member states and association agreements with third countries. However, its margin of influence has been extended by the EU Treaty, as amended by the Amsterdam Treaty, to the following measures:

* Provisions concerning various aspects of the functioning of the European Central Bank (Article 105 (6) EC) and amendments to the Statute of the European System of Central Banks (Article 107 (5) EC).
* Defining the tasks, priority objectives and organization of the Structural Funds, and defining the general rules applicable to the Funds (Article 161 EC).
* Adoption of acts regulating elections to the European Parliament (Article 190 (3)).

The advantage for Parliament of the assent procedure over the co-decision procedure is that, in contrast to the latter which operates within a series of strict time limits, in the assent procedure no time-limits are imposed upon the European Parliament within which it must act. This means that even where it might eventually approve a measure, delaying tactics might be used by the EP in order to maximize its influence in the decision-making process.

The Challenge of the Enlargement

Following the Luxembourg Summit of December 1997 the European Union was involved in a process of preparing the most ambitious enlargement ever: thirteen countries, with economic structures, histories and cultures different from those of the other 15 EU states had applied for membership. These were: Bulgaria, Cyprus, the Czech Republic, Estonia, Hungary, Latvia, Lithuania, Malta, Poland, Romania, Slovakia, Slovenia and Turkey. These states had been

Table 1.2 Dates of application for EU Membership

Cyprus	3.07.1990
Czech Republic	17.01.1996
Estonia	24.11.1995
Hungary	31.03.1994
Latvia	13.10.1995
Lithuania	8.12.1995
Malta	16.07.1990
Poland	5.04.1994
Slovakia	27.06.1995
Slovenia	10.06.1996
Bulgaria	14.12.1995
Romania	22.06.1995
Turkey	14.04.1987

Source: Europa-Enlargement, European Commission Documentation
http://www.europa.eu.int/comm/enlargement/negotiations

'applicant counties' for quite some time (see Table 1.2), but the enlargement process was lengthy and cumbersome. Accession negotiations with Hungary, Poland, Estonia, the Czech Republic, Slovenia and Cyprus started in March 1998; accession negotiations with Malta, Slovakia, Latvia, Lithuania, Romania and Bulgaria opened up in October 1999. To be eligible for entry, certain political, institutional and economic criteria had to be fulfilled. The political and institutional criteria were:[53]

- protection of human rights and respect for minorities
- fight against organized crime, drugs and illegal migration
- protection of the environment
- adoption of the aims of the EU and ability to enforce the EU legislation, and
- ability to pay the contributions to the EU budget on a regular basis

The economic criteria were:

- creation of a well-functioning market economy, and
- ability to cope with the competitive pressures within the EU

The requirement of a well-functioning market economy was to be fulfilled through trade liberalization, elimination of market-entry and market–exit barriers in industry, low inflation and reasonable budget- and current-account deficits, and sufficiently developed financial markets. The requirement of being able to cope with competitive forces was to be fulfilled through macroeconomic stability and predictability, sufficient human and physical capital, a satisfactory infrastructure, government policies aiming at improving competitiveness, and structural reform in product and labour markets to help make the economy more adaptable to changes in the international environment.

Negotiations with 10 of the applicant countries, namely Cyprus, Malta, the five Visegrad states (the Czech Republic, Hungary, Slovakia, Slovenia, Poland), and the three Baltic states (Estonia, Latvia, Lithuania), were concluded on 13 December 2002 and an Accession Treaty[54] was signed in a formal ceremony at the Athens Summit of 16 April 2003. These 10 countries formally became EU members on 1 May 2004. The two Balkan states, Bulgaria and Romania, which have been applicant countries since 1995, have set themselves the goal of satisfying entry requirements by 2007 and hope to joint then. Turkey, which has been an applicant country since 1987, was not deemed ready in December 2002 to begin accession negotiations, but it has recently made considerable progress toward satisfying the political and institutional criteria. It is expected to begin accession negotiations in October 2005 and may also joint the EU shortly after 2007.

From an economic point of view, the increase in the number of EU countries from 15 to 25 in May 2004 and to 27 in 2007, or to 28 shortly after, represents a major challenge. The 10 newcomers (NM-10) together with the 3 candidate countries (CC-3), Bulgaria, Romania and Turkey, will increase the EU area by 57.4 per cent from 3,234.6 square kilometers to 5,091.9 km^2, and the EU's population by 43.7 per cent from 382.7 million people to 550 million (see Table 1.3). Yet, given their relatively low level of economic development, these 13 countries will contribute no more than 8.2 per cent to the EU's GDP at market prices. Indeed, GDP per capita at market prices in many NM countries is 4 to 5 times lower than that prevailing in the EU-15, something that follows from Table 1.3 if one divides column (c) with column (b). Thus in 2004, while the EU-15 average GDP per head at market prices was 25,400 euro the corresponding NM-10 average was only about 6,400 euro, giving an average income difference per capita at market prices between the two groups of 19,000 euro at an annual basis. GDP per capita in purchasing power standards (PPS), which takes account of cost-of living conditions, is also in most NM countries and in all CC-3 well below that of the corresponding EU-15 average. In 2004, GDP in PPS amounted to 13,500 euro in NM-10 and 6,800 euro in CC-3 as compared to an EU-15 average of 24,300 euro. Cyprus, Slovenia and Malta are the most well-off NM counties (GDP per head in PPS at 75.0, 71.8 and 66.7 per cent of the EU-15 = 100 average). Next comes the Czech Republic (GDP per head at 64.2 per cent of the EU-15 average), followed by Hungary and Slovakia (GDP per head in PPS at 56.7 and

Table 1.3 Basic economic facts – the enlarged European Union, 2004

	(a) Area (thousand km²)	(b) Total Population (million)	(c) GDP at current market prices (billion euro)	(d) GDP per capita in PPS (euro)	(e) GDP per capita in PPS as % of EU-15 = 100
Cyprus	9.3	0.7	12.5	18,200	75.0
Czech Republic	78.7	10.2	87.0	15,600	64.2
Estonia	45.2	1.4	8.8	11,300	46.4
Hungary	93.0	10.1	81.4	13,800	56.7
Latvia	64.6	2.3	10.9	9,700	39.8
Lithuania	65.3	3.4	17.7	10,700	44.2
Malta	0.3	0.4	4.4	16,200	66.7
Poland	312.7	38.2	195.9	10,600	43.8
Slovakia	49.0	5.4	32.6	11,900	49.2
Slovenia	20.3	2.0	26.0	17,400	71.8
NM-10	738.4	74.1	477.2	13,500	55.8
Bulgaria	110.9	7.8	19.7	6,900	28.3
Romania	238.4	21.7	56.7	6,900	28.7
Turkey	769.6	68.7	244.6	6,500	26.7
CC-3	1,118.9	98.2	321.0	6,800	27.9
EU-15	3,234.6	382.7	9,730.9	24,300	100
EU-28	5,091.9	555.0	10,529.1		
Enlargement (from 15 to 28) change (%)	57.4%	43.7%	8.2%		

Sources: (a) Eurostat, *Towards an Enlarged European Union – Key Indicators on Member States and Candidate Countries,* April 2003.
(b) Eurostat database, *Long-term Indicators,* Population and Social Conditions.
(c), (d), (e) Eurostat database, *Long-term Indicators,* Economy and Finance.

49.2 per cent of the EU-15 GDP respectively). Poland, Estonia and Lithuania come next (GDP per head in PPS at about 45 per cent of that of the EU-15). Latvia is the least well-off new member state (GDP per head at 39.8 per cent of the EU-15 average in 2004). The 2 Balkan states, Bulgaria and Romania, have even lower GDP per head in PPS, namely 28.3 and 28.7 of the EU-15 average respectively, although this is expected to increase somewhat by 2007. Turkey has currently the lowest GDP per head in PPS, amounting to only 26.7 per cent of the GDP of the EU-15. Living standards in terms of percentage of population that owns a car or has access to Internet, or in terms of infant survival and life expectancy, are also in many of the newcomers and in all three candidate countries well below those in EU-15 (see Table 1.4).

In terms of structure of production, all the newcomers are more agricultural than the EU-15 states. The 10 NM countries have increased the agricultural area of the European Union by 29 per cent, the number of farmers by 56 per cent and the number of farms by 74 per cent, reducing average farm size by 39 per cent (see Table 1.5). The contribution of agriculture to their gross domestic value added (GVA) ranges from 6.1 per cent in Lithuania to 2.1 per cent in Malta, giving an average for all the new member states of 3.6 per cent as compared to only 1.9 per cent in the EU-15 (see Table 1.6). Bulgaria, Romania and Turkey are even more agricultural than the 10 newcomers, with shares of agricultural output in GVA amounting to 12.5, 12.9 and 11.1 per cent respectively. As regards agricultural employment, this is 8.7 per cent of total employment on average in the 10 NMs and 27.7 per cent on average in the 3 CC countries as compared to only 4.1 per cent in the EU-15. Given the percentage contribution of agricultural activities to GVA, the relatively large number of people engaged in agriculture in the 10 newcomers and the 3 prospective members is indicative of the low labour productivity in this sector.

Table 1.4 Living standards

	Passenger cars per 100 inhabitants	Mobile phones per 100 inhabitants	Internet users per 100 inhabitants	Infant mortality per 1000 live births	Life expectancy in years	
					Males	Females
Cyprus	37	41	20	5.6	75.3	80.4
Czech Republic	34	68	14	4.0	72.1	78.5
Estonia	30	54	32	8.4	65.6	76.4
Hungary	24	31	15	8.1	67.2	75.7
Latvia	25	26	7	11.0	64.5	75.6
Lithuania	32	28	7	8.6	67.5	77.7
Malta	50	61	25	4.4	75.1	79.3
Poland	27	25	10	7.7	70.2	78.4
Slovakia	24	40	17	6.2	69.4	77.6
Slovenia	44	76	30	4.2	72.7	80.1
Bulgaria	26	20	7	14.4	68.5	75.1
Romania	14	20	5	18.4	67.7	78.8
Turkey	7	22	4	38.7	66.4	71.0
EU-15	50	58	36	4.6	75.2	81.2

Source: Eurostat, *Towards an Enlarged European Union – Key Indicators on Member States and Candidate Countries*, April 2003.

Table 1.5 Farming structure after enlargement

	Farmers (million)	Agricultural area (million Ha)	Number of farms (millions)	Average farm size (Ha)
NM-10	3.8	38.5	5.2	7.4
EU-15	6.8	132.0	7.0	18.9
EU-25	10.6	170.5	12.2	13.2
Percentage change	+56%	+29%	+74%	−39%

Source: 'Facts and Figures on EU Trade in Agricultural Products', Press Release 16/12/2002, European Commission.

Table 1.6 Contribution of agriculture to gross domestic value-added (GVA) and sectoral employment, 2003[*]

	(a) Contribution of agriculture to GVA	(b) Sectoral employment % of total employment		
		Agriculture	Industry	Services
Cyprus	3.8	5.2	22.9	71.9
Czech Republic	2.8	4.5	39.6	55.9
Estonia	4.3	5.6	30.6	63.8
Hungary	4.1	5.3	33.4	61.3
Latvia	4.1	13.7	27.0	59.3
Lithuania	6.1	17.9	28.1	54.0
Malta	2.1	2.1	30.0	67.9
Poland	2.9	18.4	28.6	53.0
Slovakia	3.9	5.8	38.4	55.8
Slovenia	3.0	8.4	37.8	53.8
NM-10	3.6	8.7	31.6	59.7
Bulgaria	12.5	10.1	32.9	57.0
Romania	12.9	36.0	30.0	34.0
Turkey	11.1	37.0	23.3	39.6
CC-3	12.2	27.7	28.7	43.5
EU-15	1.9	4.1	28.0	67.9

(*)latest available
Sources: (a) Eurostat database, Long-term Indicators, Economy and Finance (b) Eurostat, Statistics in Focus, 'European Labour Force Survey 2003, Principal Results', 2004

As far as trade is concerned, with the exception of Poland, all the NMs are very open economies (see Table 1.7, column (a)); and trade between them and the EU-15 has shown an upward trend since the late 1990s following the accession negotiations (see Figure 1.1). However, the importance of the EU-15 market for the economies of the 10 new member states and the 3 prospective members is much greater than the importance of their markets for the EU-15 states. For example, in 2000 the NMs imported goods and services from the EU-15 equal to 108.8 billion euro and exported to the EU-15 goods and services equal to 89.0 billion euro, something that corresponds to 57.1 and 60.3 per cent of their total imports and exports respectively (see Table 1.7, columns (b) and (c)). Hungary, the Czech Republic and Poland are the most

Table 1.7 New member states and candidate countries – openness and trade with the EU-15

| | (a) | (b) | | (c) | |
| | | Trade with EU-15 Value (billion euro), 2000 | | Trade with EU-15 (percent of total trade), 2000 | |
	Openness: exports and imports relative to GDP, 2002 (%)	Exports	Imports	Exports	Imports
Cyprus	117	1.0	3.1	49.0	55.5
Czech Republic	143	21.4	23.8	68.9	61.8
Estonia	200	3.2	3.3	69.4	56.5
Hungary	150	21.9	23.0	74.3	57.8
Latvia	114	1.9	2.0	47.8	44.0
Lithuania	126	2.2	2.6	61.2	52.6
Malta	209	1.0	2.8	41.3	63.6
Poland	73	23.1	33.6	69.2	61.4
Slovakia	129	7.0	6.5	59.9	49.8
Slovenia	167	6.3	8.1	62.2	67.7
NM-10	143	89.0	108.8	60.3	57.1
Bulgaria	128	3.1	3.2	n.a.	n.a
Romania	85	7.6	8.7	n.a	n.a
Turkey	57	17.5	29.7	n.a.	n.a
EU-15	74				

Sources: (a)Eurostat – *Statistics in Focus*, Industry, Trade & Services, 'SMEs in the Candidate Countries', 2004.
(b) Eurostat, *Statistics in Focus*, External Trade, 'The 13 Candidate Countries Trade with the EU 2000', 2001.
(c)Eurostat, *Statistical Yearbook 2003 on Candidate Countries*, 2003.

Figure 1.1   NM-10 and CC-3 trade with the EU-15, value (billion euro)

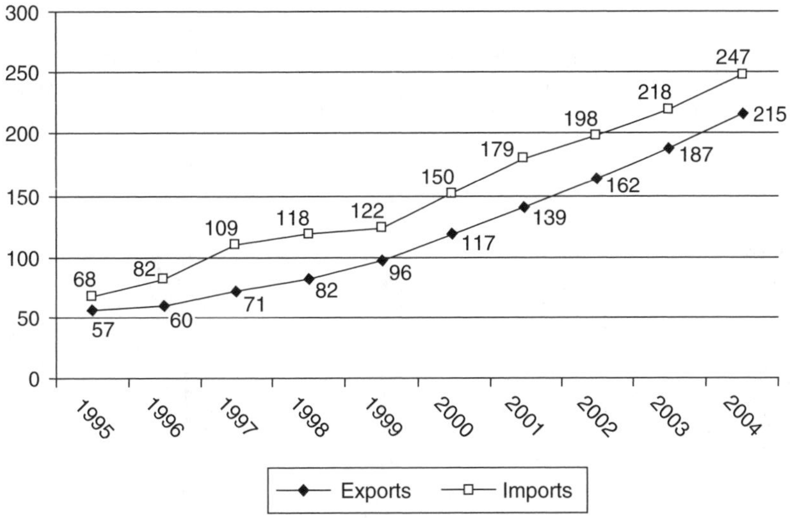

Source: Eurostat database, *External Trade Statistics*

important trade partners of the EU-15; the share of trade with the EU-15 (exports and imports together) in their total trade is above that of the rest NM countries (74.3% (57.8%) of total exports (imports) in Hungary, 68.9% (61.8%) of total exports (imports) in the Czech Republic and 69.2% (61.4%) of total exports (imports) in Poland). The EU-15 market is also important for Turkey (see column(b)). On the other hand, the NM-10 and CC-3 countries' share in the EU-15 total exports and imports is relatively small amounting to no more than 18 per cent in 2004. Moreover, there are significant differences in terms of the importance of the newcomers and prospective members as a trading bloc for the individual EU-15 member states (see Table 1.8). In 2000, out of the 150.3 billion euro (117 billion) EU-15 exports to (imports from) the NM-10 and CC-3 57.4 billion (50.6 billion) corresponded to German exports (imports), implying that about 40 per cent of total EU-15 trade with these countries involved exclusively Germany. Italy, France, Austria and the UK contributed less than 15 per cent to total EU-15 trade with the NM-10 and CC-3. Belgium, the Netherlands and Sweden contributed no more than 6 per cent, while Denmark, Spain, Finland and Ireland contributed no more than 3 per cent.

At the same time, several of the 10 new member states, including Poland, Slovakia, Lithuania and Latvia, are currently experiencing serious unemployment problems (see Table 1.9, columns (a)-(c)). In all of them, total unemployment had shown an upward trend between

Table 1.8 Trade of EU-15 with NM-10 and CC-3, 2000

| | Value (billion euro) | | % of total EU-15 trade with NM-10 and CC-3 | |
	Imports	Exports	Imports	Exports
Austria	9.4	10.1	8.0	6.7
Belgium	4.6	6.5	3.9	4.3
Denmark	2.2	2.2	1.9	1.5
Finland	2.0	4.4	1.7	2.9
Germany	50.6	57.4	43.2	38.2
Greece	3.0	5.4	2.6	3.6
France	9.7	14.9	8.3	9.9
Ireland	0.8	1.7	0.7	1.1
Italy	13.3	20.4	11.4	13.6
Luxembourg	0.2	0.3	0.2	0.2
Netherlands	6.1	8.5	5.2	5.7
Portugal	0.8	0.5	0.7	0.3
Spain	1.8	2.5	1.5	1.7
Sweden	3.6	5.3	3.1	3.5
UK	9.0	10.3	7.7	6.9
EU-15	117.0	150.3	100	100

Source: Eurostat, *Statistics in Focus*, 'The 13 Candidate Countries' Trade with the EU', 2000.

1996 and 1999 as a result of the restructuring process that was under way; and since 2003 it has been stabilized at an average level of about 10 per cent (see Figure 1.2). In many NMs the employment problem is particularly serious for the young people aged under 25 years: they are experiencing on average an unemployment rate of 20.5 per cent as compared to 16.4 per cent in the EU-15. Long-term unemployment is also a problem for all the NM-10 countries except Cyprus, but it is particularly serious for Poland and Slovakia where it amounts to 10.7 and 11.1 per cent respectively of the total labour force. Of the 3 CC countries Bulgaria experiences particularly serious unemployment problems, currently having an unemployment rate of 11.9 per cent, long-term unemployment 8.9 per cent and youth unemployment 24.4 per cent. As far as inflation is concerned, in the NM-10 countries considerable progress has been made since 1997, when all of them undertook to implement stabilization policies (see Figure 1.2). However, inflation in most of them is still high when compared with that of the EU-15 average (see column (e) of Table 1.9), something requiring attention given its adverse impact on the competitiveness of the NMs' exports. At the same time, except in Malta, Slovenia and Cyprus, total labour productivity is well below the EU-15 average (see

Figure 1.2 Unemployment and inflation in the NM-10 countries

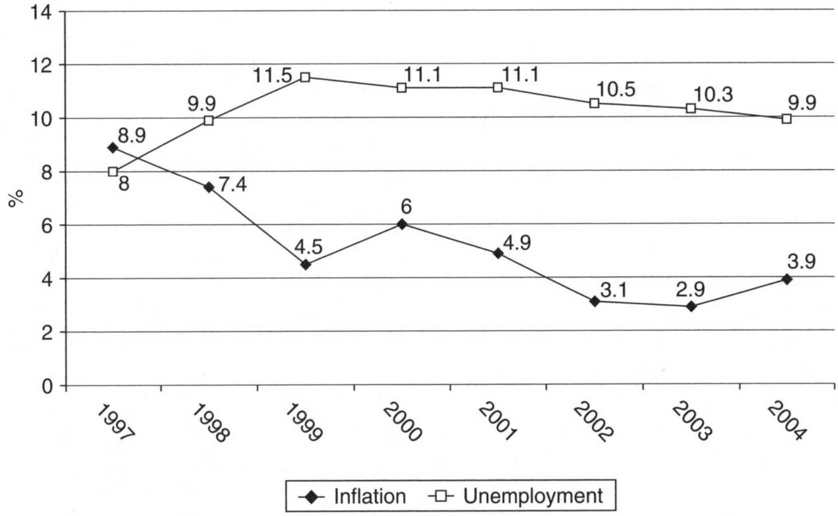

Source: Eurostat database, *Structural Indicators*

column (d)). In 2004, total labour productivity in the 10 new member states was on average no more than 60 per cent of that of the EU-15; and in the 3 CC countries it was on average no move than 35 per cent of that of the EU-15. In general, the much lower GDP per head in the newcomers and prospective members together with their low labour-productivity levels, high unemployment and inflation rates and the need to modernize their economies and adopt new technologies in industry require a lot of structural and cohesion spending.

Recognizing this need for additional resources to adapt their economies to the new environment, the EU-15 Heads of State at the Copenhagen Summit of December 2002 committed themselves to make available to the 10 NM states between 2004 and 2006 a total amount of 40.7 billion euro (see Table 1.10). Of this amount, the biggest item, almost 22 billion (Heading 2), is structural and cohesion funding. Structural and cohesion funding are financial instruments addressed to less prosperous regions and countries. Structural funds, set at 14.3 billion in total, aim at increasing regional growth, competitiveness and the creation of jobs. Cohesion funds are to be used to finance major investment in transport and the environment in the NM-10 states, assisting them to cope with the requirements of the internal market; they are set at 7.5 billion. As far as agriculture is concerned (Heading 1), a total amount of almost 10 billion euro has been made available, of which almost 5 billion concern direct

Table 1.9 Labour market conditions and inflation rates, 2004

	(a) Total unemploy-ment rate, % of labour force	(b) Long-term unemployed, % of labour force	(c) Unemploy-ment rate of persons aged under 25 years (%)	(d) Total labour productivity per person employed as % of EU-15 = 100	(e) Inflation rate
Cyprus	5.0	1.1	10.6	68.2	1.9
Czech Republic	8.3	3.8	21.1	59.8	2.6
Estonia	9.2	4.6	21.0	46.1	3.0
Hungary	5.9	2.4	14.8	64.5	6.8
Latvia	9.8	4.3	19.0	40.7	6.2
Lithuania	10.8	6.1	19.9	46.1	1.1
Malta	7.3	3.5	16.7	80.5	2.7
Poland	18.8	10.7	39.5	56.4	3.6
Slovakia	18.0	11.1	32.3	57.0	7.4
Slovenia	6.0	3.4	14.3	71.1	3.2
NM-10	9.9	5.1	20.5	59.1	3.9
Bulgaria	11.9	8.9	24.4	30.5	6.1
Romania	7.1	4.1	21.4	33.1	11.9
Turkey	10.2	2.4	20.5	39.0	n.a
CC-3	9.7	5.1	22.1	34.2	
EU-15	8.0	3.3	16.4	100	2.0

Sources: (a), (c) Eurostat database, *Long-term Indicators,* Population and Social Conditions
(b), (d), (e) Eurostat database – *Structural Indicators*

support to farmers and 5 billion are to be used for promoting rural development. Of the remaining amount, about 4 billion constitutes funding for internal policies and transitional expenditure (Heading 3) and almost 2 billion is to be used for administration (Heading 4). There is also Heading X, agreed during the negotiations that led to the signing of the Accession Treaty in December 2002, which includes a special cash-flow facility and a temporary-budget-compensation facility amounting to a total of about 3 billion euro. As regards the biggest items, namely Headings 1 and 2, of the total available resources for agriculture and structural actions (31.5 billion), about 25 per cent (8 billion) is to be made available in 2004, about 35 per cent (10.6 billion) will be made available in 2005, and the remaining 40 per cent (12.9 billion) will be released in 2006. In agriculture

Table 1.10 Enlargement funding (billion euro), 2004–2006

	2004	2005	2006	Total 2004–2006
Heading 1: Agriculture	1.9	3.7	4.1	9.7
• Common Agricultural Policy	0.3	2.0	2.3	4.6
• Rural development	1.6	1.7	1.8	5.1
Heading 2: Structural actions	6.1	6.9	8.8	21.8
• Structural Fund	3.5	4.8	6.0	14.3
• Cohesion Fund	2.6	2.1	2.8	7.5
Heading 3: Internal policies & *transitional expenditure*	1.4	1.4	1.4	4.2
Heading 4: Administration	0.5	0.6	0.6	1.7
Heading X: Special cash-flow *facility and temporary* *budgetary compensation*	1.3	1.1	0.9	3.3
Total of Headings	11.2	13.7	15.8	40.7

Source: Copenhagen European Council 12–13 December 2002, Presidency Conclusions, *Press Release* 14/2/2002, European Commission.

about 20 per cent (1.9 billion) of total resources (9.7 billion) will be made available in 2004 and about 40 per cent in 2005 and 2006 (3.7 and 4.1 billion). Serious problems may arise in this sector after 2013: from 2013 onwards, with the 10 new member states being fully incorporated into the EU, the Commission will be faced with the task of allocating the limited agricultural budget to 25 rather than to 15 states, something that will make more urgent the need for a reform of the common agricultural policy. Problems may also arise after 2007 in the area of regional and social policy. Regions with income per head less than 75 per cent of the EU average receive funding from the Cohesion Fund, while those with income per head more than 75 per cent of the EU's average are not eligible to such funding. At the moment, several regions in Portugal, Greece, Spain and Italy are recipients of such funding. When the 10 NM states will be fully incorporated into the European Union, the level of average income in the EU, on the basis of which cohesion funding is determined, will fall. A number of such regions will then find themselves outside the 75% limit, something that may create conflicts among the 25 member states.

Nevertheless, all the 10 new members, as well as the 3 candidate countries, are expected to have GDP growth rates above those in the EU-15 in the years to come, something that will help them acheive convergence with the rest of Europe in the longer run (see Table 1.11). The NM-10 on average experienced real GDP growth of 4.1 per cent

Table 1.11 Real GDP growth, GDP per capita in PPS and labour productivity – 2003–2006*

	Real GDP growth rate %				GDP per capita in PPS (EU-15 = 100)				Percentage change between 2003–2006	Labour productivity per person employed (EU-15 = 100)				Percentage change between 2003–2006
	2003	2004	2005	2006	2003	2004	2005	2006		2003	2004	2005	2006	
Cyprus	1.9	3.5	3.9	4.2	74.5	75.0	75.8	76.7	3.0	67.7	68.2	68.9	69.8	3.1
Czech Republic	3.7	3.8	3.8	4.0	63.0	64.2	65.4	66.8	6.0	58.2	59.8	61.2	62.6	7.6
Estonia	5.1	5.9	6.0	6.2	44.4	46.4	48.4	50.6	14.0	45.0	46.1	47.6	49.4	9.8
Hungary	3.0	3.9	3.7	3.8	55.4	56.7	57.9	58.9	6.3	63.4	64.5	65.5	66.7	5.2
Latvia	7.5	7.5	6.7	6.7	37.5	39.8	41.8	43.8	16.8	38.8	40.7	42.6	44.4	14.4
Lithuania	9.7	7.1	6.4	5.9	41.9	44.2	46.2	47.9	14.3	44.5	46.1	47.9	49.5	11.2
Malta	-0.3	1.0	1.5	1.8	67.6	66.7	66.2	65.7	-2.9	81.5	80.5	80.3	79.9	-2.0
Poland	3.8	5.8	4.9	4.5	42.1	43.8	45.2	46.3	10.0	54.5	56.8	58.3	59.3	8.8
Slovakia	4.0	4.9	4.5	5.2	47.7	49.2	50.4	51.9	8.8	55.1	57.0	58.3	59.9	8.7
Slovenia	2.5	4.0	3.6	3.8	70.3	71.8	72.9	74.2	5.5	69.7	71.1	72.3	73.7	5.7
NM-10	4.1	4.7	4.5	4.6	54.4	55.8	57.0	58.3	8.2	57.8	59.1	60.3	61.5	7.3
Bulgaria	4.3	5.5	6.0	4.5	27.2	28.3	29.5	30.4	11.8	29.8	30.5	31.2	31.8	6.7
Romania	4.9	7.2	5.6	5.1	27.1	28.7	29.8	30.8	13.7	31.4	33.1	34.5	35.8	14.0
Turkey	5.8	8.5	5.0	5.3	25.4	26.7	27.0	27.5	8.3	37.3	39.0	39.2	39.5	5.9
CC-3	5.0	7.1	5.5	5.0	26.6	27.9	28.8	29.6	11.3	32.8	34.2	35.0	35.7	8.9
EU-15	0.8	2.2	2.2	2.3	100	100	100	100		100	100	100	100	

* 2005, 2006 forecasts
Source: Eurostat database – *Structural Indicators*

in 2003 and 4.7 per cent in 2004 as compared to only 0.8 and 2.2 per cent respectively in EU-15; and recent estimates show that high growth rates will continue in 2005 and 2006 (real growth is expected to be at 4.5 and 4.6 per cent in 2005 and 2006 respectively in NM-10 as compared to 2.2 and 2.3 per cent (in EU-15). Labour productivity and GDP per head in PPS have also improved in all NM-10 (except Malta) since 2003 and are expected to continue on an upward trend, giving an average (predicted) increase for the whole period 2003–6 that has followed the signing of the Accession Treaty of 7.3 per cent for labour productivity and of 8.2 per cent for GDP per head. This is because most of the 10 NM states have good prospects for rapid investment. Installing new machines and adjusting to new technologies, for example, is likely to be a relatively easy process in most NMs, given their well-educated labour force (see Table 1.12, column (a), where the percentage of people having completed at least upper secondary education is on average 80.4 per cent of total population in the NM countries as compared to 64.6 per cent in EU-15). Their public-administration systems are also expected to function more efficiently in the coming years, given the major restructuring that is currently under way in their public sectors, something that will contribute further to investment growth and GDP growth. Moreover, foreign direct investment in the NM-10 countries has shown

Table 1.12 Labour force quality and hourly labour costs, 2002[*]

	(a)	(b)
	% of the population aged 25 to 64 having completed at least upper secondary education	Hourly wage cost (euro)
Cyprus	66.5	9.9
Czech Republic	87.8	5.4
Estonia	87.5	3.7
Hungary	71.4	4.9
Latvia	82.6	2.4
Lithuania	84.8	2.9
Malta	n.a.	7.6
Poland	80.8	5.3
Slovakia	85.8	3.6
Slovenia	76.8	9.7
NM-10	80.4	5.5
EU-15	64.6	23.4

[*] latest available
Sources: (a) Eurostat, *Yearbook 2004* – Population and Social Conditions
(b) Eurostat, *Yearbook 2004* – Economy and Finance

a significant upward trend since 2000, as many European firms have sought to take advantage of both the abolition by the EU-15 of the trade barriers on manufactured imports from them and the cheap labour force in these countries (see Table 1.12, column (b), where in 2002 the average hourly wage cost in the NM countries was 5.5 euro as compared with 23.4 euro in EU-15). These factors suggest that all the NM states are most likely to develop into 'dynamic economies' in the longer run and thus be able to cope with the competitive pressures within Europe. Indeed, several recent studies suggest that in the longer run, the enlargement will lead to income gains for both sides, that is, for both the newcomers and the EU-15, although for the former the benefits will be relatively larger since they start form a lower economic base. For example, a recent study by the Commission (European Commission (2001)) predicts that the enlargement of May 2004 could increase the level of real GDP of the EU-15 by 0.7 percentage points on a cumulative basis and the rate of growth of real GDP in the NM countries by between 1.3 and 2.1 percentage points. Surveys of public opinion also show that over 55 per cent of the EU-15 citizens has welcome the enlargement; and that about 65 per cent of the citizens of the NM countries would have voted 'yes' in a referendum about EU membership.[55]

At the same time, with the increase in the number of EU states from 15 to 25 in May 2004 and probably to 27 by 2007, certain institutional changes have become necessary. For this reason, the *Protocol for the Enlargement of the EU (No 1)* and the *Declaration for the Enlargement (No 20)*[57] have been annexed to the Nice Treaty. According to the *Declaration for the Enlargement*, after 2007, when the EU will consist of 27 member states, the European Parliament will have 732 MEPs, with the more populous states retaining the power in the EP's decision-making (see Table 1.13). As far as the Council's decision-making procedure is concerned, the Nice Treaty in many cases replaces unanimity with qualified–majority voting. While there are some changes, the vote-weighting population-reflected complexities regarding qualified majority voting are retained. In particular, according to the *Declaration for the Enlargement*, a total of 345 votes are to be allocated to the 27 member states, with the distribution of votes not being in full accord with the population of the states. Proportionately the member states with smaller populations will still have more votes than their populations warrant. Thus Germany, the UK, France and Italy will have 29 votes each; Spain and Poland 27 votes each; Romania 14; the Netherlands 13; Greece, Belgium, Portugal, the Czech Republic and Hungary 12 votes each; Sweden, Austria and Bulgaria 10 votes each; Denmark, Slovakia, Finland and Lithuania 7 votes each; Latvia, Slovenia, Estonia, Cyprus and Luxembourg 4 votes each; and Malta 3 votes. When the Council is acting following a Commission's

Table 1.13   Number of Members in Parliament and votes in Council after the 2007 enlargement

	Number of Members in Parliament	Number of votes in Council
Austria	17	10
Belgium	22	12
Bulgaria	17	10
Cyprus	6	4
Czech Republic	20	12
Denmark	13	7
Finland	13	7
Germany	99	29
Greece	22	12
Estonia	6	4
France	72	29
Hungary	20	12
Ireland	12	7
Italy	72	29
Latvia	8	4
Lithuania	12	7
Luxembourg	6	4
Malta	5	3
Netherlands	25	13
Poland	50	27
Portugal	22	12
Romania	33	14
Slovakia	13	7
Slovenia	7	4
Spain	50	27
Sweden	18	10
UK	72	29
Total	732	345

Source: Eurostat database – *The European Union at a Glance*, *http://www.europa.eu.int/abc/index2_en.htm*.

proposal, qualified majority will require 258 casting votes plus 14 member states; in all other cases a majority of 258 casting votes plus 18 member states will be required for a measure to be passed. In general, the *Declaration for the Enlargement* creates a new system of dual majority whereby measures are not passed unless the member states in favour constitute a percentage significantly greater than 50 per cent of the EU's total population. As far as the composition of the Commission is concerned, the *Protocol for the Enlargement of the EU* accepts the principle that "each member state has one Commissioner". According to this principle, the five largest member states, namely Germany, France, Italy, Spain and the UK, will give up their second commissioner so that from May 2004 onwards all 25 EU states will have one commissioner each. However, in 2007 the number of commissioners will fall short of the number of states. The principle 'one state one commissioner' will then have to be amended; and the composition of the Commission will be decided by the Council acting on unanimity.

Notes

1 For a historical background and the development of the European Community, see Fontaine (1990), Urwin (1995), Salmon and Nicoll (1997), Dedman (1996), McAllister (1997) and Swann (1992). See also Nicoll and Salmon (2001), Maclay (1998), Bainbridge (1998), Pierson (1996), Archer and Butler (1996), Maresceau (1997) and Bulmer (1994).

2 According to Article 97 ECSC, the Treaty of Paris that established the ECSC was due to expire in July 2002 unless steps were taken for renewing it.

3 The invitation was initially accepted and a Board-of-Trade official was dispatched but later recalled by the Spaak Committee.

4 See Bulmer (1994).

5 The UK acceded to the Communities under a Conservative government with Edward Heath as prime minister. A referendum held in 1975 under a Labour government, with Harold Wilson as prime minister, endorsed overwhelmingly, by a nearly 2:1 majority, Community membership (see Irving, 1975).

6 The documents relating to the accession of Greece were signed in Athens on 28 May 1979, while the Treaties of Accession of Spain and Portugal were signed in Madrid and Lisbon, respectively, on 12 June 1985.

7 The EC and the EFTA countries, that is Austria, Sweden, Norway, Iceland, Finland and Liechtenstein, created the European Economic Area (EEA) that came into being at the beginning of 1994. This was viewed by many EFTA countries as a preliminary step to full EC membership.

8 Norway again remained outside of the Community because of a negative verdict delivered by the Norwegian people.

9 Negotiations with these countries were concluded in December 2002.

10 The SEA is published in the *Official Journal* 1987 L 169/1. See also Moravcsik (1991).

11 See COM (85) 310, and also Armstong and Bulmer (1998).

12 See European Commission (1992).

13 According to Article A (third paragraph) of the EU Treaty 'The Union shall be founded on the European Communities, supplemented by the policies and forms of co-operation established by this Treaty'. For an analysis

and assessment of the Maastricht Treaty see Wessels (1994), O'Keefe and Twomey (1995), Marks *et al.* (1996) and Grieco (1995).

14 To avoid confusion, the provisions of the EU Treaty are identified by letters in contrast with the other three Community Treaties where provisions are identified by numbers.

15 See 'Intergovernmental Conference on the Revision of the Treaties', Italian Presidency, *Collected Texts*, General Secretariat, Council of the EU, Brussels, July 1996.

16 See 'Conclusions of the Madrid European Council', *EU Bulletin* 12–1995, Annex 15.

17 See European Commission (1999, 2000). See also Moravcsik and Nicolaidis (1999), Walker (1998), Ehlermann (1998) and Shaw (1998).

18 See Pescatore (2001) and also Johnston (2001).

19 For an analysis and evaluation of the role of the Council in the Community's decision-making process see Westlake (1997) and Bulmer and Wessels (1987). See also Nugent (2003) and O'Nuallain (1985).

20 In relation to majority voting, it is worth mentioning the Luxembourg Compromise of 29 January 1966 that was in fact an 'agreement to disagree'. It is not a legally binding agreement but it has been used in practice. According to the Luxembourg compromise a member state can exercise a veto in the Council when its vital national interests are at stake.

21 Because of the EU enlargement to 25 members the distribution of votes has been changed in the Treaty of Nice (see the discussion on pages 48–50).

22 In connection with the blocking minority, something must be said about the so-called 'Ioannina Compromise' that deals with the appropriate size of the blocking minority when qualified majority voting applies to the Council after the accession of Austria, Sweden and Finland to the European Union. The Ioannina Compromise was passed in the Council Decision of March 1994 (*Official Journal*, 1994C 105/I) as amended by the Council Decision of 1 January 1995 (*Official Journal*, 1995CI/I). According to this decision, 'if members of the Council representing a total of 23 to 25 votes indicate their intention to oppose the adoption by the Council of a decision by qualified majority, the Council will do all in its power to reach, within a reasonable time a satisfactory solution that could be adopted by at least 65 votes. During this period and always respecting the rules of procedure of the Council, the President undertakes with the assistance of the Commission any initiative necessary to facilitate a wider basis of agreement in the Council.'

23 On this, Article 202 states that 'The Council may request the Commission to undertake any studies which the Council considers desirable for the attainment of the common objectives and to submit to any appropriate proposals.'

24 See the discussion on pages 48–50. For an analysis of the role of the Commission in the EC decision-making process see, for example, Nugent (2001) and Edwards and Spence (1994).

25 See the European Parliament's Rules of Procedure, Rule 33 (5).

26 There are numerous provisions that empower the Council to act on a proposal from the Commission when making Community legislation.

27 Although the Council has the power to pass legislation in nearly all cases, the Commission retains discretion as to the content and timing of the proposal it puts forward to the Council.

28 The justification for the Commission being granted the power of proposal was that its autonomy and its expertise would result in its being best able to represent the common European interest. See for example Featherstone (1994).

29 See COM(85) 310 final.

30 Council Decision 87/373 as amended. It should be noted that all different procedures involve committees composed of national officials.

31 There are three main procedures for the Commission's exercise of powers delegated by the Council:
   • Advisory Committee, Procedure I.
   • Management Committee, Procedure II.
   • Regulatory Committee, Procedure III.
   Procedure I places no constraint on the Commission's power to pass delegated law, while Procedure III imposes the greater restriction on it.

32 See Article 3(1) SEA and the ensuing Articles which refer to the European Parliament. For an extensive discussion of the EP's functions see for example Corbett *et al.* (1995) and Westlake (1994). See also Hix and Lord (1997) and Greenwood (1997).

33 See also Council Directive 93/109 on exercising the right to vote in European Parliament elections, *Official Journal*, 1993 L329/34.

34 The Treaty of Nice has changed this to allow for the participation of the 10 new member states.

35 The Bureau has a number of administrative and financial functions laid down by the Rules of Procedure.

36 There is no requirement for this session to be convened.

37 The Court of Justice and the Court of First Instance acting in their judicial role are excluded from the jurisdiction of the Ombudsman.

38 The Parliament must act in one way or the other in 45 days otherwise the budget is deemed to be finally approved.

39 All Council decisions connected with the budgetary procedure are taken by qualified majority.

40 See Article 6 of the Rules of Procedure of the Court, *Official Journal* 1991 L 176, as amended in *Official Journal*, 1995 L 44/61.

41 Council Decision 88/591 on 24 October 1988, *Official Journal*, 1988 L319 and *Official Journal*, 189C 215/1. For an analysis of the functions and role of the Court of First Instance, see for example Pappas (1990). For the role of the Court of Justice and of European Courts more generally see Plender (1997) and Schermers and Waelbroeck (1992).

42 For a discussion of the institutional arrangements regarding the ECB and the problems involved, see Pipkorn (1994), Smits (1996), Beaumont and Walker (1999), Crowley (2001) and Gormley and De Haan (1996).

43 For the legal dimensions of European integration see Armstrong (1998). See also Craig and De Burca (1997, 1999), Wyatt and Dashwood (1993), Greaves (1996), Dashwood (1996), Burns (1996), Timmermans (1997), Boyron (1996), Weatherill and Beaumont (1999) and Chalmers (1998).

44 Article 230 is the principal device to review the legality of Community Acts. That is, direct actions for the annulment of Community Acts may be brought before the Court of Justice under Article 230.
45 See Joined Cases 16 and 17/92, *Producteurs de Fruits* v. *Council* [1962] *European Court Reports (ECR)*, 471, 478.
46 See Case C-322/88, *Grimaldi* v. *Fonds des Maladies Professionelles* [1989] *ECR*, 4407.
47 Rules of Procedure EP, Rules 53 and 54.
48 See for example Case 138/79, *Roquette Freres* v. *Council* [1980] *ECR*, 3333.
49 See Case C-65/93, *European Parliament* v. *Council*.
50 See Case C-388/92, *European Parliament* v. *Council* [1994] *ECR*, I-2067.
51 Case 1253/79, *Battaglia* v. *Commission* [1982] *ECR*, 297; Case C-331/88, *Queen* v. *Minister of Agriculture, Fisheries and Food and Secretary of State for Health, FEDESA and others* [1990] *ECR*, I-4023, 4067.
52 See *European Parliament Progress Report on the Delegations to the Conciliation Committee*, Annex II, 6. PE 223, 209.
53 See European Commission (2003).
54 Accession Treaty: *http://www.europa.eu.int/comm/enlargement/negotiations/treaty_of_accession_2003*
55 Other studies on the economic effects of enlargement include Baldwin, Francois and Porters (1997), Grabbe (2001) and Boeri and Brücker (2001). See also European Commission (2003) and the Commission's regular enlargement papers – *European Commission: Enlargement Papers, http://www.europa.eu.int/comm/economy/finance*
56 The Treaty of Nice does not reform drastically the institutional framework of the EU. The aim of the amendments provided in it is to simply absorb the new member states. The composition and the powers of the EU's political institutions cannot be viewed in isolation: political agreement on changing the number of commissioners has been inextricably linked to reform of the Council's voting system.
57 See Accession Treaty, Protocols: *http://www.europa.eu.int/comm/enlargement/negotiations/treaty_of_accession_2003*

References

Archer, C. and Butler, F. (1996) *The European Union: Structure and Process* (London: Pinter).
Armstrong, A. (1998) 'Legal Integration: Theorising the Legal Dimension of European Integration', *Journal of Common Market Studies*, vol. 36, pp. 155–74.
Armstrong, A. and Bulmer, S. (1998) *The Governance of the Single European Market* (Manchester: Manchester University Press).
Bainbridge, T. (1998) *The Penguin Companion to European Union* (London: Penguin).
Baldwin, R., Francois, J.F. and Porters, R. (1997) 'The Costs and Benefits of Eastern Enlargement', *Economic Policy*, vol. 24, pp. 127–76.
Beaumont, P. and Walker, N. (1999) *Legal Framework of the Single Currency* (Oxford-Portland: Hart Publishing).

Boeri, T. and Brücker, H., (2001) *The Impact of Eastern Enlargement on Employment and Labour Markets in the EU Member States Final Report*, Directorate General for Economic and Social Affairs, European Integration Consortium, Berlin and Milan.

Boyron, C. (1996) 'Maastricht and the Co-decision Procedure: A Success Story', *International Corporate Law Quarterly*, vol. 45, pp. 293–318.

Bulmer, S. (1994) 'History and Institutions of the European Union', in M. Artis and N. Lee (eds), *The Economics of the European Union* (Oxford: Oxford University Press).

Bulmer, S. and Wessels, W. (1987) *The European Council* (London: Macmillan – Palgrave).

Burns, H. (1996) 'Law Reform in the European Community and its Limits', *Yearbook of European Law*, vol. 16, pp. 243–75.

Chalmers, D. (1998) *European Union: Law and EU Government* (London: Ashgate)

Corbett, R., Jacobs, F. and Shackleton, M. (1995) *The European Parliament* (London: Cartermill).

Craig, P. and De Burca, G. (1997) *EC Law: Text, Cases and Materials* (Oxford: Clarendon Press).

Craig, P. and De Burca, G. (1999) *The Evolution of EU Law* (Oxford: Oxford University Press).

Crowley, P. (2001) 'The Institutional Implications of EMU', *Journal of Common Market Studies*, vol. 39, pp. 385–404.

Dashwood, A. (1996) 'The Limits of European Community Powers', *European Law Review*, vol. 21, pp. 113–28.

Deadman, M. (1996) *The Origins and Development of the European Union 1945–1995* (London: Routledge).

Edwards, G. and Spence, D. (eds) (1994) *The European Commission* (London: Cartermill).

Ehlermann, C.D. (1998) 'Differentiation, Flexibility, Closer Co-operation: The New Provisions of the Amsterdam Treaty', *European Law Journal*, vol. 4, pp. 246–70.

European Commission (1992) *Treaty on European Union*, Office for Official Publications, Luxembourg.

European Commission (1999) *Employment in Europe*, Luxembourg.

European Commission (2000) *Strategies for Jobs in the Information Society*, Brussels.

European Commission (2001) *The Economic Impact of Enlargement*, Directorate General for Economic and Financial Affairs, May.

European Commission (2003) 'Progress Towards Meeting Economic Criteria for Accession: the Assessment from the 2003 Comprehensive Monitoring Reports and Regular Report', *European Economy* – Enlargement Paper No. 19, Directorate General for Economic and Financial Affairs.

Featherstone, K. (1994) 'Jean Monnet and the Democratic Deficit in the European Union', *Journal of Common Market Studies*, vol. 149, pp. 154–5.

Fontaine, G. (1990) *Europe – A Fresh Start: The Schuman Declaration, 1950–90*, EC Official Publications, Luxembourg.

Gormley, L. and de Haan, J. (1996) 'The Democratic Deficit of the European Central Bank', *European Law Review*, vol. 21, pp. 95–112.

Grabbe, H. (2001) *Profiting from EU Enlargement* (London: Center for European Reform).

Greaves, R. (1996) 'The Nature and Binding Effect of Decisions under Article 189 EC', *European Law Review*, vol. 21, pp. 3–16.

Greenwood, J. (1997) *Representing Interests in the EU* (London: Macmillan – Palgrave).

Grieco, J. (1995) 'The Maastricht Treaty, Economic and Monetary Union and the Neorealist Research Programme', *Review of International Studies*, vol. 21, pp. 21–40.

Hix, S. and Lord, C. (1997) *Political Parties in the European Union* (London: Macmillan – Palgrave).

Irving, R. (1975) 'The United Kingdom Referendum: 1975–76', *European Law Review*, vol. 1, pp. 20–32.

Johnston, A. (2001) 'Judicial Reform and the Treaty of Nice', *Common Market Law Review*, vol. 38, pp. 499–523.

Maclay, M. (1998) *The European Union*, Sutton, Gloucestershire.

Maresceau, M. (eds) (1997) *Enlarging the European Union* (London: Longman).

Marks, P., Hooghe L. and Blank, K. (1996) 'European Integration from the 1980s', *Journal of Common Market Studies*, vol. 14, pp. 341–78.

McAllister, R. (1997) *From EC to EU: A Historical and Political Study* (London: Routledge).

Moravcsik, K.A. (1991) 'Negotiating the Single European Act', *Industrial Organization*, vol. 45, pp. 19–56.

Moravcsik, K.A. and Nicolaidis, K., (1999) 'Explaining the Treaty of Amsterdam: Interests, Influences and Institutions', *Journal of Common Market Studies*, vol. 37, pp. 59–85.

Nicoll, W. and Salmon, T. (2001) *Understanding the European Union* (Essex: Pearson Educational Ltd).

Nugent, N. (2001) *The European Commission* (London: Macmillan – Palgrave).

Nugent, N. (2003) *The Government and Politics of the European Union* (London: Macmillan – Palgrave).

O'Keefe, D. and Towney, P. (eds) (1995) *Legal Issues of the Maastricht Treaty* (London: Chancery Press).

O'Nuallain, C. (eds) (1985) *The Presidency of the European Council* (London: Croom Helm).

Pappas, S. (eds) (1990) *The Court of First Instance of the European Communities*, European Institute of Public Administration, Maastricht.

Pescatore, P. (2001) 'Nice Aftermath', *Common Market Law Review*, vol. 38, pp. 265–71.

Pierson, P. (1996) 'The Path to European Integration: A Historical Institutionalist Analysis', *Comparative Political Studies*, vol. 29, pp. 123–163.

Pipkorn, J. (1994) 'Legal Arrangements in the Treaty of Maastricht for the Effectiveness of the EMU', *Common Market Law Review*, vol. 31, pp. 263–91.

Plender, R. (ed) (1997) *European Courts: Practice and Precedents* (London: Sweet & Maxwell).

Salmon, T. and Nicoll, W. (1997) *Building European Union: A Documentary History and Analysis* (Manchester: Manchester University Press).

Schermers, H.G. and Waelbroeck, D. (1992) *Judicial Protection in the European Communities* (Deventer: Kluwer).

Shaw, J. (1998) 'The Treaty of Amsterdam: Challenges of Flexibility and Legitimacy', *European Law Journal*, vol. 4, pp. 63–86.

Smits, R. (1996) *The European Central Bank – Institutional Aspects* (Deventer: Kluwer).

Smits, R. (2005) 'The European Constitution and EMU: An Appraisal', *Common Market Law Review*, vol. 42, pp. 425–68.

Swann, D., (1992), *The Economics of the Common Market* (London: Penguin).

Timmermans, C. (1997) 'How Can One Improve the Quality of Community Legislation?', *Common Market Law Review*, vol. 34, pp. 1229–57.

Urwin, D. (1995) *The Community of Europe: A History of European Integration since 1945*, (London: Longman).

Walker, N. (1998) 'Sovereignty and Differentiated Integration in the European Union', *European Law Journal*, vol. 4, pp. 355–88.

Weatherill, S. and Beaumont, P. (1999) *EU Law: The Essential Guide to the Legal Workings of the European Union* (London: Penguin Books).

Wessels, W. (1994) 'Rationalism in the Maastrict Treaty: The Search for an Optimal Strategy of the New Europe', *International Affairs*, no. 3.

Westlake, M. (1994) *A Modern Guide to the European Parliament* (London: Pinter).

Westlake, M. (1997) *The Council of the European Union* (London: Cartermill).

Wyatt, D. and Dashwood, A. (1993) *European Community Law* (London: Sweet & Maxwell).

2 Trade Flows and Economic Integration

Athina Zervoyianni

Introduction

Integration agreements may take many different forms depending on the degree of integration of the economies involved. In the literature, eight types are usually mentioned:

- preferential trade areas (PTAs)
- free trade areas (FTAs)
- customs unions (CUs)
- single market areas (SMAs)
- common markets (CMs)
- monetary or currency unions (MUs)
- economic unions (EUs)
- political integration (PI)

Preferential trade areas represent the lowest level of integration. In a PTA lower tariff rates are imposed on import from member states than on imports from non-members. In a free trade area, tariffs on imports from member countries are eliminated entirely; member states of a FTA are free to choose whatever tariff policy they wish towards non-member countries. A customs union involves both completely free trade between participating countries and the adoption of a common external tariff *vis-à-vis* the rest of the world. In a CM, in addition to the abolition of tariffs on imports from member states and the adoption of a common external tariff, there is free movement of factors of production between member countries. SMAs are CMs that also involve complete product-market integration through the removal of all institutional and other non-tariff barriers to the free exchange of goods and services among participating countries. MUs are common markets or SMAs that also involve close cooperation in the monetary-policy field and fixed exchange rates, or a common currency and a central monetary authority that conducts monetary policy for the

57

union as a whole. In EUs in addition to monetary integration there is also cooperation in the fiscal-policy front as well as in other areas of economic policy, including employment and social security policy. In the case of political integration the participating countries operate much like a single economy: in addition to a common currency and a central monetary authority, there is centralization of national budgets as well as a common fiscal authority that is accountable to a central Parliament.

What makes countries want to participate in integration agreements? Integration agreements are sometimes proposed for political reasons. But participating countries also seek to achieve economic gains. Such gains may be derived from:

- an increase in trade flows according to comparative advantage;
- the larger size of the market and the exploitation of scale economies;
- improvement of member states' terms-of-trade with the rest of the world;
- an increase in the intensity of competition among firms;
- reduced production costs due to integration-induced technological advances
- a more efficient allocation of factors of production within the integrated area;
- a higher rate if investment and thus economic growth;
- reduction of transaction costs in money and capital markets and elimination of exchange-rate uncertainty and risk; and
- elimination of externalities arising from international macroeconomic interdependence.

In what follows we examine the benefits for member countries to be derived from the formation of customs unions. We start in the following section with an analysis of free-trade equilibrium and the effects of uniform tariffs, and then consider the trade and welfare effects of customs unions, examining both the conventional static CU theory and the dynamic effects of CUs. The final section summarizes and draws conclusions.

Equilibrium Under Free Trade and the Effects of Tariffs

Autarky and Universally Free Trade

To understand the effects of integration agreements such as FTAs, CUs, CMs and so on, on trade flows and welfare, it is helpful to first study a situation of no trade and compare it to a situation of universally free trade. To do so, use will be made of production possibility frontiers (PPFs) and community indifference curves (CICs) (see Caves *et al.* (2001) and Krugman and Obstfeld (2002)). Perfect competition will be assumed throughout.

PPFs show efficient combinations of commodities that an economy can produce given the quantities of factors of production and technology. The TT curve in Figure 2.1(a) is a PPF schedule for an economy that produces two goods, X and Z. If the production of X is OX_1, then the maximum amount of Z that can be produced is OZ_1. Indeed, the TT curve reflects several standard principles of microeconomic theory. First, some points of production, like points E and D, are not feasible: they cannot be attained given the productive capacity of the economy under consideration. Second, the country under consideration can in principle produce at points that lie below the TT curve, such as point C. This, however, would be inefficient since a greater amount of both goods could be produced at other points, like point G. The third feature of the TT curve is that it is negatively sloped. This is due to the implicit assumption that factors of production are fixed. With fixed factors of production, to produce more of X than the amount corresponding to, say, point G, the production of Z must be reduced in order to release the necessary resources. Fourth, the TT curve is concave to the origin, showing the law of increasing costs: increasing amounts of $X(Z)$ must be sacrificed as the production of $Z(X)$ continues to expand by one unit at a time.

CICs show, given incomes and prices, all alternative combinations of aggregate purchases of Z and X that secure for a country's residents, as a group, a given level of utility (Figure 2.1(b)). The concept of a 'community indifference curve' is obviously looser than that of an individual's indifference curves. Indeed, certain assumptions need to be made if a CIC is to be uniquely defined. First, all residents of the country concerned must have the same preferences and therefore the

Figure 2.1

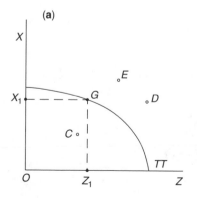
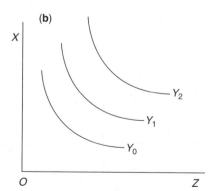

same indifference map. Second, preferences must be homothetic so that demand for a product is proportional to income. And, third, the distribution of income among individuals must remain constant. These assumptions may seem restrictive but are necessary to allow one to aggregate the individual consumers' indifference curves to obtain a unique set of community indifference curves.

Consider equilibrium in the closed-economy case, namely under autarky. In a closed economy the consumption point and the production point coincide. With perfect competition, equilibrium occurs at point E in Figure 2.2, where the community indifference curve Y is tangent to the production possibility frontier TT. Equilibrium relative prices, $P = (P_Z/P_x)$, are reflected in the absolute slope of the budget line, or price line, PP. For example, suppose that the utility function defining consumer preferences in the country under consideration is $V = V(X, Z)$. Taking the total differential of the utility function, we have $dV = V_x dX + V_z dZ$, where $V_x = \partial V(.)/\partial X$ is the marginal utility of X and $V_z = \partial V(.)/\partial Z$ is the marginal utility of Z. Along an indifference curve utility is constant, and thus setting $dV = 0$, we have $-V_x dX = V_z dZ$, or $-(dX/dZ) = (V_z/V_x)$. Utility maximization requires that the ratio of marginal utilities (V_z/V_x) equals relative prices $P = (P_z/P_x)$, that is $-(dX/dZ)_{\text{at } E} = P = P_z/P_x$. Accordingly, the slope of the PP line at point E shows the relative price of Z (PP is then the 'equilibrium' price line). The steeper the price line the more expensive is product Z relative to product X.

To study a situation of universally free trade, more than one country must be assumed. Consider the case where the world consists of two countries, a home country (country H) and a foreign country (country F). For reasons that will become evident shortly, if free trade is to result in economic gains, pre-trade price ratios in H and F, say

Figure 2.2

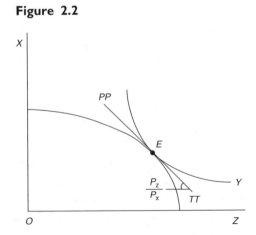

P_1 and P_1', must differ, that is $P_1 \gtrless P_1'$. From standard trade theory, this can happen for a variety of reasons. For example, P_1 may be lower than P_1' because the producers of Z in country H have lower costs of production than those in country F due to a technological advantage. Another example is the case where although the production technology is the same in both countries, the tastes of consumers in county F are biased towards good Z, while the tastes of consumers in H are biased towards good X. P_1 may also be lower than P_1' because a factor of production employed intensively in sector Z is relatively plentiful in country H and thus is less expensive there than in country F.

Indeed, suppose that tastes and production technologies are the same in both countries, but H and F differ in terms of their relative endowments of factors of production. More specifically, suppose that H and F produce the commodities X and Z with two factors of production, capital K, and labour L, but capital is relatively plentiful in country H and labour is relatively plentiful in country F. As a result, the capital/labour ratio in economy H will be greater than that in economy F, implying that $(K/L)_H > (K/L)_F$. Also, if we assume that Z is a capital-intensive good while X is a labour-intensive good, then with a constant-returns-to-scale technology, irrespective of factor prices, producers in sector $Z(X)$ will be using more capital (labour) than labour (capital) to produce one unit of $Z(X)$. Thus $(K/L)_Z > (K/L)_X$.

Under these assumptions, if both countries were to devote all their productive resources to sector Z (sector X), the quantity of $Z(X)$ produced in country H (country F) would be greater than in country F (country H). This would give production possibility frontiers like those represented by the curves TT and TT^* in Figures 2.3(a) and 2.3(b) respectively. With no trade, production and consumption in each country takes place at the point where the highest possible community

Figure 2.3

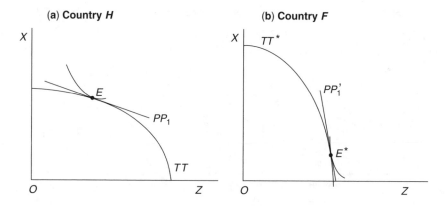

(a) Country H (b) Country F

indifference curve and the production possibility frontier are tangent to each other. Accordingly, equilibrium is at point E in country H and at point E^* in country F. Equilibrium relative prices in the pre-trade situation are represented by the lines PP_1 and PP_1'. The line PP_1 is less steep than the price line PP_1' indicating that with no trade $P_1 = (P_z/P_x)_H < P_1' = (P_z/P_x)_F$, and so Z is less expensive in country H than in country F. This follows logically: Z is a capital-intensive good and capital is relatively plentiful in country H. In a situation of no trade, one should therefore expect, other things being equal, Z to be less expensive in country H than in country F.

What effect would a trade agreement between H and F have on prices, consumption, production and welfare in each country? The first point to note is that on the assumption of no transport costs, international trade will have the effect of equalizing national price ratios: with free exchange of commodities, a common international price ratio will be established. This common price ratio will be given by the point where the sum of home and foreign residents' 'relative demands' for Z equals the 'relative supply' of Z.

Figures 2.4(a) and 2.4(c) show relative-demand and relative-supply schedules in H and F respectively. The schedules are derived from the PPF and the CIC diagrams. $S_H = (Q_z/Q_x)_H^s$ represents the relative supply of Z in country H, that is the quantity of Z supplied relative to that of X. The $D_H = (Q_z/Q_x)_H^d$ schedule represents the relative demand for Z in country H, namely the quantity of Z demanded relative to that of X. With no trade, the market in H is stabilized at price P_1. Similarly, S_F and D_F are the relative supply and relative demand schedules for country F. With no trade, the relative price of Z in country F is P_1'. In Figure 2.4(b), the lines S_W and D_W are 'world' relative demand and relative supply schedules; that is, $D_W = D_H + D_F$

Figure 2.4

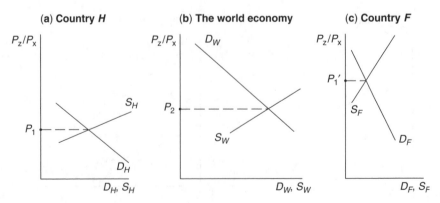

(a) Country H   (b) The world economy   (c) Country F

and $S_W = S_H + S_F$. With international trade, commodity markets will be stabilized at price P_2, where the 'world' relative demand for Z equals the world relative supply. As can be seen from the figure, the move from a situation of no trade to a situation of universally free trade involves a rise in the relative price of Z in the home country and a fall in the relative price of Z in the foreign country: in country H the relative price of Z rises from P_1 to P_2, while in country F it falls from P_1' to P_2.

In terms of Figure 2.5, the price change induced by free trade is represented by a change in the slope of the price lines PP_1 and PP_1'. We know that the steeper the price line the more expensive is commodity Z relative to commodity X. For country H, free trade implies a rise in the relative price of Z. The new (common) international price ratio under free trade can therefore be represented by the steeper price line PP_2. Faced with the new price line PP_2, firms in country H will increase the production of Z and reduce that of X. Thus, in the home country, production will shift from point E to point A. In country F, the price line becomes less steep: faced with the new price line PP_2, producers in F will now produce less of Z and more of X. The production point shifts from E^* to A^*.

How has the welfare of the residents of the two countries been affected by free trade? With trade, each country's consumption point need not be on its PPF. With free trade, H and F can reach the higher indifference curves Y_1 and Y_1^*, which are tangent to the common international price line PP_2, by importing and exporting commodities. The consumption point moves from point E to point B in country H and from E^* to B^* in country F. In the home country, OZ_2 units of Z are now produced domestically, of which, OZ_1 are consumed domestically and Z_1Z_2 are exported to country F. As regards commodity X,

Figure 2.5

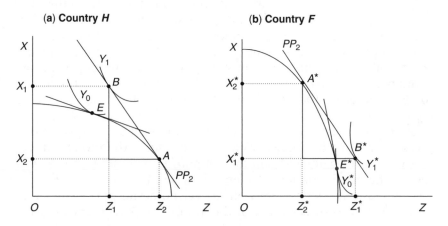

(a) Country H   (b) Country F

OX_2 is produced domestically and X_2X_1 is imported from country F. In the foreign economy the situation is exactly the opposite. $OZ_2{}^*$ is produced domestically and $Z_1{}^*Z_2{}^*$ is imported. Also, $OX_2{}^*$ is produced domestically and $X_2{}^*X_1{}^*$ is exported. Free trade increases welfare in both countries as country H's residents move from the indifference curve Y_0 to the higher indifference curve Y_1; and country F's residents move from curve $Y_0{}^*$ to curve $Y_1{}^*$.

But why is it that the move from self-sufficiency to universally free trade allows countries to increase welfare? The reason for the welfare gain is that free trade enables countries to specialize in the production of those goods in which they have a comparative advantage. Country H has a comparative advantage in the production of Z because Z is a capital-intensive product and in this country capital is relatively plentiful. Country F has a comparative advantage in the production of X because X is a labour-intensive product and labour in F is relatively plentiful. International trade, by allowing specialization according to comparative advantage, enables countries to consume more of all products, and so it results in welfare gains.

Trade barriers and the Effects of Uniform Tariffs

Trade obstacles. Despite the fact that trade theory suggests that countries benefit from free trade, national governments often impose obstacles to free trade so as to keep out foreign competition from domestic markets. There are several trade obstacles, including import tariffs, quotas on imports, production subsidies, exchange controls, import prohibition and other non-tariff barriers.

An import tariff is a tax on importing a good or a service into a country collected by customs officials at the place of entry. Tariffs can be of two forms: specific and *ad valorem*. A specific tariff is expressed as a fixed money amount per physical unit of the imported commodity. An *ad valorem* tariff is expressed as percentage of the market price of the good when it reaches the importing country. To the extent that tariffs will increase the demand for domestically-produced competing commodities, they will lead to increases in the domestic price of those commodities. From this point of view, tariffs indirectly affect adversely foreign producers and benefit the domestic producers of competing commodities.

Quotas are quantitative restrictions on imports: the government gives out a limited number of licenses to import the product under consideration legally and prohibits importing without a license. As a result, the total volume of imports allowed into a country per year is reduced. Quotas have effects on domestic prices similar to tariffs: as long as the quantity of the licensed imports is smaller than that which households and firms would import in the absence of the quota, quotas raise the price of domestically-produced competing goods above the world price. Thus, like tariffs, they discriminate in favour of domestically-produced competing commodities.

Production subsidies have the effect of reducing the costs of domestic production, and so, unlike tariffs and quotas that indirectly affect adversly foreign producers, they directly benefit domestic producers. Exchange controls restrict the amount of foreign exchange available for imports, therefore indirectly channelling domestic demand towards domestically-produced goods. Import prohibition directly seeks to protect domestic production at the expense of goods produced abroad. Non-tariff barriers to trade are institutional, technical and physical obstacles to the free movement of goods and services that indirectly discriminate against goods and services produced abroad.

Effects of uniform tariffs, partial equilibrium. To examine the welfare effects of a tariff, consider the market for a single commodity Q and assume an economy that is small relative to the rest of the world. D_h and S_h in Figure 2.6(a) are demand and supply schedules for the product. Assuming no externalities in consumption, the height of the line D_h at any point reflects the marginal utility of consumption, namely the benefit which consumers derive from the corresponding unit of Q consumed. The whole area under the demand curve represents total utility. Similarly, under the assumption of perfect competition, the height of the line S_h at each point reflects the marginal cost of producing the corresponding unit of Q and the whole area under the supply curve represents the total cost of production. With no trade, equilibrium is at point A. At point A, Q_1 is produced and purchased at

Figure 2.6

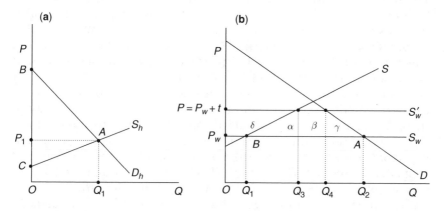

a market-clearing price P_1. Given the quantity purchased Q_1, the total utility derived by consumers from the product is area $OBAQ_1$. However the amount spent on Q is only area OP_1AQ_1. The difference between these two areas, the triangle P_1AB, is a net welfare gain arising from the fact that all units of Q, except for the last one, are purchased by consumers at a price lower than what they would have been prepared to pay for it (measured by the height of the demand curve at each unit of Q bought). Thus changes in the size of this triangle caused by trade flows can be viewed as representing a net change in 'consumers' surplus'. On the other hand, the total cost of producing the quantity Q_1 is given by area $OCAQ_1$. However producers' total revenue from selling the quantity Q_1 at price P_1 is the rectangular area OP_1AQ_1. The difference between these two areas, the triangle CP_1A, can be taken to represent 'producers' surplus'; and changes in the size of it can be seen as reflecting changes in the welfare of producers.

Figure 2.6(b) assumes trade flows. D is the demand curve for the commodity Q in the home country. S is the domestic supply curve, and S_w is the perfectly elastic world supply curve, or foreign supply curve. S_w is a flat line indicating that the home country is too small to affect international prices with its own actions: it takes P_w as given. Assuming no transportation costs, free trade will bring about equality between the domestic price and the international price of the commodity. Thus the domestic market will also be stabilized at price P_w. At this price domestic supply is OQ_1 and demand is OQ_2. The volume of imports is the difference between domestic demand and supply, namely Q_1Q_2. Total consumers' expenditure is area OP_wAQ_2. Expenditure on domestic production is area OP_wBQ_1, and expenditure on imports is area BAQ_1Q_2. Area OP_wBQ_1 also represents the domestic producers' revenue.

Now suppose that the government of the country under consideration decides to impose a tariff t per unit on imports from all sources. The tariff will shift the S_w line upwards. With perfect competition, the domestic price of Q will also rise by the full amount of the tariff. In terms of Figure 2.6(b), the domestic price of the commodity now becomes $P = P_w + t$. This price increase can be seen as having a demand effect, a production effect, a tariff-revenue effect, and a distribution effect (see Hitiris (2003) and Molle (2001)).

Starting from the demand effect, the price increase causes consumers to lower their demand: consumption falls from OQ_2 to OQ_4. As a result, there is a reduction in the surplus of consumers equal to areas $(\delta + \alpha + \beta + \gamma)$. At the same time, in response to the price increase, production in sector Q expands at the expense of other sectors. Thus the domestic supply of Q rises from OQ_1 to OQ_3. This has a production effect: producers' surplus increases by area δ. The tariff-revenue effect arises from the fact that the home country's government now collects revenue equal to the quantity of imports times the tariff, namely tO_3Q_4. This is measured by area β. The distribution effect comes from two sources. First, the tariff revenue collected by the government is paid by domestic consumers. Thus area β can be seen as an income transfer from domestic consumers to the government. Second, by raising the price of the domestically-produced competing commodities, the tariff increases producers' profits per unit of output. Accordingly, area δ can be seen as an income transfer from domestic consumers, who now pay a higher price per unit of output bought, to domestic producers who receive a higher price for each unit of output sold.

The net welfare loss from the tariff for the country as a whole is thus given by areas $(\alpha + \gamma)$. Area α is a net resource waste: the country under consideration produces the additional quantity Q_1Q_3 domestically at a higher cost rather than importing it from abroad. Area γ is a net utility loss arising from the fall in consumption at the price P, which exceeds the world price P_w. In our example, removing the tariff would increase the welfare of the home country by $(\alpha + \gamma)$.[1]

Customs Unions or Universally Free Trade?

The analysis in the previous section suggests that completely free trade allows countries to reach maximum possible welfare. From this one gets the impression that starting from a situation of uniform tariffs on imports from all countries, the removal of tariffs on imports from some countries will be unambiguously beneficial to the countries concerned and to the world as a whole. More specifically, since a CU is a step towards freer trade and since free trade is always welfare-improving, it seems reasonable to expect that a CU will unambiguously raise welfare. Viner (1950) was the first to argue that this may not be so. That this may not be the case follows from the theory of second best, a well-known principle in economics: eliminating a distortion that moves a country only partly and not fully towards an optimal situation, in our case completely free trade, may lower instead of raise welfare. As far as customs unions are concerned, the implication is that the gains a country may hope to achieve by participating in a CU will always be lower than the welfare gain it can attain by adopting a free-trade policy towards all countries.

The question then is why a country may decide to adopt the second-best solution of a CU rather than the first best solution of fully free international trade. One answer is that the first best solution of completely free international trade may not be feasible. Another possibility is that the first best solution may involve serious adjustment costs. International trade theory ignores adjustment costs by making the assumption that factors of production are completely mobile both internationally and within individual economies, that full employment always prevails, and that nominal wages and prices are fully flexible. In reality, due to factor immobility and/or short-run wage/price rigidities, removing tariffs may lead to temporary increases in national rates of unemployment and may thus involve adjustment costs in the form of short-run output losses. And, while it may be relatively easy for a country to overcome the problems arising from the required adjustments following the elimination of tariffs on imports from a small number of countries, it may be very difficult to make allowance for with the adjustments required by removing tariff barriers on imports from all sources. Indeed, CU theory is based on the implicit assumption that the option of completely free international trade is not available to member countries or is undesirable due to large adjustment costs (see Panagariya (2000)).

Now customs-union theory consists of the so-called 'conventional' theory and the 'modern' theory. Conventional CU theory is concerned with the static effects of CUs, namely the impact of the tariff changes induced by the formation of a customs union on the allocation of resources between different products and different markets and on the terms-of-trade of the union countries with the rest of the world. In this context, the criterion for evaluating CUs is economic efficiency. The possibility that the formation of the CU, through its impact on the size of the market, may influence the overall level of production in member countries is ignored. On the other hand, modern CU theory focuses on more dynamic effects, including the impact of CUs on the size of the market, on the possibility of exploiting scale economies, on competition within the union and on investment and growth.[2]

Static Reallocative Effects of Customs Unions

Static analyses of custom unions are usually based on five main assumptions. The first is that perfect competition prevails in all markets and there are no externalities in consumption and/or production. This assumption implies that prices accurately reflect the opportunity cost of production as well as the marginal utility of consumption. The second assumption is that the factors of production are perfectly mobile within each member country but not between them. Third, wages are fully flexible and so full employment exists continuously. And, fourth, there are increasing costs in production. Thus supply curves are upward-sloping. Much of this literature also makes a number of other simplifying assumptions. These are: goods can be moved from one country to another without incurring costs of transport; that all barriers to international trade take the form of tariffs on imports; and that, in all countries, there are no trade imbalances, namely the value of exports equals the value of imports.

In the context of static customs-union analysis, a CU may increase or reduce member states' welfare by causing 'trade creation', 'trade diversion' or 'trade suppression'. These three concepts were first introduced by Viner (1950) and further extended by Meade (1955), Lipsey (1957) and Bhagwati (1971). Trade creation reflects a situation where total trade in a product increases with the formation of the CU. This arises from a consumption effect and a production effect. The former results from an increase in the consumption of the product through a union-induced reduction in its market price. The production effect results from a union-induced replacement of domestic production by less expensive imports from other countries participating in the CU. Since both the consumption effect and the production effect lead to more trade, it follows from the analysis of free-trade equilibrium that trade creation must have positive welfare effects. Trade diversion has to do with changes in the origin of imports. It refers to a situation where the customs union leads a country to substitute higher-cost imports from countries that are members of the CU for lower-cost imports from the rest of the world. Trade suppression occurs when, following the establishment of the CU, world trade is reduced. Indeed, many different cases may arise depending on the height of the common external tariff adopted by the union countries, on the height of national tariffs before the establishment of the CU and on demand and supply elasticities in participating countries.

Trade Creation, Trade Diversion and Trade Suppression

In much of the static CU literature, three countries are assumed, a home country (country H) a partner country (country P) and the rest of the world (country ROW). Country H and country P are taken to be small enough to be unable to influence international prices through their own policies. Thus the rest-of-the-world supply curve, S_w, is perfectly elastic at the international price P_w.

Figures 2.7(a_1) and 2.7(a_2) reflect the initial situation in the market for commodity Q in country P and country H respectively. The two countries are assumed to be able to produce Q at costs reflected in the supply curves S_h and S_p. However, Q can be imported from the rest of the world at price P_w. Thus, to keep out foreign competition, country H and country P adopt a tariff on all imports equal to t_h and t_p per unit respectively. As a result of the tariffs, the price of Q in H is $P_h = P_w + t_h$ and in P is $P_p = P_w + t_p$. Therefore, in the pre-union situation, demand and supply is Q_1 in country H and Q_4 in country P.

Figure 2.7

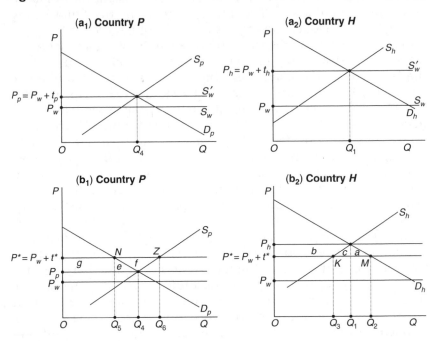

Suppose now that country P and country H decide to form a customs union. They agree to remove all tariffs on their bilateral trade and to adopt an external common tariff of such a height so as, together as a CU, to reach self-sufficiency. In Figures 2.7(b_1) and 2.7(b_2), the tariff that can achieve this is t^*. With a common external tariff of t^* per unit the price of Q within the CU becomes $P^* = P_w + t^*$, and at P^* the excess demand for Q in country H, KM, equals the excess supply of Q in country P, NZ.

As the price of Q falls in country H from P_h to P^*, consumers gain the area sum $(a+b+c)$. Producers lose area b. Thus area b is not a gain from the point of view of the home country as a whole: it is a transfer of income from producers to consumers. On the other hand, the sum of areas $(a+c)$ is a net gain to country H reflecting 'trade-creation'. Area c is the production effect of trade creation: expensive domestic production has been replaced by cheaper imports from country P. Area a is the consumption effect: country H's residents now consume the additional quantity $Q_1 Q_2$ at the lower price P^*.

In the case of country P, the formation of the CU results in a price increase. Accordingly, the surplus of domestic producers increases by the area sum $(g+e+f)$. However, the surplus of domestic consumers falls by $(g+e)$. Thus, for the country as a whole, the net welfare effect is measured by area f. This area reflects the extra profits of country P's producers from their sales to country H.

Both country H and country P gain from the creation of the CU. At the same time, as there was no rest-of-the-world trade before the formation of the CU and this continues to be zero after the CU, the establishment of the customs union has no impact on ROW; there is no trade diversion or trade suppression.

Another, more realistic, possibility is illustrated in Figure 2.8. In Figures 2.8(a_1) and 2.8(a_2), $D_P(D_h)$ and $S_P(S_h)$ are demand and supply schedules in country P (country H). The world supply schedule is S_w and the world supply price is P_w. Initially, in country P a tariff t_P per unit is imposed on all imports with the result that the entire internal demand is covered from domestic production. At the same time, country H, is protecting its industry by a tariff t_h per unit. As a result, its effective rest-of-the-world supply curve is S'_w and the domestic price of the product is P_h.

Suppose now that country H and country P decide to participate in a CU and adopt a common external tariff t^* high enough to keep out foreign competition from their combined markets. Given the tariff t^*, the price of Q within the customs union becomes P^*, and, at this

Figure 2.8

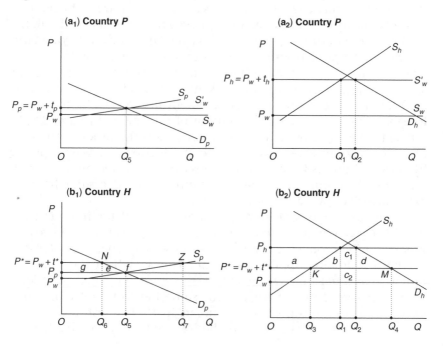

price, the excess demand for the product in H, KM, just equals the excess supply of Q in P, NZ.

With the formation of the CU, the price of Q falls in country H and increases in country P. As a result, more of Q is consumed in H and less is consumed in P. On the other hand, there is an expansion of the production of Q in country P and a contraction in country H. Thus, as far as welfare is concerned, in country P there is an increase in the surplus of producers equal to the area sum $(g+e+f)$. Consumers suffer a welfare loss since they have to pay a higher price than before for each unit of Q bought. This loss is represented by the contraction in the area below the demand curve and above the price, namely the area sum $(g+e)$. For the country as a whole, however, there is a net welfare gain equal to area f. Area f reflects the extra profit that country P's producers obtain by exporting to country H.

In country H, welfare is influenced by three effects. First is the substitution of imports from country P for domestic production: Q_3Q_1 is now imported from P instead of being produced domestically. The second effect is the increase in demand due to the price fall that follows the creation of th CU: as P_h falls to P^*, domestic consumption is increased by Q_2Q_4. And the third effect is the substitution of imports from country P for imports from the rest of the world. As a result of the first two effects, the surplus of consumers in country H increases by the area sum $(a+b+c_1+d)$, while producers suffer a reduction in their surplus equal to area a. Thus a is not a net gain from the point of view of country H as a whole. Area c_1 is also not a net gain. Prior to the establishment of the CU, country H's government was collecting tariff revenue on imports from ROW equal to $t_hQ_1Q_2$, that is areas (c_1+c_2). Now country H gets all its imports from country P and these imports are not subject to any tariff. Area c_1 is therefore a gain to the consumers of Q but a loss to country H's government in terms of tariff revenue foregone: it represents a redistribution of income within country H. The net trade-creation gain is $(b+d)$. Area b is the production effect of trade creation: expensive domestic production has been replaced by cheaper imports from country P. Area d is the consumption effect: following the formation of the CU, country H's residents purchase the extra quantity Q_2Q_4 at the lower price P^*.

As regards the substitution of imports from P for imports from ROW Q_1Q_2 is now imported at a price that exceeds the world cost of producing the product: the low-cost supplier ROW has been replaced by the higher-cost supplier country P. This switch in the source of imports has a negative welfare effect, represented by area c_2. Indeed, country H's government has lost the sum of areas (c_1+c_2), of which only c_1 has been returned to consumers in H. The rest, area c_2, is a dead-weight loss. Area c_2 reflects the welfare loss to country H from trade diversion: it arises from a change in the source of imports, from a low-cost country to a higher-cost country.

While country P unambiguously benefits from the formation of the CU, country H in principle may or may not be better off according to whether the gain from trade creation exceeds or falls short of the loss from trade diversion. This will depend on the height of the initial tariff in this country and thus the size of the original tariff revenue, on the difference between production costs in P and in the rest of the world, and on the elasticity of the demand for and supply of Q in H. In the example of Figure 2.8, the net welfare effect of the CU for country H is positive: the size of areas $(b+d)$ is greater than the size of area c_2. And the same applies to the total effect of the CU, namely $(b+d-c_2+f) > 0$, with the result that the customs union is on net terms welfare-improving.

The possibility of a trade-suppressing CU, first pointed out by Viner (1950)[3], is illustrated in Figure 2.9 (see also Nevin (1990) and Robson (1998)). S_h and D_h in Figures 2.9(a_2) and 2.9(b_2) are supply and demand schedules in country H and S_w is the world supply curve. In this country a tariff t_h per unit is initially imposed on all imports so that the domestic price of Q is P_h. Demand and supply in country P are represented by the schedules D_P and S_P in Figures 2.9(a_1) and 2.9(b_1).

Figure 2.9

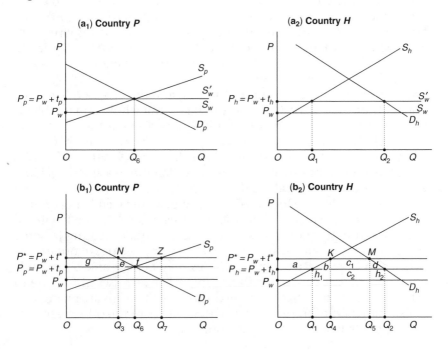

Initially, there is a tariff t_p per unit on all imports so the domestic market is supplied fully from domestic producers.

Suppose now that country P and country H form a customs union and that they agree to adopt a common external tariff of such a height so that ROW is excluded from their combined market. The required tariff rate is t^* per unit: due to the common external tariff t^*, the price of Q within the CU becomes P^* and, at this price, the excess demand in country H, KM, equals the excess supply in country P, NZ.

As far as country P is concerned, the welfare effects of the formation of the CU are similar to those in the previous example, namely producers gain the area sum $(g + e + f)$ but consumers lose the area sum $(e + f)$. There is thus a net welfare gain, represented by area f.

In country H the price of Q also rises with the formation of the CU. Domestic demand falls to OQ_5, domestic production rises to OQ_4, total imports are reduced by $(Q_1Q_4 + Q_5Q_2)$; and imports of Q_4Q_5 previously coming from ROW now come from country P. Producers in country H thus experience a welfare gain, measured by area a, while consumers experience a welfare loss, measured by the area sum $(a + b + c_1 + d)$. The net welfare loss is therefore $(b + c_1 + d)$. Areas $(b + d)$ represent a trade-suppression welfare loss: expensive domestic production has risen; and overall domestic demand has fallen. Area c_1 is a trade-diversion loss: consumers in country H now buy imports of Q_4Q_5 from the higher-cost supplier country P rather than from the low-cost supplier ROW. At the same time, country $H's$ government losses the tariff revenue which before the CU was collecting on imports from ROW. There is therefore an additional welfare loss of $t_hQ_1Q_2$ or the area sum $(h_1 + c_2 + h_2)$, of which c_2 arises from trade diversion and $(h_1 + h_2)$ results from trade suppression.

Moreover, since in our example the area sum $(b + c_1 + d + h_1 + c_2 + h_2)$ is larger than area f, the CU proves to be on the whole undesirable. It has been a trade-suppressing CU: it has caused world trade to fall by $(Q_1Q_4 + Q_5Q_2)$.

The conclusion to be drawn from Figures 2.7 to 2.9 is that small CUs cannot in general be described as either welfare-increasing or welfare-reducing: only empirical analysis can establish whether existing (prospective) CUs have increased (will increase) the well-being of their member states' residents.[4] Indeed, as Viner (1950) himself pointed out, in a multi-product analysis a CU may be trade-creating in some products and trade-diverting (or even trade-suppressing) in others. CU theory also implies that some countries may benefit and others may lose. Thus, as Panagariya (2000), among others, stresses, if CUs are to be formed in the first place, compensation mechanisms are required to re-distribute part of the gains to some countries to the other members that are made worse off from CU formation.

Terms-of-Trade Effects of Customs Unions

What if the importance of the union-countries' trade in total world trade in any given product is not so small to imply that the world price of that product remains unchanged regardless of movements in the union's demand for imports from *ROW*? In other words, what are the effects of CUs if the rest-of-the world supply curve cannot be taken as horizontal and thus the world price of the product is dependent upon the union's demand for imports from *ROW*?

By forming a CU, member countries may acquire market power: collectively they may become important buyers and sellers in world markets and this may enable them to influence world prices. There are two channels through which countries may benefit by forming a CU via their increased significance in world markets. First, acting as a group, they may be able to impose an optimal common tariff on imports from the rest of the world, without running the risk of facing retaliatory actions by it. An optimal tariff is a tariff that enables a country, or a group of countries, to reach the maximum possible level of welfare through its impact on their terms of trade with the rest of the world. Second, even without imposing an optimal common tariff, the formation of a large CU via increased market power may be followed by a reduction in the prices of the goods that the member states are importing from non-members. This may lead to welfare gains, others than those implied by the conventional trade-creation effect.

Terms-of-trade effects and the optimal common tariff. The terms of trade are defined as the ratio of the price of a country's (or a group of countries') exportable commodities to the price of its (their) importable commodities. A rise in this ratio implies a terms-of-trade improvement: the price received for exports increases relative to the price charged for imports. A terms-of-trade improvement increases the welfare of the country (or group of countries) concerned since it implies that the same volume of exports can purchase more imports.

To examine optimal tariffs and terms-of-trade effects use will be made of offer curves (OCs) following Caves *et al.* (2001), Chacholiades (1990) and Moore (2001). Offer curves are derived from the PPF and CIC diagrams we have considered earlier by asking what is the maximum level of welfare that a country can achieve by exporting and importing goods at different relative prices. Accordingly, to examine terms-of-trade effects, one needs to assume at least two commodities per country, one 'exportable' and one 'importable'.

Consider two countries, country U, the customs union, and ROW, the rest of the world, each producing two commodities X and Z under conditions of perfect competition. Country U has a comparative advantage in the production of Z and is thus an exporter of Z and an importer of X, while country ROW has a comparative advantage in the production of X and is thus an exporter of X and an importer of Z. Under these assumptions, the O_U curve in Figure 2.10(a) can be taken to represent the offer curve of country U. Each point on the O_U curve shows how many units of Z county U's residents will be willing to give up in exchange for any given quantity of commodity X at the prevailing relative price of Z, that is the price ratio (P_z/P_x). O_R in Figure 2.10(b) represents the offer curve of ROW. Each point on that curve shows how many units of X the residents of this country

Figure 2.10

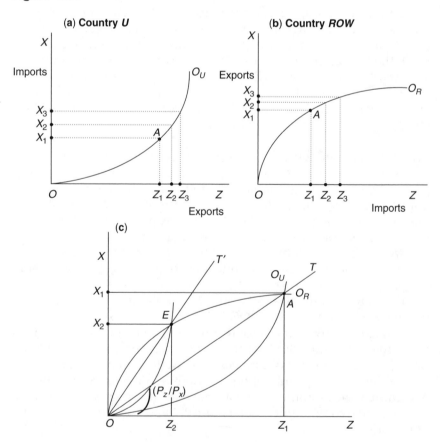

will be willing to give up in exchange for a given quantity of Z at the prevailing relative price of Z.

The shape of the offer curves follows from the law of diminishing marginal utility: the rate at which county U's (country ROW's) residents are prepared to exchange $Z(X)$ for $X(Z)$ drops as more units of commodity $X(Z)$ are consumed. For example, suppose that we start at point A in Figure 2.10(a) with exports OZ_1 and imports OX_1. Initially, to increase their consumption of X by say 1 per cent from OX_1 to OX_2, residents of country U would be prepared to give up Z_1Z_2 units of commodity Z. However, to increase their consumption of X by another per cent, say from OX_2 to OX_3, they would be prepared to reduce their consumption of Z by less than 1 per cent, that is they would be prepared to export only Z_2Z_3 units of Z in exchange for imports of X_2X_3. Thus, the O_U curve is convex to the origin. For the same reasons the O_R curve in Figure 2.10(b), the offer curve of ROW, is concave to the origin.

One can draw the two offer curves O_R and O_U in a single diagram. The point where they intersect, point A in Figure 2.10(c), is the equilibrium at which exchange takes place. Point A also determines the equilibrium relative price of Z, namely (P_z/P_x). Indeed (P_z/P_x) is reflected in the slope of a line from the origin through point A, that is in the slope of the line OT. To see this, note that at the equilibrium point A, country U is importing from ROW the quantity OX_1 and is exporting to ROW the quantity OZ_1. On the other hand, ROW is importing the quantity OZ_1 and exporting the quantity OX_1. At the equilibrium point A, trade must be balanced in the sense that the value of each country's imports must equal the value of its exports. Accordingly, $OZ_1 \times P_z = OX_1 \times P_x$ and thus $P_z/P_x = \frac{OX_1}{OZ_1}$. But the slope of the line OT at A is measured by the ratio $\frac{OX_1}{OZ_1}$. It therefore reflects the relative price of Z.

Since $Z(X)$ is country U's exportable (importable) commodity, the slope of the line OT also measures its terms of trade with ROW. A steeper price line, say OT', would imply an improvement in country U's terms of trade with ROW. For example, suppose that at the prevailing international prices, a smaller quantity of ROW's exportable commodity is demanded by country U. More precisely, suppose that at the old terms of trade, given by the slope of the line OT, country U's demand for imports from ROW drops by X_1X_2. Such a drop in country U's import demand would cause its offer curve to move leftwards. The new equilibrium would be at point E, and country U's terms of trade with ROW would improve.

In Figure 2.11(b) in the absence of a CU and with no tariffs, the highest indifference curve that country U can achieve, given the price

Figure 2.11

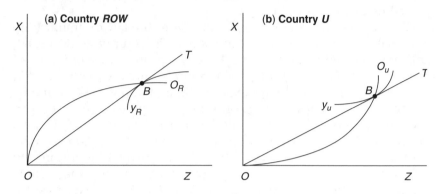

line OT, is represented by the curve y_U which is tangent to the international price line at B. Similarly in Figure 2.11(a), the curve y_R represents the maximum level of welfare that ROW can achieve given the price line OT.

Suppose now that the countries in U form a customs union, and that, being a group of countries with a common external-tariff policy, they have the power to impose tariffs without the fear of retaliation by the rest of the world, subject only to the constraint that ROW buys and sells the amounts shown on its offer curve O_R. It is then evident from Figure 2.12(a) that points on the offer curve O_R other than B, that is initial equilibrium, would represent a more favourable outcome for country U. For example, point C on O_R would lie on a higher indifference curve as far as country U is concerned; and the indifference curve $y_U{}^*$ in Figure 2.12(b), which just touches ROW's offer curve at point D, would represent the maximum level of welfare that country U could achieve given the rest of the world offer curve O_R.

Can country U get to a point like D on the indifference curve $y_U{}^*$? Country U, as a customs union, can in principle get to this point by adopting a common external tariff on imports from ROW of such a height that makes its offer curve cross O_R at point D. Adopting this tariff would reduce the union's import demand, and thus export supply given the assumption of balanced trade, at any given world prices. In terms of Figure 2.12(c), it would produce a leftwards swing in its original offer curve. And an optimal external tariff is effectively that which leads to a tariff-inclusive offer curve $O_U{}^*$. Equilibrium after the adoption of the optimal tariff would then be at D on the new international-price line OT^*. At D the highest possible ROW indifference curve, namely y_R', is tangent to the equilibrium price line OT^*. However, due to the tariff, the union's indifference curve at D,

Figure 2.12

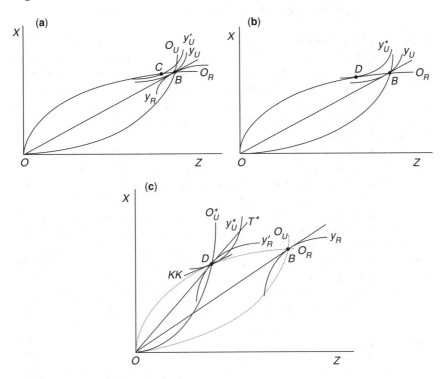

that is $y_U{}^*$, is not tangent to OT^*, it is simply tangent to the ROW's offer curve O_R. In other words, the union's external tariff has led to a reduction in the international relative price of X, which is the importable commodity of the union countries: OT^* is steeper than OT. The relative price of X within the CU has increased due to the tariff. This is reflected in the KK line, which measures the slope of the union's indifference curve $y_U{}^*$ at the point where it just touches ROW's offer curve. That is, the slope of $y_U{}^*$ at D reflects the relative price of X within the customs union. The slope of OT^* reflects international relative prices. The difference in the slopes of the two price lines, KK and OT^*, measures the optimal common external tariff of the union countries.

In effect, by being able to impose an optimal common external tariff on all imports from ROW without fears of retaliation, a large CU can increase the welfare of its member states through a terms-of-trade improvement, even if it is on balance trade-suppressing; that is, even if it causes a fall in the total volume of world trade (as has indeed been the case in Figure 2.12(c)). Such a CU, however, is bound to hurt the rest of the world: in Figure 2.12(c), ROW's welfare, or real income, has fallen at point D relative to point B since D is on a lower indifference curve as far as ROW is concerned, namely on the curve y'_R.

Partial equilibrium analysis: effects on international prices. Even if we ignore the optimal-tariff possibility, the formation of a large customs union may lead to welfare gains for the union countries by reducing the price of products that they import from the rest of the world. This point can be illustrated using a partial equilibrium analysis (see Hitiris (2003), Molle (2001), Robson (1998), Nevin (1990) and Panagariya (2000)).

Figure 2.13(a) shows the market for a single good Q, produced in country H and country P before the establishment of the CU. D_T is the demand curve for Q in country H and country P taken together, that is, $D_T = D_h + D_p$. Similarly, S_T describes the combined total supply, $S_T = S_h + S_p$. S_w is the ROW supply curve and S'_w is the effective ROW supply curve. In the absence of the CU, H and P are confronted with the ROW price P_w, which none of them individually can affect. Also, both H and P have tariffs on imports from ROW, and this gives an average tariff of $t = P - P_w$ per unit. The effective ROW supply curve is thus the flat line S'_w and the price of Q in country H's and country P's markets is $P = P_w + t$. At this price total demand in the union is OQ_2

Figure 2.13

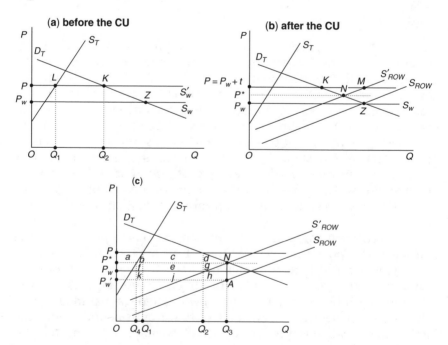

and supply is OQ_1. Imports from *ROW* are Q_1Q_2. The tariff revenue is tQ_1Q_2.

Suppose now that H and P decide to establish a customs union and that together, as a CU, become sufficiently important actors in international markets to be able to influence the price of their imports. Accordingly, instead of facing the fixed price P_w, country H and country P together as a CU now face the upwards-sloping *ROW* supply curve S_{ROW} in Figure 2.13(b). S_{ROW} must be passing through point Z, where the CU's aggregate demand curve D_T crosses the flat line S_w. However, given the union countries' tariff t, the effective *ROW* supply curve is not the schedule S_{ROW} but the schedule S'_{ROW}, which incorporates the tariff t. And, given this 'effective' *ROW* supply curve, at the initial price of the product $P = P_w + t$, there is now an excess supply of Q, equal to KM, within country H's and country P's markets. This excess supply will cause the price of Q to fall: following the formation of the customs union, the price of Q within the CU will drop from P to P^* and equilibrium will be achieved at point N.

In Figure 2.13(c), as the price of Q drops to P^*, demand within the CU rises from OQ_2 to OQ_3. The union's supply of Q falls from OQ_1 to OQ_4. Thus imports from *ROW* are now Q_3Q_4. As a result, consumers in the union countries experience a welfare gain equal to the area sum $(a+b+c+d)$. Producers lose area a and the governments of H and P lose part of their initial tariff revenue, namely area c. We thus have a net welfare gain measured by $(b+d)$. This is a conventional trade-creation gain.

However the formation of the customs union also has had an impact on world prices. With equilibrium in the CU being at point N, the price that foreign producers receive per unit of Q sold is P'_w: S'_{ROW} is the tariff-inclusive *ROW* supply curve but the price foreign suppliers receive per unit of Q sold is reflected in the supply curve S_{ROW}. In other words, while consumers within the CU pay the price P^*, foreign producers now sell at price P'_w rather than at price P_w. This reduction in international prices implies additional welfare gains for the union countries. Indeed, after the establishment of the CU, the governments of H and P collect tariff revenue equal to the volume of imports from *ROW* times the difference between the price of Q within the CU, P^*, and the world price of the product P'_w, that is $Q_4Q_3 \times (P^* - P'_w)$. This tariff revenue is measured by the area sum $(f+e+g+k+j+h)$. Before the CU, the total tariff revenue collected by H and P was $Q_1Q_2 \times (P-P_w) = (c+e)$. Thus, with the formation of the CU, country H's and country P's governments lose area c. However, we still have extra tariff revenue equal to $(f+g+k+j+h)$. Part of it, the area sum $(f+g)$, is 'paid' by consumers within the CU (as they purchase Q at a price higher than the international price). But the rest, the area sum $(k+j+h)$, is 'paid' by foreign producers in the sense that it results from the fact that the international price of Q drops from P_w to P'_w. Since for the union countries this extra tariff revenue $(k+j+h)$ represents a net welfare gain, the total welfare gain they derive from the formation of the CU is $(b+d+k+j+h)$.[5]

Dynamic Effects of Customs Unions

As stressed by Bhagwati (1993), static CU theory disregards three important dynamic effects that may result from the enlargement of the market following the formation of a customs union. First is the effect of the customs union on competition. Following the formation of the CU, the intensity of competition among firms operating within the integrated area will increase and this may lead to technological improvements and thus to greater efficiency in production. Second, the enlargement of the market may enable firms to exploit economies of scale. A third effect is the impact of the CU on investments, with the formation of the CU new markets will become available to individual firms, inducing them to expand production, something that may imply increased investment and a higher rate of economic growth.

Competition effects. The competition effect of CU formation can be illustrated using a simple demand – supply diagram along the lines suggested by Pelkmans (1982, 1984). In Figure 2.14, D_0 and S_0 are demand and supply schedules in country H prior to the CU. In the pre-union phase there is a tariff t per unit on imports from all sources and, for simplicity, ROW prices and country P's prices are assumed to be equal. Domestic demand is OQ_2 and domestic supply is OQ_1. Thus the price of Q within country H is $P_0 = P_w + t = P_h + t$.

Figure 2.14

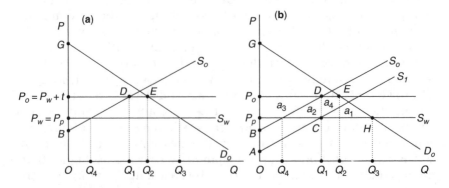

Now suppose that following the establishment of the customs union, the tariff t on imports from country P is eliminated so domestic prices drop to P_p in Figure 2.14(b). Ignoring the competition effect, one would conclude that the position of the S_0 schedule would remain unchanged, that imports of Q_3Q_4 would be obtained from country P, and that the net welfare gain to country H from the CU would be the area sum $(a_1 + a_2)$. Yet firms in country H, faced with the possibility of increased competition from other union firms, and thus with the possibility of a loss of markets, may decide to adopt more efficient production techniques that reduce production costs. If they do so, the supply curve S_0 will tend to shift to the right. In Figure 2.14(b), S_0 is assumed to shift to S_1. The result is that area a_3 is no longer a redistribution effect: it becomes a net welfare gain. In particular, with the new supply curve S_1, the surplus of producers is the triangle AP_pC. Before the CU it was BP_0D. As the surplus of producers remains the same in size, while consumers gain the areas $(a_3 + a_2 + a_4 + a_1)$ and the government loses its tariff revenue, area a_4, the net welfare gain for the country as a whole is given by $(a_3 + a_2 + a_1)$. In effect, competition increases the magnitude of the net welfare gain by area a_3.

Economies of scale. Static CU theory ignores the possibility that the formation of a customs union, by increasing the size of the market, may enable firms to exploit economies of scale. Corden (1972) was the first to analyse the implications of economies of scale for evaluating CUs and extensions of his analysis can be found in, for example, Baldwin and Venables (1995), Smith and Venables (1988) and Panagariya (2000).[6,7]

The possibility of exploiting scale economies arises as soon as imperfect competition is allowed for. With imperfect competition, firms in long-run equilibrium will not necessarily operate at a point where their average cost curve has a minimum and there may be opportunities for them to lower average costs by expanding production. The incentive for increased production should come from demand. And in the case of a CU, increased demand can come from the opening up of new markets that the removal of tariffs will imply.

To examine how scale economies may be taken into account in analysing the welfare effects of CUs, as before, three countries will be assumed, country H, country P and ROW, and the market for a single homogeneous product Q, produced under conditions of imperfect competition, will be considered. As is common in the literature, it will be assumed that while Q is produced in ROW at constant costs, it can be produced in H and P at decreasing average costs. However, whatever the scale of production, country P and country H cannot produce with average costs at or below world prices. To simplify the exposition, firms will be taken to follow an average-cost pricing policy. Many different situations can arise depending on the initial situation in the two countries in the pre-CU phase.

In Figure 2.15, $S_h(S_p)$ is the average-cost curve (and supply curve) in country H (country P) and $D_h(D_p)$ is the demand curve. S_w is the ROW supply curve and P_w is the given world-supply price. Before the CU, tariffs are assumed to achieve self-sufficiency; that is, tariff-inclusive import prices equal average domestic costs. Accordingly, in the pre-CU phase, there is a tariff t_h in country H and t_p in country P. Country H produces and consumes the quantity Q_1 at price P_h. Country P produces and consumes the quantity Q_2 at price $P_p < P_h$. Both H and P are operating on the downward-sloping part of their average cost curves implying that there are opportunities for scale economies. However, Country P has a comparative price advantage.

Now suppose that country P and country H establish a CU and also agree to adopt an external common tariff against ROW of such a level so as to continue to keep out foreign competition from their markets. After the setting up of the CU, country's P producers will start supplying the whole union, given their initial comparative price advantage. Moreover given their downwards-sloping cost curve, costs per unit of output will be lower when they produce for the entire union market than when they were producing for their local market only. As a result, the common external tariff required to exclude ROW from country H's and country P's markets will be lower than the initial national tariffs. In particular, as producers in P will now face the demand curve $D_U = D_h + D_p$, the tariff that can exclude ROW from the union market will be t^*.

Accordingly, after the creation of the CU, the union-wide quantity demanded OQ_5, is now produced in country P and sold at price P^*. At P^*, demand in country P is OQ_4 and exports to country H are Q_4Q_5. In Country H, demand and imports are $OQ_3 = Q_4Q_5$.

Both countries gain from the formation of the CU. There is a trade-creation effect for country H, given by the area sum $(a + b)$. Area a is the production effect of trade creation: less costly imports from country P have replaced country domestic production. Area b is the consumption effect of trade creation, which results from the increase in demand due to the price cut.

In addition, in country P consumers now purchase the product at a price $P^* < P_p$. This is what is known in the CU literature as the 'cost-reduction' effect: it results from the fact that an existing domestic source of supply has become less expensive; it is not a switch to a less costly source of supply abroad. The cost-reduction effect increases the

Figure 2.15

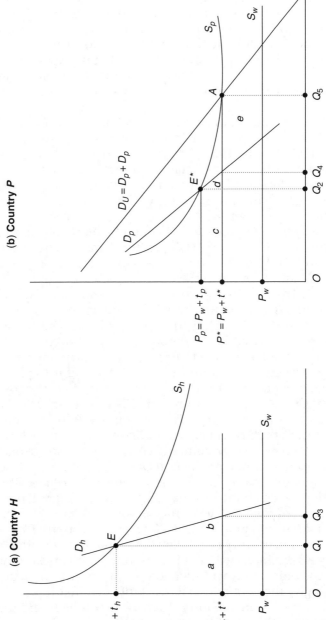

(a) Country *H*

(b) Country *P*

surplus of consumers in country P by the area sum $(c+d)$. The gain represented by area c results from the fact that the initial quantity OQ_2 is now produced at a lower cost. The gain represented by area d results from the extra consumption Q_2Q_4 induced by the fall in the price of the product. In addition to the cost-reduction gain, country P also experiences a welfare gain from the fact that its exports to country H are sold at prices higher than the world price P_w. In our example, this gain is measured by area e. Thus the net welfare effect of the CU is $(a+b+c+d+e) > 0$.

Figure 2.16 illustrates another possibility, one in which before the CU there is production in only one of the two countries (see Robson (1998) and Nevin (1990)). In particular, Q is assumed to be produced only in country P. Provided that, regardless of the scale of production, the established producers, that is those in country P, are more efficient than those in country H, it is reasonable to assume that after the formation of the CU, country P, which has the established and more efficient producers will supply the entire union market. Accordingly, in Figure 2.16, $D_h(D_p)$ is the demand schedule in country H (country P). S_h is the average-cost curve (and supply schedule) in country H and S_p is the average-cost curve (and supply schedule) in country P. The fact that S_p is below S_h for almost any Q indicates that production costs in country P are in general lower than in country H. The schedule $D_U = D_h + D_p$ is the union-wide demand curve. S_w is the ROW supply curve and P_w is the world supply price.

Initially, country H has a tariff t_h per unit on all imports. Therefore the price of Q in this country is P_h and demand is OQ_1. There is no domestic production (as P_h is less than average domestic costs), so the quantity OQ_1 is imported from ROW. Thus country H collects tariff revenue equal to $OQ_1 \times (P_h - P_w)$. In country P, on the other hand, the pre-union tariff is set at t_p. Accordingly, the tariff-inclusive import price just equals average domestic costs, so domestic demand is met entirely from domestic production OQ_2.

Now suppose that country P and country H form a CU and that they adopt a common external tariff of such a level that ROW is excluded from their markets. Since production costs in country P are in general lower than in country H, and since country P's initial price is below that in country H, it follows that after the formation of the CU country P's producers will supply the entire union market. Equilibrium in the customs union will therefore be at point B in Figure 2.16(b). Accordingly, the common external tariff required to keep out ROW from country H's and country P's markets will be t^* and the price of the product within the CU will be P^*.

In country P supply increases from OQ_2 to OQ_5. Domestic demand is OQ_4 and exports are Q_4Q_5. There is a cost-reduction gain equal to the area sum $(c+d)$ and an export gain equal to area e. As far as country P is concerned, we therefore have a net welfare gain measured by $(c+d+e)$.

Figure 2.16

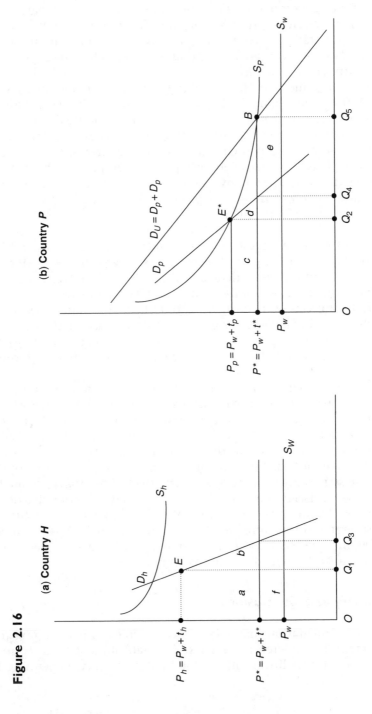

In country H, consumers gain areas $(a + b)$. However, only area b is a net gain since before the establishment of the CU area a was part of the government's tariff revenue. Also, another part of the government's initial tariff revenue, area f, is a dead-weight loss. Area f represents trade-diversion: the quantity OQ_1 is now imported from country P whose costs are higher than those of ROW; the government of country H has thus lost tariff revenue equal to f, which has not gone to consumers in H. Accordingly, country H may or may not benefit from the CU, depending on whether area b is bigger than area f. Nevertheless, in this example, the cost-reduction gain to country P is greater than the trade-diversion loss to country H. From the point of view of the two countries taken together, the net effect of the CU is therefore unambiguously positive, despite the fact that this customs union is a trade-diverting one; and any undesirable effects on country's H welfare can in principle be dealt with by means of appropriate transfer payments.

Effects of CUs on investment and output growth. The problems involved in quantifying the effects of CUs on growth are greater than those involved in measuring the other dynamic effects, including competition effects and scale-economies effects, for two reasons. First, the factors affecting investment, capital formation and so economic growth are many and vary from one country to another; second, it is often very difficult to separate the integration effect on these variables from the impact on them of other elements, including government policies.

An attempt to estimate the impact of the EC customs union on the rate of growth in member countries is a study by Marques-Mendes (1986a, b). Marques-Mendes (1986a) focused on two periods, 1961–72 and 1974–81. For the period 1961–72, when the EC consisted of six countries, the formation of the European customs union was estimated to have increased the rate of growth of European output by 0.20 per cent, suggesting an increase in welfare well above that estimated for the static effects. For the period 1974–81, when the EC consisted of nine countries, Marquez-Mendes's estimate of the dynamic gain through investment and therefore growth was larger, namely 0.64 per cent of total EC income. Henrekson and Torstensson (1997) also find significant growth effects from the EC customs union.

Summary and Conclusions

Economic integration may take many different forms, ranging from agreements for preferential tariffs to the establishment of an economic union or a full political union. Potential gains vary, depending not only on the degree of integration involved, but also on the structure of the member states' economies and initial conditions.

As early as the 1950s Europeans saw economic integration as a vehicle for the promotion of economic prosperity. Thus, with the Rome Treaty of 1957, France, Germany, Italy, Belgium, the Netherlands and Luxembourg abolished tariffs and other quantitative restrictions on trade between them and established a European customs union. Since then a voluminous theoretical and empirical literature has emerged, examining the conditions under which a customs union will be welfare improving. And, while early contributions to this literature focused on the static effects of CUs, namely the impact of CUs on the allocation of resources and on the terms-of-trade of the countries involved with the rest of the world, more recent contributions have emphasized gains from dynamic effects, including the impact of customs unions on the size of the market, on competition within the union and on growth rates.

Indeed, early contributions to the CU literature pointed to the conclusion that small CUs could not in general be described as welfare-improving or welfare-reducing, since they could lead to trade creation for some products and trade diversion, or even trade suppression, for others; and that, in any case, the welfare gains involved might not be large. This conclusion changes in the case of large CUs, namely when the member states collectively are significant buyers and sellers in international markets. The establishment of a large CU implies extra benefits for member states through improvements in their terms-of-trade with the rest-of-the world, either by enabling them to adopt an optimal external tariff *vis-à-vis* the rest of the world without running the risk of retaliatory actions by it, or through a reduction in the international price of products due to their increased significance as a group in world markets.

But even if one takes account of terms-of-trade effects, static CU theory disregards important dynamic effects of CUs. Following the formation of a CU, the intensity of competition among firms operating within the integrated area is likely to increase, inducing greater efficiency in production. The enlargement of the market resulting from the CU may also enable firms to exploit economies of scale, thus reducing production costs and selling prices. At the same time, the enlargement of the market may provide an incentive for firms to undertake additional investment, something that in the longer run will contribute to economic growth. However, quantifying the dynamic effects of CUs, especially those arising through investment and growth, is not an easy task given the many factors affecting capital formation. Yet these dynamic effects can be significant in size: dynamic gains from the formation of the EC customs union through investment and growth have been estimated to have implied an extra annual increase of EC income of 0.64 per cent as compared to only 0.15 per cent increase in welfare from the static effects.

Notes

1 Using community indifference curves and production possibility frontiers, the welfare effects of tariffs can also be analyzed for the case of a large open economy that can influence international prices. This general equilibrium framework will be employed latter, in the context of a large CU.
2 For a recent survey of the CU literature see Panagariya (2000). Other survey articles are Tovias (1994), Baldwin and Venables (1995), Bhagwati *et al.* (1998) and Panagariya (1999). See also Bhagwati (1991), Frankel (1997, 1998) and Bhagwati *et al.* (1999).
3 This case is theoretically possible but not very realistic: GATT allows CUs to be formed provided that the expected common external tariff does not exceed the average of the initial national tariffs.
4 For a survey of the empirical studies on the effects of CUs and for a discussion of the problems involved in measuring these effects see Winters (1987), Pelkmans and Gremmen (1983), Ohly (1993), Srinivasan, Whalley and Wooton (1993), Frankel (1997) and Panagariya and Duttagupta (2001). Early contributions to the empirical CU literature include Balassa (1967, 1975), Truman (1969, 1975) and Mayes (1978). In general, static welfare gains are found to be small, ranging from 0.15 to 0.5 per cent of GDP.
5 See Petith (1977) for an attempt to measure the terms-of-trade effects of the EC's customs union. His results suggest a gain from a terms-of-trade improvement of between 0.3 per cent and 0.9 per cent of GDP.
6 See Silberston (1972) for the theory of scale economies. For an estimate of the scale-economies effect of the EC customs union see Owen (1983).
7 For the different cases that may arise see Moore (2001), Molle (2001) and Robson (1998). See also Pelkmans (2001).

References

Balassa, B. (1967) 'Trade Creation and Trade Diversion in the European Common Market', *Economic Journal*, vol. 77, pp. 1–21.

Balassa, B. (1975) 'Trade Creation and Trade Diversion in the European Common Market: An Appraisal of the Evidence', in B. Balassa (ed.), *European Economic Integration* (Amsterdam: North Holland).

Baldwin, R. and Venables, A. (1995) 'Regional Economic Integration', in G. Grossman and K. Rogoff (ed.), *Handbook of International Economics*, Vol. III (Amsterdam: North Holland).

Bhagwati, J. (1971) 'Trade Diverting Customs Unions and Welfare Improvements: A Clarification', *Economic Journal*, vol. 81, pp. 580–7.

Bhagwati, J. (1991) *The World Trading System at Risk* (Princeton, NJ: Princeton University Press).

Bhagwati, J. (1993) 'Regionalism and Multilateralism: An Overview', in J. De Melo and A. Panagariya (eds), *New Dimensions in Regional Integration* (Cambridge: Cambridge University Press).

Bhagwati, J., Greenaway, D. and Panagariya, A. (1998) 'Trading Preferentially: Theory and Policy', *Economic Journal*, vol. 108, pp. 1128–48.

Bhagwati, J., Krishna, P. and Panagariya, A. (eds) (1999) *Trading Blocs: Alternative Approaches to Analysing Preferential Trade Agreements* (Cambridge, Mass.: MIT Press).

Caves, R., Frankel, J. and Jones, R. (2001) *World Trade and Payments* (New york: Addison-Wesley).

Chacholiades, M. (1990) *International Economics* (New York: McGraw-Hill).

Corden, W.M. (1972) 'Economies of Scale and Customs Union Theory', *Journal of Political Economy*, vol. 80, pp. 465–75.

Frankel, J. (1997) *Regional Trading Blocs in the World Trading System*, Institute for International Economics, Washington DC.

Frankel, J. (ed) (1998) *The Regionalism of the World Economy* (Chicago: Chicago University Press).

Henrekson, M. and Torstensson, R. (1997) 'Growth Effects of European Integration', *European Economic Review*, vol. 41, pp. 1537–1557.

Hitiris, T. (2003) *European Union Economics* (London: Prentice Hall).

Krugman, P. and Obstfeld, M. (2002) *International Economics, Theory and Policy* (New York: Addison-Wesley).

Lipsey, R. (1957) 'The Theory of Customs Union: Trade Diversion and Welfare', *Economica*, vol. 24, pp. 40–6.

Marques-Mendes, A.J. (1986a) 'The Contribution of the European Community to Economic Growth', *Journal of Common Market Studies*, vol. 24, pp. 261–77.

Marques-Mendes, A.J. (1986b) *Economic Integration and Growth in Europe* (London: Croom Helm).

Mayes, D. (1978) 'The Effects of Economic Integration on Trade', *Journal of Common Market Studies*, vol. 17. pp. 1–25.

Meade, J. E. (1955) *The Theory of Customs Unions* (Amsterdam: North Holland).

Molle, W. (2001) *The Economics of European Integration: Theory, Practice, Policy* (Aldershot: Dartmouth).

Moore, L. (2001) 'The Economic Analysis of Preferential Trading Areas', in M. Artis and N. Lee (eds), *The Economics of the European Union* (London: Oxford University Press).

Nevin, E. (1990) *The Economics of Europe* (London: Macmillan – Palgrave).

Ohly, C. (1993) 'What Have We Learned About the Economic Effects of European Integration?', Economic Paper no. 103, DGII, European Commission.

Owen, N. (1983) *Economies of Scale within the European Community* (Oxford: Clarendon Press).

Panagariya, A. (1999) 'The Regionalism: An Overview', *World Economy*, vol. 22, pp. 477–511.

Panagariya, A. (2000) 'Preferential Trade Liberalisation: The Traditional Theory and New Developments', *Journal of Economic Literature*, vol. 38, pp. 287–331.

Panagariya, A. and Duttagupta, R. (2001) 'The Gains from Preferential Trade Liberalisation in the CGES: Where From Do They Come?', in S. Lahiri (ed), *Regionalism and Globalisation: Theory and Practice* (London: Routledge).

Pelkmans, J. (1982) 'Customs Union and Technical Efficiency', *De Economist*, vol. 130, no. 4.

Pelkmans, J. (1984) *Market Integration in the European Community* (The Hague: Nijhoff).

Pelkmans J. (2001) *European Integration: Methods and Economic Analysis*, (Harlow, UK: Prentice Hall).

Pelkmans, J. and Gremmen, H. (1983) 'The Empirical Measurement of the Static Customs Union Effects', *Rivista Internationale di Scienze Economichei Commerciali*, vol. 30, pp. 612–22.

Petith, H.C. (1977) 'European Integration and the Terms of Trade', *Economic Journal*, vol. 87, pp. 262–72.

Robson P. (1998) *The Economics of International Integration* (London: Rontledge).

Silberston, A. (1972) 'Economies of Scale in Theory and Practice', *Economic Journal*, vol. 82, pp. 369–91.

Smith, A. and Venables, A. (1998) 'Completing the Internal Market in the European Community: Some Industry Simulations', *European Economic Review*, vol. 32, pp. 1451–75.

Srinivasan, T.N., Whalley, J. and Wooton, I. (1993) 'Measuring the Effects of Regionalism on Trade and Welfare', in K. Anderson and R. Blackhurst (eds), *Regional Integration and the Global Trading System* (New York: St Martin's Press).

Tovias, A. (1994) 'A Survey of the Theory of Economic Integration', in H. Michelmann and P. Soldatos (eds), *European Integration: Theories and Approaches* (Lanham, Maryland: University Press of America).

Truman, E. (1975) 'The Effects of European Integration on the Production and Trade of Manufactured Products', in B. Balassa (ed.), *Economic Integration* (Amsterdam: North Holland).

Truman, E. (1969) 'The European Economic Community: Trade Creation and Trade Diversion', *Yale Economic Essays*, vol. 9, pp. 201–57.

Viner, J. (1950) *The Customs Union Issue* (New York: Carnegie Endowment for International Peace).

Winters, A.L. (1987) 'Britain in Europe: A Survey of Quantitative Studies', *Journal of Common Market Studies*, vol. 25, pp. 315–35.

3 Factor- and Product-Market Integration and Europe's Single Market

Athina Zervoyianni and George Argiros

Introduction

The rationale behind factor-market integration in a CU is that the freedom of factors of production to move from one member state to another will equalize their marginal productivities: this will lead to more efficient allocation of resources within the union and thus higher aggregate incomes. On the other hand, the removal of non-tariff barriers to trade can be seen as a necessary prerequisite for the existence of truly integrated product markets. Indeed, the Treaty of Rome, which established the European Community, emphasized that Europe's prosperity and economic unity would crucially depend on its ability to create a fully integrated market. It therefore committed member states to implement specific provisions for the free circulation of goods, services, labour and capital within Europe.[1] The member states of the Community also recognized that in order to be made effective, these provisions of the Rome Treaty would have to be supplemented by policy actions in other related spheres, particularly in the area of competition. They thus sought to develop a comprehensive European competition policy. However, despite the Rome Treaty's provisions and the adopted relevant legislation and competition policy, the European common market was still, until the mid-1980s, largely fragmented: substantial price differences among the member states continued to exist, suggesting a considerable degree of non-competitive segmentation of markets. The reason for such segmentation was that while tariffs and quantitative restrictions on trade had been eliminated, there were many remaining and newly created institutional or non-tariff barriers. These barriers were arising from frontier controls on goods and persons at customs posts, from differences in indirect taxation and discriminatory public-procurement rules, from diverse technical specification and standards relating to products and from restrictions on freedom to engage in certain service transactions.

These barriers were imposing extra costs on products and services. They were also preventing the optimal utilization of resources and the exploitation of scale economies, encouraging at the same time oligopolistic structures. The response to these problems was the Commission's 'single market policies' for completing the European internal market.

In what follows we examine the effects of allowing for free movement of factors of production within a CU and we also study the welfare effects of removing institutional or non-tariff barriers to the free circulation of products among the member states. In addition, the Commissions' policies for completing the European internal market are discussed and evaluated. The next section deals with the welfare effects of factor-market integration, followed by a consideration of the welfare implications of removing non-tariff barriers to trade. We then focus on the 1992 Internal Market Programme, presenting the existing estimates of its possible quantitative impact, followed by a consideration of more recent internal-market policies and of Europe's economic performance relative to that of US and Japan. The final section presents a summary and conclusions.

Effects of Factor-Market Integration

The welfare effects of the integration of factor markets can be examined by comparing situations with and without factor movements. As is conventional in much of the literature, technology will be assumed to be given, perfect competition will be taken to prevail and prices and wages will be assumed to be fully flexible so that full employment of factors exists continuously.[2]

Capital Market Integration: Free Movement of Capital

Consider first the capital market. Figures 3.1(a) and 3.1(b) follow from MacDougal's (1969) general-equilibrium approach. In Figure 3.1(a), the vertical axis measures the price of capital, r. With perfect competition in all markets, the price of capital reflects the marginal product of capital. The horizontal axis measures the existing capital stock, K. The KK schedule can thus be taken to represent the relationship between the marginal product of capital and the capital stock. It is downwards-sloping indicating that, other things being equal, the marginal product of capital falls as the capital stock gets bigger. Its position and steepness are determined by the production function and thus by technology and the size of the labour force.

Figure 3.1

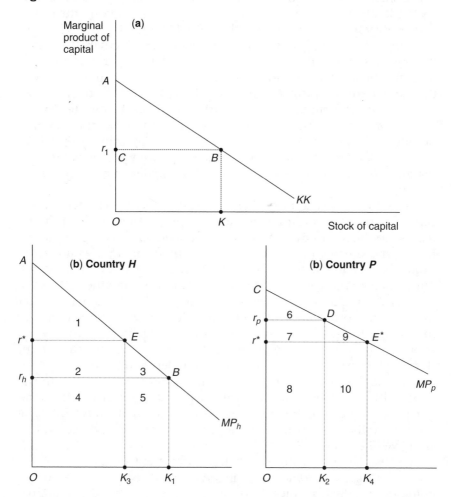

Suppose that initially capital is not free to flow from one country to another and that the capital employed in the home country is *OK*. Given the full-employment assumption, it is easy to find from Figure 3.1(a) the distribution of income. The height of the *KK* schedule at each point measures the marginal product of capital that is determined by the production function. Total domestic product, and also national product and income, is thus given by the area below the *KK* schedule, that is *OABK*. This consists of two components: capital income $OCBK = OK \times r_1$, namely the stock of capital times its price, and labour income $ACB = (OABK - OCBK)$, that is total domestic product (and national income) minus capital income.

Consider now two countries, country H and country P, and assume that initially there is no capital mobility both between them and between each one of them and the rest of the world. The schedules MP_h and MP_p in Figure 3.1(b) are marginal productivity functions in countries H and P respectively. Prior to the integration of capital markets, the quantity of capital employed in the two countries differs: the capital employed in H, and owned by the citizens of H, is OK_1 while the capital employed in country P, and owned by the citizens of P, is OK_2. Accordingly, in the pre-integration phase, the marginal product of capital is r_h in country H and r_p in country P, where $r_p > r_h$. With perfect competition, since capital owners will earn the marginal product of capital, profits will be higher in country P than in country H.

Now suppose that country H and country P decide to integrate their capital markets. Accordingly, barriers to the free movement of capital relative to the rest of the world are maintained but obstacles to capital flows between them are removed. To simplify matters, assume that capital is still completely immobile with regard to the rest of the world. This means that the total capital stock within the combined market of country H and country P will not be affected by the capital-market integration. However, after the establishment of an integrated market for capital, there will be a movement of capital from country H to country P in search for higher profit. This process will continue until the distribution of the total stock of capital between the two countries is such that its marginal productivity in H and P is equalized. In the figure, this is achieved for a marginal productivity of capital equal to r^*. Thus, following the integration of the capital markets OK_3 of the union's capital stock will be employed in country H and OK_4 will be employed in country P.

How has the establishment of free movement of capital affected each country's national income? As noted earlier, a country's domestic product is measured by the area below the marginal productivity curve. Also, with perfect competition, profits per unit of capital equal the marginal product of capital. Thus, in the pre-integration phase, domestic product in country H is the sum of areas $(1 + 2 + 3 + 4 + 5)$ while domestic product in country P is the sum of areas $(6 + 7 + 8)$. With no mobility of factors of production, domestic product is identical to national product, so, in the context of Figure 3.1, national income in country H and country P is also $(1 + 2 + 3 + 4 + 5)$ and $(6 + 7 + 8)$ respectively.

Following the integration of capital markets domestic product in country H declines: domestic production is now represented by the area sum $(1+2+4)$. However what matters for welfare is not domestic product but national income, namely domestic product plus the income that domestically-owned factors of production have earned abroad minus the income that foreign-owned factors of production have earned domestically. Capital owned by country H's residents of $K_3K_1 = K_2K_4$ is now employed in country P and earns income equal $r^*K_2K_4$. Country H's total national income is thus $(1+2+4+10)$. The increase in its national income exceeds the fall in its domestic product: area (10) is bigger than areas $(5+3)$. For country H, therefore, the net effect of the establishment of an integrated capital market is a net increase in welfare equal to $(10-5-3) > 0$. In country P, domestic product after capital-market integration is $(6+7+8+9+10)$. However, its national income is $(6+7+8+9)$. So national income also increases in country P by area (9). For the union countries as a whole, then, there is a net increase in incomes equal to $(10-5-3+9) > 0$.

While leading to higher aggregate incomes, the integration of capital markets has changed the distribution of income within each country. Given the full-employment assumption, labour's share in national income in country H was initially $(1+2+3)$. Allowing for free movement of capital between country H and country P has had the effect of reducing this share by the area sum $(2+3)$. By contrast, in country P, the share of labour in national income, which prior to integration was equal to area (6), has risen by $(7+9)$. Thus 'workers' ('capital owners') are worse off (better off) in country H and better off (worse off) in country P. However, since each country's national income has risen, any undesirable distributional effects can in principle be eliminated through appropriate transfer payments.

Labour-Market Integration: Free Movement of Labour

Figures 3.2(a) and 3.2(b) illustrate the effects of allowing for labour-market integration within a CU. As before, two countries are assumed, country H and country P. $L_h^d(L_h^s)$ is the labour demand (supply) function in country H and $L_p^d(L_p^s)$ is the labour demand (supply) function in country P. Movement of labour is taken to be costless. Also, labour markets are assumed to clear and there is no unemployment.

Prior to the elimination of the barriers to the free movement of workers between the two countries, employment in country H is OL_1 and the real wage rate is W_1^R. In country P, employment is OL_2 and the real wage rate is W_2^R. Suppose now that all barriers to labour flows across frontiers are removed. If this is the case, since factor movement is assumed to be costless, workers will move from H to P in search for higher real wages. This process will continue until real wages in

Figure 3.2

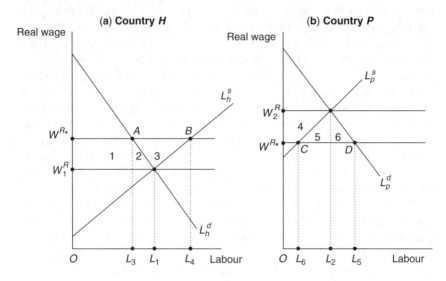

the two countries are equalized. This is achieved for a real wage rate of W^{R*}: at W^{R*} the excess demand for labour in country P, CD, just equals the excess supply of labour, AB, in country H. Indeed, with the new real wage rate, employment in country H is reduced to OL_3 and L_3L_4 of its labour force is employed in country P. Employment in country P increases to OL_5. This consists of OL_6 workers who are citizens of P and L_6L_5 workers who are citizens of country H.

How has the establishment of an integrated labour market affected welfare levels? Country P's employers gain the area sum $(4+5+6)$, the change in the area above the wage rate and below the labour demand curve. Country P's workers lose area (4), the change in the size of the area above the labour supply curve and below the wage rate. In Country H employers lose the area sum $(1+2)$. Citizens of country H working in the country, that is OL_3, gain area (1). Country H's citizens employed in P, that is $L_3L_4 = L_6L_5$, gain the area sum $(2+3)$. Accordingly, areas (4), (1) and (2) are income transfers: area (4) from country P's workers to country P's employers, area (1) from country H's employers to country H's workers employed locally and area (2) to the citizens of country H employed in country P. On the other hand, areas (5), (6) and (3) are net welfare gains as they are not compensated by losses elsewhere. Thus, both country H and country P benefit from the creation of an integrated labour market, and any undesirable income-distribution effects within each country can in principle be eliminated through appropriate government policies.[3]

Non-Tariff Barriers to Trade

Institutional or non-tariff barriers to the free circulation of goods, services and factors of production among the member states of a CU can take three different forms:

- physical barriers
- fiscal barriers
- technical barriers

Physical barriers refer to delays at borders for customs-control purposes, excessive customs documentation and related administrative burdens for companies and public administrators. Controls at border-crossing points and relevant customs documentation are helpful for tax policy and for the fight against drugs and terrorism, but these barriers add to the cost of goods as they travel from one member state to another.

Fiscal barriers arise mainly from national differences in indirect tax structures, including different coverage and/or different rates of VAT. Fiscal barriers create distortions in selling prices and also reduce competition.

Technical barriers are restrictions on the free movement of goods and services resulting from diverse national norms and regulations. Such barriers may take the form of differences in health and safety standards governing manufactured products. Differences in standards imply that products which are considered safe by one member state, and thus can legally be sold within that state, may not be allowed to enter the market of another member state. This forces firms to produce separate types of goods for the markets of individual member states. Technical barriers may also take the form of legislation relating to services that prevents national service-producing companies from trading outside national frontiers. Moreover, they include non-competitive public procurement rules that systematically discriminate in favour of local suppliers, as well as legal restrictions on companies wishing to establish subsidiaries in other member states. All these 'technical' barriers impose economic costs. By fragmenting the market, they complicate the production process and do not allow union producers to exploit scale economies. By restricting entry, they prevent firms from investing in new production processes and also reduce competition.

To examine the welfare effects of removing non-tariff barriers, it is convenient to divide them into two groups along the lines suggested by Emerson *et al.* (1990): those influencing international trade directly by adding to the costs of the products as they travel from one country to another, and those influencing more generally production costs in member states. The first category of barriers can be taken to include physical barriers and even the fiscal barriers. On the other hand, technical barriers fall in the second category.[4]

Effects of Removal of Physical or Fiscal Barriers

Consider a CU consisting of country H and country P. Figure 3.3(a) illustrates the market for commodity Q in country H. It assumes that the common external tariff adopted by country H and country P is such that the rest of the world is excluded from their markets. Accordingly, initially, all of country H's imports are coming from country P. Country P's supply curve is represented in the figure by the line S_P. However, as far as consumers in country H are concerned, the effective import supply curve is not S_P but S_P^*. This is because there is a physical or fiscal non-tariff barrier that leads to an extra cost of x per imported unit of Q. Initially, then, country H consumes OQ_2 units of the commodity, of which OQ_1 are produced domestically and Q_1Q_2 are imported from country P.

Suppose now that the non-tariff barrier causing the extra cost x per imported unit is eliminated. As the barrier is removed, the S_P schedule now becomes the effective import supply curve for country H. Thus, country H consumes OQ_3 units of the product of which OQ_4 are produced domestically and Q_4Q_3 are imported from country P. Accordingly, consumers experience a rise in welfare, equal to $(b+a_1+c+a_2)$. Producers in country H experience a fall in their surplus equal to area b. There is therefore a net welfare gain, measured by (a_1+c+a_2).

What is worth noting is that the elimination of this non-tariff barrier leads to a larger net welfare gain than the removal of a tariff barrier having an equivalent effect on trade. Suppose, for example, that the reason behind the effective import supply curve S_P^* was not the non-tariff barrier but a tariff x per physical unit of the product. Removing this tariff would lead to a net welfare gain of only (a_1+a_2), as area c in this case would correspond to tariff revenue forgone.

Figure 3.3

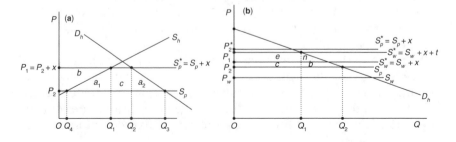

Another situation worth considering is one in which at the initial stage, trade occurs between country H and the rest of the world (*ROW*). To simplify the exposition, no home production of the good in question is assumed. This case is illustrated in Figure 3.3(b), where the rest of the world is assumed to be more efficient producer of the product in question than country P. Thus, S_w is the *ROW* supply curve and S_p represents country P's supply curve. As in the previous example, it is assumed that there is a physical or a fiscal barrier leading to an extra cost of x per unit. Accordingly, S_p^* is country P's effective supply curve, which incorporates increased cost arising from the non-tariff barrier. On the other hand, S_W^{**} is *ROW*'s effective supply curve. This incorporates increased cost arising from both the non-tariff barrier and the CU's common external tariff.

Despite the fact that imports from *ROW* are subject to a tariff while imports from country P are not, at the initial stage country H is obtaining its imports from the rest of the world because of the more favourable cost conditions there relative to those in country P. Accordingly, at the initial stage, the price of the product in country H is P_1 and domestic demand and imports are OQ_1.

Now suppose that country H and country P decide to eliminate the non-tariff barrier to trade between them but to retain that barrier relative to trade with *ROW*. This means that country H will now face the schedule S_p as its 'effective' import-supply curve. As a result, the price of the product in country H will fall to P_2, and country H will be importing OQ_2 from country P. The welfare implications are straightforward. There is a trade-creation gain; an increase in consumer's surplus measured by areas $(e+n+c+b)$. And there is a trade-diversion loss measured by area e. Area e was previously country H's tariff revenue from imports from *ROW*. The net effect in the figure is a sizeable welfare gain, equal to $(n+b+c)$.

Effects of Removing a Technical non-Tariff Barrier

The welfare effects illustrated in Figures 3.3(a) and 3.3(b) are based on the assumption that the costs of producing goods remain unchanged following the elimination of the non-tariff barrier. Yet removing non-tariff barriers, in particular technical barriers resulting from diverse national standards and regulations, is most likely to reduce production costs: union firms will no longer have to produce different products for the different markets of individual member states. The welfare effects involved are illustrated in Figures 3.4–3.9 (see also Molle (2001), Pelkmans (2001) and Hansen and Nielsen (1997)).

In Figure 3.4, which is similar in spirit to Figure 2.14(b), perfect competition is assumed and the industry's supply curve is also the

Figure 3.4

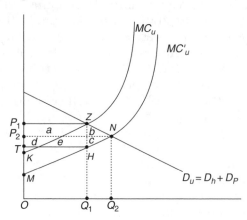

marginal cost curve. The $D_U = D_h + D_p$ schedule represents the union countries' demand curve. MC_U is the union's marginal cost curve (and supply curve) before the elimination of the technical barrier. The common external tariff of the union is assumed to be such that *ROW* is excluded from its markets. Thus, at the initial stage, the quantity OQ_1 is produced and consumed within the union at price P_1.

Suppose now that the union countries decide to harmonize technical regulations and standards and that, as a result of such actions, there is a general reduction in production costs, causing the union's marginal cost curve MC_U to shift to MC_U'. As the price of the product within the union falls to P_2, consumers experience an increase in their surplus by $(a + b)$. The surplus of producers is the area MP_2N, or equivalently $(MTH + d + e + c)$. Before the removal of the technical barrier it was KP_1Z. As $MTH = KP_1Z$, the surplus of union producers also increases by $(d + e + c)$. The welfare gain for the union as a whole is therefore $(a + b + d + e + c)$.

Additional gains from removing non-tariff technical barriers may arise if it is possible to exploit economies of scale. This is illustrated in Figure 3.5. In this figure, imperfect competition and average-cost pricing by firms is assumed. The technical barrier is taken to effectively imply that producers encounter restrictions on exports, with the result that they are unable to exploit their decreasing costs as the size of their output is confined to that implied by their local market. In particular, the existence of the technical barrier is taken to constrain the level of production to OQ_1. With average-cost pricing, this implies a price of P_1. If the technical barrier was to be eliminated, firms could increase exports and raise production, to say OQ_2. This would cause a fall in the price of the product to P_2, leading to welfare gains.

Figure 3.5

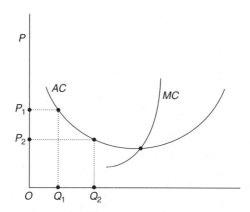

Removing technical barriers may, through greater market integration, also lead to a general reduction in market power and thus force individual firms to lower price-cost margins (see Jacquemin (1982))[5] and Allen *et al.* (1998)). This will reduce product prices and increase welfare. Such a situation is illustrated in Figure 3.6. At the initial stage, Q is produced in country H by a monopoly firm that is assumed to be protected from foreign competition by the existence of a technical barrier. MC_1 is the firm's marginal cost curve and AC_1 is the average cost curve. D_1 is the domestic demand curve and MR_1 is the marginal revenue curve. In the initial situation, profit maximization implies that the quantity OQ_1, corresponding to the point where $MC_1 = MR_1$, will be produced and that the price charged per unit will be P_1. The firm's total revenue is thus OQ_1KP_1 and its profit per unit is ZK.

Suppose now that the technical barrier protecting the monopoly firm from foreign competition is eliminated and so the 'effective' import supply curve is the schedule S_P. The effective market price in the domestic economy will thus become P_2. Given the new price P_2, demand in country H rises from OQ_1 to OQ_3. The firm lowers production to OQ_2, where $P_2 = MC_1$, and the excess of domestic demand over domestic production, Q_2Q_3, is covered by imports from country P. The result is an increase in the surplus of consumers in country H, equal to the area sum $(a+b)$. The firm's profit per unit falls to NH and its total revenue falls by $(a+c)$. For the country as a whole, the net welfare gain is $(b-c) > 0$.

Figure 3.6 takes the position of the cost curves and of the demand curve to remain unchanged after the elimination of the technical barrier. Yet, following the removal of the non-tariff barrier, the increase in the intensity of competition among firms may stimulate

Figure 3.6

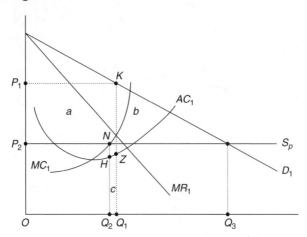

research and development (R&D) and innovation as each producer will now have an incentive to reduce production costs and improve the quality of the goods offered. The welfare implications of this possibility are illustrated in Figure 3.7 (see Emerson *et al.* (1990) and also Scherer (1987)). The initial situation is similar to that shown in Figure 3.6, namely OQ_1 is produced at the point where $MC_1 = MR_1$, the price charged per unit is P_1, the firm's total revenue is OQ_1KP_1 and per unit profit is KH. When the technical non-tariff barrier is eliminated, the monopoly firm is faced with the price P_2 due to competition from other countries participating in the CU. However, the increase

Figure 3.7

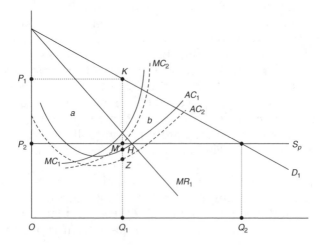

in competition may induce the firm to engage in R&D to reduce production costs, in which case its marginal cost curve MC_1 and the average cost curve AC_1 will shift to the right of their initial position, for example to MC_2 and AC_2. The net welfare gain here is greater than that in Figure 3.6: the total revenue of the firm falls by area a only (and profit per unit falls to ZM); and the surplus of domestic consumers increases by the area sum $(a+b)$. Thus, country H as a whole experiences a net gain in welfare of b.

The R&D induced by increased competition through the elimination of technical non-tariff barriers, in addition to lowering marginal costs, may also lead to improved product quality, which in turn may lead to increased demand. Increased demand may also result from a 'learning effect': as the availability of a product in the union market will increase with the elimination of technical barriers, consumers will 'learn about' this product and so they may be inclined to buy it, something that will lead to an expansion in demand (see Emerson *et al.* (1990) and Molle (2001)). This possibility is shown in Figure 3.8. The initial situation is the same as in Figure 3.7: domestic production and demand is OQ_1. After the elimination of the technical barrier, the monopoly firm fixes its price at the level P_2. However, the increase in the intensity of competition, by stimulating research and development, in addition to reducing production costs also leads to a new demand schedule D_2 due to better product quality. Learning effects, due to the increased availability of the product resulting from the elimination of the technical barrier, may also work in the same direction, moving the D_1 schedule further to the right. Accordingly, while the firm's total revenue falls by area a, the surplus of consumers in country H increases by the sum of areas $(a+b+c)$.

Figure 3.8

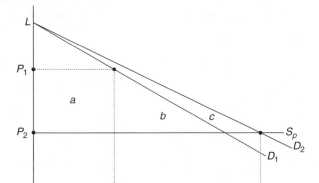

In addition to enabling firms to exploit scale economies and to stimulating more R&D to reduce production costs and improve product quality, the removal of a technical non-tariff barrier, by eliminating international price discrimination, may also lead to further welfare gains to consumers. The welfare effects involved can be illustrated with the aid of Figures 3.9(a) and 3.9(b) (see also Robson (1998), Pelkmans (2001) and Hansen and Nielsen (1997)). In Figure 3.9(a) a monopoly firm based in country H is considered. It is assumed that the firm produces a given quantity of Q, which is absorbed partly by the local market and partly by the market of country P. In the initial phase, the two markets are segmented due to the existence of a non-tariff technical barrier. To simplify matters, the firm's total production and sales are assumed to remain unchanged after the removal of the technical barrier. Country H's demand function is represented by the D_h schedule. Country P's demand function is represented by the schedule D_p. Demand elasticities differ, with D_p being more elastic than D_h. The marginal revenue curve corresponding to the demand curve D_h is MR_h and that corresponding to D_p is MR_p.

With segmentation of the two markets and given the different demand elasticites, the firm will practice price discrimination: profit maximization requires the firm to organize its sales to the local and country P's markets in such a way that $MR_p = MR_h$. Accordingly, with the two marginal-revenue curves crossing at point A in Figure 3.9(a), OQ_1 is sold locally at price P_1 and Q_1Q is sold in country P's market at price P_2.

When the technical non-tariff barrier causing the segmentation of markets is removed, the market is integrated and so the firm will be forced to adopt uniform-price practices. Indeed, in Figure 3.9(b), as the two demand curves cross at point B, integration of markets will lead to an equilibrium price of P^*, implying that prices drop in country H's market and increase in country P's market. The firm's

Figure 3.9

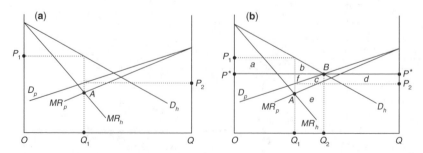

sales in the local market are now OQ_2 while its sales in country P are Q_2Q. Accordingly, consumers in country H experience a welfare gain measured by areas $(a+b)$. Consumers in country P experience a welfare loss equal to the area sum $(c+d)$. The firm's revenue from its sales to country P increases by $(d-e)$. Its revenue from its sales in the local market increases by $(c+f+e-a)$. Therefore, from the point of view of the monopoly firm the overall effect of product-market integration is $(d+c+f-a)$. This must be negative, otherwise there would be no reason for price discrimination. However, from the point of view of the residents of H and P taken together, the overall welfare effect of the elimination of the technical barrier is a gain, equal to $\{(a+b)-(c+d)+(c+d+f-a)\} = (b+f)$.

Europe's Single Market and the 1992 Internal Market Programme

As early as 1975, the existing non-tariff barriers to the free circulation of goods, services and factors of production among the member states of the community were seen as producing a serious handicap on European industry and a major obstacle to developing an integrated internal European market. Thus attempts were made to remove them; but such attempts failed to yield spectacular results.

Attempts to complete the internal market started to intensify from the beginning of the 1980s mainly as a result of Europe's continuing poor industrial performance. Indeed, during the period 1973–85, the competitiveness of European industry deteriorated considerably relative to that of Japan and the US, and many academic economists, as well as the European Commission itself, were convinced that, to a certain extent, this was due to the existing non-tariff barriers to the internal market and, more generally, to the fact that the European market remained fragmented.

The Commission's 1985 White Paper on Completing the Internal Market

In January 1985, the EC Heads of State formally recognized the potential benefits from a unified European market and asked the Commission to prepare specific proposals for completing the internal market. The Commission considered the situation, and in June 1985 published a White Paper setting out the required programme.[6]

The Commission's White Paper, entitled *Completing the Internal Market*, first sought to identify the remaining non-tariff barriers to the free mobility of goods, services, labour and capital within the

EC, namely the physical, fiscal and technical barriers. The Commission classified the measures that needed to be taken for achieving the Community single market under three headings:

- removal of physical barriers created by customs posts at frontiers and other control posts;
- removal of technical barriers, whether they applied to goods or to services, created by different national product or service regulations and standards for health and safety reasons, or for environmental or consumer protection; and
- removal of fiscal barriers created by different laws on taxation.

Having identified the barriers, the Commission then proceeded to prepare an action plan, the Internal Market Programme (IMP), for completing the European market by adopting a large set of legislative measures for the removal of these non-tariff barriers. The White Paper also specified measures to be taken in other community-policy areas to facilitate the process of completing the European market. In particular, it recommended that extra funds should be made available to the poorer EC regions to help improve their infrastructure. It also recommended a strengthening of Europe's Social Policy, Environmental Policy and the EMS.[7]

The White Paper proposed as deadline for the implementation of the proposed legislation, and the removal of the remaining non-tariff barriers, the 31st December 1992. This formally became an EC objective in 1986 through the Single European Act (SEA).[8] The SEA made changes to the Rome Treaty to allow the Council of Ministers to take decisions by qualified majority rather than unanimity on matters relating to the internal market. It also made the completion of the internal market by 1 January 1993 a Treaty obligation.

The 'New Approach' to Removing Technical Barriers

A large part of the Commission's legislative proposals for removing non-tariff barriers concerned technical barriers. Technical barriers were many and varied from one country to another. For many years the most important tool for eliminating such barriers, in particular for eliminating divergences in national provisions and rules governing products and services, was the harmonization of laws based on Article 100EEC. There were, however, two difficulties with this legislative mechanism. In procedural terms, the passage of Directives was in some cases problematic because of the unanimity required by Article 100: any member state could block a proposed Community legislation. In substantive terms, the type of Directives that the Commission normally devised in the 1970s and early 1980s was 'vertical product-related', which laid down all the technical details that manufacturers had to comply with if their products were to circulate freely in the Community market.[9] This harmonization strategy (called 'traditional') had attracted over the years a lot of criticism. The criticism was related to the following issues:

- the results of harmonization work were very poor, given the speed and intensity of regulation in member states;
- the approach adopted by Community authorities on harmonization was incremental and particularistic;
- the process for developing and testing draft Directives, in particular the decision-making procedure, was time-consuming and cumbersome;
- the implementation period by member states was very long;
- the excessive uniformity required for the harmonized products prevented innovation and competition; and
- the requirement that all the detailed technical specifications had to be decided by the Council was often causing bottlenecks in it.

In order therefore for the internal market to be realized by the end of 1992, a new regulatory strategy had to be developed. This new strategy was set out in the Commission's White Paper and was accepted by the Council in its Resolution of May 1985 on a 'New Approach to Technical Harmonization and Standards' (NATHS).[10] Four key elements were to make up the Community's new strategy:

- The Mutual Information Directive (MID)
- The principal of mutual recognition
- Harmonization of only 'essential' health and safety requirements
- The promotion of European standardization

The first step towards the preparation of the new approach was the adoption of the MID, namely Directive 83/189/EEC[11], on the establishment of an 'information procedure' in the field of technical standards and regulations. Under this procedure, each member state (actually each national standardization organization) was obliged to notify the Commission and all the other standardization institutions in member states about all national standardization projects and draft Regulations. During the examination phase member states were obliged not to implement the proposed technical regulation. There was also a standstill period when the Commission was giving notice of its intention of submitting a proposal for a Directive or Regulation on the subject. And there was a required suspension period of six months if the standing committee set up under the Directive proposed that the European-standards organizations were to draw up a European standard. In addition, a safeguard clause was introduced providing for the possibility that a member state could ignore the communication and standstill requirements of the Directive in case of urgent needs related to the protection of its citizens. In fact, the MID made it possible to prevent the adoption by member states of national regulations under Community law. The Directive also had the additional value of fostering transparency in the national-standard-setting processes. On the other hand, it kept the responsibility of member states intact as regards their own standards, as long as there was no possibility of developing European standards. This was very much in line with the principle of subsidiarity that at the time was taking a prominent role in the process of European integration.

The 'principle of mutual recognition' was developed as a result of the *Cassis de Dijon* jurisprudence of the Court of Justice.[12] According to this jurisprudence, a product that had been lawfully produced and marketed in one member state was to be considered capable of circulating freely in the European single market. The same applied *mutatis mutandis* to services. Indeed, the *Cassis* jurisprudence introduced the 'equivalence' of member states' standards. Obstacles to free circulation throughout the EC's single market resulting from disparities between national regulations concerning the marketing of products or provision of services were to be accepted insofar as they could be considered necessary for satisfying 'mandatory requirements', that is consumer or environmental protection, fairness of commercial transactions and so on. Harmonization efforts were therefore concentrated on those measures that were considered necessary for satisfying mandatory requirements.

This led naturally to the third element of the new approach, namely that legislative harmonization was to be limited to the adoption of 'essential' health and safety requirements with which products put on the market ought to conform in order to qualify for free circulation throughout the Community. It was the task of the competent (private) standardization institutions to implement, through technical specifications, these essential safety requirements. Such technical specifications were not mandatory and retained their character of voluntary standards. National authorities were obliged to recognize that products manufactured in conformity with the harmonized standards were presumed to conform to the 'essential requirements'.

The success of the new approach was based on the assumption that it was possible to develop European essential requirements. Where this was not the case, however, the principle of equivalence between the national standards was to prevail. The essential requirements had to be worded precisely enough to create, on transposition into national law, binding obligations that could be enforced. They also ought to be formulated in such a way so as to enable the certification institutions to certify straightaway that products conform to the requirements even when there were no standards. Indeed, the precise wording of the essential requirements was necessary to create some degree of certainty in the market since industry had to be reasonably sure when the free circulation of products throughout the EC would be forthcoming. Consumers were also to benefit from such precision.

The fourth element of the new approach was the promotion of European standardization. Standardization was seen as a very important element both because it would reduce barriers to intra-Community trade, and because it would increase the competitiveness of European industry.[13] The principal Community bodies which were to participate were the European Standardization Committee (CEN) and the European Standardization Committee for Electrical Products (CENELEC). The relationship between these standardization organizations and the Commission was regulated in a *Memorandum of Agreement* in which it was agreed that CEN and CENELEC would take up the elaboration of standards and the Community would guarantee their financial status. The openness to pluralist participation (particularly on the part of consumers) of the standard-setting procedures was seen as a precondition for the legitimization of putting product safety (at the level of standardization) in private hands.

Delegating the process of developing technical standards to these organizations also meant a greater involvement of industry itself in the whole process. This was expected to result in higher-quality standards because of industry's greater experience in this field compared with that of civil servants. Of course, a system of checks and balances was needed in that respect to ensure that the general interest would not be weakened.

However, according to the harmonization system established by the new approach, the marketability of goods throughout the Community was to be dependent not only upon the connection of products with the development of the relevant European or national standards, but also upon the proof of conformity of products with these standards. The fact that a product complied with European or national standards was not enough to create a 'presumption of safety'. Presumptions of safety bound up with compliance with standards ought to be mutually recognized. This was more so in cases where manufacturers were choosing to show direct compliance with the mandatory requirement itself by some other means. The Model Directive[14] was adopted containing a typology of possible controls. In particular, conformity was to be assessed by:

- Certificates and marks of conformity issued by a third party
- Results of tests carried out by a third party
- A declaration of conformity issued by the manufacturer, in which case a surveillance system would be required

This certification was to play a pivotal role for the access of the new approach because it was by way of certification that the producer was to show that he had observed the mandatory requirements. A single conformity mark would certify this conformity, the 'CE-mark'.

Thus the certification represented a general methodological framework to unblock the harmonization programme and to promote greater mobility of goods by defining essential requirements and by drawing up European standards. It also promoted competition and innovation because it combined stipulated safety objectives with flexibility on the particular product type which could comply with those safety requirements, and also flexibility on the standards through which this compliance could be achieved.

Estimates of the Effects of the IMP: The Cecchini Report – Method and Findings

Immediately after the signing of the SEA, a major study, carried out on behalf of the Commission, attempted to quantify the benefits of creating a single European market. This study, entitled *The Costs of Non-Europe* came to be known as the Cecchini Report from the President of the relevant committee.[15] Its findings are discussed in Cecchini (1988), Emerson *et al.* (1990) and Pelkmans and Winters (1988). In addition to the Cecchini Report, other studies have also sought to measure the effects of removing non-tariff barriers to the free circulation of goods, services and factors of production within Europe, pointing out, at the same time, the merits and shortcomings of the analysis of the Cecchini Report. Examples[16] of such studies are Baldwin (1989, 1992), which concentrates on the growth effects of the Commission's Internal Market Programme, and Neven (1990), which emphasizes distributional aspects. At the same time, the *Single Market Review*,[17] a study undertaken by the Commission a few years after the adoption of the Internal Market Programme, attempted to assess the effects of the IMP from an *ex post* perspective.

The Cecchini Report did not attempt to examine directly the degree to which each of the specific measures of the IMP would change the production, consumption and marketing of products and services and so on, within Europe. Instead, it sought to estimate the IMP impact by measuring departures from what a truly integrated market would have looked like.[18] Thus, it first sought to identify the barriers that were to be removed through the implementation of the SEA's provisions. It then collected information on the characteristics of the various European industries, on the potential for scale-economies and on price dispersion across industries as well as on business opinion regarding how industries were likely to be affected by market integration. On the basis of this information, it provided microeconomic and macroeconomic estimates of the potential gains from the completion of the European internal market.

The estimates of the potential microeconomic gains are summarized in Table 3.1. These estimates are based on a four-step evaluation of the impact of removing non-tariff trade barriers. Step I focuses on the benefits resulting from the removal of barriers that affect trade directly. Step II focuses on the benefits arising from the removal of barriers affecting overall production. Step III concentrates on gains from exploiting scale economies, and step IV estimates gains from increased competition and reduction of monopoly profits.

According to the Cecchini Report these benefits were to be brought about through the effects of: (a) removing frontier-control barriers, (b) removing market-entry barriers, and (c) eliminating cost-increasing barriers. Removing frontier-control barriers would result in a fall in the cost of customs procedures, including border stoppages and related costs arising from excessive customs documentation. The removal of such barriers would lower prices both directly and indirectly by increasing competition among firms and providing European producers with an incentive to improve efficiency. The second group of effects would arise in cases where barriers hindered foreign-market entrance. These barriers were typically found in public procurement and also in private-sector industries where national standards and regulations were preventing entry by non-local firms. By improving market access, elimination of such barriers would accentuate competition directly. This would in turn lower oligopolistic profits. It could also lead to increased investment to exploit scale economies, something that would have a favourable impact on members states' GDP and exert downward impact on prices. The third group of effects would create welfare gains by removing costs resulting from diverse health and safety standards for goods, and from differences in national regulations concerning services, especially finance and transport, something that would directly reduce prices and thus increase consumers' welfare. There would also be indirect effects through a strengthening of competition.

The Cecchini Report estimated the total potential microeconomic gain for the EC as a whole (EU-12 in 1988) to be between 174 and 258 billion ECU at 1988 prices, implying a mid-point estimate of 5.3 per cent increase of GDP. As Table 3.1 shows, the gains from the removal of border-control barriers, the physical barriers, were estimated to be smaller than those arising from the removal of cost-increasing barriers and market-entry barriers. In particular, the benefits from step I were estimated to be between 0.2 and 0.3 per cent of GDP. The benefits from step II were estimated to be between 2.0 and 2.4 per cent of GDP. The benefits from step III were found to be in the range of 2.1 per cent of GDP, while those relating to step IV were estimated to be in the range of 1.6 per cent of GDP. Accordingly, removing technical and fiscal barriers were expected to result in an increase in the EC's GDP of between 5.7 and 6.1 per cent .

Table 3.1 Estimates of microeconomic gains from the Internal Market Programme

	Step I	Step II	Step III	Step IV	Total (I + II + III + IV)	
Gains in billions of ECU	8–9	57–71	61	46	(a) for EU7 at 1985 prices	127–187
					(b) for EU12 at 1988 prices	174–258
					(c) mid-point of (a) and (b)	216
Gains as % of GDP	0.2–0.3	2.0–2.4	2.1	1.6	(a) for EU7 at 1985 prices	4.3–6.4
					(b) for EU12 at 1988 prices	4.3–6.4
					(c) mid-point of (a) and (b)	5.3

Step I: Gains from the removal of barriers affecting trade
Step II: Gains from the removal of barriers affecting overall production
Step III: Gains from exploiting economies of scale
Step IV: Gains from intensified competition and reduction of monopoly profits

Source: Based on Cecchini (1988).

While the IMP was a programme aimed mainly at improving efficiency in the supply-side of the economies of the member states, the Cecchini Report emphasized that the microeconomic effects would be accompanied by substantial macroeconomic gains. In particular, it was maintained that the improvements in the supply-side of the member states' economies, by increasing investment, consumers' real purchasing power and the competitiveness of European products, would directly increase aggregate demand and GDP in the Community. In addition, by improving productive capacity, the supply-side changes would lead to a reduction of inflation and enhance the ability of member states to raise employment in the longer run.

Table 3.2 shows the Report's estimates of the potential macroeconomic gains. Two sets of estimates were produced: estimates 'with accompanying measures' and estimates 'without accompanied measures'. Accompanying measures referred to active economic policy in the area of public-sector investment and/or taxation. Indeed, three options were considered. In the first, shown as (a) in Table 3.2, accompanied measures were calibrated in such a way so that the margin for manoeuvre created by the microeconomic gains from market integration was fully used in the area of the budget. The result in such case would, according to the Report, be a 7.5 per cent increase in the EU-12 GDP, a 4.3 per cent drop in consumer prices, 5.7 million new jobs, but a trade-balance deficit of 0.5 per cent of GDP. The second option, option (b), assumed that member states would use the full margin for manoeuvre made possible by the supply-side effects of the IMP to attain external equilibrium. This option would reduce the size of potential government-led growth and/or reductions in taxes

Table 3.2 Estimates of macroeconomic gains from the Internal Market
Programme

	Estimates without accompanied measures	Estimates with accompanied measures	
GDP percentage change (%)	4.5	a. Budget balance	7.5
		b. External balance	6.5
		c. Price reduction	7.0
Consumer Prices (%)	−6.1	a. Budget balance	−4.3
		b. External balance	−4.9
		c. Price reduction	−4.5
Employment (million of new jobs)	1.8	a. Budget balance	5.7
		b. External balance	4.4
		c. Price reduction	5.0
Budget deficit (% of GDP)	2.2	a. Budget balance	0.1
		b. External balance	0.7
		c. Price reduction	0.4
External balance (% of GDP)	1.0	a. Budget balance	−0.5
		b. External balance	0.0
		c. Price reduction	−0.2

Source: based on Cecchini (1988).

and so would result in a 6.5 per cent increase in GDP, a 4.9 per cent
reduction in prices and 4.4 million new jobs. In the third option,
option (c), the accompanied economic policy was so arranged as to
exploit only 30 per cent of the fall in consumer prices arising from
the IMP. This option would enable a 7 per cent increase in GDP, a
4.5 per cent reduction in prices, 5 million new jobs and an external
deficit of 0.2 %. But even 'without accompanied measures', that is
passive economic policies, the Cecchini Report predicted significant
macroeconomic gains from the completion of the European internal
market, namely a 4.5 per cent increase in GDP, a 6.1 per cent drop in
consumer prices and 1.8 million new jobs.

Assessment of the Cecchini Report

It could be argued that a major advantage of the Cecchini Report
was that the estimates (of the benefits) were derived from detailed
information about member states' industrial sectors and were checked
against the results of surveys of business opinion regarding the impact

of the IMP. The Report, however, had several weaknesses. First, estimates were based on the assumption that all the required legislation would be adopted and implemented by 1 January 1993. Yet, by the end of 1992 the Commission admitted that only 93 per cent of the 300 new Directives had been adopted.[19] Second, the estimates were derived from comparisons with a hypothetical case of full integration and were not therefore a genuine prediction of the effects of the IMP. For this reason, some authors maintained that the Commission's results were overoptimisitc.[20] And, third, certain key aspects had been omitted from the Report. These were: the impact of the IMP on the distribution of income within member states; the external effects of completing the European internal market; the distribution of the gains between individual member states; and the dynamic effects of the internal market.

The redistribution effects of completing the internal market had not been seriously assessed by the Cecchini Report. The Report maintained that the implementation of the IMP could cause temporary increases in unemployment, but the temporary nature of the unemployment increases was questioned by a number of authors.[21] In particular, fears of permanent increases in unemployment and long-run deterioration of employment conditions in Europe were expressed. The external effects of the IMP had also been largerly ignored in the Cecchini Report. As far as these effects were concerned, the argument was that the completion of the internal market could have substantial trade-diversion effects and could thus reduce welfare in the rest of the world. Indeed, a popular argument was that the increased competitive pressures induced by the IMP would make low-productivity member states raise external-protection levels to keep their domestic industries in business (see, for example, Dornbusch (1989)). A counter-argument, however, was that the completion of the internal market would promote world trade as its expansionary impact on the community's GDP would lead to an increase in European imports from the rest of the world. The issue of how gains from the IMP would be shared by individual member states had also not been properly addressed in the Cecchini Report: the Report made no attempt to provide quantitative estimates of the distribution of gains among member states and maintained that all members would benefit from the IMP. On this issue, immediately after the publication of the Report, two different views were put forward. The first was that some member states, including Spain, Portugal, Greece, the UK and Ireland, would see their market shares, and thus welfare, decline following the completion of the IMP as more efficient producers from other European states would displace their local industries. The second view was that the gains would be larger in countries that before the IMP were protecting their domestic markets with relatively high barriers.

Neven's (1990) study represented an attempt to examine explicitly how the benefits from free movement that would follow the creation of the internal market would be distributed among the member states. His findings were supportive of the latter view: they suggested that Northern European countries would gain little from the IMP with the main beneficiaries being the Southern European countries. According to Neven's results, Southern European countries would benefit from fuller exploitation of their comparative advantage in labour-intensive commodities and from gains from unexploited scale economies that had already been substantially exploited in Northern Europe.

Neven's findings suggested that the UK would benefit from the single market because of a better exploitation of its comparative advantage. This view was also shared by Pelkmans and Winters (1988) who emphasized that the important issue for British industry was whether or not it could expect to increase sales as a result of the completion of the internal market. Indeed, they classified UK industries into three groups according to the frequency with which they were reporting non-tariff barriers to the European internal market. Group I included frequent-barriers sectors, namely those in which over 70 per cent of firms were reporting non-tariff barriers. Group III included few-barriers sectors, in which under 30 per cent of firms were reporting institutional obstacles to the free movement of goods within the European Community. An intermediate category, for 'intermediate barriers' sectors, group II, was also considered. For each of these industries, the UK's share in Community trade was calculated. This share was then taken to be an indication of revealed comparative advantage: the higher the share the more competitive the British industry. Comparing UK shares in Community trade with the frequency with which barriers were being reported, Pelkmans and Winters came up with three main findings. First, relatively few barriers existed to intra-European trade of UK firms in sectors like motor vehicles, paper and publishing, and footwear, clothing and leather. By contrast, aerospace, computers, chemicals, non-ferous metals, wood and furniture had very high incidences of reported barriers. Second, the barriers to intra-EC trade were more frequent in more sophisticated industries, in particular in high-technology sectors. Third, UK trade shares were higher in sectors that were reporting most barriers. Making the reasonable assumption that the completion of the European internal market would lead to greater liberalization of trade in the frequent-barriers sectors than in the low barriers sectors, Pelkmans and Winters' argument was that UK industry was well-placed to benefit from the IMP.

In addition to ignoring the distribution of benefits from the IMP among member states, the Cecchini Report only examined the initial static effects of the IMP and did not make any allowance for an increase in long-run growth rates. Baldwin (1989), among others, emphasized that in addition to the static effects, there would also be a medium-term bonus as the static efficiency gains would induce higher saving and investment, something that would contribute to further output increases.

Baldwin's estimates indicated that the total output increase from the IMP, when both the static effects and the medium-term dynamic effects were taken into account, could be between 3.3 per cent and 11.8 per cent of GDP for France, between 3.4 per cent and 14.9 per cent of GDP for Germany, between 3.4 per cent and 14.2 per cent for the Netherlands, between 3.1 per cent and 12.5 per cent for Britain and between 3.5 per cent and 25.4 per cent for Belgium. This medium-term bonus would be achieved even if there were no permanent increases in the underlying growth rate. Moreover, as Baldwin pointed out, growth rates could be permanently increased. His efforts to quantify this suggested that the IMP could add between 0.2 and 0.9 percentage points to the member states' long-term growth rate.[22]

The 1996 Single Market Review

At the same time, the findings of the *Single Market Review* (SMR), a set of 38 studies commissioned by the European Commission (see European Commission (1996) and Monti (1996)), suggested that to a large extent the IMP had the effects predicted by the Cecchini Report. The *SMR* did the same type of work as the Cecchini Report but from an *ex post* perspective; its findings can be summarized as follows:

- In European product markets, increased competition was confirmed, resulting in cost and price reductions and output expansion.
- Intra-European trade creation had occurred and no extra European trade diversion was found.
- Price reductions were particularly significant in high-tech sectors, such as aerospace as well as in certain food sectors and in some electrical sectors, including electrical machinery, where public procurement prevented entry by non-domestic firms.
- Further price convergence was achieved.

Other attempts to assess the impact of the IMP from an *ex post* perspective include Sapir (1995) and Allen, Gasiorek and Smith (1998). Sapir (1995) concentrated only on product markets and his results were similar to the findings of the SMR, suggesting that the IMP had led to further trade creation and that this trade creation had been directed to both EU and non-EU countries. Allen, Gasiorek and Smith (1998) examined both product and service markets and attempted to explore the extent to which the IMP had affected competitive behaviour, combining econometric evidence with simulations from a computable general equilibrium model. Again their results reinforce those of the SMR: the IMP was found to have had a considerable effect on competition and market efficiency; and it had been followed by large cost reductions in all member states, although it was the smaller EU countries that had gained the most from the IMP, with potential welfare gains for these countries amounting to 10–20 per cent of GDP.

Strengthening the European Internal Market: Recent Developments and Performance

Internal Market Policies after 1996

Following the publication of the *Single Market Review* in June 1996, several policy documents on the internal market were published by the Commission. In all these documents the Commission stressed the significant contribution of internal-market measures to competitiveness, growth and employment. Its study *Internal Market - Ten Years Without Frontiers* (European Commission (2003a)), in which the achievements of the IMP were analyzed in detail, suggested 877 billion euro additional wealth and 2.5 million new jobs since 1993. However, in its Communication[23] on the effectiveness of the single market to the Dublin European Council of 13–14 December 1996, it maintained that certain barriers still remained, with the result that the internal market could not deliver its full potential. Indeed, in this Communication, it pointed out that actions to improve the functioning of the European single market would be required to ensure a smooth transition to the single currency by January 1999 and a successful EU enlargement to 25 member states.

On 4 June 1997 the Commission thus presented an 'action plan' for improving the internal market (see European Commission (1997a)). The Commission's *Single Market Action Plan* (SMAP) contained specific measures aiming at:

- making internal-market rules more effective
- dealing with market distortions resulting from tax barriers and anti-competitive behaviour
- removing remaining sectoral obstacles to market integration
- enhancing the social dimension of the European internal market, thus establishing an integrated market for the benefit of all EU residents

These targets were to be pursued together, but specific measures were to be implemented in three phases within a period of 18 months, from June 1997 until the date of the launching of the third stage of EMU, namely 1 January 1999. In phase 1, attention was to focus on actions that required no extra EU legislation and so they could be implemented in the very short run. Such actions included measures to speed up the process of incorporating single-market Directives into national-law systems, simplification of standardization and mutual recognition rules, implementation of already endorsed liberalization measures in telecommunication and electricity and also in public procurement, and establishing a dialogue with European citizens and businesses regarding problems related to the internal market that needed to be resolved. In phase 2, actions requiring legislation already proposed but not yet endorsed by the European Parliament and Council were to be taken, including the liberalization of gas supply. In phase 3, agreement was to be reached on actions in areas where preparatory work by the Commission had not yet been completed or in areas where proposals by the Commission already existed but adopting them would require strong political determination by member states and/or significant time and effort by EU organs. Full agreement by member states on such actions was to be reached by 1 January 1999.

The SMAP was endorsed by the Amsterdam European Council of 16–17 June 1997. In Amsterdam, member states recognized the importance of the single market for jobs and growth and asked the Commission to publish regularly reports on the progress in implementing the SMAP, starting from December 1997. The Commission also undertook the obligation to publish on a regular basis a *Single Market Scoreboard*[24] containing indicators that would reflect the member states' commitment to the action plan.

In January 1999, in its assessment of the SMAP, the Commission pointed out that considerable progress towards achieving all endorsed targets had been made but further effort was needed in the areas of patents and conformity marking, where progress had been slow, as well as in the areas of tax barriers and state-aid expenditure, where major distortions still existed. Progress on the European Company Statute had also not been satisfactory. In response to these weaknesses, and stressing that the internal market should be seen as a means to benefit EU citizens, the Commission presented in November 1999 its strategy for further improving internal-market performance over the next five years (see European Commission (1999)). The Commission's *Internal Market Strategy* (IMS) contained a large number of specific actions, aimed at fulfilling four objectives:

- improving quality of life in EU
- enhancing efficiency of the EU's product and capital markets
- improving business environment and competition
- exploiting the achievements of internal-market policies in a changing world

These targets, and also the measures to be taken to meet them, were to be reviewed and updated annually, so as to take account of the actual situation in the single market and of opinions by households and businesses regarding problems.

The IMS was adopted by the European Council at the Helsinki Summit of December 1999 and a first review of the strategy was undertaken by the Commission in May 2000. In its first review of the IMS[25], the Commission noted that overall progress had been slow, but it identified new priority actions to be taken to help EU meet the targets set out at the Lisbon Summit[26], in particular to promote technology improvements and foster innovation. In its second annual review of the IMS in April 2001[27], the Commission found that performance was poor: only 55 per cent of planned actions had been implemented on time. It thus urged EU organs and member states to improve progress by working together more effectively. The targets and priorities set out for the next 18 months remained the same as in the 2000 Review, and they reflected mainly the Lisbon Summit agenda. A third review of the IMS was undertaken by the Commission in April 2002.[28] In several key areas, initiatives had been completed on time, but overall performance was roughly the same as in the April 2001 Report (only 52 per cent of the measures had been implemented). Strategic targets remained the same; and the Commission stressed the need to move more quickly.

On 7 May 2003, the Commission presented a new internal-market strategy (NIMS), the *Internal Market Strategy – Priorities 2003–2006* (see European Commission (2003b)), covering a three-year period, partly as a response to the slowdown in economic growth, job creation, intra-EU trade and price convergence that the EU-15 member states had been facing since 2001. The NIMS aims at strengthening the internal market by pressing ahead with structural reforms so as to enable EU member states to boost competitiveness and investment, maximize the gains from the enlargement and realize the Lisbon objective of becoming dynamic knowledge-based economies by 2010. The strategy involves actions for:

- integrating service markets
- ensuring high quality in the areas of transport, telecommunication and post by opening up markets to competition
- making more open the public procurement markets
- improving conditions for businesses, including effective protection of patents and intellectual property rights and favourable legislation for small and medium-sized enterprises
- reducing the impact of tax obstacles
- simplifying the regulatory environment

- providing better information to EU citizens and businesses about their rights in the internal market and about available opportunities
- meeting the challenge of an ageing EU population by increasing the security, affordability and portability of pensions and by integrating national health-service sectors
- effectively enforcing internal-market rules

The NIMS is regarded by many internal-market participants and Community organs, including the Council and the European Parliament, as a key EU policy-coordination program to be implemented alongside the other two major EU policy-coordination programs, the *Broad Economic Policy Guidelines* and *Employment Guidelines*.[29] All three programs, cover the same period and are to be regarded as complements. The first annual implementation report of the NIMS[30] was not very encouraging in the sense that only 27 out of the 45 measures were completed on time. However, the second annual implementation report of the NIMS[31] showed good progress, with two-thirds of the legal steps towards achieving the endorsed targets completed. A third implementation report is due to be published in April 2006.[32]

The EU's Economic Performance Relative to Japan and the USA

Economic performance in the EU relative to that in its main competitors, the US and Japan, has been mixed since the adoption in 1999 of the Commission's additional internal-market measures. With the exception of 2001, real GDP growth has been higher in the US than in the European Union since 1999, with forecasts showing that this will continue in 2005 and 2006 (see Table 3.3). Labour productivity growth in the US also has been rising at a higher rate than in the EU-25 (see Table 3.4); and US unit-labour-cost growth has slowed down considerably after 2001 compared with unit-labour-cost growth in the EU (see Table 3.6), suggesting a deterioration of the relative competitiveness of the EU economy. On the other hand, in terms of real GDP growth and labour productivity, the EU's performance has been better than that of Japan's. Japan experienced slow GDP growth on average in 1999–2004; and labour productivity remained below that of EU-15 throughout 1999–2004. As far as employment growth is concerned, performance in 2001–2003 had been poor in the EU-25 but worse in Japan and the US (see Table 3.7). Average employment growth in the EU-15 member states slowed down from 2 per cent in 2000 to 0.3 per cent in 2003. In Japan, and also in the US, negative employment-growth rates prevailed in both 2001 and 2002. Gross fixed capital formation as per cent of GDP was also higher in the EU than in the US during the entire period 1999–2004

Table 3.3 Real GDP growth: EU, US and Japan (%)

	1999	2000	2001	2002	2003	2004	2005*	2006*
EU-25	2.9	3.6	1.7	1.1	0.9	2.2	2.3	2.4
EU-15	2.9	3.6	1.7	1.0	0.8	2.2	2.2	2.3
US	4.4	3.7	0.8	1.9	3.0	4.4	3.0	2.9
Japan	−0.1	2.4	0.2	−0.3	1.4	2.6	2.1	2.3

* forecasts

Source: Eurostat database, General Economic Background.

Table 3.4 Labour productivity per person employed: EU, US and Japan (in PPS, EU-25 = 100)

	1999	2000	2001	2002	2003	2004	2005*	2006*
EU-25	100	100	100	100	100	100	100	100
EU-15	109.0	108.4	108.2	107.9	106.8	106.4	106.2	106.0
US	135.6	134.6	134.9	137.3	139.0	143.7	144.4	145.1
Japan	94.7	95.5	95.9	96.0	96.9	100.2	100.3	100.8

* forecasts

Source: Eurostat database, General Economic Background.

Table 3.5 Gross fixed capital formation: EU, US and Japan (% of GDP)

	1999	2000	2001	2002	2003	2004	2005*	2006*
EU-25	20.4	20.7	20.3	19.5	19.2	19.5	19.7	20.0
EU-15	20.2	20.6	20.1	19.4	19.1	19.3	19.6	19.8
US	18.7	19.0	18.3	17.1	17.2	18.1	18.6	18.8
Japan	26.3	26.3	25.8	24.2	23.9	23.9	23.6	23.4

* forecasts

Source: Eurostat database, National Accounts.

Table 3.6 Unit labour cost growth: EU, US and Japan (annual percentage change)

	1999	2000	2001	2002	2003	2004
EU-25	−0.0	0.4	0.5	−0.6	−0.3	*n.a.*
EU-15	−0.0	0.5	0.5	−0.4	−0.3	−0.9
US	0.4	1.8	−0.3	−2.4	−1.9	−1.0
Japan	−0.4	−0.7	−0.1	*n.a.*	*n.a.*	*n.a.*

Source: Eurostat database, General Economic Background.

Table 3.7 Employment growth: EU, US and Japan (annual percentage change)

	1999	2000	2001	2002	2003*
EU-25	1.2	1.4	1.1	0.3	0.2
EU-15	1.7	2.0	1.3	0.5	0.3
US	2.2	2.2	−0.1	−0.8	0.0
Japan	−0.8	−0.1	−0.6	−1.4	−0.2

* latest available
Source: Eurostat database, General Economic Background.

Table 3.8 Trade integration of goods: EU, US and Japan (average of exports and imports of goods as per cent of GDP)

	1999	2000	2001	2002	2003*
EU-25	*n.a.*	*n.a.*	9.7	9.2	9.0
EU-15	9.2	11.1	10.8	10.4	10.2
US	9.3	10.2	9.2	8.8	9.0
Japan	7.7	8.5	8.6	8.7	9.2

* latest available
Source: Eurostat database, Economic Reform.

(see Table 3.5). It slowed down in 2002–2003, but since 2004 it has started to rise again. Fixed capital formation in Japan has also slowed down after 2000, but it remained above that in the EU throughout 1999–2004. This is expected to continue in 2005 and 2006. Japan has also experienced a steady increase in its trade of goods with the international economy (see Table 3.8). Extra-EU trade as per cent of GDP in goods as well as in services has fallen since 2000 (see Table 3.9). The EU is also showing poor performance in high-tech exports (see Table 3.10). High-tech exports in the EU-15 had been

Table 3.9 Trade integration of services: EU, US and Japan (average of exports and imports of services as percent of DP)

	1999	2000	2001	2002	2003*
EU-25	*n.a.*	*n.a.*	3.4	3.3	3.2
EU-15	3.2	3.6	3.6	3.5	3.4
US	2.6	2.6	2.5	2.5	2.5
Japan	2.0	2.0	2.1	2.2	2.2

* latest available
Source: Eurostat database, Economic Reform.

Table 3.10 High-tech exports (share of total exports)

	1999	2000	2001	2002	2003*
EU-25	19.7	20.6	20.5	18.2	17.8
EU-15	18.9	19.6	19.8	17.6	17.2
US	30.0	29.8	28.6	27.9	26.9
Japan	25.1	26.9	24.7	23.0	22.7

* latest available
Source: Eurostat database, Innovation and Research.

Table 3.11 Gross domestic expenditure on R&D (per cent of GDP)

	1999	2000	2001	2002	2003*
EU-25	1.86	1.88	1.92	1.93	1.95
EU-15	1.90	1.93	1.98	1.99	2.00
US	2.63	2.70	2.71	2.64	2.76
Japan	2.96	2.99	3.07	3.12	*n.a.*

*latest available
Source: Eurostat database, Innovation and Research.

below those in both Japan and the US throughout 1999–2003; and in 2002–2003 their share in total exports fell. On the other hand, R&D expenditure as per cent of GDP has been rising in the EU since 1999, although it is still below that in both the US and Japan (see Table 3.11). Spending on human resources in the EU as per cent of GDP was well above that of Japan's throughout 1999–2002, and also that of the US in 1999–2001 (see Table 3.12). On the other hand, in the area of patents and IT-ICT expenditure, the European Union is still lagging well behind the US and Japan (see Tables 3.13 and 3.14). But the EU-15 countries are catching up rapidly in broadband penetration

Table 3.12 Spending on human resources (per cent of GDP)

	1999	2000	2001	2002*
EU-25	5.00	4.94	5.10	5.23
EU-15	5.04	4.97	5.09	5.22
US	4.93	4.93	5.08	5.35
Japan	3.53	3.59	3.57	3.60

*latest available
Source: Eurostat database, Innovation and Research.

Table 3.13 Patents

	Number of patent applications to the European Patent Office per million inhabitants				Number of patents granted by the US Patent and Trade Mark Office per million inhabitants			
	1999	*2000*	*2001*	*2002**	*1999*	*2000*	*2001*	*2002**
EU-25	118.33	133.61	141.96	133.59	*n.a.*	*n.a.*	60.25	59.92
EU-15	140.95	158.72	168.33	158.46	63.00	66.66	71.79	71.34
US	141.96	162.26	177.28	154.51	307.90	300.51	306.56	301.41
Japan	131.66	159.54	186.89	166.66	246.42	247.09	261.53	273.93

*latest available
Source: Eurostat database, Innovation and Research.

Table 3.14 IT-ICT expenditure (per cent of GDP)

	2002	*2003*	*2004*
EU-15	3.2	3.1	3.0
US	4.7	4.6	4.6
Japan	3.5	3.5	3.6

Source: Eurostat database, Industry, Trade and Services.

Table 3.15 ICT use, EU-15

	Broadband lines subscribed (in percentage of population)	*Internet access by households (percentage of households who have internet at home)*	*E-commerce turnover (as percentage of enterprises' total turnover)*	*E-government on-line availability (as percentage of 20 basic public services)*
2002	2.3	39	0.9	36
2003	4.5	43	1.1	45
2004	7.6	45	2.2	*n.a.*

Source: Eurostat database, Innovation and Research.

rates, internet access by households, e-commerce and e-government availability (see Table 3.15). The number of science and technology graduates in the EU-15 is also growing, approaching that of Japan (see Table 3.16).

Table 3.16 Science and technology graduates (per 1000 of population aged 20–29 years)

	1999	2000	2001	2002	2003*
EU-25	9.4	10.2	11.0	*n.a.*	*n.a.*
EU-15	10.2	11.0	11.9	12.3	12.9
US	9.3	9.7	9.9	10.0	10.9
Japan	12.6	12.6	12.8	13.0	13.2

*latest available
Source: Eurostat database, Innovation and Research.

Summary and Conclusions

The Treaty of Rome emphasized in 1957 that Europe's unity and economic prosperity would crucially depend on its ability to create a fully integrated market: a market, which, in addition to the abolition of tariffs, would also involve factor-market integration, through the removal of all obstacles to the free circulation of capital and labour, as well as product-market integration, through the removal of all non-tariff barriers to trade across member states. It therefore committed the EC states to implement specific provisions in this respect.

However, despite the Rome Treaty's provisions and the adoption of relevant legislation, until the mid-1980s in Europe there was considerable non-competitive segmentation of markets: many institutional or non-tariff barriers had remained and new ones had been created. These barriers had large negative welfare effects and, as many studies were showing, removing them would lead to welfare gains. Indeed, a number of economists in the 1980s were convinced that the poor performance of European industry was, to a certain extent, due to the existing non-tariff barriers to the internal market. These barriers were arising from frontier controls on goods and persons at customs posts, from differences in indirect taxation and discriminatory public-procurement rules, from diverse technical specification and standards concerning products, and from restrictions on freedom to engage in certain service transactions. Such non-tariff barriers were increasing production costs and creating distortions in selling prices; they were reducing competition; and they were preventing firms from exploiting economies of scale and from introducing new production processes.

The response to this problem was the Commission's White Paper on the *Completion of the Internal Market*. The White Paper prepared an action plan, the 1992 *Internal Market Programme* for creating a fully integrated European market by 1 January 1993. The Cecchini Report, a study carried out on behalf of the Commission, undertook to estimate the benefits from creating such a market. The Report found that the benefits involved would be substantial: microeconomic gains were estimated to imply a 5.3 per cent increase in the member states' GDP, while macroeconomic effects, even without accompanied measures, were estimated to result in a further 4.5 per cent increase in GDP, as well as 6.1 per cent reduction in consumer prices and 1.8 million new jobs. Following the IMP, other 'action plans' have also been adopted by the Commission to further strengthening the European Single market: the *Single Market Action Plan* was launched in 1997; the *Internal Market Strategy* was launched in 1999; and the *Internal Market Strategy Priorities 2003–2006* was launched in 2003.

To what extent have the estimated gains from the Commission's internal-market measures become a reality? To what extent has the performance of European industry improved since the implementation of the measures? Commission studies suggest that there has been increased competition in European markets resulting in expansion of output; the volume of both intra-EU and extra-EU trade has increased; prices have fallen, particularly in sectors where national public procurement rules and regulations were preventing entry by non-domestic firms; and further price convergence across member states has been achieved. Other researchers, however, argue that the full benefits from internal markets measures will require a long time to fully materialize and that we should wait until at least 2006, when the third report on the implementation of the Commission's latest strategy for strengthening the internal market, the *Internal Market Strategy 2003–2006*, will come out. Yet others stress that if member countries are to exploit fully the benefits from the internal market, structural reform in the labour market is needed and, that if such reform is not implemented, European industry stands little chance of significantly improving its performance. Nevertheless, structural reform in labour markets involves serious political and social costs and this explains the slow progress that EU member states have shown in this front.

Notes

1   See for example Deadman (1996) and Swann (1992).
2   See for example Pelkmans (2001), Robson (1998), Molle (2001) and Hitiris (2003) or similar textbooks. Much of the existing literature on factor flows makes restrictive assumptions and points to *ex ante* wage differences and *ex ante* marginal-productivity-of-capital differences as the main determinants of labour and capital mobility. The theoretical and empirical models employed often do not distinguish between fixed capital and

portfolio capital and between skilled and unskilled labour and also they do not allow for growth.

3 The assumptions in Figure 3.2 are unrealistic, especially in the case of European labour markets: in European labour markets there are rigidities and the labour force is unionized. See Razin and Sadka (1995) for a model of labour flows with wage rigidities. See also Agiomirgianakis and Zervoyianni (2001a,b) for models with labour mobility and unions.

4 For an analysis of the likely welfare effects of removing non-tariff barriers see the studies in Jacquemin and Sapir (1989, 1991). See also Hansen and Nielsen (1997) and McDonald and Dearden (1999).

5 See also, Cubbin (1987), Zimmermann (1987) and Smith and Venables (1988).

6 See European Commission (1985).

7 See Pelkmans and Robson (1987) for a discussion of the Commission's White Paper.

8 See European Commission (1987).

9 See *OJ (Official Journal)* 1969 C 76/1, 'General Program on the Removal of Technical Obstacles to Trade'.

10 See *OJ* 1985 C 136/1.

11 See *OJ* 1983 L 109/8, as amended by Directive 88/182 EEC (OJ 1988 L 81/75) and Directive 94/10 EC (OJ 1994 L 100/30).

12 See *European Court Reports*, p. 645, 1979 3, and *Common Market Law Review*, p. 494, 1979: Case 120/78 *Rewe-Zentral AG* v. *Bundesmonopolverwalrung für Branntweein.*

13 See Pelkmans (1987) for an analysis.

14 See *OJ* 1985 C 136/2, Council Resolution of 7 May, 1985.

15 See European Commission (1988).

16 Other studies include Smith and Venables (1988) and Peck (1989) which concentrate on the effects of the 1992 Internal Market Programme on ologopolistic structures; Bos and Nelson (1988) and Westway (1992) which focus on the issue of indirect taxation; Grilli (1989) and Llewellyn (1992) which deal with the impact on banking and financial services; and Page (1991), Hufbauer (1990), Sapir (1992), Haaland and Norman (1992) and Milner and Allen (1992) which examine the external implications of the IMP. For book-length treatments see Winters (1992), Siebert (1990), Swann (1992b) and Winters and Venables (1991). For an analysis of the merits and shortcomings of the Cecchini Report see also Italianer (1990, 1994), Pelkmans (1992), Flam (1992), Hoeller and Louppe (1994), Peck (1989) and Dornbusch (1989).

17 See European Commission (1996).

18 See Mayes (1997) for a discussion.

19 See European Commission (1996).

20 See Kay (1989) and Peck (1989).

21 See, for example, Cutler (1989) and Grahl and Teague (1990).

22 For the effects on growth see also Baldwin and Seghezza (1996).

23 See the *Update on the Internal Market*, http://europa.eu.int/comm/internal_market/en/update/impact/major.htm

24 See European Commission (1997b).

25 See European Commission (2000).
26 At the Lisbon Summit of March 2000 the EU Heads of State and Government decided to implement economic- and social-reform measures with the aim of making the EU a dynamic knowledge–based economy that would be capable of generating jobs and of ensuring sustainable development and social cohesion. See Chapter 6.
27 See European Commission (2001a).
28 See European Commission (2002a).
29 See European Commission (2003c, 2003d).
30 See European Commission (2004a). This report was published together with the implementation reports on *Broad Economic Policy Guidelines* and on *Employment Guidelines* as part of an "implementation package". See also European Commission (2004b, 2004c, 2005c).
31 See European Commission (2005a,b).
32 For other policy papers by the Commission focusing on issues related to the Internal Market, including competitiveness and industry, see European Commission (2001b,c, 2002b, 2003e,f,g,h, 2004d, 2005d).

References

Agiomirgianakis, G. and Zervoyianni, A. (2001) 'Globalisation of the Labour Markets and Macroeconomic Equilibrium', *International Review of Economics and Finance*, vol. 10, pp. 109–33.

Agiomirgianakis, G. and Zervoyianni, A. (2001) 'Macroeconomic Equilibrium with Illegal Immigration', *Economic Modelling*, vol. 18, pp. 181–201.

Allen, C., Gasiorek, M., and Smith, A. (1998) 'The Competition Effects of the Single Market in Europe', *Economic Policy*, vol. 27, pp. 439–86.

Baldwin, R.E. (1989) 'The Growth Effects of 1992', *Economic Policy*, vol. 9, pp. 247–82.

Baldwin, R.E. (1992) 'Measurable Dynamic Gains from Trade', *Journal of Political Economy*, vol. 100, pp. 162–74.

Baldwin, R.E. and Seghezza, F. (1996) 'Growth and European Integration: Towards an Empirical Assessment', CEPR Discussion Paper no. 1393, Centre for Economic Policy Research, London.

Bos, M. and Nelson, H. (1988) 'Indirect Taxation and the Completion of the Internal Market of the EC', *Journal of Common Market Studies*, vol. 27, pp. 27–44.

Cecchini, P. (1988) *The European Challenge 1992: The Benefits of a Single Market* (Aldershot: Wildwood House).

Cubbin, J. (1988) *Market Structure and Performance: The Empirical Research* (New York: Harwood Academic).

Cutler, T.K. (1989) 1992 – *The Struggle for Europe: A Critical Evaluation of the European Community*, (Oxford: Berg Publishers).

Deadman, M. (1996) *The Origins and Development of the European Union: 1945–1995* (London: Routledge).

Dornbusch, R. (1989) 'Europe 1992: Macroeconomic Effects', *Brookings Papers on Economic Activity*, vol. 1989, no. 2, pp. 341–62.

Emerson, M., Aujean , M., Catinat., M., Goybet, P. and Jacquemin, A. (1990) *The Economics of 1992: The EC's Commission Assessment of the Economic Effects of the Completion of the Internal Market* (Oxford: Oxford University Press).

European Commission (1985) *Completing the Internal Market*, White Paper from the Commission to the Council, COM(85) 314.

European Commission (1987) 'The Single Act: A New Frontier', *EC Bulletin*, Supplement, Luxembourg.

European Commission (1988) 'Research on the Costs of Non-Europe: Basic Findings', vols. 1–16, Document, Luxembourg.

European Commission (1996) 'Economic Evaluation of the Internal Market – the Single Market Review', *European Economy*, no. 4, Office for Official Publications, Luxembourg.

European Commission (1997a) *Single Market Action Plan*, 18 June 1997, http://europa.eu.int/comm/internal_market/en/update/strategy/action/plan.htm

European Commission (1997b) *Internal Market Scoreboard – Edition 1*, http://europa.eu.int/comm/internal_market/score/index_en.htm

European Commission (1999) *Internal Market Strategy for the Next Five Years*, COM(99) 624, 24 November 1999.

European Commission (2000) *Review of the Strategy for Europe's Internal Market*, COM(00) 257, 7 March 2000.

European Commission (2001a) *Second Annual Review of the Internal Market Strategy*, 17 April 2001, http://www.europa.eu.int/comm/internal_market/en/update/ strategy/review01.htm

European Commission (2001b) *Supporting National Strategies for the Future of Health Care and Care for the Elderly*, COM(01) 723, 5 February 2001.

European Commission (2001c) *Budgetary Challenges Posed by Ageing Populations: The Impact on Public Spending on Pensions, Health and Long-term Care for the Elderly and Possible Indicators of the Long-term Sustainability of Public Finances*, Economic Policy Committee/ECFIN/665/01.

European Commission (2002a) *Third Annual Review of the Internal Market Strategy*, 11 April 2002, http://www.europa.eu.int/comm/internal_market/en/update/ strategy/index.htm

European Commission (2002b) *Communication on Industrial Policy in an Enlarged Europe*, COM(02) 714 , 11 December 2002.

European Commission (2003a) *The Internal Market – Ten Years Without Frontiers*, Commission Staff Working Paper , SEC(03) 1417, 7 January 2003.

European Commission (2003b) *Internal Market Strategy – Priorities 2003–2006*, COM(03) 238, 7 May 2003.

European Commission (2003c) 'Broad Economic Policy Guidelines', *European Economy*, no. 4, Office for Official Publications, Luxembourg.

European Commission (2003d) *Employment Guidelines*, COM(03), 8 May 2003.

European Commission (2003e) *Green Paper on Entrepreneurship*, COM(03) 27, 21 January 2003.

European Commission (2003f) *Communication on Innovation Policy*, COM(03) 112, 11 March 2003.

European Commission (2003g) *Investing in Research: An Action Plan for Europe*, COM(03) 226, 30 April 2003.

European Commission (2003h) *EU Productivity and Competitiveness: An Industry Perspective – Can Europe Resume the Catching-Up Process?*, Enterprise Publications, Office for Official Publications, Luxembourg.

European Commission (2004a) *Report on the Implementation of the Internal Market Strategy 2003–2006*, COM(04) 22, 21 January 2004.

European Commission (2004b) 'Broad Economic Policy Guidelines 2003–2005', *European Economy*, no. 4, Office for Official Publications, Luxembourg.

European Commission (2004c) *Joint Employment Report 2004–2005*, January 2004, http://europa.eu.int/comm/employment_social/employment_strategy/employ_en.htm

European Commission (2004d) *European Competitiveness Report*, Commission Staff Working Paper , SEC(04) 1397, 8 November 2004.

European Commission (2005a) *Second Implementation Report of the Internal Market Strategy 2003–2006*, COM(05) , 27 January 2005.

European Commission (2005b), *Internal Market Scoreboard – Edition 14*, http://europa.eu.int/comm/internal_market/score/index_en.htm

European Commission (2005c) 'Integrated Guidelines 2005–2008', *European Economy*, no. 4, 2005, Office for Official Publications, Luxembourg.

European Commission (2005d) *EU Sectoral Competitiveness Indicators*, Enterprise and Industry Publications, Office for Official Publications, Luxembourg.

Flam, H. (1992) 'Product Markets and 1992: Full Integration, Large Gains', *Journal of Economic Perspectives*, vol. 6, pp. 7–30.

Grahl, J. and Teague, P. (1990) *1992: The Big Market* (London: Lawrence and Wishart).

Grilli, V. (1989) 'Financial Markets and 1992', *Brookings Papers on Economic Activity*, vol. 1989, no. 2, pp. 301–24.

Haaland, J. and Norman, D. (1992) 'Global Production Effects of European Integration', CEPR Discussion Paper no. 669, Centre for Economic Policy Research, London.

Hansen, J. and Nielsen, J. (1997) *An Economic Analysis of the EC* (London: McGraw-Hill).

Hitiris, T. (2003) *European Union Economics* (London: Prentice Hall).

Hoeller, P. and Louppe, M. (1994) 'The EC's Internal Market: Implementation and Economic Effects', *OECD Economic Studies*, no. 23, Winter.

Hufbauer, G. (ed.) (1990) *Europe 1992: An American Perspective* (Washington D.C.: Brookings Institute).

Jacquemin, A. (1982) 'Imperfect Market Structure and International Trade: Some Recent Research', *Kyklos*, vol. 35, pp. 75–93.

Jacquemin, A. and Sapir, A. (1989) (eds) *The European Internal Market: Trade and Competition* (Oxford: Oxford University Press).

Jacquemin, A. and Sapir, A. (1991) 'Competition and Imports in the European Market', in A. Winters and J. Venables (eds), *European Integration: Trade and Industry* (Cambridge: Cambridge University Press).

Itallianer, A. (1990) '1992: Hype or Hope, a Review', *Economic Paper no. 77*, DGII, February.

Itallianer, A. (1994) 'Whither the Gains from European Integration', *Revue Economique*, vol. 45(3), May.

Kay, J. (1989) 'Myths and Realities', in *1992: Myths and Realities* (London: Centre for Business Strategy, London Business School).

Llewellyn, D. (1992) 'Banking and Financial Services' in D. Swann (eds), *The Single European Market and Beyond* (London: Routledge).

MacDougal, G. (1969) 'The Benefits and Costs of Private Investment From Abroad: A Theoretical Approach', in J. Bhagwati (ed.), *International Trade* (Harmondsworth: Penguin).

Mayes, D. (1997) 'The Problems of the Quantitative Estimation of Integration Effects', in A. El-Agraa (eds), *Economic Integration Worldwide* (New York: St Martin's Press).

McDonald, F. and Dearden, S. (1999) *European Economic Integration* (London: Longman).

Milner, C. and Allen, D. (1992) 'The External Implications of 1992', in D. Swann (ed.), *The Single European Market and Beyond*, pp. 162–92 (London: Routledge).

Molle, W. (2001) *The Economics of European Integration: Theory, Practice, Policy* (Aldershot: Dartmouth-Ashgate).

Monti, M. (1996) *The Single Market and Tomorrow's Europe*, Office for Official Publications, Luxembourg.

Neven, D.J. (1990) 'Gains and Losses from 1992', *Economic Policy*, vol. 10, pp. 14–62.

Page, S. (1991) 'Europe 1992: Views of Developing Countries', *Economic Journal*, vol. 101, pp. 1553–66.

Peck, M.J. (1989) 'Industrial Organisation and the Gains from Europe 1992', *Brookings Papers on Economic Activity*, vol. 2, pp. 277–99.

Pelkmans, W. (1987) 'The New Approach to Technical Standardisation', *Journal of Common Market Studies*, vol. 25, pp. 249–60.

Pelkmans, W. (1992) 'EC-92 as a Challenge to Economic Analysis', in S. Borner and H. Grubel (eds), *The EC After 1992* (London: Macmillan – Palgrave).

Pelkmans, W. (2001) *European Integration – Methods and Economic Analysis* (London: Prentice Hall).

Pelkmans, W. and Robson, P. (1987) 'The Aspirations of the White Paper', *Journal of Common Market Studies*, vol. 25, pp. 143–65.

Pelkmans, W. and Winters, A.L. (1988) *Europe's Domestic Market* (London: Routledge).

Razin, A. and Sadka, F. (1995) 'Revisiting Migration: Wage Rigidities and Income Distribution', CEPR Discussion Paper no. 1091, Centre for Economic Policy Research, London.

Robson, P. (1998) *The Economics of International Integration* (London: Allen & Unwin).

Sapir, A. (1992) 'Europe 1992: The External Trade Implications', *International Economic Journal*, vol. 6, pp. 1–16.

Sapir, A. (1995) 'Europe's Single Market: The Long March to 1992', CEPR Discussion Paper no. 1245, Center for Economic Policy Research, London.

Scherer, F.M. (1987) 'Antitrust, Efficiency and Progress', *New York University Law Review*, vol. 62, pp. 998–1020.

Siebert, H. (ed.) (1990) *The Completion of the Internal Market* (Tubingen: Mohr).

Smith, A. and Venables, A. (1988) 'Completing the Internal Market in the European Community: Some Industry Simulations', *European Economic Review*, vol. 32, pp. 1451–1475.

Swann, D. (1992a) 'The Single Market and Beyond: An Overview', in D. Swann (eds), *The Single European Market and Beyond*, pp. 3–26 (London: Routledge).

Swann, D. (eds) (1992b) *The Single European Market and Beyond* (London: Routledge).

Westway, T. (1992) 'The Fiscal Dimensions of 1992' in D. Swann (eds), *The Single European Market and Beyond*, pp. 82–105 (London: Routledge).

Winters, A.L. (eds) (1992) *Trade Flows and Trade Policy After 1992* (Cambridge: Cambridge University Press).

Winters, A.L. and Venables, A. (eds) (1991) *European Integration: Trade and Industry* (Cambridge: Cambridge University Press).

Zimmermann, K.F. (1987) 'Trade and Dynamic Efficiency', *Kyklos,* vol. 40, pp. 73–87.

4 Macroeconomic Interdependence, Cooperation and Currency Unions

Athina Zervoyianni

Introduction

A currency or monetary union (MU) imposes constraints on member states' macroeconomic policies. By becoming a member of such a union, a country loses its ability to use monetary policy for 'stabilization' purposes, namely to influence aggregate demand. Indeed, permanently fixed exchange rates or a common currency require common control over member states' money supply. To fulfil this requirement, either a central monetary authority must be created or the member states' monetary authorities must explicitly coordinate their actions. National fiscal authorities also lose much of their scope for independent action. In the absence of a MU, the fiscal authorities of a country have the option of financing a budget deficit by borrowing from the central bank. In a currency union this option is no longer available: national budget deficits can be financed only by borrowing from the public, that is by new issues of government debt. In addition, a country participating in a MU loses much of its power to conduct an independent exchange-rate policy against non-union currencies. This is because, with capital mobility, exchange rates are closely linked to each other through international arbitrage in the foreign exchange markets. Thus restricting the value of the exchange rate of any two currencies has implications for the exchange rate of each of these currencies relative to all the other currencies.

Because MU membership involves costs, a crucial issue is under what conditions the benefits from participating in a monetary union exceed the costs. To this question there are four different approaches in the literature: the optimum-currency-areas theory; conventional Keynesian and new-classical approaches; the game-theoretic approach; and the seigniorage issue.

In what follows we analyse these approaches, and we also assess their implications for the desirability of monetary integration in Europe.

The next section focuses on optimum-currency-areas theory, followed by an examination of the conventional Keynesian and new-classical approaches. We then examine the case for macroeconomic cooperation using the basic tools of game theory, followed by a consideration of the seigniorage issue. A summary and conclusions are provided in the final section.

Optimum Currency Areas and Similarity of Structures and Shocks

The optimum-currency-areas (OCAs) theory concentrates on the costs of monetary integration, pointing to the existence of certain structural economic characteristics as criteria for determining whether or not a country is a good candidate for participation in a monetary union. The criteria set out in this literature include:

- the degree of labour and capital mobility
- the degree of openness to trade
- the level of diversification of the economy
- the similarity of the economies concerned in terms of responses to external shocks and nature of underlying disturbances

The classic contributions to the OCAs theory are Mundell (1961), McKinnon (1963) and Kenen (1969). These three papers represent the 'core' theory of OCAs and much of the existing empirical work has been based upon them.[1] Starting with Mundell (1961), he viewed labour mobility as the key criterion in the choice for and against a currency union (CU). He argued that fixed exchange rates in a CU were costly, mainly because of asymmetric shocks and nominal rigidities. If labour mobility existed between the member states, this would substitute for exchange rate flexibility and the losses from forming a currency union caused by nominal rigidities and asymmetric disturbances would be partly nullified.[2] Mundell also viewed the degree of capital mobility within the currency union as a factor equally important to labour mobility. His argument was that high capital mobility would imply that countries could finance balance-of-payments deficits without having to resort to exchange-rate depreciations. The fixity of exchange rates within the CU would thus not be a problem, provided that high mobility of capital existed between participating states.

McKinnon (1963), on the other hand, viewed openness to trade as the most important criterion in the choice of a currency union. He pointed out that very open economies were likely to suffer quite severe disruptions to trade and production from currency depreciations and appreciations. He also argued that flexible exchange rates were relatively ineffective in very open economies as exchange-rate changes could destabilize the domestic price level without having large beneficial effects on real wages or the terms of trade. Thus relatively open economies would stand to gain more from forming a CU than relatively closed economies. Openness to trade has also been emphasized more recently by a number of other authors, including Melitz (1995, 1996) and Bayoumi (1994). Bayoumi (1994), in particular, has stressed that with the same structure of underlying disturbances, a country will generally prefer to join in a CU with countries whose products is using more rather than less.

Another structural characteristic proposed by the OCAs literature is the degree of diversification of a country's production and imports. Kenen (1969) was the first to point out that countries with high product diversification would be better able to maintain a CU than those with no diversification, since the latter countries would in general be subject to larger disturbances. In the same context, he argued that high product diversification meant stable export earnings and thus stable balance of payments. This, in turn, would imply no need for exchange-rate changes to maintain external equilibrium. By contrast, low product diversification would cause a country to be heavily dependent on developments in export markets and thus be relatively more dependent on exchange-rate changes to maintain external equilibrium.

On the other hand, much of the OCAs literature views the similarity of the countries concerned in terms of responses to external shocks and nature of underlying disturbances as the most important factors to investigate in the choice of a CU.

To illustrate the argument, consider two countries in a MU, say 'Germany' and 'France', as well as the rest of the world, *ROW*, along the lines suggested, for example, by Levin (1983). On the assumption that Germany and France have already adopted a common currency whose exchange rate relative to non-union currencies is left to float freely and that prices are given in the short run, their goods markets can be taken to be described by equations (1a) and (1b):

$$\textit{Germany} \quad y = y^d = \sigma e - \delta r + cy + \gamma y^* + \omega y_{ROW} - u \qquad (1a)$$

$$\textit{France} \quad y^* = y^{*d} = \sigma e - \delta r^* + cy^* + \gamma y + \omega^* y_{ROW} + u \qquad (1b)$$

$$0 < c, \gamma, \omega < 1, \omega > \omega^*$$

$$r = r^* = r_{ROW} \qquad (1c)$$

In equation (1a) the demand for products produced in Germany, y^d, and therefore total German output, y, is negatively related to the domestic interest rate, r, and is positively related to domestic income, y, and, through the trade balance, to income in France, y^*, and in the rest of the world, y_{ROW}. Similarly, in (1b), the demand for products produced in France, y^{*d}, and therefore total French output, y^*, is negatively related to r^* and is positively related to y^* and, through the trade balance, to y and y_{ROW}. y^d and y^{*d}, also through the trade balance, depend on the value of the exchange rate of France's and Germany's common currency relative to the ROW currency. This exchange rate, denoted by e, is defined as units of the common currency per unit of the ROW currency. Thus, an increase (fall) in its value reflects a depreciation (appreciation) of Germany's and France's common currency against the ROW currency. As prices are assumed to be given in the short run, a higher e improves the competitiveness of products produced within the union and so increases economic activity and output there. c is the marginal propensity to consume domestically-produced goods in each country, and γ is the propensity to import from partner countries. Perfect capital mobility and static exchange-rate expectations are assumed, so, from equation (1c), the same interest rate effectively prevails in all three countries. The parameters ω and ω^* in equations (1a) and (1b) can be taken to reflect the symmetry in the union economies' responses to changes in the international environment. As $\omega > \omega^*$, Germany and France differ in terms of the sensitivity of their economies to external shocks: movements in economic activity, and thus income, in ROW do not affect them to the same extent. u represents a stochastic asymmetric shock, which is negative correlated across countries.

Solving equation (1b) for e and substituting the resulting expression into equation (1a), the condition for equilibrium in the union countries' goods markets can be written as in equation (1):

$$y = y^* + \frac{1}{(1-c+\gamma)}\{(\omega - \omega^*)y_{ROW} - 2u\} \tag{1}$$

which is represented in Figure 4.1(a) by the upward-sloping line GG.

As far as monetary equilibrium is concerned, this is achieved when the union's money shock, m_U, equals total money demand, m_U^d, which is the sum of money demand in the two union countries, namely $(m^d + m^{*d})$:

$$m_U = m_U^d = \phi(y + y^*) - \lambda r_{ROW} \tag{2}$$

Figure 4.1

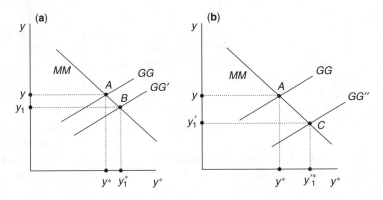

m_U is controlled by the union's central monetary authority. m_U^d is positively related to aggregate income, and thus production within the union $(y+y^*)$ through a transactions motive for holding money, and is negatively related to union interest rates and therefore, from equation (1c), to the world interest rate r_{ROW}. In Figure 4.1(a) equation (2) is shown as the downwards-sloping line MM: an increase in income in Germany, y, would create excess demand for money in the union and this would require a fall in income in France, y^*, to maintain equilibrium. Simultaneous equilibrium in the union's goods and money markets occurs at A, where the GG and MM schedules intersect. On the other hand, adding (1a) and (1b) and using (1c) and (2), one can obtain an expression for the equilibrium value of the exchange rate of the common currency:

$$e = \sigma_1[\varphi_1 m_U + \lambda_1 r_{ROW} - (\omega + \omega^*)y_{ROW}] \tag{3}$$

where

$$\varphi_1 = [1-(c+\gamma)](1/\varphi) > 0$$
$$\lambda_1 = \lambda\varphi_1 + 2\delta > 0, \sigma_1 = (1/2\sigma) > 0$$

Suppose now that output in the rest of the world falls. Since Germany and France differ in terms of their vulnerability to changes in economic activity in non-union countries, this will have an asymmetric impact on their economies: the fall in y_{ROW} will have a relatively small negative impact on aggregate demand and output in France, but a relatively large negative effect on aggregate demand and output in Germany. However, exchange-rate changes between the two union countries are not possible. At the same time, with perfect capital mobility, from equation (3), the common currency has to depreciate relative to the *ROW* currency to maintain global equilibrium. This depreciation of the common currency more than offsets the impact of the fall in y_{ROW} on output in France while it is not enough to fully offset the impact of the shock on output and thus income in Germany. Accordingly, in Figure 4.1(a), y falls to y_1 and y^* rises to y_1^* as the *GG* line shifts to the right of its initial position, to the position occupied by, say, the schedule *GG'*.

As can be seen from equation (1), similar considerations hold even if $\omega = \omega^*$ but there is an asymmetric stochastic disturbance u, negatively correlated between countries. Such a disturbance would lower aggregate demand and output in Germany and would increase aggregate demand and output in France. If exchange-rate changes between the two union countries were possible, equilibrium would be restored through a depreciation of the German mark relative to the French franc. Within a CU however exchange-rate changes between the union currencies are not possible. At the same time, from equation (3), the common currency has to remain unchanged relative to the *ROW* currency to maintain global equilibrium. Accordingly, in Figure 4.1(b), the *GG* schedule shifts to the right, with the result that output in both countries is destabilized.

Indeed, the conclusion to be drawn from Figures 4.1(a) and 4.1(b) is that in countries in which common shocks have an asymmetric impact due to diverse economic structures and in countries in which asymmetric shocks occur within alike economic structures, a one-size-fits-all monetary policy is not recommendable. Such countries will not be good candidates for participation in a CU (see Bayoumi (1994) and Bayoumi and Eichengreen (1993)).

While this is a valid point, it could be argued that the OCAs theory has two main limitations. The first is that it may not be easy to accurately quantify all the structural characteristics identified as relevant by the OCAs literature. Second, no single economy is likely to have all the structural characteristics required to make it an ideal member of a currency union. In the process of determining the net outcome of a move to a MU, one therefore needs to know which characteristics are more important than the others.

Recently, attempts have been made in the literature to deal with both problems. On the one hand, there have been attempts to integrate the theory of OCAs with the theory of international trade and/or derive models of OCAs using a general equilibrium approach with regionally differentiated goods.[3] Using such a framework, the various structural criteria proposed by the OCA for assessing MUs can be integrated and compared. These models also make it possible to analyse the incentives involved in forming MUs in more detail than in earlier models. Moreover, since the early 1990s, a large number of studies have attempted to operationalize the OCAs theory, mainly as a way of providing evidence on EMU's costs and benefits.[4] Bayoumi and Eichengreen (1997), for example, have applied the core implications of OCAs theory to cross-country data constructing optimum-currency-areas indices for the European countries.

At the same time, since the start of the discussions leading to the signing of the Maastricht Treaty the issue of asymmetric shocks and asymmetric responses has been examined extensively.[5] In an attempt to explore the likelihood of asymmetric shocks within the EU, several authors, including Cohen and Wyplosz (1989), Weber (1991) and Stockman (1988), have addressed the issue of whether fluctuations in aggregate variables across European countries have been synchronized. Cohen and Wyplosz (1989) have focused on growth rates of real output, real wages and prices and concluded that fluctuations in these variables across Germany and France have been broadly symmetrical. Weber (1991) has extended the Cohen-Wyplosz analysis to the other European Community countries, reaching a similar conclusion. Stockman (1988) has examined industrial-production growth in two-digit manufacturing industries in seven European states and found that industry-specific shocks have been no less important than nation-specific shocks. These studies, however, have been criticized by many, including Bayoumi and Eichengreen (1993, 1996), Chamie, DeSerres and Lalonde (1994) and Demertzis, Hughes-Hallett and Rummel (1998), on the grounds that examining fluctuations in aggregate variables provides no information about the nature of shocks since it is impossible to distinguish between the impact of the shocks and the dynamic responses to them. Much of this more recent literature suggests that not all types of shocks have been well correlated across Europe and that the distinction between core and periphery plays an important role. In particular, the results of Bayoumi and Eichengreen (1993), who use data until 1988 and vector auto-regressions to separate in output and price equations the structural demand and supply shocks from the dynamic responses to them, indicate that the degree of shock asymmetry in wider Europe is higher than in the US regions and increases in magnitude as we move from the core to the periphery. More specifically, they find that while real demand and supply shocks in Germany and in the other core European countries (that is, France, Belgium, Denmark and the Netherlands) have been reasonably well-correlated, those between Germany and the broader set of EU states are less well-correlated and poorly correlated compared to most regions of the US. Bini-Smaghi and Vori (1993) arrive at a similar conclusion in that they find that, while the EC-6 are likely to experience predominantly symmetric shocks, it is unlear whether this conclusion can be extended to the rest of the European states. Chamie *et al.* (1994), on the other hand, challenge even the distinction between core and peripheral countries in the EU, as implied by OCA criteria. In particular, employing the Bayoumi-Eichengreen methodology of using vector auto-correlation techniques, they first identify nominal and real demand shocks as well as supply shocks and then distinguish between common and specific components of these shocks, arguing that the relative importance of the common component can be taken as a measure of the degree of cross-country symmetry of shocks. Their results indicate that, out of the thirteen European countries considered, only Germany and Switzerland are related to the common component of supply and real demand shocks to a degree broadly comparable to that found in the US regions; and that the shocks affecting Belgium, France, the Netherlands, Spain and the UK, although related to the common component, have a strong country-specific element. Extending their sample period beyond 1988, Bayoumi and Eichengreen (1996) find similar results: as far as supply shocks are concerned, cross-country correlation is found to be statistically significant only between Germany and Belgium, Austria, France and the Netherlands. The results of Demertzis *et al.* (1998) also reveal the importance of the nature of shocks considered. Examining correlation of shocks within and between groups of EU countries, they reach the conclusion that in terms of supply shocks there is little difference between core and periphery: while real demand disturbances are found to be largerly synchronized within both the core and the periphery of the EU, supply shocks are not, in either the core or the periphery.

It could be argued, however, that the correlation of shocks across Europe in the past does not provide a sensible indicator of the appropriateness of the EU as an optimum currency area since the process of economic integration is likely to cause changes in the pattern of national and regional fluctuations in the member states' economies. Indeed, economic integration, through closer international trade links between member states, may lead to more specialization at the country level as member states will tend to concentrate on the production of goods in which they have a comparative cost advantage. More specialization in production will in turn increase the likelihood of idiosyncratic or asymmetric shocks. For this reason Krugman (1991, 1993), among others, has argued that deeper trade integration in the EU, which has been made possible by the internal-market measures, will over time increase the probability of shock asymmetry across member states. Nevertheless, as Frankel and Rose (1997, 1998) have pointed out, increased trade resulting from the integration process may in principle operate in an opposite direction; it may produce more rather than less symmetric shocks. This will be the case if real demand disturbances predominate, since economic integration will tend to increase the common component of such shocks. It will also be the case if economic integration mainly results in greater intra-industry or intra-regional trade, since in such case, as economic integration progresses, the correlation of national business cycles will tend to become tighter than before. The econometric results of Frankel and Rose (1997, 1998), Artis and Zhang (1999), Fatàs (1997) and Bayoumi and Eichegreen (1997) seem to support this view. Frankel and Rose (1997, 1998) examine empirically the relationship between higher trade intensity and degree of correlation of national business cycles, using data from 20 industrialized countries covering a period of 30 years. Their findings indicate that closer international trade linkages have historically resulted in greater, rather than less, correlation of national economic activity across countries: they find a strong positive relationship between increased trade flows and the cross-country correlation of aggregate macroeconomic variables. These results suggest that the process of European integration can be expected to lead over time to more highly syncronized business cycles, thus making participation of member states in the eurozone even more desirable in the future. Fatàs (1997) reaches the same conclusion. He studies the behaviour of employment-growth rates across the EU states since the establishment of the EMS, focusing on how it has evolved over time. His results indicate that the correlation of employment-growth rates across European countries has been increasing over time while those across European regions has been decreasing. This again suggests that over time European integration can be expected to reduce the magnitude of the national component of business cycles. The findings of Artis and Zhang (1999) and Bayoumi and Eichengreen (1997) point to the same conclusion.

As for asymmetries across countries concerning the impact of common shocks, including common policy changes, much of the evidence indicates that there are still considerable differences among the EU economies. For example, Dornbusch *et al.* (1998), using econometric models developed by the EU countries' central banks, examine how a common interest-rate change by the European Central Bank is transmitted to the EU economies. They find that the transmission mechanism is not the same across the member states, with the result that the impact on key national macroeconomic variables, such as output and inflation, differs in size by 50 per cent or more.[6]

Phillips-Curve Theory and the Effects of Monetary Integration

Conventional approaches to the effects of monetary integration seek to avoid the problem of trying to single out important structural characteristics by attempting to explicitly identify and evaluate the relative costs and benefits of MU membership.

Starting from the benefits, the most obvious advantage that a MU offers to participating countries is the elimination of exchange-rate uncertainty and risk. With the exception of dealers in foreign exchange, everyone would agree that exchange-rate instability is undesirable. Indeed, firms do not know where to construct new plants or which projects to invest in if no confident prediction can be made about exchange rates at least three to five years ahead. Especially in the case of the EU exchange-rate uncertainty is a particularly important problem, given the intention of member states to create a unified internal market.

In addition to eliminating exchange-rate uncertainty and risk, a monetary union also offers several other benefits to member states. One of them is that the foreign exchange reserves required to cover the group as a whole are smaller than those needed if each country was to maintain an independent currency. The reason is obvious: in a MU there is no need to hold reserves to cover balance of payments deficits with the other member states. Foreign reserves are needed only for regulating exchange rates with the rest of the world. It is also quite unlikely that all the members of a MU will be experiencing balance of payments deficits with the rest of the world at the same time. Thus, a monetary union can be expected to need lower foreign exchange reserves than those required by member countries operating individually. Other benefits include:[7] lower information and transaction costs in international trade; dynamic efficiency gains; a greater weight of member states in international negotiations concerning the global management of exchange rates; and, that intervention in foreign exchange markets by the group as a whole will be more effective than individual actions by the national central banks.

As far as the costs of a monetary integration are concerned, within the context of conventional Keynesian thinking, most analyses are based on the Phillips-curve theory. According to it, a stable negative relationship always exists between the rate of unemployment, U, and the rate of wage inflation, $\rho = (\Delta W/W)$. Such a relationship is represented in Figure 4.2(a) by the curve PC. The rationale behind the PC curve is that the lower the level of unemployment the more inclined are trade unions to demand higher wages. The PI schedule describes the relationship between wage inflation and price inflation

Figure 4.2

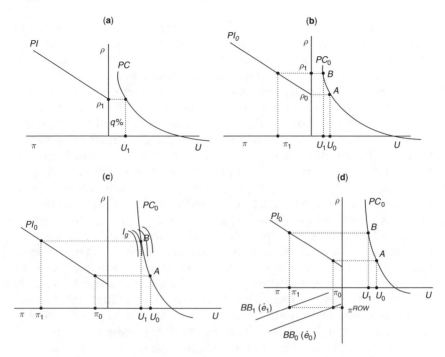

$\pi = (\Delta P/P)$: higher wage costs lead to increased market prices. So price inflation is equal to wage inflation minus labour-productivity growth. Thus, the fact that the intercept of the PI schedule with the vertical axis is positive indicates a positive change over time in labour productivity: because of labour productivity growth of q per cent, price inflation in Figure 4.2(a) is zero when wage inflation is ρ_1.

The implication of the Phillips curve is that national governments face a stable trade-off between inflation and unemployment and can thus choose whatever combination of U and π they consider desirable by adopting appropriate economic policies. Suppose, for example, that the economy is initially at A in Figure 4.2(b), with unemployment U_0 and zero price-inflation, but that the government considers U_0 as unacceptably high and wants to reduce it. According to the Phillips-curve theory, a reduction in unemployment can be achieved through an expansionary monetary or fiscal policy. An expansionary fiscal or monetary policy would raise aggregate spending in the economy and thus the demand for labour and so aggregate employment. However, observing the increased demand for labour, workers would be inclined to revise upwards their wage claims. This would lead to higher price inflation. Thus as unemployment would fall to U_1, price inflation would no longer be zero and equilibrium would be at point B on the original Phillips curve PC_0.

As far as the costs of monetary integration are concerned, the argument is that when exchange rates are flexible, each country can achieve whatever combination of inflation and unemployment it wishes without having to worry about external equilibrium. In particular, in Figure 4.2(c), suppose that society's preferences over inflation and unemployment are represented by the set of indifference curves I_g. Then, assuming a stable Phillips curve, point B, where PC_0 is tangent to the lowest possible indifference curve, represents maximum 'social' welfare. This implies an unemployment rate of U_1. Accordingly, in Figure 4.2(d), adopting, for example, an expansionary fiscal policy to raise aggregate demand, the government reduces unemployment to U_1 but price inflation is raised to π_1 and thus the competitiveness of domestic products in world markets falls. To restore competitiveness at its initial level, the government then uses monetary policy to devalue the domestic currency relative to foreign currencies. That is, domestic price inflation increases from π_0 to π_1, but the rate of depreciation of the domestic currency, $\dot{e}$, also goes up by the same amount, from say $\dot{e}_0$ to $\dot{e}_1$, and this prevents the real exchange rate from falling and thus the competitiveness of domestic products from deteriorating. Accordingly, the BB schedule in Figure 4.2(d) can be taken to represent a balance-of-payments equilibrium line, namely combinations of π and rest-of-the world inflation π^{ROW} that maintain competitiveness at its original level for a given $\dot{e}$ and other rest-of-the-world macroeconomic variables. Thus, as $\dot{e}$ rises from $\dot{e}_0$ to $\dot{e}_1$, the BB_0 schedule shifts up to the position occupied by the BB_1 schedule, and this maintains external equilibrium.

Now participation in a monetary union implies that a country will no longer be free to determine independently its own inflation rate since a MU requires coordination of national monetary policies and permanently fixed exchange rates or a common currency. Assume then that the country concerned has already reached maximum social welfare, point B in Figure 4.2(c), and is considering the possibility to participate in a MU together with other countries. Participation in the MU may require this country to lower its inflation rate to the level represented, for example, by π_0. To achieve this lower inflation rate, contractionary demand-management policy needs to be adopted. Accordingly, the government reduces public spending or increases taxes, so inflation does fall to π_0. However, the new inflation rate π_0 is accompanied with higher unemployment U_0, and participation in the MU implies that monetary policy cannot be used to offset the adverse effect of the contractionary fiscal policy on unemployment. In terms of Figure 4.2(c), the 'cost' of MU membership is then the additional unemployment $(U_0 - U_1)$.[8]

It is obvious that the above argument relies on the hypothesis of a stable trade-off between inflation and unemployment. New-classical approaches to the costs of MU emphasize that the hypothesis of such a stable trade-off is not supported by the empirical evidence: the empirical evidence indicates that a stable trade-off, if it exists, is only temporary, that is in the long run the Phillips curve is either very steep or vertical as workers are concerned about their real wages rather than their nominal wages. Indeed, while empirically based traditional Phillips curves do well in explaining postwar inflation in a number of countries, especially in the USA, their stability over time and across regimes is unclear: traditional Philips curves in many countries have been overpredicting inflation after the 1980s. Some researchers have found that by making some adjustments, such as changing the measure of full-employment output in the empirical equations, or introducing imperfect competition, the basic relationship still holds.[9] Others, however, have simply found no evidence of traditional-type Phillips curves.

To illustrate the point about a vertical Phillips curve in the context of the new-classical thinking, suppose that we start in Figure 4.3 from point A on the Phillips curve PC_0 with zero price inflation and an unemployment rate of U_0. The government wants to reduce unemployment below that level, say to U_1, and so it adopts an expansionary demand-management policy. This initially leads to an increase in labour demand, which in turn leads to a rise in nominal wages. Workers, believing that price inflation will continue to be zero, initially perceive this rise in nominal wages as a rise in real wages. As real wages are believed to have increased, labour supply in the economy increases and unemployment falls to U_1. But, with the

Figure 4.3

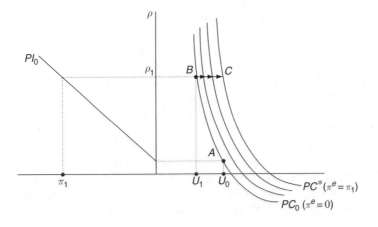

new unemployment rate U_1, price inflation is now π_1. Workers eventually realize that inflation has gone up and that their real wages have not actually risen. Accordingly, those who have entered into wages contracts on the belief of higher real wages will leave the labour market. Eventually, the economy will move from point B to point C. More generally the original Phillips curve PC_0, whose position reflects an expected inflation rate π^e of zero, will shift rightwards overtime as workers will adjust their expectations of inflation to actual inflation. And it will eventually stabilize at the position occupied by the PC^* curve that reflects an expected inflation of $\pi^e = \pi_1$. In the long run, then, the Phillips curve is vertical at the level of unemployment U_0, which results when the perceived rate of inflation is equal to the actual rate. This is the 'natural' rate of unemployment. The natural rate of unemployment cannot be changed through demand-management policies: it requires measures that improve the productive capacity of the economy.

The natural-rate hypothesis has important implications for the costs of participation in a MU. With a vertical long-run Phillips curve, the main disadvantage of not having an independent monetary policy, and thus a flexible exchange rate, is the inability of a country to choose independently its own inflation rate. The existence of such a choice however is not really an advantage if the inflation rate offered by MU membership is low and stable. This argument is illustrated in Figure 4.4 using a quadrant diagram suggested by De Grauwe (1975). The upper part of the diagram refers to the home country, say the UK, and the lower part to the partner country, say Germany. PC^{UK} is the Phillips curve for the UK and PC^G is the Phillips curve for Germany. While the position of the two Phillips curves differs, both are vertical at the natural level of unemployment (U_N^{UK} and U_N^G respectively). The line $PI^{UK}(PI^G)$ reflects the relationship between wage inflation and price inflation in the UK (Germany). The intercepts of the curves with the vertical axis reflect labour-productivity growth.

In the absence of MU, the UK and Germany can determine their national inflation rates independently. Suppose that the UK chooses the inflation rate π_1^{UK}. Then wage inflation is ρ_1^{UK}. Germany chooses a price-inflation rate of π_1^G and this implies wage inflation of ρ_1^G. Price inflation is lower in Germany than in the UK, but exchange-rate changes make the two national inflation rates consistent with each other: with $\pi_1^{UK} > \pi_1^G$ the pound will be depreciating in the foreign exchange markets relative to the Germany mark and this will maintain balance of payments equilibrium in each country.

If Germany and the UK were to establish a monetary union, they would lose their power to independently determine their own rates of inflation since inflation rates would no longer be able to diverge.

Figure 4.4

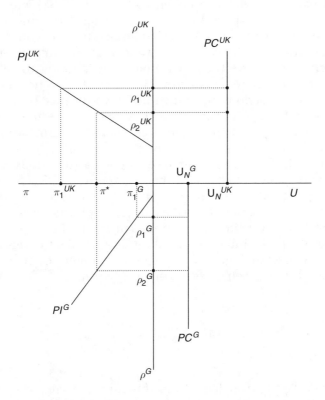

Assume, for example, that the agreed common inflation rate lies between the initial national inflation rates, say at π^*. The UK would then have to accept a lower wage-inflation rate ρ_2^{UK} than it would have otherwise chosen. But this would be the only cost of monetary integration: participation in the MU would involve no unemployment costs for the UK.

The Game-Theoretic Approach to Monetary Integration: Macroeconomic and Strategic Interdependence, Nash and Cooperative Outcomes

Unlike traditional approaches, the game-theoretic approach to the effects on the member states of establishing a MU emphasizes international macroeconomic interdependence and strategic interactions among national governments in formulating economic policy.

This literature owes much to the Japanese economist Koichi Hamada who, in a series of papers published in the late 1970s and 1980s, considered the welfare consequences of international interdependence. In particular, Hamada (1974, 1976, 1979, 1985) and Hamada and Sakurai (1978) explored what kind of macroeconomic outcomes were likely to occur as a result of international interdependence when individual countries' governments were manipulating their policy instruments to achieve their own objectives ignoring the effects of their actions on other countries. He showed that uncoordinated monetary-policy actions by individual governments could lead to outcomes that nobody wanted, such as global recessions or inflationary situations, and that there were gains to be made from the coordination of national macroeconomic policies.[10]

The game-theoretic literature makes explicit assumptions about the behaviour of policy-makers and the constraints they face in setting monetary policy, with most papers being based on three main assumptions. The first is that policy-makers in each country have targets for output and inflation and their aim is to minimize fluctuations of the output level and the inflation rate around these target values. Accordingly, they will set their monetary-policy instruments so as to maximize the value of a 'social welfare' function of the form:

$$V = -c(y - y^T)^2 - (\pi - \pi^T)^2 \tag{4}$$

$$V^* = -c^*(y^* - y^{*T})^2 - (\pi^* - \pi^{*T})^2 \tag{5}$$

$$0 < c, c^* < \infty$$

Equations (4) and (5) are logarithmic functions, where $y(y^*)$ is (the log of) the actual level of output in, say, the UK (Germany) and $y^T(y^{*T})$ is (the log of) the target level of output, which can be taken to be 'potential' output. Similarly, $\pi(\pi^*)$ is the actual rate of inflation in the UK (Germany) and $\pi^T(\pi^{*T})$ is the target value for the inflation rate. Equations (4) and (5), then, simply say that positive or negative deviations of current output levels, $y(y^*)$, from potential-output levels, $y^T(y^{*T})$, are equally undesirable. The same applies to inflation: positive or negative deviations of $\pi(\pi^*)$ from $\pi^T(\pi^{*T})$ are equally undesirable.

These types of welfare functions give indifference curves that have a centre. For example, suppose that output and inflation in the UK are at their target levels and that this combination of y and π is represented by point B in Figure 4.5. As both positive and negative deviations of y (or π) from point B are equally undesirable, the UK indifference map can be represented by the set of the indifference curves I_{UK}. These indifference curves represent lower welfare levels as we move away from the centre, point B. The centre of the curves, B, is the 'bliss point' since it shows the maximum level of welfare that the UK can achieve. Similar considerations hold for Germany: B^* is

Figure 4.5

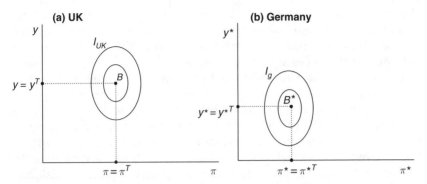

its bliss point and indifference curves represent lower welfare levels as we move away from the centre.

Going back to equations (4) and (5), the constants c and c^*, where $0 < c, c^* < \alpha$, reflect the relative priority that the authorities attach to the objective of output stability. For example, a relatively large $c(c^*)$ would represent a situation where the UK (German) policy-makers were concerned mostly about unemployment and therefore output. A value of $c(c^*)$ less than unity, on the other hand, would reflect a situation in which the authorities were concerned less about output than about inflation. Obviously, national policy-makers may differ in terms of the priority they attach to the output objective relative to the inflation objective. Thus the value of the parameter c in the UK's welfare function may or may not be the same as the value of c^* in the German welfare function. The same applies to the target values for output and inflation: $y^T(\pi^T)$ may or may not be equal to $y^{*T}(\pi^{*T})$. But even if the position of the German bliss point differs from that of the UK, the indifference curves of Germany (the UK) will still have a circular shape reflecting the fact that both positive and negative deviations of $y^*(\pi^*)$ from $y^{*T}(\pi^{*T})$ are equally undesirable.

The game-theoretic approach to the effect of MU does allow for the fact that demand-management policies, if not accompanied by measures that improve the productive capacity of the economy, have no long-run effects on employment. However, it is also recognized that there are times when national economies are hit by exogenous (unanticipated) shocks. These shocks may be transitory, that is, the economy eventually returns to its initial pre-shock state, but they may cause output and inflation to deviate from their target levels in the short run because of labour-market imperfections and/or wage contracts. In particular, the argument is that, unlike other variables, wages are set by trade unions and firms in infrequent time intervals and so cannot instantaneously change in response to any disequilibrium in the labour market. Accordingly, nominal wages can be taken as predetermined at any point in time. Under such circumstances, transitory shocks have real effects in the short run. Monetary policy also has real effects in the short run and can therefore be adjusted to reduce the adverse effects of the shocks on output, although at the expense of higher inflation.

It is also assumed that individual economies are large enough to be able to influence through their own policies the economic performance of at least some of their trading partners and this is taken into account by national governments when formulating economic policy. In effect, the game-theoretic literature emphasizes strategic interactions between national policy-makers in setting monetary policy. Under such circumstances, there are two forms of policy decisions to consider. The first is Nash non-cooperative behaviour. Under a Nash regime, governments in individual countries act independently in the field of economic policy, treating the policy decisions of governments in other countries as given and ignoring the effects that their own policy actions will have on the welfare of these other countries. The second form of macroeconomic-policy design is cooperation. Under a cooperative regime, policy-makers in individual countries agree to coordinate their actions in pursuing their objectives and seek to maximise a joint welfare function, which is a weighted sum of the national welfare functions. Monetary integration obviously reflects the second form of policy decisions since participating countries explicitly cooperate in the monetary field. On the other hand, a situation of no MU and flexible exchange rates can be taken to be represented by the Nash non-cooperative model.

To illustrate the point that the game-theoretic literature is making about monetary integration, a simple two-country log-linear model will be employed in the spirit of Canzoneri and Grey (1985), Currie *et al.* (1989) and Canzoneri and Henderson (1988, 1991). Consider two countries, the 'UK' and 'Germany', and assume that they are of the same economic size and symmetric in all respects. Also assume that both are initially at their respective bliss points, but that this equilibrium is disturbed by an adverse productivity shock. To simplify the exposition, y^T, y^{*T}, π^T and π^{*T}, that is the logarithm of potential-output levels and of target inflation rates, will be normalized to zero. Also, a one-to-one relationship between money growth and inflation rates will be assumed to exist. This allows us to write the policy-makers' objective functions as in equations (6) and (7):

$$v = -cy^2 - \dot{m}^2 \tag{6}$$

$$v^* = -cy^{*2} - \dot{m}^{*2} \tag{7}$$

where $\dot{m}$ $(\dot{m}^*)$ is the rate of money growth in the UK (Germany) and $y(y^*)$ is UK (German) output.

To compare outcomes with and without monetary cooperation macroeconomic interdependence is crucial: one needs to establish how changes in each country's monetary policy will affect not only its own output but also the other country's output. In other words, one needs to establish the sign of the partial derivatives:

$$\frac{\partial y}{\partial \dot{m}}, \frac{\partial y^*}{\partial \dot{m}^*}, \frac{\partial y}{\partial \dot{m}^*}, \frac{\partial y^*}{\partial \dot{m}}$$

The sign of the first two partial derivatives poses no problem: most of the macroeconomic models of open economies predict that in the presence of wage contracts, domestic output responds positively to unanticipated increases in the growth rate of the domestic money stock. The sign of the other two partial derivatives is more problematic as in the literature there is no agreement on the international spillover effects of national monetary policies. Indeed, two opposing forces are in operation here. On the one hand, for any given $\dot{m}^*$, an increase in the UK's money-growth rate $\dot{m}$, by raising UK output and thus moving the UK balance of payments into deficit through increased imports, would cause the pound to depreciate relative to the German mark in the foreign exchange markets or the German mark to appreciate relative to the pound. This would, in turn, reduce the relative competitiveness of German products, and therefore the demand for them, and so German output y^*. On the other hand, for any given $\dot{m}^*$, the rise in $\dot{m}$, through its positive impact on UK output, would tend to lead to increased demand for imports from Germany and thus to higher German output. Accordingly, the sign of $\frac{\partial y^*}{\partial \dot{m}}$ may in principle be negative or positive depending on which of these two effects dominates. Similar considerations apply to the sign of the partial derivative $\frac{\partial y}{\partial \dot{m}^*}$. However, since the empirical evidence suggests that, especially in European markets, the competitiveness effect is relatively strong, in what follows it will be assumed that the first effect dominates. Accordingly, the relationship between (the log of) each country's output/income and the two monetary-policy instruments $\dot{m}$ and $\dot{m}^*$ will be taken to be described by equations (8) and (9):

$$y = b_1 \dot{m} - b_2 \dot{m}^* - u \tag{8}$$

$$y^* = b_1 \dot{m}^* - b_2 \dot{m} - u^* \tag{9}$$

$$b_1, b_2 > 0, \ |b_1| > |b_2|, \ u \gtrless u^*$$

As $b_2 > 0$, equations (8) and (9) indicate that the international spillover effect of national monetary policies is negative. The terms u and u^* represent adverse (unexpected) productivity shocks, leading to lower output. Obviously, Germany and the UK may or may not be experiencing the same productivity shocks, that is $u \gtrless u^*$. Inserting equations (8) and (9) into equations (6) and (7), we can write the objective functions as:

$$v = -c[b_1 \dot{m} - b_2 \dot{m}^* - u]^2 - \dot{m}^2 \tag{10}$$

$$v^* = -c[b_1 \dot{m}^* - b_2 \dot{m} - u^*]^2 - \dot{m}^{*2} \tag{11}$$

As will be realized shortly, equations (10) and (11) give indifference curves that are ellipses in $(\dot{m}^*, \dot{m})$ space with inflexion points along upward-sloping lines.

For the moment we shall assume that $u = u^*$, namely we shall consider a symmetric productivity shock affecting the UK and Germany equally. This is illustrated in Figure 4.6. The BP line is a $45°$ line, and point O represents equilibrium before the occurrence of the productivity shock. In other words, we start from an initial equilibrium position with $y = y^T$, $y^* = y^{*T}$ and $\dot{m}^* = \dot{m}$. Since the adverse productivity shock will tend to lower output in both countries, the initial combination of money-growth rates, represented by point O, will no longer be optimal after the occurrence of the shock. Following the productivity shock, the best combination of $\dot{m}$ and $\dot{m}^*$ from the UK's point of view is represented by point B. Relative to point O, point B involves no change in money-supply growth in the UK and a fall in money-supply growth in Germany. This is the best outcome for the UK. As, at point B, $\dot{m}$ remains unchanged, inflation in the UK also remains unchanged and so there is no welfare loss through the inflation channel. At the same time, as the international spillover effect of national monetary policies is negative, the fall in $\dot{m}^*$ has a positive effect on y and thus offsets the adverse impact of the productivity shock on UK output. For the same reasons, the best outcome for Germany is a situation of no change in its money-supply growth together with a fall in money-supply growth in the UK. This is represented by point B*. The fact that B and B* are equally close to point O reflects the assumption that Germany and the UK are affected by the shock in exactly the same way, that is, that $u = u^*$. One can also draw indifference curves around the new bliss points B and B*, and a set of such curves, II and II*, are shown in Figure 4.6(a). These indifference curves represent lower welfare levels as we move away from the centre, B or B*.

Figure 4.6

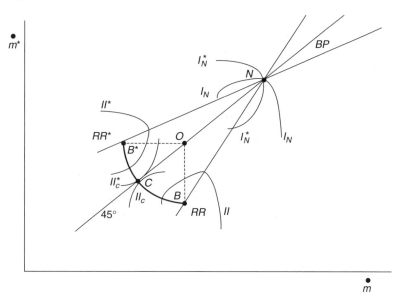

Consider macroeconomic outcomes with monetary cooperation. Connecting the points of tangency between the UK's and Germany's indifference curves, one obtains a locus of Pareto-efficient outcomes or the 'contract curve', BB^* in Figure 4.6. Moving along this curve a country cannot improve its welfare without causing a deterioration of other countries' welfare. This means that monetary cooperation between the UK and Germany will lead to an outcome at some point on the contract curve BB^*. The UK (Germany) would be better off with an outcome closer to $B(B^*)$ than with an outcome closer to $B^*(B)$; and, the relative bargaining strength of the two countries will determine exactly where on the contract curve equilibrium under monetary cooperation will occur. Here however we are implicitly assuming that the UK and Germany are symmetric and of the same economic size, and so they can be taken to have the same bargaining strength. Thus, given that the productivity shock affects both of them equally, full monetary cooperation will lead to point C of the contract curve, halfway between B and B^*. Notice that point C lies on the 45° line BP, implying that Germany and the UK adopt common monetary policies. This Pareto-efficient outcome $\overset{\bullet}{m}{}^* = \overset{\bullet}{m}$ could in principle be achieved by simply fixing the German mark/sterling rate even without the UK and Germany having to establish a genuine MU. However, as will be seen shortly, this arises from the assumption that the two countries are experiencing the same productivity shock and does not hold in general.

We now come to the interesting question of what Germany and the UK would lose by not coordinating their monetary policies. With no monetary cooperation, given the symmetry of the two countries, the most probable outcome will be Nash non-cooperative equilibrium. Under Nash non-cooperative behaviour, policy-makers in Germany and the UK will act independently in setting monetary policy. Accordingly, the Bank of England (Bank of Germany) will choose that value of $\dot{m}$ ($\dot{m}^*$) which maximizes its own objective function treating $\dot{m}^*$ ($\dot{m}$) as given. In particular, policy-makers in the UK will find the partial derivative of equation (10) with respect to money-supply growth in the UK and set it equal to zero. German policy-makers will adopt a similar policy: they will set the partial derivative of equation (11) with respect to money-supply growth in Germany equal to zero. We thus have the following first-order conditions for a maximum:

$$\frac{\partial v}{\partial \dot{m}} = cb_1[b_1 \dot{m} - b_2 \dot{m}^* - u] + \dot{m} = 0 \tag{12a}$$

$$\frac{\partial v^*}{\partial \dot{m}^*} = cb_1[b_1 \dot{m}^* - b_2 \dot{m} - u^*] + \dot{m}^* = 0 \tag{13a}$$

Equations (12a) and (13a) lead to two equations in two variables, $\dot{m}$ and $\dot{m}^*$, that represent the best each country can do by treating the other country's policies as given:

$$\text{UK} \qquad \dot{m} = \frac{1}{1+cb_1^2}[cb_1b_2 \dot{m}^* + cb_1u] \tag{12b}$$

$$\text{Germany} \quad \dot{m}^* = \frac{1}{1+cb_1^2}[cb_1b_2 \dot{m} + cb_1u^*] \tag{13b}$$

These equations are known as reaction functions or reaction curves: the UK's (Germany's) reaction curve shows the UK's (Germany's) best reply to changes in German (UK) monetary policy and to unanticipated shocks. Obviously, since they are the outcome of the maximization of equations (10) and (11), the reaction curves must pass through the relevant bliss points. Moreover, given the assumption that the international spillover effect of monetary policies is negative, the reaction curves must be upward-sloping in ($\dot{m}^*$, $\dot{m}$) space. In particular, with $b_2 > 0$ an expansionary monetary policy in Germany (an increase in $\dot{m}^*$) would have a negative effect on UK output. Since UK output is assumed to be at its target level initially, this would lead to a welfare loss. To maintain output at its initial level, UK policy-makers would respond to the rise in $\dot{m}^*$ with a monetary expansion; that is, they would raise $\dot{m}$. Similarly an expansionary monetary policy in the UK would lower German output and, to maintain German output at its initial level, German policy-makers would respond with a rise in their own money-growth rate. Accordingly, the reaction curves will have positive slopes.[11]

The reaction functions are represented in Figure 4.6 by the schedules RR and RR^*. At points where they cross the indifference curves, Germany's and the UK's indifference curves must have an inflexion point since the reaction functions are the direct outcome of the maximization of equations (10) and (11). Thus with $b_2 > 0$, the indifference curves in the $(\dot{m}^*, \dot{m})$ plane have inflexion points along upward-sloping lines.

Equilibrium in the absent of monetary cooperation is at the point where the two reaction curves intersect. This is point N. We can draw indifference curves passing through this non-cooperative equilibrium point. Thus, under a Nash non-cooperative regime, the level of welfare in the UK is represented by the indifference curve $l_N l_N$ and that in Germany by the indifference curve $l_N^* l_N^*$. What is important is that non-cooperative behaviour on the part of policy-makers in Germany and the UK leads to a Pareto-inefficient outcome. At point N, the indifference curves of Germany and the UK are not tangent to each other and this means that there is room for welfare improvements. Moreover, point N is less close to both B and B^* than point C, implying that monetary cooperation between Germany and the UK would unambiguously increase the welfare of both.

The conclusion to be drawn from the above analysis is that countries can gain and never lose by coordinating their monetary policies or forming a monetary union. The intuition is simple. When Germany and the UK coordinate their monetary policies, they explicitly take into account the spillover effects that their own policy actions would have on each other. Thus, in setting monetary policy in response to the productivity shock, UK (German) policy-makers recognize that a monetary expansion in Britain (Germany) would lower output in Germany (UK) and that this would aggravate the unemployment problem there (caused by the productivity shock), inducing German (UK) policy-makers to adopt policies that eventually would affect adversely the UK (Germany). Monetary cooperation 'internalizes' the externalities caused by international macroeconomic interdependence and this enables each country to reach a higher level of welfare.

However, the above analysis relies on the assumption that the productivity shock affects the UK and Germany equally. What if

Germany and the UK are not experiencing the same productivity shocks? Would monetary cooperation or monetary union still be desirable? To examine this issue one needs to consider the effects of an asymmetric shock, namely a productivity shock that has a larger negative effect on, say, UK output than on German output, and therefore $|u| > |u^*|$. Point O in Figure 4.7 represents equilibrium in the UK and Germany before the occurrence of such an asymmetric productivity shock. As long as the international spillover effect of national monetary policies is negative, so that, say a monetary expansion in Germany (UK) lowers aggregate demand and output in the UK (Germany), the UK's (Germany's) bliss point after the occurrence of the shock will still lie to the right (left) of the 45° schedule BP. But, because here the shock has a greater impact on UK output than on German output, the fall in Germany's money-growth rate required to enable the UK to attain bliss will be larger than the fall in the UK money-supply growth required to enable Germany to attain bliss. This is reflected in the position of the bliss points B_1 and B_1^* relative to point $O : OB_1$ exceeds OB_1^*, reflecting the asymmetric nature of the shock. On the other hand, the fact that here we are dealing with an asymmetric shock does not affect the slopes of the two reaction curves: provided that the international spillover effect of national monetary policies is negative, the two reaction curves will still be

Figure 4.7

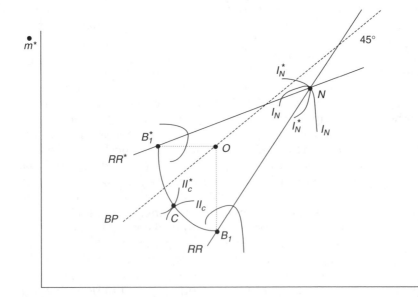

upwards-sloping in $(\dot{m}^*, \dot{m})$ space. The two reaction curves will also still have to pass through the relevant bliss points. Thus, RR is the UK's reaction curve and RR^* is Germany's reaction curve.

Nash non-cooperative behaviour by policy-makers in Britain and Germany would lead to point N, where the schedules RR and RR^* intersect. Notice that here Nash equilibrium is not on the 45° line BP, implying that the UK and Germany will have different rates of money-supply growth at N. However, non-cooperative behaviour still leads to a Pareto-inefficient outcome: the UK's and Germany's indifference curves at N are not tangent to each other, implying that there is room for welfare improvements.

Under a cooperative regime, the rate of money-supply growth in Germany and the UK would be determined jointly: Germany and the UK would jointly set $\dot{m}$ and $\dot{m}^*$ so as to maximize the weighted sum of their objective functions. Accordingly, equilibrium would be established at some point on the contract curve $B_1 B_1^*$, like point C in Figure 4.7 (which lies half-way between B_1 and B_1^*). The indifference curves at C are tangent to each other, implying that point C is a Pareto-efficient outcome. What this implies is that Germany and the UK can gain by explicitly cooperating in the field of monetary policy even if they are experiencing asymmetric shocks. Notice, however, that here Germany and the UK cannot attain point C by simply maintaining a fixed DM/pound exchange rate: point C requires common control over national money supplies, that is a MU with a central monetary authority or full cooperation between the national central banks.

Can monetary cooperation be counter-productive? More specifically, are there any circumstances under which the UK and Germany could lose by explicitly coordinating their monetary policies or forming a MU? Extending a model developed by Barro and Gordon (1983) for a closed economy to the two-country case, Rogoff (1985), among others, has shown that this is possible if policy-makers' target levels for output, and thus employment, are too ambitious.

The original Barro–Gordon framework ignores stochastic shocks focusing on the effects of discretionary monetary policy. Its starting point is a Phillips curve that takes account of expected inflation:

$$\dot{p} = -(1/\alpha)(U - U^N) + \dot{p}^e$$

or

$$U = U^N - \alpha(\dot{p} - \dot{p}^e) \tag{14}$$

where $\dot{p}$ and $\dot{p}^e$ are, respectively, the actual and expected inflation rate and U^N is the natural rate of unemployment. Equation (14) implies that anticipated changes in inflation, and therefore in money-supply growth, have no impact on unemployment. Only when the actual rate of inflation exceeds that expected, can unemployment be reduced below the natural-rate level. Obviously, if the private sector forms expectations rationally, predictions of future inflation cannot be systematically wrong. Thus, with no stochastic shocks, we will have $\dot{p}=\dot{p}^e$ and so $U = U^N$, that is, actual unemployment will be at its natural-rate level.

As far as the government is concerned, it cares about both inflation and unemployment and will seek to maximize a social welfare function of the form:

$$v = -c(U - U^T)^2 - \dot{p}^2, U^T < U^N \qquad (15)$$

The target rate of inflation is implicitly assumed to be zero. On the other hand, the government's target rate of unemployment is ambitious in the sense that it is lower than the natural rate U^N. Indeed, crucial to the Barro–Gordon analysis is the assumption that due to, for example, externalities and imperfections in the labour markets, the level of employment considered by the authorities as socially optimal is higher than the natural level of employment.

To consider the desirability of monetary cooperation under such circumstances we shall use a simple Barro–Gordon model for the two-open-economy case in the tradition of Rogoff (1985), Currie and Levine (1991) and Canzoneri and Henderson (1988). Assume two countries, say 'UK' and 'France'. Policy-makers' preferences are of the form:

$$V = -c(U - U^T)^2 - \pi_c^2 \qquad (16)$$
$$V^* = -c(U^* - U^{*T})^2 - \pi_c^{*2} \qquad (17)$$
$$U^T, U^{*T} < U^N$$

where U^T, the target rate of unemployment, is lower than the natural rate U^N. π_c and π_c^* in equations (16) and (17) are consumer price index (CPI) inflation rates, defined as:

$$\pi_c = \dot{p} + v_1 \dot{e} \qquad (18a)$$
$$\pi_c^* = \dot{p}^* - v_1 \dot{e} \qquad (19a)$$
$$v_1 > 0$$

where $\dot{p}$ and $\dot{p}^*$ is domestic price inflation in the UK and France respectively, $\dot{e}$ is the rate of depreciation of sterling relative to the French franc, and v_1 can be taken to reflect the importance of imported goods in total private-sector consumption in each country. Equations (18a) and (19a) take into account that CPI inflation rates are influenced both by the rate of change in the prices of domestically-produced goods and by the rate of change in the domestic-currency price of imports and therefore by the rate of depreciation of the domestic currency relative to other currencies. In our case, the relevant exchange rate is the rate of depreciation of the pound relative to the French franc, denoted by $\dot{e}$. Accordingly, π_c and π_c^* can be taken to be functions of the form shown in equations (18a) and (19a).

Under a floating exchange-rate regime, increases in money-supply growth in the UK relative to money-supply growth in France would tend to lead to a depreciation of the pound relative to the French franc in the foreign exchange markets. Accordingly, we can write:

$$\dot{e} = v_2(\dot{m} - \dot{m}^*) + z_0.$$

$$v_2, z_0 > 0$$

Using this expression for $\dot{e}$, and assuming for simplicity a one-to-one relationship between domestic-price inflation in each country and money-supply growth, we can write equations (18a) and (19a) as:

$$\pi_c = \dot{m} + v(\dot{m} - \dot{m}^*) + v_0. \tag{18}$$

$$\pi_c^* = \dot{m}^* - v(\dot{m} - \dot{m}^*) - v_0. \tag{19}$$

where $v = v_1 v_2$, $v_0 = v_1 z_0$. Also, assuming Phillips curves that take account of inflation expectations we have:

$$\dot{p} = -1/\alpha(U - U^N) + \dot{p}^e \tag{20a}$$

$$\dot{p}^* = -1/\alpha(U^* - U^N) + \dot{p}^{*e} \tag{21a}$$

Inverting equations (20a) and (21a) and replacing each country's domestic price inflation with money-supply growth, we can write:

$$U = U_N - \alpha(\dot{m} - \dot{m}^e) \tag{20}$$

$$U^* = U_N^* - \alpha(\dot{m}^* - \dot{m}^{*e}) \tag{21}$$

Inserting equations (20) and (18) into equation (16), and equations (21) and (19) into equation (17), we have the UK's and France's objective functions as:

$$V = -c[-\alpha(\dot{m} - \dot{m}^e) + (U^N - U^T)]^2 - [\dot{m} + v(\dot{m} - \dot{m}^*) + v_0]^2 \tag{22}$$

$$V^* = -c[-\alpha(\dot{m}^* - \dot{m}^{*e}) + (U^{*N} - U^{*T})]^2 - [\dot{m}^* - v(\dot{m} - \dot{m}^*) - v_0]^2 \tag{23}$$

Consider macroeconomic outcomes with and without monetary cooperation. Without monetary cooperation, policy-makers will behave as Nash players: policy-makers in the UK will set $\dot{m}$ so as to maximize equation (22) taking $\dot{m}^*$ and $\dot{m}^e$ as given, and policy-makers in France will set $\dot{m}^*$ so as to maximize equation (23), taking $\dot{m}$ and $\dot{m}^{*e}$ as parametric. Accordingly, we have the following first-order conditions for a maximum:

$$\frac{\partial V}{\partial \dot{m}} = c\alpha(U - U^T) - \pi_c(1 + \nu) = 0 \tag{24a}$$

$$\frac{\partial V^*}{\partial \dot{m}^*} = c\alpha(U^* - U^{*T}) - \pi_c^*(1 + \nu) = 0 \tag{24b}$$

where π_c, π_c^*, U and U^* are defined in equations (18) to (21). However, with rational expectations, the private sector will anticipate the policy-makers' behaviour and therefore, in the absence of stochastic shocks, on average $\dot{m}^e = \dot{m}$ and $\dot{m}^{*e} = \dot{m}^*$. This will have two implications. On the one hand, from equations (20) and (21) unemployment will be at its natural level, that is $U = U^N$ and $U^* = U^{*N}$. On the other hand, as $U = U^N$ and $U^* = U^{*N}$, from equations (24a) and (24b) we obtain:

$$\alpha c(U^N - U^T) - \pi_c(1 + \nu) = 0$$
$$\alpha c(U^{*N} - U^{*T}) - \pi^{c*}(1 + \nu) = 0$$

Accordingly, assuming that $U^T = U^{*T}$ and $U^N = U^{*N}$, equilibrium CPI inflation rates in the absence of monetary integration are:

$$\pi_c^N = \pi_c^{*N} = \left(\frac{\alpha c}{1 + \nu}\right)(U^N - U^T) \tag{25}$$

Now suppose that the UK and France are in a monetary union and set monetary policy cooperatively so as to maximize a joint welfare function, which is the weighted sum of their own objective functions, subject to equations (18) to (21). Assuming equal weights and $U^T = U^{*T}$, the function to be maximized is:

$$V^c = 1/2(V + V^*) = -1/2\{c(U - U^T)^2 + \pi_c^2 + c(U^* - U^T)^2 + \pi_c^{*2}\} \tag{26}$$

The first-order conditions for a maximum are:

$$\frac{\partial V^c}{\partial \dot{m}} = \alpha c(U - U^T) - \pi_c(1 + \nu) + \pi_c^* \nu = 0 \tag{27a}$$

$$\frac{\partial V^c}{\partial \dot{m}^*} = \alpha c(U^* - U^T) - \pi_c^*(1 + \nu) + \pi_c \nu = 0 \tag{27b}$$

But with rational expectations, on average we will have $\dot{m}^e = \dot{m}$ and $\dot{m}^{*e} = \dot{m}^*$. Accordingly, $U = U^* = U^N$ and thus from equations (27a) and (27b) equilibrium CPI inflation rates are:

$$\pi^C = \pi^{*C} = ac\ (U^N - U^T) \tag{28}$$

Welfare in both France and the UK is lower under monetary cooperation than under no cooperation: inflation rates are higher under a fully cooperative monetary regime than under a Nash non-cooperative regime ($\pi_c^c, \pi_c^{*c} > \pi_c^N, \pi_c^{*N}$), while in both cases unemployment remains at its natural-rate level. Accordingly, here we have a situation where, in the absence of exogenous stochastic shocks, monetary union between the UK and France would lead to welfare losses rather than welfare gains and so would be undesirable.

What is the intuitive explanation behind this result? As equations (18) and (19) indicate, with no stochastic shocks and ambitious employment targets (that is, $U^T < U^N$), when policy-makers launch unilateral monetary expansions, CPI inflation rates will increase not only through higher prices for domestically-produced goods but also through higher prices for imports via the depreciation of the exchange rate. When, on the other hand, policy-makers in the UK and France launch a coordinated monetary expansion to increase employment above the natural-rate level, they know that there will be no undesirable effects on CPI inflation rates through exchange-rate changes. Accordingly, they will have a greater incentive to pursue expansionary policies when acting together than when they act independently. As the private sector knows that, actual CPI inflation rates will be higher under monetary integration than under a non cooperative monetary regime. And, in the context of the model examined here, where we have rational expectations and monetary neutrality, social welfare will be lower.

Seigniorage

The term seigniorage refers to the command over real resources that the government of a country with an independent monetary policy can obtain by printing money. The resource cost of printing money is very small. At the same time, money is accepted as a means of payments. Accordingly, a government with an independent currency can supply the private sector with money in exchange for real resources, that is, goods, services, labour and physical capital, which are costly to produce. In addition to being able to buy goods and services, a government with an independent currency can also use the newly created money to meet interest obligations on its debt held by households and firms (see Fischer (1982), Hansen and Nielsen *et al.* (1997), Sibert (1994) and Romer (2001)).

Seigniorage can thus be viewed as a 'tax' on the private sector's holdings of money balances. Accordingly, a government may choose to have a relatively large money-growth rate, and therefore high inflation, if, due to an underdeveloped tax system, the cost of collecting revenue through ordinary taxation exceeds the cost of accumulating public-sector revenues through seigniorage. This option will no longer exist if the country joins a genuine monetary union: in a MU, common control is exercised over the money supply in individual countries and the seigniorage revenue from the creation of the common currency goes to the union's central monetary authority. Thus the argument is that countries, which before becoming union members relied a lot on seigniorage as a source of taxation, may as members of a MU experience problems with financing government expenditure. Indeed, faced with the inability to finance expenditure through seigniorage, the government of these countries may have to cut back on public spending, with possibly undesirable consequences for the domestic economy.[12] The implication for the EU is that in the case of member states that over the years have been dependent on seigniorage as a means of financing public expenditure participation in the EMU will transfer all the fiscal burden on ordinary taxation, something that, at least in the short run, may create distortions in the existing tax systems through increases in the tax base or the tax rates.[13] Indeed, on the basis of this argument, it can be argued that the 10 new EU member states should be allowed to follow more flexible policies that will permit them to have relatively higher inflation rates and an optimum level of seigniorage revenue through the inflation tax.

The seigniorage basic argument follows from the definition of the government budget constraint. Ignoring government debt, the government budget constraint in nominal terms can be written as:

$$G - T = \dot{M}$$

and in real terms as:

$$(G^R - T^R) = \dot{M} \left(\frac{1}{P}\right) \tag{29}$$

where M is the money supply, $\dot{M} = (dM/dt)$ is the change over time in M, $G^R(G)$ is real (nominal) government spending, $T^R(T)$ is real (nominal) tax revenue, and P is the domestic price level. As we are ignoring government debt, equation (29), can be interpreted as saying that any increase in government spending over revenue from ordinary taxation can be financed by revenue from seigniorage. The real value of seigniorage is the right-hand side of equation (29), namely $\dot{M}\left(\frac{1}{P}\right)$. Now in a genuine monetary union there is common control over money-growth rates. Accordingly, if the union places a heavy weight on low-inflation policies, and thus on non-expansionary monetary policies, participation in it will reduce the permissible magnitude of $\dot{M}\left(\frac{1}{P}\right)$ for some member countries and thus, other things being equal, the revenue from seigniorage. This can be viewed as a 'cost' arising from monetary integration.

While the possibility of not been able to finance government spending by revenue from seigniorage should be taken into account in assessing the overall effects of MU membership, in practice any welfare loss involved may be small as a country cannot obtain unlimited revenues from seigniorage. More specifically, there is a limit to the extent to which additional increases in the money-supply growth rate can generate extra revenues from seigniorage. To see this equation (29) can be written as:

$$\mu\left(\frac{M}{P}\right) = (G^R - T^R) \tag{29a}$$

where $\mu = (\dot{M}/M)$ is the rate of money-supply growth and (M/P) is the supply of real money balances. In equilibrium, the supply of real money balances must equal the demand for real money balances $(M/P)^d$ so we can write equation (29a) as:

$$S = \mu\left(\frac{M}{P}\right)^d = (G^R - T^R) \tag{29b}$$

where S is seigniorage. Now the demand for real money balances can be taken to depend positively on real output and negatively on the opportunity cost of holding money, namely the nominal interest rate:

$$\left(M\big/P\right)^d = -\lambda r + \varphi Y$$

where λ and ϕ are positive constants. But the nominal interest rate can be expressed as the real interest rate r^R plus the rate of inflation $dP/dt \times 1/P = \dot{p}$ and thus:

$$\left(M\big/P\right)^d = -\lambda(r^R + \dot{p}) + \varphi Y \tag{30}$$

In a non-growing economy, real output Y and the real interest rate r^R will be constant in the long run, so successive increases in the growth rate of the money supply will affect seigniorage through two channels. On the one hand, an increase in μ will raise the revenue from seigniorage corresponding to the private sector's initial holdings of, or demand for, real money balances. On the other hand, the resulting increase in the inflation rate will reduce the private sector's demand for real money balances, $(M/P)^d$, and thus the magnitude of seigniorage revenues for any given μ. In a non-growing economy therefore the net effect of an increase in the money-supply growth rate on seigniorage in long-run equilibrium would be:

$$\frac{dS}{d\mu} = \left(M\Big/P\right) - \mu\lambda\left(\frac{d\dot{p}}{d\mu}\right), \text{where} \frac{d\dot{p}}{d\mu} > 0 \tag{31}$$

From equation (31) it follows that whether an increase in the rate of money-supply growth will be accompanied in the long run by an increase in the public sector's seigniorage revenues is unclear. This depends, among other things, on the size of the interest elasticity of money demand, namely the value of λ, and the initial rate of growth of the money supply, namely the value of μ. In particular, an initially high money-growth rate together with a relatively large interest-rate elasticity of money demand can lead to a situation where further increases in money-supply growth reduce rather than increase the government's revenue from seigniorage.

This seems to be verified by the empirical literature. Gros and Vandille (1995), for example, represents an attempt to measure the effects of lower money growth, and therefore inflation, and of financial-market integration under the EMU on the revenues from seigniorage for European states that in the past relied most heavily on this source of revenue for financing government spending. Four Southern European EU member states, which throughout the years have had high inflation rates and weak fiscal positions, have been considered, namely Greece, Italy, Portugal and Spain, along with Germany so as to assess the difference in seigniorage revenues. The other EU countries have not been analysed as they have experienced only moderate inflation rates and their ratio of money base to GDP has been much lower than in the four EU countries examined. The results of Gros and Vandille indicate that during the 1980s[14] the governments of Southern European countries were indeed obtaining considerable cash flows from seigniorage. However, they suggest that disinflation under EMU would have relatively small effects on seigniorage revenues. For Greece disinflation under the EMU is found to lead to a loss of seigniorage revenues of 1.94 per cent of GDP and financial-market integration to a loss of revenue of only 0.39 per cent, that is a total EMU effect of 2.34 per cent of GDP. For Portugal, only the financial market integration effect is found to lead to a loss of revenue, making the full EMU effect to be only about 1 per cent of GDP loss in revenue. For Spain and Italy the full effect is found to be even smaller, namely 0.75 per cent of GDP for Spain and 0.13 per cent of GDP for Italy.

On the other hand, while the role of the interest-rate elasticity of money demand in a government's ability to extract revenue from the private sector by issuing money is important, the framework described by equations (29) to (31) can be criticized on the grounds that it ignores government debt and output growth. Following De Grauwe (2003) the argument could be presented as follows. With non-zero existing debt, the government budget constraint can be written as in (32a):

$$\dot{B} + \dot{M} = (G - T) + rB \qquad (32a)$$

where the deficit can be financed either by money creation, $\dot{M}$, or by new issues of government bonds, $\dot{B} = dB/dt$ with rB being interest payments on government debt. Because here we assume a growing economy, it is convenient to express all variables as ratios to GDP and write equation (32) as:[15]

$$\dot{b} + \dot{m} = (g - t) + rb - bx \qquad (32)$$

where $g = G/Y$ denotes government spending as per cent of nominal GDP, $t = T/Y$ is tax revenue as per cent of GDP, $m = (\dot{M}/Y)$ is the change over time in high-power money as per cent of GDP, and $x = (\dot{Y}/Y)$ is GDP growth. Long-run equilibrium requires that the debt to GPD ratio stabilizes at a constant value so that $\dot{b} = 0$. Accordingly we have:

$$\dot{m} + (t - g) = (r - x)b \qquad (33)$$

Equation (33) says that in an economy in which the interest rate exceeds the growth rate of GDP, a stable debt-to-GDP ratio requires either a high enough rate of money creation or a large enough primary surplus $(t - g)$. In the absence of monetary integration, a government can use both sources of revenue to stabilize the debt-to-GDP ratio. Indeed, as De Grauwe (2003) notes, 'optimal' public finance implies that a government should use the two sources of revenue, t and $\dot{m}$, in such a way that the marginal cost of raising revenue by increasing taxes just equals the marginal cost of raising revenue through inflation and seigniorage (see also Mankiw (1987) and Grilli (1989)).[16] This implies that countries with underdeveloped tax systems may find it rational to raise revenue mainly through seigniorage, and therefore through inflation. Now if such countries were to participate in a MU together with more developed countries that had a lower rate of money growth, they would have to lower their own money-growth rate. But then, since these countries might not be in a position to raise significant revenue from sources other than money creation, they would have to cut back on government spending if they were to stabilise their debt to GDP ratios. This would be a 'cost' of participation in an MU (see Dornbusch *et al.* (1998)).

This issue is of relevance to the 10 new EU member states (EU-10). Raising public revenue through ordinary taxation is not always an easy task in EU-10 . On the other hand, many of the EU-10 countries, while having achieved lower inflation rates since 1997, will have to cut inflation, and thus money-supply growth, even further if they are to be eligible for EMU entry. This would reduce the amount of seigniorage revenue that their governments could extract from the private sector. Given the difficulties in raising public revenue through ordinary taxation, EMU membership may therefore require them to undertake additional drastic cuts in public spending.

Summary and Conclusions

Monetary integration involves both benefits and costs. The benefits are obvious. The most obvious is the elimination of exchange-rate uncertainty and risk, which in the case of the EU is particularly important given the intention to create a genuine internal market that involves no distinction between the domestic market of one member state and those of the other member states. As far as the costs are concerned, participating countries cannot conduct an independent monetary and exchange-rate policy and also lose much of their scope for independent action in the fiscal-policy front.

Within the context of the OCAs theory, certain structural character-istics, including the degree of capital and labour mobility, openness to trade, the level of diversification of domestic production and exports, and the similarity of the countries concerned in terms of responses to external shocks and nature of underlying disturbances, are taken as criteria for determining whether or not a group of countries are good candidates for participating in a MU. Of these criteria, capital mobility, openness to trade and diversification of production and imports pose no problem in the case of the EU, but labour mobility within Europe has always been limited and is not expected to increase much in the near future. Problems also arise in the case of the criterion of similarity of underlying disturbances and responses to external shocks. Indeed, since the start of the discussions leading to the Maastricht Treaty, the issue of asymmetric shocks and asymmetric responses in Europe has been the focal point of many empirical studies. A large part of this literature finds that the distinction between core and periphery plays an important role in determining the degree of correlation of shocks across member states, implying that only a sub-group of EU member states can be taken to constitute a truly optimum currency area. Some studies also find that there are significant differences among the EU countries in terms of responses to shocks. However, it may be argued that the correlation of shocks across Europe in the past and the existing economic structures and responses to shocks are not appropriate criteria for determining whether or not the EU can develop into an OCA: the integration process in Europe may well lead over time to fewer asymmetric shocks and more similar economic structures and responses to shocks.

On the other hand, conventional approaches to the costs of monetary integration seek to explicitly identify and evaluate the relative costs and benefits of participation in a MU. Analyses that follow Keynesian thinking are based on the Philips-curve theory, stressing that membership will imply higher unemployment if the country concerned is required to lower its inflation rate. Analyses that follow new-classical thinking claim that a MU involves no adverse effects in terms of unemployment as in the long run the Phillips curve is vertical, arguing that the main cost of not having a flexible exchange rate and an independent monetary policy is the inability of a country to decide on its own inflation rate.

The game-theoretic approach to the effects on member countries of a MU emphasizes macroeconomic interdependence and strategic interactions between national policy-makers in implementing economic policy. Two possible forms of policy decisions in this case are: Nash non-cooperative behaviour and cooperation. A situation of no MU and flexible exchange rates represents Nash non-cooperative behaviour, while monetary union reflects the second form of policy decisions since participating countries explicitly cooperate in the monetary field. Within such a framework, because monetary cooperation internalizes the externalities caused by international macroeconomic interdependence, countries can gain by forming a MU, not only when the stochastic shocks they experience are symmetric, but also when the shocks are asymmetric. This conclusion of the game-theoretic approach reverses the OCAs theory's argument that European countries facing asymmetric shocks should not actually participate in the EMU. It also provides a theoretical rationale for EU countries that are not in the core category, and thus experience shocks which are not well-correlated with those of the other countries, to become members of the EMU. Can monetary unification ever be counterproductive? The game-theoretic literature tells us that this may happen if, the policy-makers' target level for output, and thus employment, is too ambitious: in such circumstances, in the absence of stochastic shocks, inflation rates may be higher under a fully cooperative regime than under a Nash non-cooperative regime.

Finally, to the factors that need to be taken into account in assessing the overall effects of MU membership, one should add the issue of seigniorage: the command over real resources that the government of a country with an independent monetary policy can obtain by printing money. This option will no longer exist if a country decides to join a genuine monetary union, since in such a union common control is exercised over money supply in individual countries. A related issue is the importance of seigniorage revenues for stabilizing the debt-to-GDP ratio in the long run. The seigniorage issue is relevant to several of the 10 new EU member states which have relatively underdeveloped tax systems and which in the post had relied a lot on seigniorage as a means of financing public spending.

What overall conclusion can then be derived regarding the desirability of macroeconomic cooperation and MU membership? The issue is complex and a single statement would be over-simplistic. Yet one could claim that economies with strong trade and financial links, with not very dissimilar economic structures or underdeveloped tax systems and with not very unrealistic employment targets may gain overall by cooperating in the macroeconomic-policy field and thus entering into a MU.

Notes

1 See Ishiyama (1975), Masson and Taylor (1993), Tavlas (1993, 1994), Eichengreen (1993b) and De Grauwe (1996, 2003) for a discussion of the OCAs literature.
2 The existence of nominal rigidities is central to much of the OCAs literature: with full flexibility of prices and wages, the costs of participation in a CU would be zero making the OCAs literature pointless. See Bayoumi and Eichengreen (1996).
3 See Melitz (1995, 1996), Bayoumi (1994) and Demopoulos and Yannacopoulos (1999, 2001).
4 See, for example, De Grauwe and Vanhaverbeke (1993), Descressin and Fatàs (1995), Bayoumi and Eichengreen (1993, 1996, 1997, 1998) and Eichengreen (1992, 1993a).
5 Asymmetric shocks have been seen by many as a major problem for EMU: see Favero et al. (2000).
6 For differences in transmission mechanisms and structures see also Demertzis and Hughes-Hallett (1998a,b).
7 See European Commission (1990) and Gros and Thygesen (1992).
8 See De Grauwe (2003), El-Agraa (1998), Robson (1998) and Pelkmans (2001) or similar textbooks for this type of analysis.
9 See, for example, Gordon (1998), Stock (1998), Rudebusch and Svensson (1999), Gali et al. (2001), Stock and Watson (1999) and Mills et al. (1995,

1996, 1997). See Ball *et al.* (1988), Ball and Mankiw (1994), Mankiw (2001), Clarida *et al.* (1999) and McCallum (1997) for a survey. See also Blanchard and Katz (1997) for the natural rate of unemployment.

10   See Currie and Levine (1985), Currie *et al.* (1989) and Canzoneri and Henderson (1988, 1991) for extensions of Hamada's framework. See also Zervoyianni (1993, 1997).

11   From (12b) and (13b) and given that $b_1, b_2 > 0$ and $|b_1| > |b_2|$, the slopes of the reaction functions in the $(\dot{m}^*, \dot{m})$ plane are:

$$UK \; \frac{d\,\dot{m}^*}{d\,\dot{m}} = \frac{(1+cb_1^2) > 0}{b_2 b_1} > 1, \quad Germany \; \frac{d\,\dot{m}^*}{d\,\dot{m}} = \frac{b_2 b_1}{(1+cb_1^2)} \begin{array}{c}>0\\<1\end{array}$$

12   See Sibert (1994) for an analysis.

13   See Torres (1990) and Gavazzi and Pagano (1988).

14   For the issue of seigniorage in the EMS period see Giavazzi and Giovannini (1989), Dornbusch (1988) and Grilli (1989).

15   See De Grauwe (2003). The debt to GDP ratio, b, is simply B over Y. Thus taking time derivatives we have $\frac{d(B/Y)}{dt} = \frac{1}{Y}\frac{dB}{dt} - \frac{B}{Y^2}\frac{dY}{dt}$, or $\dot{b} = \frac{1}{Y}\dot{B} - \left(\frac{B}{Y}\right)\left(\frac{\dot{Y}}{Y}\right) = \frac{1}{Y}\dot{B} - bx$. Multiplying all terms by Y and moving $\dot{B}$ to the left-hand side of the equation we have $\dot{B} = Y\dot{b} + Yxb$. Using this expression for $\dot{B}$ we can write equation (32a) as $\left(\frac{\dot{M}}{Y}\right) + \dot{b} + bx = \left(\frac{G}{Y} - \frac{T}{Y}\right) + r\left(\frac{B}{Y}\right)$, which gives equation (32).

16   See Fisher (1982) and Dornbusch (1988).

References

Artis, M., and Zhang, W. (1999) 'Further Evidence on the International Business Cycles and the ERM: Is There a European Business Cycle?', *Oxford Economic Papers*, vol. 51, pp. 120–32.

Ball, L. and Mankiw, N.G. (1994) 'A Sticky Price Manifesto', *Carnegie-Rochester Conference on Public Policy*, vol. 41, pp. 127–51.

Ball, L., Mankiw, N.G. and Romer, D. (1988) 'The New Keynesian Economics and the Output–Inflation Trade Off', *Brookings Papers on Economic Activity*, vol. 1, pp. 1–65.

Barro, R.J. and Gordon, D.B. (1983) 'Rules, Discretion and Reputation in a Model of Monetary Policy', *Journal of Monetary Economics*, vol. 12, pp. 101–21.

Bayoumi, T. (1994) 'A Formal Model of Optimum Currency Areas', *IMF Staff Papers*, vol. 41, pp. 537–58.

Bayoumi, T. and Eichengreen, B. (1993) 'Shocking Aspects of Monetary Union', in F. Torres and F. Giavazzi (eds), *Adjustment and Growth in the European Monetary Union* (Cambridge: Cambridge University Press).

Bayoumi, T. and Eichengreen, B. (1996) 'Operationalising the Theory of Optimum Currency Areas', CEPR Discussion Paper no. 1484, Centre for Economic Policy Research, London.

Bayoumi, T. and Eichengreen, B. (1997) 'Ever Closer to Heaven? An Optimum-Currency-Area Index for European Countries', *European Economic Review*, vol. 41, pp. 761–70.

Bayoumi, T. and Eichengreen, B. (1998) 'Exchange Rate Volatility and Intervention: Implications of the Theory of Optimum Currency Areas', *Journal of International Economics*, vol. 45, pp. 191–209.

Bini-Smaghi, L. and Vori, S. (1993) 'Rating the EC as an Optimal Currency Area', *Temi di Discussioni*, no. 187, January, Banca di Italia, Rome.

Blanchard, O. and Katz, L. (1997) 'What We Know and Do Not Know About the Natural Rate of Unemployment', *Journal of Economic Perspectives*, vol. 11, pp. 51–72.

Canzoneri, M. and Gray, A. (1985) 'Monetary Policy Games and the Consequences of Non Co-operative Behaviour', *International Economic Review*, vol. 26, pp. 547–63.

Canzoneri, M. and Henderson, D. (1988) 'Is Sovereign Policymaking Bad?', *Carnegie-Rochester Series on Public Policy*, vol. 28, pp. 93–140.

Canzoneri, M. and Henderson, D. (1991) *Monetary Policy in Interdependent Economies: A Game-theoretic Approach* (Cambridge, Mass.: MIT Press).

Chamie, N., DeSerres, A. and Lalonde, R. (1994) 'Optimum Currency Areas and Shock Asymetry: A Comparison of Europe and the United States', Working Paper no. 94/1, Bank of Canada.

Clarida, R., Gertler, M. and Gali, J. (1999) 'The Science of Monetary Policy: A New Keynesian Perspective', *Journal of Economic Literature*, vol. 37, pp. 1661–707.

Cohen, D. and Wyplosz, C. (1989) 'The European Monetary Union: An Agnostic Evaluation', in R. Bryant, D. Currie, J. Frenkel, P. Masson and R. Porters (eds), *Macroeconomic Policies in an Interdependent World*, (Washington, DC: Brookings).

Currie, D. and Levine, P. (1985) 'Macroeconomic Policy Design in an Interdependent World', in W. Buiter and R. Martson (eds), *International Economic Policy Coordination* (Cambridge: Cambridge University Press).

Currie, D., Holtham, G. and Hughes, G. (1989) 'The Theory and Practice of International Policy Co-ordination: Does Co-ordination Pay?', CEPR Discussion Paper no. 325, Centre for Economic Policy Research, London.

Currie, D. and P. Levine (1991) 'The International Co-ordination of Monetary Policy', in C. Green and D. Llewellyn (eds) *Surveys in Monetary Economics*, vol. 1 (Cambridge, Mass.: Blackwell).

De Grauwe, P. (1975) 'Conditions for Monetary Integration: A Geometric Interpretation', *Weltwirtschaftliches Archiv*, vol. 111, pp. 634–46.

De Grauwe, P. (1996) 'The Economics of Convergence Towards Monetary Policy in Europe' in F. Torres (eds) *Monetary Reform in Europe* (Lisbon: Universidade Catolica Editoria).

De Grauwe, P. (2003) *The Economics of Monetary Union* (Oxford: Oxford University Press).

De Grauwe, P. and Vanhaverbeke, W. (1993) 'Is Europe an Optimum Currency Area? Evidence from Regional Data', in P. Masson and M.P. Taylor (eds), *Policy Issues in the Operations of Currency Unions* (Cambridge: Cambridge University Press).

Demertzis, M. and Hughes-Hallett, A. (1998a) 'Does a Core–Periphery Regime Make Europe into an Optimum Currency Area?', in P. Weltens (ed.), *European Monetary Union* (Berlin: Springer Verlag).

Demertzis, M. and Hughes-Hallett, A. (1998b) 'Asymmetric Transmission Mechanisms and the Rise in European Unemployment: A Case of Structural Differences or of Policy Failures?', *Journal of Economic Dynamics and Control*, vol. 22, pp. 869–86.

Demertzis, M., Hughes-Hallett, A. and Rummel, O.J. (1998) 'Is a Two-Speed System in Europe the Answer to the Conflict Between the German and the Anglo-Saxon Models of Monetary Control?', in S. Black and M. Moersch (eds), *Competition and Convergence in Financial Markets: The German and Anglo-American Model* (New York: Elsevier, North Holland).

Demopoulos, G. and Yannacopoulos, N. (1999) 'Conditions for Optimality of a Currency Area', *Open Economies Review*, vol. 10, pp. 289–305.

Demopoulos, G. and Yannacopoulos, N. (2001) 'On the Optimality of a Currency Area of a Given Size', *Journal of Policy Modeling*, vol. 23, pp. 17–24.

Descressin, J. and Fatàs, A. (1995) 'Regional Labour Market Dynamics in Europe and Implications for EMU', *European Economic Review*, vol. 39, pp. 1627–55.

Dornbusch, R. (1988) 'The European Monetary System, the Dollar and the Yen', in F. Giavazzi *et al.* (eds), *The European Monetary System* (Cambridge: Cambridge University Press).

Dornbusch, R., Favero, C. and Giavazzi. F. (1998) 'Immediate Challenges for the European Central Bank: Issues in Formulating a Single Monetary Policy', *Economic Policy*, vol. 26, pp. 15–64.

Eichengreen, B. (1992) 'Is Europe an Optimum Currency Area? in S. Borner and H. Gruebel (eds), *The European Community After 1992: The View from Outside* (London: Macmillan – Palgrave).

Eichengreen, B. (1993a) 'Labour Markets and European Monetary Unification', in P. Masson and M.P. Taylor (eds), *Policy Issues in the Operations of Currency Unions* (Cambridge: Cambridge University Press).

Eichengreen, B. (1993b) 'European Monetary Unification', *Journal of Economic Literature*, vol. 31, pp. 1321–57.

El-Agraa, A.M. (eds) (1998) *The European Union* (London: Prentice-Hall).

European Commission (1990) 'One Market, One Money', *European Economy*, no. 44.

Fatàs, A. (1997) 'EMU: Countries or Regions? Lessons from the EMS Experience', *European Economic Review*, vol. 41, pp. 743–51.

Favero, C., Freixas, X., Persson T. and Wyplosz, C. (2000) *One Money, Many Countries*, Monitoring the European Central Bank 2 (London: Centre for Economic Policy Research).

Frankel, J. and Rose, A. (1997) 'Is EMU More Justifiable Ex Post or Ex Ante?', *European Economic Review*, vol. 41, pp. 753–60.

Frankel, J. and Rose, A. (1998) 'The Endogeneity of the Optimum Currency Areas Criteria', *Economic Journal*, vol. 108, pp. 1009–25.

Fischer, S. (1982) 'Seigniorage and the Case for a National Money', *Journal of Political Economy*, vol. 90, pp. 295–307.

Gali, J., Gertler, M. and Lopez-Salido, J.D. (2001) 'European Inflation Dynamics', *European Economic Review*, vol. 45, pp. 1237–70.

Giavazzi., F. and Giovannini, A. (1989) *Limiting Exchange Rate Flexibility* (Cambridge, Mass.: MIT Press).

Giavazzi., F. and Pagano, M. (1988) 'The Advantage of Tying One's Hands: EMS Credibility and Central Bank Credibility', *European Economic Review*, vol. 32, pp. 1055–82.

Gordon, R.J. (1998) 'Foundations of the Goldilocks Economy', *Brookings Papers on Economic Activity*, vol. 2, pp. 297–346.

Grilli, N. (1989) 'Seigniorage in Europe', in M. de Cecco and A. Giovannini (eds), *A European Central Bank?* (Cambridge: Cambridge University Press).

Gros, D. and Vandille, G. (1995) 'Seigniorage and EMU: The Fiscal Implications of Price Stability and Financial Integration', *Journal of Common Market Studies*, vol. 33, pp. 175–96.

Gros, D. and Thygesen, T. (1992) *European Monetary Integration: From the European Monetary System Towards Monetary Union* (London: Longman).

Hamada., K. (1974) 'Alternative Exchange Rate Systems and the Interdependence of Monetary Policies', in R. Z. Aliber (ed.), *National Monetary Policies and the International Monetary System* (Chicago: University of Chicago Press).

Hamada., K. (1976) 'A Strategic Analysis of Monetary Interdependence', *Journal of Political Economy*, vol. 84, pp. 677–700.

Hamada., K. (1979) 'Macroeconomic Strategy Coordination Under Alternative exchange Rates', in R. Dornbusch and J. Frenkel (eds), *International Economic Policy* (Baltimore: Johns Hopkins University Press).

Hamada., K. (1985) *The Political Economy of Monetary Interdependence*, (Cambridge Mass: MIT Press).

Hamada., K. and Sakurai, M. (1978) 'International Transmission of Stagflation under Fixed and Flexible Exchange Rates', *Journal of Political Economy*, vol. 86, pp. 877–95.

Hansen, J. and Nielsen, J. (1991) *An Economic Analysis of the EC* (London: McGraw-Hill).

Ishiyama, Y. (1975) 'The Theory of Optimum Currency Areas: A Survey', *IMF Staff Papers*, vol. 22, pp. 344–83.

Kenen, P. (1969) 'The Theory of Optimum Currency Areas: An Eclectic View', in R. Mundell and A. Swoboda (eds), *Monetary Problems of the International Economy* (Chicago: Chicago University Press).

Krugman, P. (1991) *Geography and Trade* (Cambridge, Mass.: MIT Press).

Krugman, P. (1993) 'Lessons of Massachusetts for EMU', in F. Giavazzi and F. Torres (eds), *The Transition to Economic and Monetary Union in Europe* (New York: Cambridge University Press).

Levin, J.H. (1983) 'A Model of Stabilisation Policy in a Jointly Floating Currency Area', in J.S. Bhandari and B.H. Putman (eds), *Economic Interdependence and Flexible Exchange Rates* (Cambridge, Mass.: MIT Press).

Mankiw, G. (1987) 'The Optimal Collection of Seigniorage', *Journal of Monetary Economics*, vol. 29, pp.374–41.

Mankiw, G. (2001) 'The Inexorable and Mysterious Trade-off Between Inflation and Unemployment', *Economic Journal*, vol. 108, pp. 45–61.

Masson, P.R. and Taylor, M. (1993) 'Currency Unions: A Survey of the Issues', in P. Masson and M. Taylor (eds), *Policy Issues in the Operation of Currency Unions* (Cambridge: Cambridge University Press).

McCallum, B. (1997) 'A Comment', *NBER Macroeconomics Annual*, pp. 355–9, National Bureau of Economic Research, Cambridge, Mass.

McKinnon, R. (1963) 'Optimum Currency Areas', *American Economic Review*, vol. 53, pp. 717–25.

Melitz, J. (1995) 'A Suggested Reformulation of the Theory of Optimum Currency Areas', *Open Economies Review*, vol. 6, pp. 281–98.

Melitz, J. (1996) 'The Theory of Optimum Currency Areas, Trade Adjustment and Trade', *Open Economies Review*, vol. 7, pp. 99–116.

Mills, T., Pelloni, GL. and Zervoyianni, A. (1995) 'Unemployment Fluctuations in the US: Further Tests of the Sectoral-Shifts and Reallocation-Timing Hypotheses', *Review of Economics and Statistics*, vol. 77, pp. 295–304.

—(1996) 'Sectoral Shifts and Unemployment Fluctuations in the UK', *Economics Letters*, vol. 52, pp. 55–60.

—(1997) 'Unemployment Fluctuations in the UK: 1958–1992', *Applied Economics Letters*, vol. 4, pp. 253–56.

Mundell, R. (1961) 'A Theory of Optimum Currency Areas', *American Economic Review*, vol. 51, pp. 657–65.

Pelkmans, J. (2001) *European Integration: Methods and Economic Analysis* (London: Prentice-Hall).

Robson, P. (1998) *The Economics of International Integration* (London: Allen & Unwin).

Rogoff, K. (1985) 'Can International Policy Coordination be Counter-Productive?' *Journal of International Economics*, vol. 18, pp. 199–217.

Romer, D. (2001) *Advanced Macroeconomics* (New York: McGraw-Hill).

Rudebusch, G.D. and Svensson, L. (1999) 'Policy Rules for Inflation Targeting', in J. Taylor (ed), *Monetary Policy Rules* (Chicago: University of Chicago Press).

Sibert, A. (1994) 'The Allocation of Seigniorage in a Common Currency Area', *Journal of International Economics*, vol. 37, pp. 111–22.

Stock, J. (1998) 'Comment', *Brookings Papers on Economic Activity*, vol. 2, pp. 347–60.

Stock, J. and Watson, M. (1999) 'Forecasting Inflation', *Journal of Monetary Economics*, vol. 44, pp. 293–335.

Stockman, A. (1988) 'Sectoral and National Aggregate Disturbances to Industrial Output in Seven European Countries', *Journal of Monetary Economics*, vol. 21, pp. 387–409.

Tavlas, G.S. (1993) 'The New Theory of Optimum Currency Areas', *The World Economy*, vol. 6, pp. 663–85.

Tavlas, G.S. (1994) 'The Theory of Monetary Integration', *Open Economies Review*, vol. 5, pp. 211–30.

Torres, F.S. (1990) 'Portugal, the EMS and 1992: Stabilization and Liberalization', in P. De Grauwe and L. Papademos (eds), *The European Monetary System in the 1990s* (London: Longman).

Weber, A. (1991) 'EMU and Asymmetries and Adjustment Problems in the EMS: Some Empirical Evidence', *European Economy*, vol. 1, pp. 187–207.

Zervoyianni, A. (1993) 'Insider – Outsider Conflicts and Policy Games in Interdependent Economies', *Dynamis Quaderno* 9/1993, Instituto di Ricerca Sulla Dinamica dei Sistemi Economici, Milan.

Zervoyianni, A. (1997) 'Monetary Policy Games and Coalitions in a Two-Country Model with Unionised Wage Setting', *Oxford Economic Papers*, vol. 49, pp. 57–76.

5 Performance of the EMS, the ERM-II and the New EU Member States

Athina Zervoyianni

Introduction

The European Monetary System (EMS) was created in 1978 by the six founding members of the Community, namely Germany, France, Italy, Belgium, the Netherlands and Luxembourg. It began to operate in March 1979, and its primary aim was to create a 'zone of monetary stability' in Europe by restricting the margin of fluctuations between the member states' exchange rates to ±2.5 per cent around 'central rates'.

Indeed, despite a number of central-rate realignments shortly after the creation of the EMS, bilateral exchange rates between the European currencies had remained remarkably stable throughout the 1980s and had shown much less variability, in both nominal and real terms, than currencies outside the system. During the 1980s and early 1990s the EMS currencies had also shown low variability relative to non-European currencies. At the same time, all the ERM countries managed to achieve the twin goal of reducing inflation and increasing inflation convergence.

The European Monetary System proved unable to survive following the 1992–93 crisis in currency markets: in August 1993 member states took the decision to widen the ERM exchange-rate bands from 2.25 per cent above or below the ECU central rates to ±15 per cent. Yet, even after August 1993, the wider ±15 per cent ERM band continued to be seen by many Europeans as representing an important 'common' monetary framework; and it provided the background against which negotiations among the EU member states started for establishing the process for the adoption of a single currency in January 2002.

The EMS experience is also of relevance to the 10 new EU member states (Cyprus, the Czech Republic, Estonia, Hungary, Latvia, Lithuania, Malta, Poland, Slovakia and Slovenia) that joined the European Union in May 2004. All of them have declared a strong desire to participate in the eurozone and adopt the common currency as quickly as possible. To do so they are expected to link their currencies to the euro through the 'new exchange-rate mechanism', the ERM-II (a ±15 fluctuation band around central euro rates), and remain in it for at least 2 years before applying for EMU membership. Indeed, some of them already peg their currencies to the euro and others are seeking for the most appropriate exchange-rate regime during the transition period towards full EMU membership.

In what follows we discuss the developments that led to the creation of the EMS, and we consider its performance. We also consider the features of the 'new exchange-rate mechanism' and the challenge of ERM-II membership for the new member states. The next section concentrates on the pre-EMS attempts towards monetary cooperation in Europe and discusses the EMS's main aspects. We then assess the performance of the European Monetary System. The issue of inflation during the EMS period is addressed, examining the extent to which the European Monetary System contributed to the reduction of average inflation in Europe and inflation divergence. Thus, within a game-theoretic framework, we consider the impact that the EMS might have had on inflation by changing the nature of interactions between European policy-makers and the credibility of monetary policies. The factors that might have been responsible for the disintegration of the EMS in August 1993 are then discussed, followed by a consideration of the new exchange-rate mechanism and the challenge of ERM-II membership for the newcomers. The final section contains a summary and conclusions.

Early Attempts at Monetary-Policy Cooperation in Europe and the EMS

Provisions for Macroeconomic and Monetary Policy Coordination in the Rome Treaty

The Treaty of Rome was not very explicit on the macroeconomic and monetary integration of Europe. References to issues of macro-economic policy coordination were made only in Articles 103–107. Articles 103 and 104 described the general objectives of the EC in the field of macroeconomic and monetary policy, while Articles 105 to 107 described the instruments to be used to attain these objectives. More specifically, Articles 103 and 104 of the Rome Treaty stated that the objectives of the Community would be:

• to ensure balance of payments equilibrium in member states
• to maintain confidence in EC currencies
• to ensure a high level of employment and low inflation rates

To achieve these objectives, three instruments were to be used:

- coordination of national economic policies
- stability of exchange rates
- financial assistance to member states facing structural balance-of-payments problems

To promote macroeconomic policy coordination, a Monetary Committee was set up immediately after the signing of the Rome Treaty. Its task was to review the monetary and financial situation of the EC countries and to report regularly to the Commission.

The Rome Treaty therefore imposed no constraints on member states' macroeconomic and monetary policies. This could be explained by the economic circumstances of the late 1950s, namely the satisfactory performance of the European economies (that is, the low unemployment and inflation rates, the high rates of GDP growth, favourable trade balances and adequate foreign exchange reserves) and the smooth functioning of the international monetary system.

The international monetary system in operation in the late 1950s was the Bretton Woods system of fixed exchange rates. This system was agreed by the major developed countries at an international conference at Bretton Woods in New Hampshire in 1954. Under this system, non-US countries were committed to maintaining exchange rates for their currencies relative to the dollar. The numerical values of these fixed exchange rates were called par values, and all the non-US central banks were to intervene in the foreign-exchange markets to keep market exchange rates within a margin of 1 per cent above or below these par values. They would thus purchase dollars to prevent their currencies from appreciating and sell dollars to prevent their currencies from depreciating. On the other hand, the USA was pursuing an independent monetary policy, setting interest rates without reference to the exchange rate. However, under the Bretton Woods agreement, US monetary authorities would accept dollars in exchange for gold. To manage the system, the International Monetary Fund (IMF) was created, and all countries participating in the Bretton-Woods system became members of the IMF.

Until the early 1960s this system was functioning smoothly: inflation in the USA was low and the European currencies were stable relative to the dollar and therefore stable relative to each other. This situation started to change in the mid-1960s. Because of the Vietnam War, the USA began in 1967 to pursue a highly expansionary monetary policy that led to creeping inflation and a growing balance-of-payments deficit. This created doubts about the dollar's ability to maintain its par value relative to the other currencies and led to speculative movements of capital away from dollar-denominated assets. Eventually, in March 1968, the US monetary authorities were forced to announce that they would no longer accept dollars in exchange for gold. This announcement was followed by large exchange-rate fluctuations that destabilized the relative value of the European currencies. In particular, in June 1969 the French franc was devalued by 11.1 per cent relative to the dollar, while the German mark was revalued by 9.29 per cent. The result was a revaluation of the deutschmark–french franc (DM/FF) exchange rate by more than 20 per cent.

This large change in the bilateral exchange rate of the two most important EC currencies was seen by many as endangering the common agricultural policy and more generally the integration process in Europe. Thus, in the early 1970s the first attempts towards creating a 'zone of monetary stability' in Europe emerged. These attempts took the form of the Werner Plan.

The Werner Plan and the 'European Snake'

In March 1970 the Council of Ministers asked the Commission to set up a committee to prepare plans for a 'full economic and monetary union' among the member states. The committee, known as the Werner Committee from its Chairman Pierre Werner (then Prime Minister and Minister of Finance of Luxembourg), consisted of member states' representatives. The Werner Committee took the desirability of monetary unification as given and concentrated on how it could best be achieved. On this matter, two different views were advanced. The first, supported by the Germans and the Dutch, was that before attempting monetary unification, member states had to achieve convergence of economic performances by coordinating their macroeconomic policies. The second view, supported mainly by the French, was that commitment to maintain stable exchange rates would inevitably lead to macroeconomic and monetary convergence and that the fixing of European exchange rates was the best way to attain monetary unification. In the end, the Werner Committee proposed the creation of full monetary union by 1980 but recommended that the process should be gradual, consisting of two phases.[1]

In the first phase the emphasis would be given to the achievement of greater economic convergence. In particular, during the first phase, which was to extend from 1971 to 1973, the exchange rates of the member states' currencies were to be maintained within narrower margins than those imposed by the Bretton Woods system. Also governments were to consult with each other before proceeding to changes in their fiscal- and monetary-policy stance. In addition, short-term credit facilities were to be created to help member states maintain stable exchange rates between their currencies.

In the second phase, a full monetary union was to be established. This second phase, which was to start in January 1974, was to involve the establishment of a European Fund for Monetary Cooperation (EMCF). The EMCF would hold and manage part of the member states' foreign exchange reserves and was to be eventually transformed into a system of Community central banks that would decide on monetary policy for Europe as a whole.

The Werner Plan was adopted by the EC Council of Ministers in March 1971. The first phase of monetary union was to start in June 1971, but this did not happen because of adverse developments in foreign exchange markets. In particular, in March 1971 doubts about the dollar's ability to maintain its par value relative to other currencies led to large speculative movements of short-term capital away from dollar-denominated assets, causing turbulence in foreign exchange markets. The result was that in Germany and the Benelux countries foreign exchange markets closed for two weeks while France was forced to adopt drastic foreign-exchange controls. The pressures on the dollar in foreign exchange markets continued, and in December 1971 the member states of the IMF signed the Smithsonian Agreement under which measures were taken to resolve the crisis. These measures involved:

- A devaluation of the dollar against all the other national currencies, that is a reduction in its parity rates.
- A widening of the IMF's permissible fluctuation margins from 1 per cent above or below parity rates to 2.25 per cent above or below these rates.

Because of these developments in the world economy, the first phase of the Werner Plan started almost a year later than was originally planned, namely in April 1972. The arrangements during this phase were:

- Market exchange rates between member states' currencies were to fluctuate within a margin of ±1.125 per cent around parity rates instead of the new IMF margin of ±2.25 per cent. This arrangement came to be known as the 'European Snake' or 'snake in the tunnel': the 'tunnel' represented the permissible fluctuation margins of each European currency with the dollar, that is the ±2.25 per cent limit, while the 'snake' represented the narrower margins of intra-European rates, that is the ±1.125 per cent limit.
- A European Monetary Cooperation Fund was created. This was to provide short-term funds to member countries to intervene in foreign exchange markets in order to keep rates within the ±1.125 per cent margin.
- Participating countries were allowed to leave the 'European Snake' temporarily or permanently if this was considered at any time appropriate.

The European Snake did not last long as the oil crisis of 1973 made the attainment of stable exchange rates between member states a very difficult task. Indeed, the oil crisis had severe consequences for inflation and the balance-of-payments of almost all the industrial countries, including Europe: between 1973 and 1976 the average rate of inflation in Europe increased by more than 50 per cent. Moreover, it did not affect all the Community states to the same extent, and this increased the gap between member states' inflation rates and thus made impossible the maintenance of stable intra-European exchange rates. The UK and Ireland, which, anticipating membership of the European Community, entered the European Snake in May 1972, were forced to leave the system in June 1972. Denmark withdrew from it in July 1972. Italy left it in January 1973 and France withdrew from it in January 1974. France rejoined the system in July 1975, but again withdrew from it in March 1976. Only Germany and the Benelux countries decided to maintain stable exchange rates with each other and let their currencies float jointly against the dollar. Accordingly, when in January 1975 the Marjolin Committee, a committee of Commission officials, was asked to assess the situation, it concluded that the degree of convergence of member states' economies was much lower than what it was in 1969 and therefore the Werner Plan had to be dropped.

The EMS

Discussions about monetary integration in Europe started again in 1977. The main argument in favour of monetary unification was that the potential gains from the creation of the European common market could not materialize in an environment of exchange-rate variability and uncertainty. Another argument was that stable European exchange rates would lead to a reduction of average inflation in the Community, because, given the nominal rigidities in the member states' labour and product markets, floating exchange rates were in general inflationary. Yet another argument was that monetary integration would allow Community countries to simultaneously adopt expansionary monetary policies and thus create a high level of aggregate demand that was necessary to combat unemployment.[2] Accordingly, in December 1978 the Council of Ministers adopted a resolution on the establishment of a European Monetary System (EMS). The EMS, began to operate in March 1979. Entry into the system was not compulsory for the members of the Community, and it was also possible for a country to participate in only some of the operations of the system.[3]

The EMS had three components: the European currency unit (ECU); the Exchange Rate Mechanism (ERM) which consisted of bilateral exchange-rate fluctuation margins; and a system of credit facilities.

The ECU was a composite currency, consisting of all the EC currencies properly weighted. The weight of each national currency in the ECU was intended to reflect the share of the GDP of the member state concerned in Community GDP. In the EMS agreement there were provisions for adjusting these weights. Such adjustments were undertaken following the enlargements, namely in September 1984 when Greece became a member of the Community, in September 1989 when Spain and Portugal joined, and in September 1996 when Austria, Finland and Sweden joined the EU.

Each currency participating in the ERM had a reference rate expressed in ECUs, the 'ECU central rate' of exchange. From this rate, bilateral central rates were derived for each pair of currencies in the system. From April 1979 until July 1993, bilateral market rates were allowed to fluctuate only within narrow margins: 2.25 per cent above or below the bilateral central rates. Italy and Ireland were initially allowed to use a larger margin of fluctuation,[4] namely ±6 per cent. Spain (June 1989), Portugal (April 1990) and the UK (October 1990) were also allowed the wider ±6 per cent margin. In August 1993, these margins were raised to 15 per cent above or below the bilateral central rates. While adjustments of the ECU central rates were possible under the original EMS rules, the decision to realign central rates required the consent of all the ERM countries and the Commission.[5]

When two currencies were to hit their bilateral permissible margin, the two relevant central banks were obliged to intervene in foreign exchange markets to keep the rate within the permitted fluctuation limit. In particular, the central bank of the country whose currency had appreciated to its margin would intervene by buying the weak currency that had depreciated, while the central bank of the country whose currency had depreciated would intervene by selling the strong currency that had appreciated. For financing intervention at the margins, a very short-term financing facility (VSTF) had been created. VSTF was automatically available; debts had to be repaid within a three-month period. Countries could also undertake 'intra-marginal' intervention; that is, they could intervene in foreign exchange markets even if their currencies had not been appreciated or depreciated to their full margins. In addition to VSTF, other longer-term financing was also available to member states.

Growth, Employment and Inflation in the EMS Years

According to a Commission's is document on the EMS,[6] the European Monetary System had been created to achieve 'a greater measure of monetary stability', 'convergence of economic development among the members of the Community', 'co-ordination of national macro-economic policies' and 'growth with stability'. These were vague terms, but, as pointed out by many, including Ungerer *et al.* (1983) and Fratianni and von Hagen (1990b), they could be given a more specific interpretation from other studies and existing official documents. Thus, 'monetary stability' was meant to signify both external stability and internal stability, namely exchange-rate stability and stability of costs and prices. The term 'convergence' was meant to express the target of both reducing inflation differentials and lowering the divergence between the member states' GDP growth rates and levels of employment.[7] 'Growth with stability' meant low unemployment and low inflation. So, in effect, the explicit and implicit objectives of the EMS were:[8]

- to stabilize exchange rates
- to contribute to the reduction of average inflation in Europe
- to reduce inflation differentials
- to promote integration and the coordination of macroeconomic policies in Europe
- to promote economic growth and contribute to the reduction of unemployment in member countries

To consider how far the EMS, as was originally conceived, succeeded in achieving these objectives a sensible first step would be to look at what the empirical evidence has to say about the achievements of the system, that is to look at pre-EMS and post-EMS data on nominal and real exchange rates, on inflation performances and in particular average inflation and inflation convergence in Europe, and on GPD growth and employment growth in member states.

Exchange Rates

As far as exchange rates are concerned, there is little doubt that countries participating in the ERM had, on average during the 1980s and early 1990s, more stable exchange rates in both nominal and real terms than countries outside the system. The findings of a large number of econometric studies in fact indicate that the EMS had contributed to a reduction of exchange-rate risk and uncertainty.[9]

GDP Growth and Employment

The same does not hold for real GDP growth and employment growth. Table 5.1 reports real GDP growth rates and employment growth in three major EMS countries, namely France, Italy and Germany during two periods, 1971–80 and 1981–90. The data show that the EMS years,

Table 5.1   Real GDP growth and employment growth in major EMS countries

	Real GDP growth (%)			Employment growth (%)		
	France	Italy	Germany	France	Italy	Germany
Average 1971–80	3.3	3.6	2.7	0.5	1.0	0.2
Average 1981–90	2.5	2.3	2.2	0.3	0.6	0.5
1981	1.2	0.8	0.1	−0.4	0.0	−0.1
1982	2.6	0.6	−0.9	0.1	0.6	−1.2
1983	1.5	1.2	1.8	−0.3	0.3	−1.4
1984	1.6	2.8	2.8	−0.2	0.0	0.2
1985	1.5	3.0	2.0	−0.8	0.9	0.7
1986	2.4	2.5	2.3	0.4	0.7	1.4
1987	2.5	3.0	1.5	0.8	0.2	0.7
1988	4.6	3.9	3.7	0.9	1.1	0.8
1989	4.2	2.9	3.6	1.7	0.7	1.5
1990	2.6	2.0	5.7	1.0	1.6	3.0

Source: Eurostat, European Economy 2001, Statistical Annex.

the period 1981–90, were characterized by slower real GDP growth. In France and Italy, real GDP growth fell from an average annual rate of 3.3 per cent and 3.6 per cent respectively during 1971–80 to an average annual rate of 2.5 per cent and 2.3 per cent during the EMS period. Even in Germany, where the reunification process boosted aggregate demand and growth in the late 1980s, average real GDP growth fell during the period 1981–90 by 0.5 percentage points relative to its level in 1971–80. Employment growth in Europe had been equally poor during the EMS years: relative to 1971–1980 France and Italy experienced a reduction of employment growth by an average annual rate of 0.2 per cent and 0.4 per cent respectively. Only Germany experienced an average annual increase of 0.3 per cent in 1981–90 relative to 1971–80, but this was due to the German unification which led to 1.5 per cent employment growth in 1989 and to 3 per cent employment growth in 1990. Indeed, excluding the years 1989 and 1990, the average annual rate of employment growth in Germany during the EMS period, namely 1981–90, falls to 0.1 per cent.

Table 5.2 compares the GDP-growth performance of the EUR-11 countries, that is countries linked directly or indirectly to the ERM, with that of three non-EMS OECD countries, namely the USA, Japan and the UK. The EUR-11 countries and the USA had in 1971–80 similar GDP growth rates, that is an average annual rate of 3.3 per cent and 3.1 per cent respectively. Japan's growth rate was 4.3 per cent on average and the UK's growth rate was 1.9 per cent. During the EMS

Table 5.2 Real GDP growth in EUR-11, United States, Japan and United Kingdom (%)

	EUR-11	US	Japan	UK
Average 1971–1980	3.3	3.1	4.3	1.9
Average 1981–1990	2.4	3.2	4.2	2.7
1981	0.5	2.5	2.8	−1.3
1982	0.7	−2.1	3.0	1.8
1983	1.5	4.3	2.3	3.7
1984	2.3	7.3	3.9	2.4
1985	2.2	3.8	4.4	3.8
1986	2.5	3.4	4.8	4.2
1987	2.7	3.4	4.6	4.4
1988	4.2	4.2	6.7	5.2
1989	3.9	3.5	5.1	2.1
1990	3.6	1.7	4.8	0.7

Source: Eurostat, *European Economy* 2001, Statistical Annex.

years of 1981–90, GDP growth in EUR-11 fell to 2.4 per cent. By contrast, during the same period, GDP growth increased to 2.7 per cent in the UK and remained roughly unchanged at 3.2 per cent and 4.2 per cent in the USA and Japan respectively.

Figure 5.1 shows the behaviour of unemployment in the EC countries and in non-EC OECD countries in the period 1968–96. In 1979–82, that is just after the creation of the EMS, the EC and the non-EC

Figure 5.1 EC and non-EC OECD countries, 1968–1996: unemployment rates

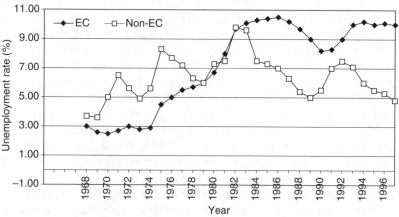

Source: OECD database, Labour Statistics.

OECD countries had similar rates of unemployment. Subsequently their unemployment performances began to diverge considerably. In the non-EC countries unemployment started to decline after 1982 and by 1993 it had fallen to 7 per cent. In the EC group unemployment continued to rise after 1982, and by 1993 it had reached 10 per cent.

It could be argued that this poor employment and real GDP growth performance of Community countries might not have been connected to the European Monetary System: it could have been the result of adverse supply-side shocks (see De Grauwe (2003)) or unfavourable structural influences on the European countries' labour markets, including the wage bargaining system. Calmfors and Driffill (1988) were the first to stress the link between macroeconomic performance and the system of wage bargaining. In particular, they classified the OECD countries according to the degree of centralization of their wage bargaining process and, studying data for the 1970s and 1980s, came up with two major findings. First, countries with highly centralized or highly decentralized bargaining systems were showing the best outcomes in terms of both unemployment and inflation; second, countries with an intermediate degree of centralization of the wage bargaining process had the worst macroeconomic performance. An intuitive explanation for these results is not difficult to find. In countries with a highly centralized wage bargaining process, where bargaining is conducted at the national level, unions recognize wider interests, taking into account macroeconomic considerations, including the inflationary consequences of excessive wage claims. This lowers their wage demands. In highly decentralized systems, where wage negotiations occur at the firm level, competitive forces are at work: workers are in a position to observe directly that unjustifiable wage increases can lead to a large loss of profitability of the firm and thus a fall in employment. This reduces their incentives to opt for excessive wages. In countries with intermediate positions, where wage bargaining occurs at the sectoral level, neither of these two factors operates. Thus, in such countries there is the least restraint on wage claims.

De Grauwe (1990) was the first to make the point that the classification of countries into an EMS group and a non-EMS group could coincide with the classification of countries according to the degree of centralization of their wage bargaining process. If this were the case, then the poor employment and real-growth performance of the EMS countries during the 1980s and early 1990s could have reflected an inefficient wage bargaining system. To address this issue, De Grauwe (1990) examined 'misery indices', consisting of the sum of cumulative inflation rates and unemployment rates, for both non-EMS countries and EMS countries. These countries were also ranked according to the degree of centralization of wage bargaining from 1 to 17. The index of centralization (ICWB) was that of Calmfors and Driffill (1988). De Grauwe's results indicated that four out of the six EMS countries considered were falling in the unfavourable intermediate group of centralization of wage bargaining.

Inflation

The upper half of Table 5.3 presents data on consumer-price (CPI) inflation in the EMS countries during the period 1979–90. The table shows that average EMS inflation reached a maximum in 1980–81, that is just after the establishment of the system, but from 1982 onwards it started to decline steadily. The drop in inflation between 1980 and 1988, namely before the participation in the ERM of the Spanish peseta, the Portuguese escudo and the UK pound, had been substantial. In 1980, average EMS inflation was 11.9 per cent. By 1988, it had fallen to 2.7 per cent, implying an inflation reduction of 9.2 percentage points. The inflation reduction was particularly remarkable in the case of the high-inflation EMS countries, Italy and Ireland: in Italy inflation fell from 21.2 per cent in 1980 to 6.4 per cent in 1990, while in Ireland it fell from 18.2 per cent in 1980 to 3.4 per cent in 1990. As far as inflation convergence was concerned, the standard deviation of inflation rates also reached a maximum in 1980 at 5.7 per cent but was reduced to 1.2 per cent in 1990. This large reduction in EMS average inflation and inflation divergence during the 1979-90 period can also be seen from Figure 5.2.

Accordingly, the picture emerging from the data is that during the 1980s and until the early 1990s, the EMS countries managed to achieve the twin objective of lowering average inflation and inflation divergence. However, as many commendators, including Fratianni and von Hagen (1990b), Weber (1991) and De Grauwe (1994) were arguing in the early 1990s, the issue was how much of this satisfactory inflation performance had been due to the EMS itself and how much had been due to other forces operating during that period. To address this issue a first step would be to compare the inflation experience of the EMS countries with that of the non-EMS countries. Thus, Figure 5.3 shows the behaviour of CPI inflation in both the EMS countries and in all the industrial countries during the 1980s. The average inflation performance of all the industrial countries seems very similar to that of the EMS countries.

This can also be seen from the bottom part of Table 5.3. Like in the EMS group, average inflation in the major non-EMS industrial countries namely Canada, Japan, UK and the US, reached a maximum in 1980, at 12.4 per cent, dropping to 5.7 per cent in 1990. The inflation reduction between 1980 and 1988 was for this group only 0.2 per cent lower than that for the EMS group. The standard deviation

Table 5.3 CPI inflation rates in EMS and major non-EMS industrial countries, 1979–1990

	1979	1980	1981	1982	1983	1984	1985	1986	1987	1988	1989	1990
EMS												
Belgium	4.5	6.7	7.6	8.7	7.7	6.3	4.9	1.3	1.6	1.2	3.1	3.4
Denmark	9.6	12.3	11.7	10.1	6.9	6.3	4.7	3.7	4.0	4.6	4.8	2.6
France	10.8	13.3	13.4	11.8	9.6	7.4	5.8	2.5	3.3	2.7	3.5	3.4
Germany	4.1	5.4	6.3	5.3	3.3	2.4	2.2	-0.1	0.2	1.3	2.8	2.7
Ireland	13.2	18.2	20.4	17.1	10.5	8.6	5.4	3.8	3.1	2.2	4.0	3.4
Italy	14.8	21.2	17.8	16.5	14.7	10.8	9.2	5.9	4.7	5.9	6.7	6.4
Luxembourg	–	–	–	–	–	–	–	–	–	–	–	–
Netherlands	4.2	6.5	6.7	5.9	2.8	3.3	2.2	0.1	-0.7	0.7	1.1	2.5
Average	8.7	11.9	12.0	10.8	7.9	6.4	4.9	2.5	2.3	2.7	3.6	3.5
Standard Deviation	4.2	5.7	5.2	4.3	3.9	2.7	2.2	2.0	1.8	1.8	1.6	1.2
Major non-EMS industrial countries												
Canada	9.1	10.2	12.5	10.8	5.8	4.3	4.0	4.2	4.4	4.0	5.0	4.8
Japan	3.7	7.7	4.9	2.7	1.9	2.3	2.0	0.6	0.6	0.7	2.3	3.1
UK	13.5	18.0	11.9	8.6	4.6	5.0	6.1	3.4	4.1	4.9	7.8	9.5
USA	11.3	13.5	10.3	6.2	3.2	4.3	3.6	1.9	3.7	4.0	4.8	5.4
Average	9.4	12.4	9.9	7.1	3.9	4.0	3.9	2.5	3.2	3.4	5.0	5.7
Standard Deviation	3.6	3.9	3.0	3.0	1.5	1.0	1.4	1.4	1.5	1.6	1.9	2.3

Source: IMF, *International Financial Statistics.*

Figure 5.2 Average inflation and standard deviation of inflation rates in EMS countries

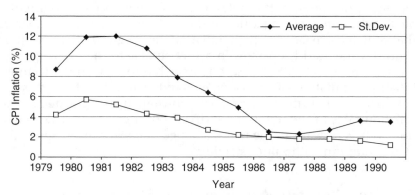

Source: Table 5.3.

Figure 5.3 Average inflation in EMS countries and in all industrial countries

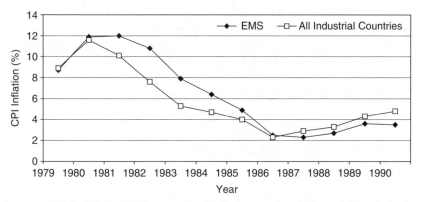

Sources: Table 5.3 for EMS countries; IMF, *International Financial Statistics* for all industrial countries.

of inflation rates for this group also fell, from 3.9 per cent in 1980 to 2.3 per cent in 1990.

It therefore appears that the statistical evidence supporting the hypothesis that the EMS helped member states fight inflation and achieve convergence of inflation rates is weak. But if this is the case, then one must ask whether there are any theoretical arguments suggesting that the EMS group should have experienced a larger reduction in both average inflation and divergence of inflation rates than the non-EMS group in the 1980s after the second oil-price shock.

More specifically, there are two issues to address. The first has to do with the mechanism of the EMS itself: is there anything special in exchange-rate systems like the EMS implying that such systems can lead to better inflation performances than other exchange-rate regimes? This question is of relevance to EU member states currently outside the eurozone, in particular those of the 10 new member states that still have relatively high inflation rates, given that for these countries the ERM-II operates in a way similar to the exchange-rate mechanism of the EMS. The second issue has to do with the counter-inflation reputation of the German Bundesbank: to what extent, if any, had German monetary policy contributed to the reduction of inflation rates in the non-German EMS countries? Again, the reputa-tion issue is relevant to the new exchange-rate mechanism, given the ECB's commitment to price stability.

The Game-Theoretic Approach to the EMS: Impact on Inflation Outcomes

There are two channels through which the creation of the European Monetary System could have affected inflation outcomes in parti-cipating states. First, its creation changed the rules determining the nature of interactions among European policy-makers by altering the policy instruments available to them. Second, the creation of the EMS could have changed expectations about future price levels as well as the credibility of the member states' central banks.

Impact of EMS on Inflation by Changing the Rules Determining the Nature of Interactions among European Policy-makers

Collins (1988) is one of the best-known attempts to address the first issue, namely the effect of the EMS on inflation performances through its impact on the rules defining interactions among European policy-makers. In particular, Collins employs the basic tools of game theory to ask whether EMS membership *should* have helped European countries to reduce their inflation rates in the 1980s, following the second oil-price shock, ignoring any impact that the creation of the EMS might have had on inflationary expectations and on the credibility of monetary policies.

Two countries are assumed in Collins' framework, called 'France' and 'Germany', and inflation outcomes under a non-EMS regime are compared with inflation outcomes under an EMS monetary regime. The non-EMS regime is taken to involve Nash non-cooperative behaviour by each country's policy-makers. That is, policy-makers in France (Germany) are assumed to act independently in the field of monetary policy, ignoring the spillover effects of their actions on the macroeconomic performance of Germany (France). The EMS regime is modelled in two different ways: a 'cooperative EMS with realignments', and an 'EMS with leadership'. In the first version of the EMS, which is a good representation of how the European Monetary System had operated during the period from 1979 to 1985, it is assumed that France and Germany set both monetary policy and the bilateral exchange rate for their currencies cooperatively. In the second EMS regime, Germany is assumed to have leadership in monetary-policy matters setting its money supply independently, while France simply adjusts its own monetary policy to that of Germany so as to maintain a stable exchange rate for its currency relative to the German mark. This is a good representation of how the EMS had operated between 1985 and 1992.

The first component of Collins' framework can be represented by a set of (log-linear) Phillips-curve-type equations determining output levels:

$$y_F = \nu(\dot{p}_F - \dot{p}_F^e) + y_F^N, \; y_G = \nu(\dot{p}_G - \dot{p}_G^e) + y_G^N$$

where y_F^N and y_G^N are natural levels of output, $\dot{p}_F^e$ ($\dot{p}_G^e$) is the expected rate of domestic-price inflation in France (Germany) and $\dot{p}_F$ ($\dot{p}_G$) is the actual rate of domestic-price inflation. Static expectations are assumed throughout ($\dot{p}_F^e = \dot{p}_G^e = 0$) and $\dot{p}_F$ and $\dot{p}_G$ are taken to be directly influenced by money-supply growth rates. Thus:

$$y_F = \nu_1 \dot{m}_F + y_F^N \tag{1}$$

$$y_G = \nu_1 \dot{m}_G + y_G^N \tag{2}$$

Equations (1) and (2) say that by controlling the rate of growth of the money supply, monetary authorities in each country can control (the log of) domestic output. Thus, in what follows, to simplify matters, the constant ν_1 will be set equal to unity and (the log of) the natural level of output equal to zero, and instead of treating $\dot{m}_F$ ($\dot{m}_G$) as the French (German) authorities' policy instrument we will take this instrument to be $y_F(y_G)$. In other words, following Collins (1988) output will be taken to be both an instrument of policy and a target.

The next component of the model is a set of objective functions describing the preferences of policy-makers in France and Germany. The objective functions are given by equations (3) and (4):

$$V_F = -(y_F)^2 - \phi(\pi_F)^2 \tag{3}$$

$$V_G = -(y_G)^2 - \phi(\pi_G)^2 \tag{4}$$

$$0 < \phi < \alpha$$

where π_F is consumer-price-index (CPI) inflation in France and π_G is consumer-price-index inflation in Germany. Accordingly, equations (3) and (4) say that French and German policy-makers dislike fluctuations in both output and the overall rate of inflation, with ϕ reflecting the relative weight they attach to CPI fluctuations.

The last component of the model is a set of equations describing the determinants of CPI inflation:

$$\pi_F = \pi_F^0 + \gamma y_F + \alpha(y_F - y_G) \tag{5}$$

$$\pi_G = \pi_G^0 + \gamma y_G - \alpha(y_F - y_G) \tag{6}$$

Actual CPI inflation in each country is assumed to be influenced by three factors: past inflation, aggregate-demand influences and exchange-rate changes. Past inflation reflects the assumption that there is inflation 'inertia' so that current inflation has a predetermined component. This predetermined portion of inflation, which in Collins (1988) study is also called 'base inflation rate', is represented in equations (5) and (6) by the terms π_F^0 and π_G^0 respectively. Indeed, to capture the post-1979 oil-price shock situation, when high inflation rates were prevailing, Collins' framework considers disinflation from an initial inflationary situation. Thus both π_F^0 and π_G^0 are assumed to be positive. Also, both countries are assumed to seek to reduce their CPI inflation rates. However, France is taken to have higher base inflation than Germany, as was indeed the case in the early 1980s. Accordingly π_F^0 is assumed to be greater than π_G^0. The second term in equations (5) and (6) reflects domestic influences on consumer-price inflation through aggregate demand. The assumption is that, other things being equal, when domestic output rises (relative to its natural-rate level), aggregate demand, and therefore labour demand, rises as well and this enables workers to press for higher wages. In the absence of productivity growth, this leads to more inflation. The last term in the inflation equations reflects international influences on national CPI inflation rates, namely the impact on CPI of changes in the FF/DM exchange rate through the domestic-currency price of imports. In particular, the hypothesis here is that when, for example, output in France rises relative to output in Germany, the demand for imports in France also rises relative to that in Germany, and this moves the French balance of payments into deficit. The deficit in France causes the French franc to depreciate relative to the German mark. The depreciation leads to a rise (fall) in the domestic-currency price of imports in France (Germany) and thus to an increase (fall) in French (German) CPI inflation. Accordingly, in equations (5) and (6), as y_F rises relative to y_G, π_F increases while π_G falls.

Notice that the last term in the CPI-inflation equations implies that France and Germany can jointly control the FF/DM exchange rate by controlling the output differential $(y_F - y_G)$. This means that the case of 'EMS with realignments', where France and Germany cooperatively set the FF/DM exchange rate, can be represented by a situation where their central banks cooperatively choose a value for the money-supply growth differential $(\dot{m}_F - \dot{m}_G)$ which ensures that the output differential $(y_F - y_G)$ is compatible with the chosen value of the FF/DM exchange rate. Similarly, the case of 'EMS with leadership can be represented by a situation in which France 'sets' y_F equals y_G so that $y_F = y_G$, and thus the FF/DM rate remains unchanged.

As we assume two countries, 'average inflation', π_A, is simply half the sum of π_F and π_G. On the other hand, the 'divergence' of national inflation rates, π_D, can be measured by half the difference between π_F and π_G:

$$\pi_A = \frac{1}{2}(\pi_F + \pi_G) \tag{7}$$

$$\pi_D = \frac{1}{2}(\pi_F - \pi_G) \tag{8}$$

The determinants of π_A and π_D follow from equations (5) and (6). In particular, adding equations (5) and (6) we have:

$$(\pi_F + \pi_G) = (\pi_F^0 + \pi_G^0) + \gamma(y_F + y_G)$$

Subtracting equation (6) from equation (5) we obtain:

$$(\pi_F - \pi_G) = (\pi_F^0 - \pi_G^0) + (\gamma + 2\alpha)(y_F - y_G)$$

Multiplying all variables in each of the above equations by half, we obtain 'average inflation' and 'inflation divergence' as follows:

$$\pi_A = \pi_A^0 + \gamma y_A \tag{9}$$
$$\pi_D = \pi_D^0 + (\gamma + 2\alpha)y_D \tag{10}$$

where π_A^0 denotes average base inflation and π_D^0 measures the initial divergence of inflation rates. Since France is assumed to have higher base inflation than Germany, we have $\pi_D^0 > 0$. Notice that equations (9) and (10) tell us that, given π_A^0 and π_D^0, average inflation and inflation difference depend respectively on average output, y_A, and the divergence of output levels, y_D.

Consider inflation outcomes under a non-EMS Nash regime. Under this regime, policy-makers in France will set money-supply growth so as to maximize their own objective function, ignoring the spillover effect of their policies on Germany. In the context of equations (1) to (10) this means that France maximizes $V_F(.)$ with respect to y_F taking y_G as given, and Germany maximizes $V_G(.)$ with respect to y_G taking y_F as given. Accordingly, the first-order conditions for a maximum are:

$$\frac{\partial V_F}{\partial y_F} = 0 \tag{11a}$$

$$\frac{\partial V_G}{\partial y_G} = 0 \tag{12a}$$

Equations (11a) and (12a) give standard reaction functions (RR_F and RR_G in Figure 5.4) showing how each country will respond to changes in the other country's monetary policy. Indeed, to consider inflation outcomes under this regime, what one needs to know is, on the one hand, whether the reaction curves are downwards-sloping or upwards-sloping in (y_F, y_G) space, and, on the other, the position of each country's bliss point, namely the point where welfare is at its highest possible level.

Starting with the slope of the reaction curves, we know from equations (5) and (6) that, other things being equal, a fall in output in France would lead, through the exchange-rate channel, to a rise in Germany's CPI inflation and that this would have a negative impact on German welfare. To prevent CPI inflation from rising, German policy-makers would then have to reduce the rate of growth of the German money supply. In the context of equations (1) to (10), this would require a fall in German output. Thus, under a non-EMS non-cooperative Nash regime, any given fall in y_F will be accompanied by a fall in y_G. Accordingly, Germany's reaction function will be positively sloping in (y_F, y_G) space. For the same reasons, the reaction function of France will also be positively sloping in (y_F, y_G) space.

As far as the position of the bliss points is concerned, the model of equations (1) to (10) considers disinflation from an initial infla-tionary situation. Since both countries want to reduce CPI inflation and since base inflation in France is higher than in Germany, the French (German) bliss point can be represented in Figure 5.4 by point $B_F(B_G)$. Compared with the initial situation in the two countries repres-ented by point O, point B_F involves no change in French monetary policy, and therefore French output, but a rise in German output. This is the best of all worlds for France. As y_F remains unchanged there are no adverse effects on welfare through the output channel. At the same time as y_G rises, the German balance of payments moves into deficit and this leads to a depreciation of the German mark relative to the French franc which reduces import prices in France and thus enables France to lower its CPI-inflation rate. For the same reasons, point B_G represents Germany's bliss point. Relative to point O, point

Figure 5.4

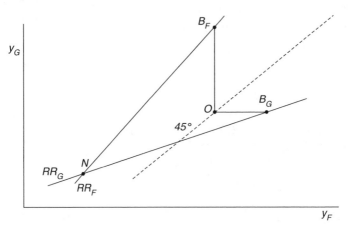

B_G involves no change in German output but a rise in French output. The rise in y_F, through its impact on the balance of payments in France via increased import demand, leads to a depreciation of the French franc relative to the German mark. This reduces CPI inflation in Germany by lowering import prices. Since base inflation is lower in Germany than in France, B_G is closer than B_F to point O: the rise in German output required to enable France to achieve zero CPI inflation is larger than the rise in French output required to enable Germany to achieve zero CPI inflation.

Since the two reaction functions are upward-sloping in (y_F, y_G) space and since they must pass through the relevant bliss points, equilibrium under a non-cooperative, non-EMS regime is at point N in Figure 5.4 where the two reaction curves intersect.

Both y_F and y_G are lower at point N than at point O, the initial equilibrium. This means from equation (9) that average inflation must have fallen. Also, since y_F falls by a larger amount than y_G, it follows from equation (10) that there should be greater convergence of the two national inflation rates at point N. That is, initially Germany had lower CPI inflation than France. Following the adoption by the German and French policy-makers of contractionary non-cooperative monetary policies, output has fallen more in France than in Germany. Accordingly, the gap between the two national inflation rates must have narrowed. Both π_A and π_D therefore fall under this regime.

To confirm that this is indeed the case, note that equations (11a) and (12a) yield:

$$y_F + \phi(\gamma + \alpha)\pi_F = 0 \tag{11b}$$

$$y_G + \phi(\gamma + \alpha)\pi_G = 0 \tag{12b}$$

Combining these we can write:

$$\frac{1}{2}(y_F + y_G) + \frac{1}{2}\phi(\gamma + \alpha)(\pi_G + \pi_F) = 0$$

or equivalently,

$$y_A + \phi(\gamma + \alpha)\pi_A = 0 \tag{13}$$

Subtracting equation (12b) from equation (11b) and multiplying all variables by half, we also have that:

$$\frac{1}{2}(y_F - y_G) + \frac{1}{2}\phi(\gamma + \alpha)(\pi_G - \pi_F) = 0$$

or, equivalently that:

$$y_D + \phi(\gamma + \alpha)\pi_D = 0 \tag{14}$$

Solving equations (13) and (14) for y_A and y_D, and inserting the resulting expressions into the expression for π_A and π_D in equations (9) and (10), we obtain the following equilibrium values for average inflation and inflation divergence under this regime:

$$\pi_A^{NC} = b_1 \pi_A^0 \tag{15}$$

$$\pi_D^{NC} = b_2 \pi_D^0 \tag{16}$$

where

$$b_1 = 1/[1 + \phi\gamma(\gamma + \alpha)], \, b_2 = 1/[1 + \phi(\gamma + \alpha)(\gamma + 2\alpha)]$$

Since b_2 is less than unity, π_D is less than π_D^0. So, even under this non-EMS regime there is greater convergence of inflation rates following the adoption by the two countries of disinflation policies. Also, even without monetary cooperation, there is a large reduction of average inflation: b_1 is less than unity, implying that π_A is less than π_A^0.

Consider next a cooperative EMS with realignments. Under this regime France and Germany set both monetary policy and the FF/DM exchange rate cooperatively to maximize a joint objective function, V, which is the weighted sum of the two national objective functions. Assuming equal weights, we have:

$$V = 1/2\,(V_F + V_G) = -1/2[(y_F^2 + \phi\pi_F^2) + (y_G^2 + \phi\pi_G^2)] \tag{17a}$$

To set monetary policy cooperatively, policy-makers in France and Germany must cooperatively set average output y_A; and to set the FF/DM rate cooperatively they must cooperatively set the output differential $y_D = y_F - y_G$ because, given our discussion of equations (5) and (6), this is what determines the FF/DM rate.

Now from the definitions of π_A and π_D, it follows that inflation in France is simply the sum of average inflation and inflation divergence, while inflation in Germany is average inflation minus inflation divergence:

$$\pi_F = (\pi_A + \pi_D), \quad \pi_G = (\pi_A - \pi_D)$$

We also have for y_F and y_G that:

$$y_F = (y_A + y_D), \quad y_G = (y_A - y_D)$$

Accordingly, we can write equation (17a) as:

$$V = -\{(y_A^2 + y_D^2) + \phi(\pi_A^2 + \pi_D^2)\} \tag{17}$$

Given equations (9) and (10), equation (17) effectively implies that the maximization problem under this regime reduces to choosing average' output and the 'divergence' between output levels. Thus the first-order conditions for a maximum are:

$$\frac{\partial V}{\partial y_A} = \frac{\partial V}{\partial y_D} = 0$$

which lead to equations (18) and (19):

$$y_A + \phi\gamma\pi_A = 0 \tag{18}$$
$$y_D + \phi(\gamma + 2\alpha)\pi_D = 0 \tag{19}$$

Solving (18) and (19) for y_A and y_D and inserting into equations (9) and (10), we arrive at the following expressions for equilibrium average CPI inflation and inflation divergence under this regime:

$$\pi_A^R = c_1\pi_A^0 \tag{20}$$
$$\pi_D^R = c_2\pi_D^0 \tag{21}$$

where

$$c_1 = 1/[1 + \phi\gamma^2], c_2 = 1/[1 + \phi(\gamma + 2\alpha)^2]$$

Equations (20) and (21) say that there is a reduction in average inflation as well as greater convergence of inflation rates: c_1 and c_2 are less than unity, implying that π_A is lower than π_A^0 and π_D is lower than π_D^0.

Finally, consider an EMS regime with leadership. Under this regime Germany sets monetary policy independently so as to maximize its own welfare function while France adjusts its money-supply growth so as to maintain a stable FF/DM exchange rate. In the context of the model of equations (1) to (10), this implies that France simply sets y_F equal to y_G while Germany maximizes V_G with respect to y_G subject only to the constraint that France will set $y_F = y_G$.

Since France sets y_F equal to y_G, it follows from equations (5) and (6) that CPI inflation rates reduce to:

$$\pi_F = \pi_F^0 + \gamma y_F \tag{22}$$

$$\pi_G = \pi_G^0 + \gamma y_G \tag{23}$$

Also, given equation (23) and the fact that Germany maximizes its own welfare with respect to y_G, we have the following first-order condition for a maximum of equation (4):

$$\frac{\partial V_G}{\partial y_G} = (y_G + \phi\gamma\pi_G) = 0 \tag{24}$$

Combining (24) with (23) yields equilibrium inflation in Germany as:

$$\pi_G = \frac{1}{(1+\phi\gamma^2)}\,\pi_G^0 \tag{25}$$

Since France will pursue a policy of setting y_F equal to y_G, from equations (22), (24) and (25) one can obtain equilibrium inflation in France as:

$$\pi_F = \pi_F^0 - \frac{\phi\gamma^2}{(1+\phi\gamma^2)}\,\pi_G^0 \tag{26}$$

From equations (25) and (26) and also (7) and (8) we obtain the following equilibrium values for average CPI inflation and inflation divergence:

$$\pi_A^L = c_1[\pi_A^0 + \phi\gamma^2\pi_D^0] \tag{27}$$

$$\pi_D^L = \pi_D^0 \tag{28}$$

Equations (27) and (28) say that there is no move towards convergence. But average inflation falls relative to its initial level as was also the case in the two other regimes: from (27) and the definition of π_A^0 and π_D^0 we have that

$$\pi_A^L - \pi_A^0 = -\frac{\phi\gamma^2}{(1+\phi\gamma^2)} < 0$$

Comparison across Regimes

Comparing inflation outcomes across regimes we have that:

$$\pi_A^{NC} < \pi_A^{R}, \pi_A^{L} \text{ with } \pi_A^{R} < \pi_A^{L}, \tag{29}$$

which suggests that the impressive reduction in inflation that the EMS countries on average experienced in the 1980s was not the result of the creation of the EMS itself: inflation in Europe would have fallen even more without the European Monetary System.

The explanation for this result is straightforward if one considers equations (1) to (10). Under the Nash non-EMS regime there is no monetary cooperation between the two countries and each has an incentive to manipulate the FF/DM exchange rate through monetary policy so as to reduce its CPI inflation rate via lower import prices. But the exchange rate is a variable common to both countries. Thus, any attempt by either Germany or France to independently manipulate this variable through monetary policy for their own benefit will prove futile. Germany perceives that it can reduce its CPI inflation by appreciating the German mark relative to the French franc through a contractionary monetary policy. But the appreciation of the DM relative to the FF intensifies the inflation problem in France and so induces France to adopt an even more contractionary monetary policy than it would adopt otherwise. This, in turn, leads to an appreciation of the French franc relative to the German mark, which increases Germany's CPI inflation and so induces the monetary authorities there to cut money-supply growth further. Such a process leads to very contractionary monetary policies and therefore a large fall in inflation rates. On the other hand, under the EMS 'leadership regime' the FF/DM exchange rate remains stable, and under the cooperative-EMS regime there is explicit cooperation between the German and the French monetary authorities. Under these two regimes, therefore, Germany and France do not engage in competitive deflation by trying to manipulate the FF/DM exchange rate. Thus, national inflation rates, and therefore average inflation, are higher relative to the non-EMS regime.

Indeed, the conclusion to be drawn from a framework like that of Collins (1988) is that there is nothing special in exchange rate regimes like the EMS which implies that they can lead to better inflation performances than non-cooperative exchange-rate regimes. Also, the model implies that the inflation divergence within Europe would have fallen even in the absence of the EMS, thus suggesting that there is nothing particular about exchange rate regimes like the EMS that can achieve convergence of national inflation rates following a disinflation.

But would welfare levels in Europe have also been higher without the EMS during the disinflation of the 1980s? In the spirit of Collins (1988), this issue is examined using Figures 5.5–5.7. Under the non-EMS Nash regime, shown in Figure 5.5, welfare in France is represented by the indifference curve $I_F I_F$. This indifference curve has an inflexion point at N, indicating that French policy-makers maximize their own objective function taking Germany's monetary policy and thus output y_G, as given. Similarly, welfare in Germany at point N is represented by the indifference curve $I_G I_G$. This indifference curve is tangent to a vertical line that goes through N, indicating that German monetary authorities maximize their own objective function taking monetary policy in France, and thus output y_F, as given. It is evident from the figure that there is room for welfare improvements: the outcome at N is not Pareto-efficient since the indifference curves are not tangent to each other.

Consider now welfare levels under the two EMS regimes. Starting with the leadership-EMS regime shown in Figure 5.6, France will operate along a $45°$ line passing through the the intial equilibrium point O. This line, labelled LL in the figure, reflects the fact that France simply sets y_F equal to y_G in order to stabilize the French franc exchange rate relative to the German mark. On the other hand, Germany will choose y_G so as to maximize its own objective function taking into account the fact that France will operate along the schedule $y_F = y_G$. Thus Germany will choose that point on the $45°$ line passing through O that gives the highest possible German welfare. This is point L: at point L Germany's indifference curve is tangent to the LL line given that Germany explicitly maximizes its welfare only under

Figure 5.5

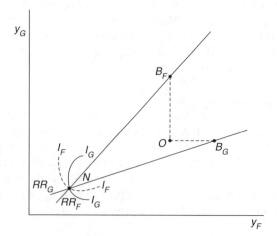

Figure 5.6

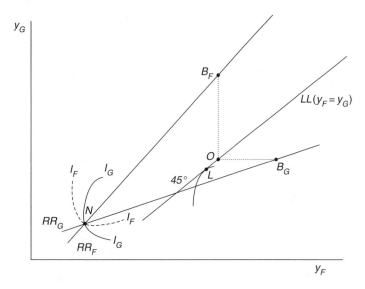

the constraint that France will operate along the line $y_F = y_G$. France's indifference curve (not shown) cannot be tangent to the $45°$ line at this point since policy-makers there do not explicitly maximize an objective function. Nevertheless, point L is closer than point N to both points B_F and point B_G, implying that welfare in both France and Germany is higher under the EMS leadership regime than under the non-EMS, non-cooperative Nash regime.

Welfare outcomes under the cooperative EMS with realignments are shown in Figure 5.7. To establish such outcomes, two points must be taken into account. First, this regime involves explicit co-operation between policy-makers in France and Germany. This means that in equilibrium, Germany's and France's indifference curves must be tangent to each other. Second, in setting monetary policy cooperatively, policy-makers in the two countries will explicitly take into account the fact that inflation is initially higher in France than in Germany. This means that the equilibrium outcome will involve a more contractionary monetary policy in France than in Germany. In terms of Figure 5.7, equilibrium under this regime will occur at a point along the schedule CC. This schedule is flatter than a $45°$ line passing through O, and so it indicates that a one-unit fall in y_F will be followed by less than one-unit fall in y_G. In other words, the CC schedule reflects the condition that monetary policy will be more contractionary in France than in Germany. Given that the equilibrium point must be somewhere along the CC line and given

Figure 5.7

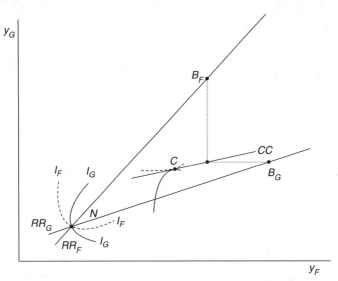

that at this point France's and Germany's indifference curves must be tangent to each other, the equilibrium outcome under this regime can be represented by a point like C. As is evident from the figure, welfare in both countries is higher at C than at N: point C is closer than point N to the bliss points B_F and B_G.

Indeed the conclusion to be drawn from Collins' framework is that although inflation in Europe during the 1980s would have fallen more without the EMS, the associated welfare loss would have been larger in the absence of the European Monetary System.

Credibility and Reputation in the EMS

In the framework analyzed above the possibility that the EMS may have influenced inflation outcomes by altering the private sector's inflationary expectations and/or by changing the credibility of member states' central banks is ignored: it implicitly assumes that expectations about future prices have no impact on the private sector's decisions.

Taking into account expectations leads us to the so-called 'EMS-Credibility Hypothesis'. This hypothesis is based on two propositions. The first has to do with the way the EMS was effectively operating after 1985 and, in particular, Germany's role in the system. The second proposition has to do with monetary policy in Germany and, in particular, the counter-inflation reputation of the Bundesbank during the EMS period. Giavazzi and Pagano (1988), Giavazzi and Giovannini

(1988) and Melitz (1988) were the first to point out that Germany's role within the EMS after 1985 was very similar to the role that the USA was playing under the Bretton Woods system: despite the initial objectives of the EMS, Germany had a leading role in the EMS and the remaining countries were 'tying their hands' on monetary policy. That is, they were simply targeting their exchange rates to the German mark and thus were passively adjusting to Germany's monetary-policy actions.[10]

That Germany was pursuing a largerly independent monetary policy was apparent from data on domestic credit: domestic credit expansion in Germany was endogenous in the sense that it attempted to sterilize the effect of the changes in net official foreign assets that occurred from intervention under the ERM on its total money supply. In particular, money-supply changes can occur either because of changes in domestic credit, DC, or because of changes in the stock of foreign exchange reserves, $FERs$:

$$\Delta M^s = \Delta DC + \Delta FERs$$

Changes in foreign-exchange reserves were occurring in all the EMS countries due to intervention in the foreign exchange markets to stabilize exchange rates. In Germany, however, the Bundesbank was preventing such changes in FERs from affecting the total money stock through offsetting changes in domestic credit. In other words, money supply in Germany was not influenced by the ERM exchange-rate margins. This was not so in the non-German ERM countries which were allowing changes in FERs to influence their total money stock and, moreover, most of them were not even announcing monetary targets.[11] So, in effect, the first component of the EMS-credibility hypothesis is that the European Monetary System operated as a deutschmark zone, with Germany pursuing an independent monetary policy.

The second element in the hypothesis is the counter-inflation reputation of the Bundesbank. A government or a central bank has such a reputation when the public assigns a high probability to the consistent pursuit of low-inflation policies. A counter-inflation reputation can be generated by a record of continuously low inflation. Looking at inflation data since the 1960s, one can see that on average inflation in Germany has been lower than in most of the other European countries, including France, Italy and the UK. And, through this consistently low-inflation performance, the Bundesbank had managed to establish a counter-inflation reputation: the private sector was certain that German monetary authorities would consistently pursue low-inflation policies.

A counter-inflation reputation can help a government a lot in the case of disinflation, given that inflationary pressures can be maintained by self-fulfilling expectations. Indeed, if a government wishes to reduce inflation quickly with low unemployment costs, it is important to stabilize inflation expectations. A simple announcement by the government that it intends to lower inflation may not be enough to achieve this objective: only if it has a reputation for sticking to pre-announced policies and a firm counter-inflation reputation it will be able to convince the private sector for its intention, and thus be able to change inflationary expectations directly, by simply announcing its willingness to reduce inflation. A government with a poor inflation history and/or a poor reputation for commitment to preannounced policies may not be able to persuade the public that inflation will fall by merely announcing its intention to reduce inflation. Such an announcement will not be credible.

How can a government who has low reputation for resisting inflationary pressures and faces credibility problems establish a counter-inflation reputation? For such a government one option is to enter into an institutionalized exchange-rate regime that involves fixing the external value of its currency to that of a low-inflation country. That is, a government who faces credibility problems may be able to acquire credibility by announcing an exchange-rate target relative to a partner country whose own central bank has a firm counter-inflation reputation. Such a policy, provided that it involves external commitment to other countries and so it is credible, will persuade the private sector that domestic inflation will fall to match that of the low-inflation partner country. Accordingly, inflationary expectations will automatically be reduced and thus actual inflation will be lowered quickly and at low costs in terms of unemployment.[12,13]

The EMS-credibility hypothesis follows from this proposition and can be stated as follows: through EMS membership, monetary authorities in inflation-prone European countries 'acquired' the counter-inflation reputation of the Bundesbank. This enabled them to fight inflation and to do so at low costs in terms of unemployment.

The EMS credibility argument has been formalized by several authors, including Krugman (1990). Krugman's model is a two-country version of the Barro–Gordon framework. It is thus based on the proposition that a Phillips-curve relationship between inflation and unemployment exists only when changes in inflation are unanticipated. This means that the actual level of output in each country is equal to its natural-rate level plus a component reflecting unanticipated inflation. Accordingly, consider two countries, called 'Germany' and 'Italy', with Phillips curves given by equations (30) and (31):

$$\text{Germany } y_G = v(\dot{p}_G - \dot{p}_G^e) + y_F^N \tag{30}$$

$$\text{Italy } y_I = v(\dot{p}_I - \dot{p}_I^e) + y_I^N \tag{31}$$

where y_G, y_I and y_G^N, y_I^N are actual levels of output and natural levels of output respectively, and $\dot{p}_G, \dot{p}_I$ and p_G^e, p_I^e are actual and expected inflation rates. Policy-makers in each country have a target level of unemployment, and therefore output, which is higher than the natural-rate level. They also want zero inflation and have objective functions, which they will attempt to maximize, of the form:

$$\textit{Germany} \quad V_G = -(y_G - y_G^T)^2 - \phi\, \dot{p}_G^2 \tag{32}$$
$$y^T > y_N$$

$$\textit{Italy} \quad V_I = -(y_I - y_I^T)^2 - \phi^*\, \dot{p}_I^2 \tag{33}$$
$$y_G^T > y_G^N, y_I^T > y_I^N, \ \phi, \phi^* > 0, \phi > \phi^*$$

where $y_G^T(y_I^T)$ is the target level of output in Germany (Italy) and $\phi(\phi^*)$ measures the German (Italian) policy-makers' aversion to inflation. The German monetary authorities are assumed to be more inflation-averse than the Italian policy-makers and so $\phi > \phi^*$.

Consider inflation outcomes under a flexible exchange-rate regime, that is a non-EMS regime, and under a 'fixed exchange-rate regime with leadership'. Under the non-EMS regime, policy-makers in Germany and Italy will independently choose their own inflation rate through monetary policy, given any expected inflation already incorporated into wage contracts. Thus, German policy-makers will set money-supply growth, and therefore $\dot{p}_G$, so as to maximize V_G treating $\dot{p}_I$ and their domestic private-sector's inflation expectations, p_G^e, as parametric. Accordingly, assuming that $y_G^T = y_I^T = y^T$ and $y_G^N = y_I^N = y^N$ the first-order condition for a maximum of equation (32) is:

$$\frac{\partial V_G}{\partial \dot{p}_G} = \nu(y_G - y^T) + \phi\, \dot{p}_G = 0$$

which using equation (30), leads to equation (34):

$$\dot{p}_G = \left(\frac{1}{\phi + \nu^2}\right)[\nu^2\, p_G^e + \nu(y^T - y^N)] \tag{34}$$

This positive relationship between $\dot{p}_G$ and p_G^e that results from the German policy-makers' actions is represented by the schedule MM_G in Figure 5.8(a), in which $\dot{p}_G = \pi_G$ and $p_G^e = \pi_G^e$. Its slope as well as its intercept with the vertical axis, depends on Germany's inflation

Figure 5.8

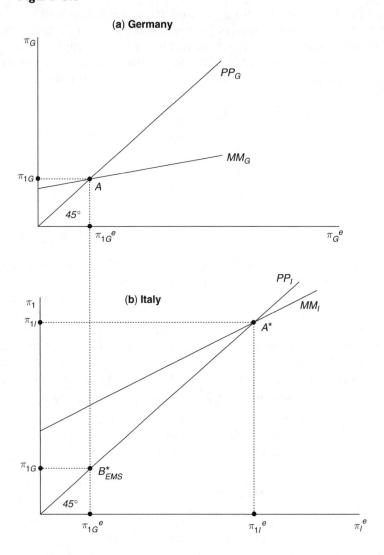

aversion, namely the value of ϕ. Similarly, for Italy the first-order condition for a maximum is:

$$\frac{\partial V_I}{\partial \dot{p}_I} = \nu(y_I - y^T) + \phi^* \dot{p}_I = 0$$

which yields inflation as:

$$\dot{p}_I = \left(\frac{1}{\phi^* + \nu^2}\right) [\nu^2 \dot{p}^e_I + \nu(y^T - y^N)] \qquad \qquad \therefore \qquad (35)$$

Equation (35) is represented in Figure 5.8(b) by the schedule MM_I where $\dot{p}_I = \pi_I$ and $\dot{p}_I^e = \pi_I^e$. As $\phi^* < \phi$, this schedule has a larger slope and intercept than the MM_G schedule.

In forming expectations, the private sector will take into account the policy-makers' behaviour. In particular, the Italian private sector will anticipate that the monetary authorities there will attempt to maximize V_I taking $\dot{p}_I^e$ as given and will form expectations accordingly. The same applies to the private sector in Germany. Accordingly, with rational expectations and no stochastic shocks, at any point in time equations (36a) and (36b) will hold:

$$\dot{p}_G = \dot{p}_G^e \tag{36a}$$

$$\dot{p}_I = \dot{p}_I^e \tag{36b}$$

These two equations describing the behaviour of the private sector in Germany and Italy are represented in Figures 5.8(a) and 5.8(b) by the 45° schedules PP_G and PP_I.

Under a non-EMS regime, equilibrium in Germany would occur at point A where the MM_G and PP_G schedules intersect. Similarly, equilibrium in Italy would occur at point A^*. In both countries output is at its natural-rate level. However, the equilibrium rate of inflation is lower in Germany than in Italy because the private sector there knows that German policy-makers are more inflation-averse than the Italians, that is $\phi^* < \phi$. Since both countries have the same output level but Germany has a lower inflation rate, 'social welfare' is higher in Germany than in Italy.

Now fixing the value of the Italian lira relative to the German mark under the EMS would require Italy to set monetary policy to match Germany's inflation performance. Thus, if Italy were to participate in the EMS and were able to persuade its own private sector that it would achieve Germany's inflation performance, it would be able to obtain the German expected rate of inflation and move its economy to point B^*_{EMS}. That is, the Italian private sector would realize that, because of commitment to the EMS, Italy's inflation rate would have to fall to the German level. Accordingly, it would set $\dot{p}_I^e$ equal to $\dot{p}_G^e$, thus enabling Italy to reach the better German outcome at point B^*_{EMS}. In effect, the EMS credibility hypothesis suggests that EMS membership must have helped the non-German European central banks to reduce inflation rates in the 1980s by 'borrowing' the Bundesbank's reputation for resisting inflationary pressures through fixing exchange rates to the German mark.

The Crisis in the Currency Markets of 1990–92

After a major realignment of the ECU central rates in 1987, three more European currencies entered the exchange-rate mechanism of the EMS: the Spanish peseta (June 1989), the British pound (October 1990) and the Portuguese escudo (April 1990). At the same time, Sweden, Austria and Finland, anticipating entry into the Community, decided to unilaterally link their currencies to the ERM. However the EMS proved unable to survive following the crisis in the currency markets of 1992–93. The unusually high German interest rates following the East–West German unification together with the abolition of capital controls in almost all European countries after 1988 led to the disintegration of the EMS.

Indeed, following the Capital Liberalization Directive of 1988, all 'core' Community countries, namely Germany, France, Italy and Belgium, removed entirely capital controls. Capital controls were also substantially reduced in other EMS countries, including Spain, Portugal and the Irish Republic. Against this background, the West–East German unification was of great importance. Neither the Germans nor the other EMS countries showed willingess to realign central bilateral DM exchange rates within the ERM, namely revalue the German mark relative to all the other curriencies to allow for the increasing strength of the DM in the markets that the East–West German unification implied. At the same time, the unification process led to a massive rise in the German budget deficit and to upward pressures on prices. To cope with the domestic inflationary pressures, the Bundesbank took the decision to raise interest rates. With almost full freedom of capital movements throughout Europe, this led to speculative attacks on all the non-German ERM currencies. Thus, in September 1992, after strong pressure on the Italian lira and the British pound, Italy and the UK withdraw from the ERM. The French franc then came under pressure, requiring massive intervention in the foreign exchange markets by both the French and the German governments to maintain the bilateral ERM exchange-rate margins. At around the same time, the Spanish peseta and the Portuguese escudo also came under pressure and were eventually devalued in November 1992 by 6 per cent. Shortly after the decision to devalue the Spanish peseta and the Portuguese escudo, namely in February 1993, the Irish pound was devalued by 10 per cent. In May 1993 the peseta and the escudo were further devalued by 8 per cent and 6.5 per cent respectively. Pressures on all the ERM currencies continued throughout the following months, forcing the European finance ministers in August 1993 to take the decision to widen the ERM bands to ±15 per cent around central ECU rates. Only the Netherlands guilder maintained the original ±2.25 per cent margin against the German mark.[14]

Despite these developments, even after August 1993 the ±15 per cent ERM band continued to be seen by many Europeans as representing an important 'common' monetary framework. And it provided the background against which negotiations started among the member states for establishing the process for the adoption of the single currency in January 2002.

ERM-II and the New EU Member States

At the Amsterdam Summit of June 1997, the European Council adopted a Resolution on the establishment of a 'new exchange-rate mechanism' in stage three of EMU. This new exchange-rate mechanism, called ERM-II, came into force on 1 January 1999. Its aim was to replace the ERM for those EU member states that remained outside the euro area; that is, to maintain stability between the euro and the non-eurozone EU currencies.

The ERM-II operating procedures were established on 1 September 1998 through an agreement between the ECB and the central banks of the EU states not belonging to the euro area. This agreement was amended on 14 September 2000 to take account of the adoption of the single currency by Greece on 1 January 2001. It was also amended on 29 April 2004 to take account of the EU's enlargement: the central banks of the 10 new member states became signatories of the agreement. This has been necessary because for these countries, although no specific timetable is envisaged, EU membership implies EMU membership (no indefinite opt outs, like in the case of Denmark and the UK, are permitted); and, according to the Maastricht Treaty, EMU membership requires exchange-rate stability of the national currency concerned for at least a two-year period prior to entry.

The ERM-II operates much like the exchange-rate mechanism of the EMS: for each participating currency outside the eurozone there is a central rate *vis-à-vis* the euro; and a standard permissible fluctuation margin is set at 15 per cent above or below that rate. Intervention at the margins is automatic and unlimited, although the ECB and the national central banks of the non-euro area states have the option to suspend it if it creates risks for price stability. Intervention is conducted in euros and in the non-eurozone currencies concerned. For this purpose the ECB and the national central banks of the non-euro area countries have opened for each other a very short-term financing facility similar to the VSTF of the EMS (see European Commission (2004)). Thus finance is initially for three months, but it can be automatically extended once for another three-month period. Like in the EMS, the parties involved in ERM-II may agree to conduct coordinated intra-marginal intervention, or to proceed to coordinated actions to influence interest rates. Each participating non-eurozone EU state has the option to narrow the fluctuation margin for its own currency but this requires the consent of the ECB; and, at the request of any of the parties involved in the ERM-II agreement, realignment of central rates is possible.

Greece participated in ERM-II between 1 January 1999 and 1 January 2001. Denmark has been participating in ERM-II since January 1999 (the Danish krone fluctuates against its euro central rate within the narrower band of ±2.25 per cent). Sweden and the UK have not yet become ERM-II members. As for the 10 new EU member states, Estonia, Lithuania and Slovenia have already joined the ±15 per cent ERM-II band (on 27 June 2004). These three countries manage to achieve low inflation (3.0 per cent, 1.1 per cent and 3.6 per cent respectively in 2004). They also have low government debt as per cent of GDP (4.8 per cent, 21.1 per cent and 30.9 per cent respectively in 2004) as well as small government budget deficits (0.5 per cent surplus in Estonia and 2.6 per cent and 2.3 per cent deficit in Lithuania and Slovenia respectively in 2004). Indeed, Estonia, Lithuania and Slovenia have set themselves to adopt the single currency by January 2007. And for this to be so, ERM-II participation for at least two years prior to EMU entry is necessary.

Accordingly, the real challenge as far as ERM-II membership is concerned, is for the other seven new member states, namely, Slovakia, Hungary, Poland, the Czech Republic, Latvia, Malta and Cyprus. These states have expressed a strong desire for a quick entry into EMU but most of them are far from meeting the Maastricht convergence criteria, especially the inflation criterion (Hungary, Slovakia, Latvia and to a lesser extent Poland) and the deficit criterion (Poland, Hungary, the Czech Republic, Malta and Cyprus).

Several academics and policy-makers take the view that ERM-II membership would be beneficial for these countries. It would offer them a mechanism for stability and flexibility; and it could assist them to achieve a combination of nominal and real convergence (see Backé and Thimann (2004)). Indeed, maintaining stable exchange rates *vis-à-vis* the euro would allow the newcomers to 'acquire' the credibility and counter-inflation reputation of the ECB along the lines suggested in the analysis of the EMS credibility hypothesis. This would help them to reduce inflation quickly; and lower inflation would enable them to achieve lower interest rates, something that could lead to more investment and higher growth. Also, along the lines of Collins' framework discussed earlier, ERM-II entry would expose policymakers in these countries to new strategic interactions with the other EU policy-makers: the 'EMS-realignment' and 'EMS-leadership' framework discussed earlier would be relevant to ERM-II membership for the 10 new EU member states with the ECB in place of the German central bank in the leadership case and the eurozone countries as the other strategic player in the realignment case. ERM-II entry could then enable the new member states to achieve a reduction of inflation with smaller losses in terms of welfare than would be the case under a non-ERM-II Nash regime. Moreover, ERM-II entry could allow their governments to proceed more easily to the necessary budget-deficit cuts, without incurring much political cost.

At the same time, the ±15 per cent-wide ERM-II band offers flexibility; and many argue that, because of this flexibility it might be desirable for the 10 new member states to remain in the ERM-II for quite some time before attempting EMU entry. This follows from the consideration that a steep adjustment path as far as inflation is concerned may not only be harmful for real growth in these countries but also not feasible due to the Balassa-Samuelson (B-S) effect (see, for example, Kenen and Meade (2003) and De Grauwe and Schnabl (2004a,b)). According to the B-S effect, many of the new member states are likely to experience higher inflation than the EU-15 for some years to come. This is because, while many of them have achieved large productivity gains in the traded-goods sectors, productivity gains in the non-traded goods sectors have been small. At the same time because of wage equalization across sectors, wage increases in non-traded goods sectors have followed those in traded-goods sectors. As a result in non-traded goods sectors, where productivity growth has been low, prices have been rising, causing overall inflation in these countries to have a tendency to remain above that of the other EU states. Additional real growth in the new EU member states may also prevent them from being able quickly to reduce inflation further. Under such circumstances the flexibility offered by ERM-II is an advantage: the ±15 per cent-wide ERM-II band would allow for the current price discrepancies between the EU-10 and the EU-15, ensuring at the same time the newcomers' overall commitment to price stability. This flexibility was absent in the EMS from 1985 onwards and in fact led to its disintegration. ERM-II membership would also imply lower risk premia in foreign-exchange markets for the new member states. This would be beneficial for trade and investment, something that could enable higher growth rates (see De Grauwe and Schnabl (2004c)).

Yet some claim that the new member states could face increased instability in ERM-II as large short-term capital movements might follow the liberalization of financial markets in these countries. They are thus in favour of a 'euroization', namely a unilateral (immediate) adoption of the euro by the new member states, rather than a gradual process of convergence and of participation in the ERM-II (see, for example, Begg *et. al.* (2003)). However, euroization is not permissible under the Maastricht Treaty's rules.

Summary and Conclusions

The EMS began to operate in March 1979 and had a number of explicit and implicit objectives including: to stabilize exchange rates; to contribute to the reduction of average inflation in Europe and inflation differentials; and to contribute to output growth and employment growth in member states.

As far as the objective of stabilizing exchange rates is concerned, there is little doubt that countries participating in the ERM had on average during the 1980s and early 1990s more stable exchange rates, in both nominal and real terms, than countries outside the system. On the other hand, the EMS did not seem to have contributed much to economic growth and employment growth: the period 1980-90 was characterized by slower real GDP growth in Europe and poor employment performance. It could be argued, however, that the growth and employment performance of the European economies in the EMS years had been influenced by adverse supply-side shocks and/or unfavourable structural factors in Europe's labour markets, something that would in any case produce unsatisfactory results regarding real growth and employment, even in the absence of the EMS.

As far as the objective of reducing average European inflation and inflation divergence is concerned, the inflation reduction in the ERM countries between 1980 and 1990 was substantial on average and particularly impressive in the case of the high-inflation member states. However, the issue is to what extent this performance was due to the EMS itself because, during the same period, lower inflation rates and a reduction in the standard deviation of inflation rates also characterized all industrial OECD countries.

In principle, there are two channels through which monetary regimes like the EMS could have affected inflation outcomes in participating states. The first is by changing the nature of interactions among national policy-makers. As far as this channel is concerned, the game-theoretic literature seems to conclude that inflation in Europe in the 1980s could have fallen even more and convergence could have been greater without the EMS, but the associated welfare loss would have been larger in the absence of the European Monetary System. On the other hand, the EMS might have affected inflation outcomes in Europe by influencing the private sectors' expectations about future price levels and strengthening the credibility of the member states' central banks. This is the so-called EMS credibility hypothesis, based on the dominant role of the deutschmark in the EMS after 1985, and can be stated as follows: through EMS membership, monetary authorities in high-inflation European countries acquired the counter-inflation reputation of the Bundesbank. This enabled them to reduce inflation and to do so at low costs in terms of unemployment.

The European Monetary System operated smoothly throughout the 1980s, despite a large number of realignments of the ECU central rates, but it proved unable to cope with the crisis in the currency markets of 1992-93. The East–West German re-unification (which led to unusually high German interest rates), and the unwillingess of the EMS countries to proceed to a revaluation of the DM within the ERM to allow for the strength of the German mark in the markets following the re-unification led to the disintegration of the EMS: in August 1993, the ERM bands were extended to ±15 per cent around central rates, making the European Monetary System a looser monetary scheme. However, for many, the wide ERM bands remained, even after 1993, an important common monetary framework; and, they constituted the basis for establishing the process towards EMU and the adoption of a single currency in January 2002.

The EMS experience is of relevance to the new EU-10 states. Indeed, Estonia, Latvia and Lithuania have already joined the new exchange-rate mechanism, the ERM-II, which has replaced the EMS for EU member countries that remain outside the eurozone. The ERM-II operates much like the ERM: there is a standard fluctuation margin of ±15 per cent around central euro exchange rates, with intervention at the margins being automatic and unlimited. Some claim that the ERM-II offers flexibility together with stability and, from this point of view, it would be beneficial for the newcomers to join it and remain in it for quite some time. Others, however, argue that ERM-II membership could be risky as large short-term financial-capital flows might follow the liberalization of capital markets in the new member states. They propose instead an immediate (unilateral) adoption by these countries of the euro, rather than a process of becoming ERM-II members and attempting convergence before applying for EMU entry. Yet this is not possible under the Maastricht Treaty's provisions: all non-eurozone countries must participate in ERM-II for at least two years before applying for EMU membership.

Notes

1 See European Commission. (1970) and Hitiris and Zervoyianni (1983).
2 See for example Ludlow (1982) and Vanthoor (1999) for a discussion of these issues.
3 For a discussion of the institutional features of the EMS in the original agreement, see for example Van Ypersele (1985), Fratianni and Peeters (1978) and Bladen-Hovell (1994).

4 Italy adopted the ±2.25 per cent band in January 1990.
5 Realignments of the central ECU rates were very frequent from the time of the creation of the EMS until the mid-1980s. After 1985 they became less frequent. See Vanthoor (1999).
6 See European Commission (1979).
7 See Van Ypersele (1979), Artis (1986) and Cohen and Wyplosz (1999).
8 Analyses of the achievements of the EMS can be found in Ungerer *et al.* (1986), Gros and Thygesen (1988), Artis (1986), Fratianni (1988, 1992), Fratianni and von Hagen (1990b), Weber (1991), Eichengreen and Wyplosz (1993) and Bladen-Hovell (1994).
9 See for example Diebold and Pauly (1988), Artis and Taylor (1994), Nieuwland *et al.* (1994), Engel and Hakkio (1996), Sarno (1997) and Frömmel and Menkhoff (2001).
10 See for example Giavazzi and Giovannini (1988, 1989), Mastropasqua *et al.* (1988), Weber (1991), Artis and Nachane (1990), Karfakis and Moschos (1990) and Rubio *et al.* (2001) for evidence that the EMS had worked in an asymmetric way. See, however, Fratianni and von Hagen (1990a) and De Grauwe (1991) for some different conclusions.
11 See for example von Hagen and Fratianni (1990) and Cohen and Wyplosz (1991) for evidence of the hypothesis that German monetary policy was operating quite independently during the 1980s.
12 See Giavazzi and Pagano (1988), Melitz (1988), Currie *et al.* (1992) and Bladen-Hovell (1994).
13 However, the findings of, for example, Svensson (1993) raise doubts as to whether the ERM has had a significant impact on inflationary expectations. The results of Bleany and Mizen (1997) also provide rather mixed evidence (the hypothesis holds only for the core EMS countries), while the findings of Sumner (2000) point against the hypothesis that the Bundesbank's reputation was a tradable good among the ERM countries.
14 See for example Cobham (1996) for a discussion of the factors cited in the literature as explanations of the EMS crisis in 1992–93. See also Thygesen (1993), Padoa-Schioppa (1988) and Eichengreen (2001).

References

Artis, M. (1986) 'The European Monetary System: An Evaluation', *Journal of Policy Modelling*, vol. 9, pp. 175–98.
Artis, M. and Nachane, D. (1990) 'Wages and Prices in Europe: A Test of the German Leadership Hypothesis', *Weltwirtschaftliches Archiv*, vol. 126, pp. 59–77.
Artis, M. and Taylor, M.P. (1994) 'The Stabilising Effect of the ERM on Exchange Rates and Interest Rates: Some Non-parametric Tests', *IMF Staff Papers*, vol. 41, pp. 123–48.
Backé, P. and Thimann, C. (2004) 'The Acceding Countries' Strategies Towards ERM-II and the Adoption of the Euro: An Analytical Review', ECB Occasional Paper No. 10, European Central Bank, Frankfurt am Main.

Barro, R. and Gordon, D. (1983) 'Rules, Discretion and Reputation in a Model of Monetary Policy', *Journal of Monetary Economics*, vol. 12, pp. 589–610.

Begg, D., Eichengreen, B., Halpern, L., von Hagen, J. and Wyplosz, C. (2003) *Sustainable Regimes of Capital Movements in Accession Countries*, CEPR Policy Paper No. 10, Centre for Economic Policy Research, London.

Bladen-Hovell, R. (1994) 'The European Monetary System', in M. Artis and N. Lee (eds), *The Economics of the European Union: Policy and Analysis*, (Oxford: Oxford University Press).

Bleany, M. and Mizen, P. (1997) 'Credibility and Disinflation in the European Monetary System', *Economic Journal*, vol. 107, pp. 1751–67.

Calmfors, L. and Driffill, J. (1988) 'Bargaining Structure, Corporatism and Macroeconomic Performance', *Economic Policy*, vol. 6, pp. 13–61.

Cobham, D. (1996) 'Causes and Effects of the European Monetary Crises of 1991–1993', *Journal of Common Market Studies*, vol. 14, pp. 585–605.

Cohen, D. and Wyplosz, C. (1991) 'The European Monetary Union: An Agnostic Evaluation', in R. Bryant *et al.* (eds), *Macroeconomic Policies in an Interdependent World* (Washington DC: International Monetary Fund).

Collins, S. (1988) 'Inflation and the European Monetary System', in F. Giavazzi *et al.* (eds), *The European Monetary System* (Cambridge: Cambridge University Press).

Currie,D., Levine, P. and Pearlman J. (1992) 'European Monetary Union or Hard EMS?', *European Economic Review*, vol. 36, pp. 1185–204.

De Grauwe, P. (1990) 'The Cost of Disinflation and the European Monetary System', *Open Economies Review*, vol. 1, pp. 147–73.

De Grauwe, P. (1991) 'Is the EMS a DM-Zone?', in A. Steinherr and W. Weiserbs (eds), *Evolution of the International and Regional Monetary Systems* (London: Macmillan – Palgrave).

De Grauwe, P. (1994) 'Towards EMU without the EMS', *Economic Policy* vol. 17, pp. 147–85.

De Grauwe, P. and Schnabl, G. (2004a) 'Nominal Versus Real Convergence to EMU Accession – EMU Entry Scenarios for the New Member States', University of Leuven Working Paper, July.

De Grauwe, P. and Schnabl, G. (2004b) 'EMU Strategies for the New Member States', *Intereconomics*, vol. 39, pp. 241–47.

De Grauwe, P. and Schnabl, G. (2004c) 'Exchange-Rate Regimes and Macroeconomic Stability in Central and Eastern Europe', CESifo Working Paper No. 1182, April.

Diebold, F.X. and Pauly, P. (1988) 'Has the EMS Reduced Member- Countries' Exchange-Rate Volatility?', *Empirical Economics*, vol. 13, pp. 81–102.

Eichengreen, B. (2001) 'The EMS Crisis in Retrospect', CEPR Discussion Paper no. 2704, Centre for Economic Policy Research, London.

Eichengreen, B. and Wyplosz, C. (1993) 'The Unstable EMS', *Brookings Papers on Economic Activity*, vol. 1, pp. 51–143.

Engel, C. and Hakkio, C.S. (1996) 'The Distribution of Exchange Rates in the EMS', *International Journal of Finance and Economics*, vol. 1, pp. 55–67.

European Commission (1970) 'Report to the Council and the Commission on the Realisation by Stages of Economic and Monetary Union in the Community', Bulletin of the European Communities, *Supplement no. 11* (The Werner Report) Brussels.

European Commission (1979) 'The European Monetary System', *European Economy*, no. 3, July.

European Commission (2004) 'New Exchange Rate Mechanism (ERM-II)', http://europa.eu.int/scadplus/leg/en/lvb/125047.htm

Fratianni, M. (1988) 'The European Monetary System: How Well Has It Worked?', *Cato Journal*, vol. 8, pp. 477–501.

Fratianni, M. (1992) *The European Monetary System and European Monetary Union* (Boulder, Col.: Westview Press).

Fratianni, M. and von Hagen, J. (1990a) 'German Dominance in the EMS: The Empirical Evidence', *Open Economies Review*, vol. 1, pp. 67–97.

Fratianni, M. and von Hagen, J. (1990b) 'The European Monetary System Ten Years After', *Carnegie-Rochester Series on Public Policy*, vol. 32, pp. 173–242.

Fratianni, M. and Peeters, T. (eds) (1978) *One Money for Europe* (London: Macmillan – Palgrave).

Frömmel, M. and Menkhoff, L. (2001) 'Risk Reduction in the EMS? Evidence From Trends in Exchange-Rate Properties', *Journal of Common Market Studies*, vol. 39, pp. 285–306.

Giavazzi, F. and Giovannini, A. (1987) 'Models of the EMS: Is Europe a Greater Deutschmark Area?' in R. Bryant and R. Porters (eds), *Global Macroeconomics: Policy, Conflicts, Cooperation* (London: Macmillan – Palgrave).

Giavazzi, F. and Giovannini, A. (1988) 'The Advantages of Tying One's Hands: Discipline and Central Bank Credibility', *European Economic Review*, vol. 32, pp. 1055–82.

Giavazzi, F. and Giovannini, A. (1989) *Limiting Exchange Rate Flexibility: The European Monetary System* (Cambridge, Mass.: MIT Press).

Giavazzi, F. and Pagano, M. (1988) 'The Advantages of Tying One's Hands: Discipline and Central Bank Credibility', *European Economic Review*, vol. 32, pp. 1055–82.

Gros, D. and Thygesen, N. (1988) 'The EMS: Achievements, Current Issues and Directions for the Future', CEPS Paper no. 35, Centre for European Policy Studies, Brussels.

Hitiris, T. and Zervoyianni, A. (1983) 'The European Monetary System', in J. Lodge (ed), *Institutions and Policies of the European Community* (London: Francis Pinter).

Karfakis, C. and Moschos, D. (1990) 'Interest Rate Linkages within the European Monetary System: A Time Series Analysis', *Journal of Money, Credit and Banking*, vol. 22, pp. 388–94.

Kenen, P. and Meade, E. (2003) 'EU Accession and the Euro: Together or Far Apart?' *International Economics Policy Briefs*, Number PB03–9, Institute for International Economics, Washington, DC.

Krugman, P. (1990) 'Policy Problems of a Monetary Union', in P. De Grauwe and L. Papademos (eds), *The European Monetary System in the 1990s* (London: Longman).

Ludlow, P. (1982) *The Making of the European Monetary System* (London: Butterworths).

Mastropasqua, C., Micossi, S. and Rinaldi, R. (1988) 'Interventions, Sterilisation and Monetary Policy in the EMS Countries, 1979–87', in F. Giavazzi *et al.* (eds), *The European Monetary System* (Cambridge: Cambridge University Press).

Melitz, J. (1988) 'Monetary Discipline and Cooperation in the European Monetary System: A Synthesis', in F. Giavazzi *et al.* (eds), *The European Monetary System* (Cambridge: Cambridge University Press).

Nieuwland, F., Verschoor, W. and Wolff, C. (1994) 'Stochastic Trends and Jumps in EMS Exchange Rates', *Journal of International Money and Finance*, vol. 13, pp. 699–727.

Padoa-Schioppa., T. (1988) 'The European Monetary System: A Long-term View', in F. Giavazzi *et al.* (eds), *The European Monetary System* (Oxford: Oxford University Press).

Rubio, O.B., Rivero, S.S. and Rodriguez, F.F. (2001) 'Asymmetry in the EMS: New Evidence Based on Non-Linear Forecasts', *European Economic Review*, vol. 45, pp. 451–73.

Sarno, L. (1997) 'Exchange Rate and Interest-Rate Volatility in the European Monetary System: Further Results', *Applied Financial Economics*, vol. 7, pp. 255–63.

Sumner, M. (2000) 'Incredibility and Inflation in the EMS', *Economic Journal*, vol. 110, pp. 662–3.

Svensson, L. (1993) 'Assessing Target Zone Credibility, Mean Revision and Devaluation Expectations in the ERM, 1979–1992, *European Economic Review*, vol. 37, pp. 763–802.

Thygesen, N. (1993) 'Towards Monetary Union in Europe: Reforms of the EMS in the Perspective of Monetary Union', *Journal of Common market Studies*, vol. 31, pp. 447–72.

Ungerer, H., Evans O., Mayer, T. and Nyberg, P. (1983) 'The EMS: The Experience 1979-1982', Occasional Paper no. 19, International Monetary Fund, Washington DC.

Ungerer, H., Evans, O., Mayer, T. and Young, P. (1986) 'The European Monetary System: Recent Developments', Occasional Paper no. 48, International Monetary Fund, Washington, DC.

Vanthoor, W.V. (1999) *A Chronological History of the European Union*, 1946–1998 (London: Edward Elgar).

Van Ypersele, J. (1979) 'Operating Principles and Procedures of the EMS', in F. Trezise (ed), *The EMS: Its Promise and Prospects* (Washington DC: Brookings).

Van Ypersele, J. (1985) *The European Monetary System* (Cambridge: Woodhead).

Von Hagen, J. and Fratianni, M. (1990) 'German Dominance in the EMS: Evidence from Interest Rates', *Journal of International Money and Finance*, vol. 9, pp. 358–75.

Weber, A. (1991) 'Reputation and Credibility in the European Monetary System', *Economic Policy*, vol. 12, pp. 58–102.

6 EMU: Benefits, Costs and Real Convergence

Athina Zervoyianni

Introduction

The development that led the Heads of State of Community countries to consider seriously the possibility of creating a monetary union was the signing of the Single European Act (SEA) in 1986. Among the SEA's objectives was the establishment of an integrated European financial market. This effectively required permanently fixed exchange rates; and permanently fixed exchange rates required monetary union. Thus in June 1988 the European Council mandated a committee, headed by the President of the Commission Jacques Delors, to evaluate the monetary situation in member states and prepare a report on how the Community should proceed to Economic and Monetary Union (EMU). The report was completed in April 1989 and proposed a single process, set out in three stages. The first stage was to involve:[1]

- greater cooperation between national central banks aiming at improvement of economic convergence
- complete freedom of capital transactions
- removal of all impediments to the private use of the ECU
- inclusion of all community currencies in the ERM
- completion of the internal market and a doubling of structural funds

The first stage of the Delors Plan was accepted by the European Council at the Madrid Summit of June 1989 and started on 1 July 1990. The other two stages required a new treaty to establish the basic institutions and structure of the economic and monetary union. According to the Delors proposals for EMU, during this second stage:

- the progress of the first stage in the areas of monetary cooperation, economic convergence and internal market would be reinforced
- exchange-rate realignments within the EMS would be made only in exceptional circumstances
- rules for the size and financing of national budget deficits would be formulated

Finally, in stage three:

- intra-European exchange rates would be irrevocably fixed and eventually national currencies would be replaced by a single community currency
- a European System of Central Banks would be set up and would be responsible for determining the value of the single community currency *vis-à-vis* the dollar and yen
- national public-sector deficits would not be allowed to be financed by printing money
- the Council of Ministers, in cooperation with the European Parliament, would have the right to propose adjustments to the budgets of national governments when they deemed to threaten monetary stability

The second and third stages of EMU were debated at a number of inter-governmental conferences but were finalized at the December 1991 Summit, which produced the Treaty on Economic and Monetary Union, signed in Maastricht on 7 February 1992. The EMU Treaty was based on five implicit principles:[2]

- that greater monetary cooperation among the EC countries was desirable
- that there were benefits to be derived from moving from the EMS to full monetary union
- that a stable EMU required rules restricting the use of national fiscal policies
- that the process of establishing EMU should be gradual and not all European states needed to join at the same speed
- that EMU would help member states achieve real convergence

The adoption of a single currency became formally an objective to be achieved by January 1999. The UK, Denmark and Sweden were allowed to adopt the single currency whenever they wished.

Evaluation of the EMU Treaty requires evaluation of the principles upon which it is based. Indeed, there are four issues to consider. First, what are the advantages of moving towards full monetary union in Europe? Second, what are the benefits and costs of an EMU relative to the previous monetary framework in Europe, namely, the EMS? Third, what are the benefits and costs of a gradual transition to EMU relative to other more radical strategies for achieving monetary integration? And, fourth, to what extent has EMU promoted real convergence? These issues are examined in what follows. The next section considers the advantages of moving towards full monetary union in Europe, and examines the benefits and costs of EMU relative to the EMS. We then move on to focus on the EMU Treaty's provisions, before examining the alternative strategies for achieving full monetary union. The issue of real versus nominal convergence in Europe is then considered, and the final section contains a summary and concluding comments.

EMU or Monetary Regimes like the EMS? Benefits and Costs

Advantages of Adopting a Single Currency

One of the advantages of moving towards full monetary union and the adoption of a single currency in Europe is related to international macroeconomic interdependence. As the game-theoretic approach to monetary integration suggests, when countries are economically interdependent, monetary-policy actions taken by individual governments in an uncoordinated manner can lead to inefficient macroeconomic outcomes.[3] Only by cooperation can the externalities resulting from international interdependence be internalized and the most efficient outcome reached. This point is particularly relevant for the European economies: the inefficiencies resulting from the absence of cooperation are greater the more integrated countries are, given that integration increases the degree of international interdependence. Within Europe, trade and financial linkages among national economies are strong, implying that more monetary cooperation should in principle be welfare-improving.

Other advantages[4] of moving towards irrevocably fixed exchange rates, and thus full monetary union in Europe, include:

- elimination of exchange-rate risk and uncertainty within the EMU area and no speculative attacks on national currencies
- no transaction costs
- price comparisons will be made easier
- saving on, and more efficient use of, foreign exchange reserves
- liquidity gains
- evolution of the euro as a competitor to the dollar and yen

The elimination of exchange-rate risk and the associated drop in uncertainty within the euro area will enable European firms to decide more efficiently on the location of their plants; and it may also induce them to undertake more investments, something that will increase growth rates and employment levels (see Molle and Morsink (1991a,b), Gros (1996b) and Belke and Gros (1998)). Moreover, elimination of exchange-rate fluctuations can have beneficial effects on trade volumes (see, for example, De Grauwe and Skudelny (2000)). At the same time, as estimated by the European Commission (see European

Commission (1990)), total savings following the adoption of the currency from the reduction of non-bank transaction costs can be between 0.2 and 0.5 per cent of EU's total GDP. This percentage becomes larger, about 1 per cent, if one adds other types of trans-actions, such as inter-bank transactions and company internal costs, including personnel and equipment costs (see European Commission (1996) and Collignon (1997)). In addition, the adoption of the single currency will facilitate price comparisons across member states, something that will enhance competition among firms and will thus lead to price reductions. Welfare gains may also result from the more efficient use of the member states' pooled foreign-exchange reserves, since reserves will no longer be required for supporting exchange-rate margins inside the euro area (see Artis (1994)); and liquidity gains for individual member states may arise from access to an enlarged EU financial market. Political gains may further be derived: the development of the euro as competitor to the dollar and yen will strengthen the bargaining power of Europeans in negotiations regarding the global management of exchange rates; and it may also strengthen their negotiating power in other fields as well, such as international trade, international migration and environmental protection.

Benefits and Costs of EMU Relative to the EMS

In examining the benefits and costs of the move from the EMS to an EMU, it is worth taking into account the difference between these two regimes. The EMS was an asymmetric system of monetary control: after 1985 it operated mainly as a DM-zone, in the sense that Germany was effectively setting monetary policy for Europe as a whole while all the other ERM countries were simply adjusting their monetary policy to that of Germany in order to stabilize the exchange rate of their currencies relative to the German mark. The EMU is a symmetric system of monetary control, in which participants have equal powers and responsibilities. Moving from an asymmetric system of monetary control like the EMS to a symmetric one like an EMU may involve both benefits and costs.[5]

Benefits. One of the benefits of moving from the EMS to an EMU lies in the fact that asymmetric systems of monetary control cannot efficiently deal with shocks that do not affect all countries simultan-eously. De Grauwe (1994) and Wyplosz (1997) were among the first to note that the problem with asymmetric exchange-rate regimes in such circumstances is that the 'centre country', which in the case of the EMS was Germany, by stabilizing its own money stock without paying attention to macroeconomic outcomes in the other member

Figure 6.1

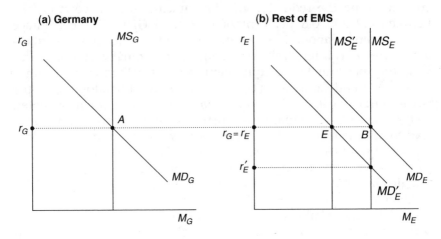

(a) Germany

(b) Rest of EMS

countries, can induce inefficient monetary–policy responses in these other countries.

This point is illustrated in Figure 6.1 along the lines suggested by De Grauwe (1994, 2003a). Figure 6.1(a) describes the money market in Germany. The vertical axis measures the level of German interest rates and the horizontal axis measures (real) money balances. The MS_G schedule represents the money-supply function. The downward sloping MD_G schedule represents German money demand: its position is determined by the level of output (an increase (fall) in German output shifts it to the right (left)). For a given level of output, equilibrium in Germany's money market is achieved at point A. As Germany was pursuing an independent monetary policy under the EMS, its money stock, and therefore the position of the MS_G schedule, was not influenced by the ERM exchange-rate margins: Germany prevented changes in foreign exchange reserves (caused by intervention in the foreign exchange markets to maintain the ERM margins) from affecting its money stock through offsetting changes in domestic credit.

Figure 6.1(b) describes the money market in the rest of the EMS countries. The MD_E schedule represents money demand for a given level of output, and the MS_E schedule represents money supply. Under the EMS, the non-German European countries were fixing their exchange rates relative to the German mark and did not sterilize the impact of interventions in foreign exchange markets on their money stock. Thus, their money supply was endogenous, and this meant that shocks affecting their economies eventually led to shifts in the MS_E schedule. With perfect capital mobility, to preserve equilibrium in the money and assets markets, fixed exchange rates within the

EMS required equality between interest rates in Germany and i rates in the rest of Europe. Accordingly, the equilibrium point in the non-German EMS countries is represented by point B.

Consider, for example, an exogenous (temporary) drop in investment demand in all the EMS countries except Germany. Such an asymmetric shock would lower aggregate demand and output in the non-German EMS economies, shifting their money-demand schedule to the left. With the MD_E schedule shifting to the left, for example to MD'_E, the rate of interest in these countries would temporarily drop below the German interest rate, to r'_E. This, however, would cause disequilibrium in the foreign exchange markets: as r_E would fall relative to r_G, assets denominated in DMs would become more attractive relative to assets denominated in the other EMS currencies. As a result, the demand for DMs (other European currencies) would rise (fall), tending to cause a depreciation of the non-German EMS currencies relative to the deutschmark.

To prevent the depreciation from occurring, the non-German EMS central banks would sell marks to their private sectors in exchange for their own national currencies. This would have the effect of reducing money supply in these countries, thus shifting the MS_E schedule to the left. On the other hand, the position of the MS_G schedule would remain unchanged: the impact of foreign-exchange market interventions on Germany's money supply would be sterilized. With no change in Germany's money supply, interest rates there would also remain unchanged. Accordingly, under the EMS, equilibrium in the non-German European states would be achieved at point E, with the new money supply schedule MS'_E.

The point to be noted is that under the European Monetary System, an adverse aggregate demand shock originating in the non-German EMS Countries was followed by a reduction in their money supplies: instead of expanding their money supply to offset the impact of the shock on their output, the non-German EMS countries were contracting their money supplies, with the result that the impact of the shock on their economies was intensified. More generally, Figure 6.1 suggests that following unanticipated shocks originating in their own economies, the non-German EMS countries were forced to adopt inappropriate monetary policies. During recessionary periods (booms) in some European countries, money supply in the whole of Europe was contracting (expanding).

It could be argued that macroeconomic outcomes would have been more efficient in an EMU. For example, in the case of Figure 6.1, the central monetary authority would recognize the need for a fall in interest rates to help the non-German countries cope with the recession, and would thus proceed to an increase in the money supply.

Indeed, in a number of occasions, the ECB's governing board has stated that the European Central Bank will rely on euro-wide aggregate data and that interest rates will respond to average macroeconomic developments in the euro-zone.[6] Thus a popular argument in the early 1990s was that the non-German European states were eager to enter EMU precisely because its symmetry would help them recover part of the monetary autonomy that they seemed to have lost in the EMS.[7]

Costs. At the same time, as early as in 1991, the proposition was put forward that without securing the full independence of a European Central Bank, the move from the EMS to an EMU would imply costs (see Currie (1992) and Currie *et al.* (1992,1996)). This argument was based on the principle that the leading central bank in Europe under the EMS, the Bundesbank, had a reputation for being inflation-conscious. It also had a reputation for precommitment: when it was announcing that it would adopt certain policies or follow a specific money-supply rule, this was fully believed by the private sector.

The role of the Bundesbank in the EMS was to be played in an EMU by the European Central Bank (ECB) in whose board the governors of all the national central banks would participate. As a result, fears were expressed at the time of signing the Maastricht Treaty that, because some of the member states' CBs did not have the counter-inflation reputation and credibility of the Bundesbank, the ECB would cause an 'inflationary bias': average inflation in Europe would be higher in an EMU than under the EMS.

This point can be illustrated along the lines suggested by Krugman (1990) using a Barro–Gordon type of framework. In Figures 6.2(a) and 6.2(b), two countries are assumed, 'Germany' and 'REU' (the rest of Europe). The $PP_G (PP_{REU})$ schedule is a 45° line, describing the behaviour of the private sector in Germany (rest of Europe). When private economic agents form expectations rationally and there are no stochastic shocks, expected inflation in Germany (REU), $\pi_G^e (\pi_{REU}^e)$, and actual inflation, $\pi_G (\pi_{REU})$, will be equal. The MM_G and MM_{REU} schedules represent the policy-makers' behaviour showing how the German and the REU policy-makers will set monetary policy, and thus actual inflation, to maximize their objective functions given the private sector's expectations about inflation. Increases in expected (current) inflation will increase (lower) unemployment through the Phillips curve. Along the lines of the Barro–Gordon framework, policy-makers will seek to maintain unemployment below its natural-rate level and will thus respond to any increase in expected inflation by adopting an expansionary monetary policy that raises actual inflation. However, because policy-makers are also concerned about inflation, a one-unit increase in $\pi_G^e (\pi_{REU}^e)$ will be accompanied by less-than-one

Figure 6.2

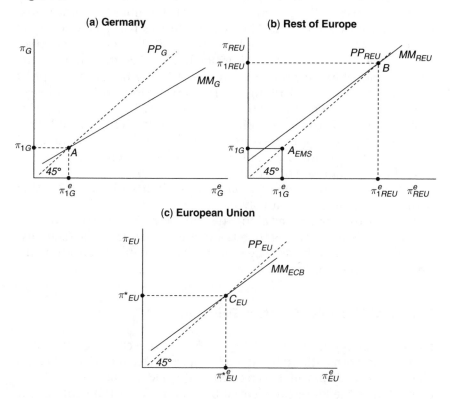

(a) Germany

(b) Rest of Europe

(c) European Union

unit increase in $\pi_G(\pi_{REU})$. Thus the MM_G and MM_{REU} schedules are upward-sloping in (π, π^e) space, but their slope is less than unity. Also the MM_G schedule is less steep than the MM_{REU} schedule, implying that German policy-makers are more inflation-averse than REU policy-makers: an increase in expected inflation that reduces employment below its natural level will be followed by a smaller increase in the money supply (and thus actual inflation) in Germany than in the rest of the EU.

Under a floating exchange-rate regime, equilibrium is attained at the point where the MM and PP schedules in each country intersect. Germany reaches equilibrium at A, while REU attains equilibrium at B. On the other hand, under the EMS, the REU monetary authorities are able to adopt the counter-inflation reputation of the Bundesbank. Thus $\pi^e_{1REU} = \pi^e_{1G}$ and REU achieves equilibrium at point A_{EMS}. The average inflation performance of Germany and REU is better under the EMS regime than under floating exchange rates, but unemployment is the same under both regimes.

Now suppose that Germany and REU have established a monetary union and that in the governing board of the union's central bank, the ECB, both German and REU representatives participate on equal terms. The ECB's concern about inflation will then be stronger than that of the REU monetary authorities but weaker than that of the German monetary authorities. In terms of Figure 6.2(c), the slope of the schedule MM_{ECB} describing the ECB's behaviour, will lie between the slopes of the German and the REU schedules. Accordingly, equilibrium in an EMU will be at point C_{EU}. For both Germany and REU, the outcome at C_{EU} is less attractive than the corresponding at A_{EMS}: relative to point A_{EMS}, point C_{EU} involves no change in output levels but a higher rate of inflation.

The argument that seems to follow logically from Figure 6.2 is that if the EMU were not to involve costs relative to the EMS, the ECB would have to be organized along the lines of the Bundesbank, with its statutes explicitly declaring that its aim was to maintain price stability. The ECB would also have to be independent of national governments and of political interference.

The EMU Treaty's Monetary Provisions

Monetary policy is discussed in the first two sections of the EMU Treaty. The Treaty stipulates that a European System of Central Banks (ESCB) and a ECB will be created in the EMU. The ESCB will be composed of the European Central Bank and the central banks of the member states. The basic tasks to be carried out by the ESCB will be:

- to define the monetary policy of the European Union
- to supervise commercial banks and other financial institutions operating within Europe and contribute to the smooth functioning of the financial system
- to hold and manage the member states' foreign-exchange reserves
- to conduct foreign exchange operations *vis-à-vis* non-European currencies

As far as the ECB is concerned, its decision-making bodies are an executive board and a governing board. The executive board consists of bankers appointed by the common accord of member states; the governing board consists of the executive board and the governors of the national central banks. The Treaty stipulates that the governing board of the ECB will formulate the monetary policy of the European Union, including decisions relating to intermediate monetary objectives and key interest rates. The executive board will implement monetary policy.

The Treaty also states that in exercising its powers the ECB will take no instructions from government in member states or from other community institution. It further stipulates that the primary objective of the ECB, and of the ESCB, will be to maintain price stability. At the same time, without prejudice to the price stability objective, the ECB will support the general economic policies of the Community.[8] The Treaty is not, however, explicit as to what these other objectives of the ECB will be. It is also not very explicit as regards the second task to be carried out by the ECB, namely its obligation to supervise credit institutions and the financial system.

As far as the EU's exchange-rate policy *vis-à-vis* the rest of the world is concerned, the Maastricht Treaty stipulates that it will be decided by the Council of Ministers of Finance. This creates an inconsistency between the provisions regarding exchange-rate policy in the EMU and those concerning monetary policy[9]. In particular, according to the provisions regarding monetary policy, the ECB will have the sole responsibility for deciding and implementing monetary policy in the EMU. On the other hand, according to the provisions regarding exchange-rate policy, the responsibility for adopting a particular policy for euro/dollar and euro/yen exchange-rates is given to national governments, since the Council of Ministers consists of representatives of national governments. The Treaty thus seems to have neglected that monetary and exchange-rate policy are inter-related under free capital mobility and so the Council's decisions about Europe's exchange-rate policy, in principle, could conflict with the ECB's decisions regarding the money supply in the EU. Indeed, immediately after the signing of the Maastricht Treaty, the argument was put forward that because of this inconsistency of the Treaty, the ECB would not be in a position to make credible policy announcements and/or would not be able to develop a counter-inflation reputation like that of Bundesbank under the EMS; and, that as a result, the creation of the EMU would be accompanied with a rise in average inflation in Europe.[9]

Some authors were also warning in the early 1990s that a European Central Bank could produce more inflation even if it had the same economic priorities and policy preferences as the Bundesbank because at that time the natural rate of unemployment was lower in Germany than in the rest of Europe (see De Grauwe (1994, 2000)). This proposition can be illustrated using Figure 6.3. Like in Figure 6.2, point A_{EMS} in Figure 6.3(a) represents equilibrium in Europe under the EMS, with the Bundesbank as the leading central bank, effectively setting monetary policy for all member states. Its reaction function, represented by the MM_{BUN} schedule, corresponds to the MM_G schedule in Figure 6.2(a)

Figure 6.3

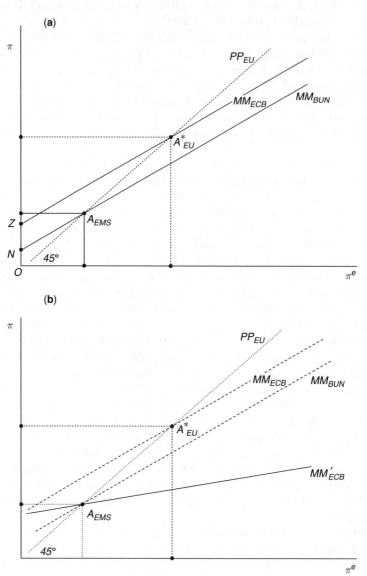

and its slope reflects Bundesbank's high priority of maintaining low inflation. The ECB's reaction function is represented in Figure 6.3(a) by the MM_{ECB} schedule. The European Central Bank is assumed to have the same policy preferences as the German monetary authorities, being as inflation conscious as the Bundesbank. The MM_{ECB}

line thus has the same slope as the MM_{BUN} schedule. But, while the slopes of the MM_{BUN} and MM_{ECB} schedules reflect exclusively the policymakers' degree of inflation consciousness, their intercepts with the vertical axis also reflect the size of the corresponding natural levels of unemployment. This is because, in the context of a Barro-Gordon framework assumed here and in the absence of stochastic shocks, when $\pi^e = 0$ actual inflation will be positively related to the natural rate of unemployment since the larger the natural rate the more inclined are monetary authorities to adopt expansionary policies, something that produces higher actual inflation. With the natural level of unemployment in the EU assumed on average higher than in Germany, the MM_{ECB} line lies uniformly above the MM_{BUN} schedule.

Consider then what happens when the ECB takes over from the Bundesbank and becomes the common central bank of Europe. The governing board of the ECB credibly announces that it will continue the Bundesbank's commitment to preserving low inflation. The private sector regards the ECB as a continuation of the Bundesbank and so it perceives that its reaction function, MM_{ECB}, will have the same slope as that of the German policymakers, MM_{BUN}. However, the ECB will be faced with an average natural rate of unemployment U_{EU}^N that exceeds the German rate U_G^N. As $U_{EU}^N > U_G^N$, for any expected rate of inflation, the intercept of the MM_{ECB} schedule with the vertical axis (OZ in the figure) will be larger than that of the MM_{BUN} schedule (ON).

It follows that equilibrium under EMU will be at A_{EU}^*: at point A_{EU}^* the MM_{ECB} schedule crosses the $45°$ line, PP_{EU}, representing the EU's private-sector behaviour. The equilibrium at A_{EU}^* is less attractive than that at A_{EMS}: unemployment in all member states is back at its natural level while average inflation is higher. Indeed, as De Grauwe (1994) was stressing in the early 1990's, with $U_{EU}^N > U_G^N$ the ECB would be pursuing on average more expansionary policies than the Bundesbank, something that would lead on average to higher EU inflation. And if the ECB were to produce the same inflation rate in the EMU as the Bundesbank in the EMS, its governing board would have to be tougher on inflation than the German monetary authorities. This is illustrated in Figure 6.3(b). An inflation outcome identical to the corresponding at point A_{EMS} would require the ECB to have the reaction function MM'_{ECB}. The MM'_{ECB} schedule is less steep than the MM_{ECB} and MM_{BUN} lines implying that the ECB is tougher on inflation than the Bundesbank. But the intercept of the MM'_{ECB} schedule with the vertical axis is as large as that of the MM_{ECB} schedule and so is consistent with the hypothesis that $U_{EU}^N > U_G^N$.

EMU Strategy: How to Achieve Monetary Unification?

Monetary unification can in principle be achieved in three ways: through 'currency competition'; through the immediate adoption of a single currency; and through a gradual process of convergence of the monetary policies and of the macroeconomic performances of participating countries.[10]

At the December 1991 summit the Heads of State of Community countries chose the third strategy for achieving monetary unification in Europe, although they agreed on a precise date for the introduction of a single currency. The issue, then, is what are the benefits and costs of this strategy for attaining EMU relative to the other two options. This issue is also relevance to the 10 new EU states which are currently searching for the optimal strategy for attaining monetary unification with the rest of Europe.

Currency Competition Strategy

The currency competition strategy has two variants. The first is known as the 'pure currency competition method'. Under this method all capital controls in participating countries are abolished and all national currencies are accepted as media of exchange in each member state. Then, free competition among the national currencies will guarantee that eventually only one of them will survive and this effectively will become the currency of the union. This strategy has the advantage that the progress towards monetary unification does not depend on successive negotiations by national governments: monetary unification is established through the market process. However, it does have a serious drawback. The country whose currency survives as the union's common currency emerges as 'leader', who can set monetary policy independently without having to take into account the effects of its policies on the other member states, and who also obtains seigniorage from the creation of international money.

The second variant of the currency competition strategy, known as the 'parallel currency method', attempts to avoid this problem. The parallel currency method involves the creation of a 'basket currency' consisting of all the national currencies properly weighted. The basket currency is allowed to circulate alongside national currencies. Then, provided that it is more stable than the national currencies, the market will eventually select the basket currency as the union's common currency. So, again, monetary unification will be established through the market process. During the negotiations that led to the Maastricht Treaty, the UK was in favour of this strategy and formulated a plan, the 'Hard ECU Plan', for achieving EMU in this way.[11] The UK's main argument in favour of the Hard ECU Plan was that the timing and pace of European monetary unification would be decided by the European people rather than being imposed on them by Community organs. This argument was criticized, however, on the grounds that the markets did not always behave in a way that would ensure maximum social welfare. There was also the problem that if the establishment of a parallel currency, a basket currency, were to lead to monetary unification, this currency would have to out-compete both the weak and the strong national currencies. Being a weighted average, the basket currency would obviously out-compete the weak national currencies, but it would not necessarily out-compete the strong national currencies. In other words, it was not certain that the market would find the parallel currency sufficiently attractive to select it as the union's currency in preference to any other. Consequently, this strategy could fail to lead to monetary union.

Indeed, during the early and mid 1990s, it was doubtful that such a strategy would work in the case of the European Union. If the parallel currency strategy was to lead to monetary unification in Europe, the ECU would have to be viewed by the private sector as more attractive than all the national currencies. In the early and mid-1990s, the evidence was suggesting that this was unlikely to be the case. In particular, statistical data were showing that between 1991 and 1995, contrary to prior expectations, the ECU had remained rather marginal as a currency of denomination and that the great bulk of inter-government and inter-CBs transaction's in Europe was conducted in national currencies. The ECU also had been used rather little as a unit of account by member states' private sectors; and it had not played any significant role as a denomination-currency in international bond markets (see Buiter and Sibert (1997)).

All these factors suggested that the parallel currency method was most unlikely to lead to monetary unification in member states. Thus, they effectively had to choose between an immediate replacement of national currencies with a common currency and a gradual process of convergence of national monetary policies and of macroeconomic performances.

Immediate Replacement of National Currencies by a Common Currency versus a Gradual Process of Inflation Convergence

The option of attempting to establish monetary union through a gradual process of convergence of macroeconomic policies and performances was seen in the early 1990s by some academics and policy-makers as risky. Along the lines suggested by DeGrauwe (1996, 2000), Figure 6.4 can be used to present the argument.

Figure 6.4

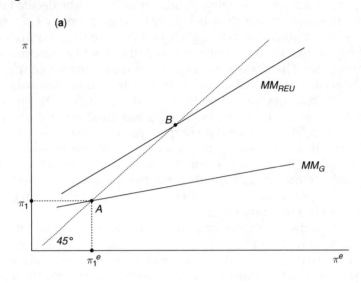

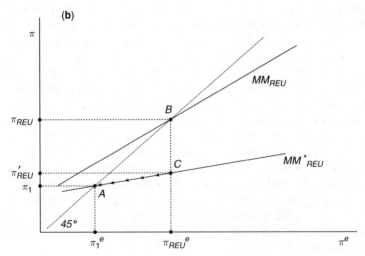

Consider 'Germany' (G) and the 'rest-of-Europe' (REU). G and REU have decided to establish an EMU with a common currency, the euro, and a common central bank, the ECB, which will have the responsibility for issuing euros and also the same credibility and counter-inflation consciousness as the Bundesbank. G and REU also agree to choose one of the following two strategies for achieving monetary union. The first is to announce that on 1 January 2002 all national currencies will be replaced by the euro. The other strategy is the gradual one: one in which there is a period of coordination of national monetary policies and of greater convergence of inflation rates and macroeconomic performances before the adoption of the common currency.

In Figure 6.4(a) the schedule MM_G describes the economic priorities of policy-makers in G and the schedule MM_{REU} describes the economic priorities of policy-makers in REU, with their slopes implying that German monetary authorities are tougher on inflation than monetary authorities in the other European states. As the private sector knows that, equilibrium prior to 1 January 2002 is at point A in G and at point B in REU where the $45°$ line describing the private sector's behaviour crosses the respective MM schedules.

If the first strategy to establish EMU is followed, on 1 January 2002 the decision to adopt the euro will be implemented. The private sector in REU, being aware that only euros will now circulate in Europe and that the supply of them will be controlled by the ECB which is as inflation-conscious as the Bundesbank, adjusts their inflation expectations downwards: π^e in the whole of Europe drops to π_1^e; and REU countries immediately move to point A, achieving lower actual inflation without unemployment costs.

Consider what could happen if the process towards achieving EMU was gradual. In the spirit of De Grauwe (1996, 2000), assume that a gradual process of establishing EMU would imply that, before the adoption of the euro and the creation of the ECB, inflation in REU would have to be reduced, at least to match the German rate. Thus, following the agreement to proceed gradually towards EMU, monetary authorities in REU announce their intention to lower inflation to the German level. Such announcement of a policy of gradual convergence can be taken to imply a change in the priorities of REU's monetary authorities over inflation and unemployment. However, announcements by the monetary authorities in the rest of Europe may not be credible enough: private agents may be uncertain about how committed the REU monetary authorities are to the new policy. They may not believe them before they have seen that the authorities have proceeded to the adoption of contractionary monetary policies and are therefore prepared to see rising unemployment.[12] In terms of Figure 6.4(b), this means that the REU may need to move in the short run from point B to point C if the private sector is to believe that the policy-makers' priorities there have actually been modified. Point C lies on a new MM schedule, the line MM_{REU}^*, whose slope reflects the REU's monetary authorities increased inflation consciousness: the slope of the MM_{REU}^* schedule is the same as that of the MM_G schedule in Figure 6.4(a). However, point C does not lie on the $45°$ line; it lies below this line. Accordingly, at C actual inflation in REU is lower than expected inflation (we have $\pi'_{REU} < \pi^e_{REU}$), implying that unemployment there is above its natural-rate level. The private sector in REU observes that, and is now convinced that the REU's policy-makers priorities have changed: they are now prepared to accept a large increase in unemployment above its natural-rate level in order to achieve lower inflation. Over time this will lead to a fall in the expected inflation rate $\pi_{REU}{}^e$. Thus, gradually REU will move along the path CA on the MM^*_{REU} schedule, from point C towards point A (the final equilibrium point). However, the movement over time from C to A along MM^*_{REU} will involve costs: along the path CA, which lies off the $45°$ line, the actual level of unemployment in REU will exceed the natural-rate level.

Indeed, this analysis can explain why some economists are not in favour of a gradual strategy towards EMU for the new EU member states (EU-10) and propose instead a 'euroization', namely an immediate adoption by these countries of the euro. The current situation in Europe could be represented in Figure 6.4 as follows: a schedule like the MM_G line could be taken to describe the eurozone countries, with its steepness reflecting the ECB's high degree of inflation conscious-ness; and a schedule like the MM_{REU} line could be taken to describe the EU-10, whose CBs' credibility and inflation consciousness is lower than that of the ECB. A gradual strategy towards EMU member-ship would imply, along the lines considered above, that the EU-10 might have to move initially to a point like C, off the $45°$ line, and then travel gradually from point C to A, incurring in the process unemployment costs. By contrast, euroization could imply a move of the EU-10 immediately to a point like A in Figure 6.4(b), making EMU participation less costly as far as unemployment is concerned. However, euroization is not possible under the Maastricht Treaty's rules.

Real Convergence: Where Do We Stand?

In December 1991, the Heads of State of Community countries adopted a gradual but irreversible strategy towards EMU, in the sense that the euro would in any case circulate on 1 January 2002. At the same time, criteria for entry were adopted. More specifically, the EMU Treaty stipulated that:

- In stage II of EMU, which was to start on 1 January 1994, a European Monetary Institute (EMI) would be created.
- In stage III a single currency would be adopted and the EMI would be replaced by the ECB. This stage would start on 1 January 1997 if the Heads of State of member countries were to decide that a large enough number of member states had met a set of convergence criteria to make the system viable.

- If by the end of 1997 the date for the start of stage III had not been set, this stage would automatically start on 1 January 1999.
- The UK, Denmark and Sweden would not be obliged to move to stage III without a separate decision to do so by their Parliaments

The convergence criteria were defined in nominal terms: entry requirements concerned inflation rates, nominal long-term interest rates, the ERM and government deficits and debts. In particular, if a member state was to qualify for entry:

- its inflation rate would have to be no higher than 1.5 per cent above the average inflation rate of the three best-performing ERM members
- its long-term nominal bond rates would have to be no higher than 2 per cent above the average rate of the three best performing countries
- it had to participate in the ERM for at least two years before entry into the EMU, and should not have devalued its currency during the same period
- it should not have 'excessive' budgetary deficits and debt

Inflation convergence can be considered a prerequisite for the success of a monetary union: it is necessary if loss of competitiveness in individual economies is to be avoided when there is a single currency. Indeed, as noted by many (see, for example, Artis (1994), Hasse (1995) and Currie (1998)), the first two criteria can be seen as a reassurance of a country's ability to have low inflation on a continual basis. The argument is that sustainability of low inflation can be assessed by two factors: by past inflation performance; and, by expectations about future inflation performance. The first factor is reflected in current inflation, while the second factor is reflected in long-term interest rates since long-term interest rates are indicators of expected inflation. As far as the interest rate criterion is concerned, there was also the argument in the early 1990s that interest rates would reflect the verdict of markets regarding the degree of macroeconomic convergence achieved within Europe (see Bini-Smaghi *et al.* (1994)).

As for the third criterion, in the early 1990s there was no consensus as to whether it had to be taken seriously, given that, following the 1992–93 EMS crisis, the ERM fluctuation margins were increased to 15 per cent above or below the ECU central rates. Some analysts were arguing at the time that a country's convergence with the rest of Europe could hardly be assessed by its ability to maintain such wide margins (see Buiter (1995) and Currie (1998)). A counter-argument, however, was that participation in the narrow bands of the ERM (that is, the ±2.25 per cent band) could be seen as an indication of a country's willingness to accept institutional-based co-operation schemes and thus its commitment to participate in the EMU (see Cobham (1991), Artis (1992, 1994) and De Grauwe (1996)). For some national currencies, the central rates of the ERM could also be used as a reference point for determining the irrevocably fixed exchange rates within the EMU, which were to hold between January 1999 and until the adoption of the common currency. For this reason, Italy returned to the ERM (narrow bands) in 1997, and Finland and Greece joined the ERM in 1996 and 1998 respectively. As far as the two-year devaluation rule was concerned, it had the objective of preventing competitive devaluations before entry into the EMU.

The last criterion was translated into binding rules for the size of public deficits and debt; this criterion has been heavily criticized. Also heavily criticized has been the Maastricht Treaty's insistence on nominal convergence: the Maastricht Treaty has neglected real convergence, which, from a longer-term perspective, can be considered more important than nominal convergence. Some argue that nominal convergence will necessarily lead to real convergence; others, however, note that this may not be the case and/or that little attention has been paid to the question of exactly how quickly this may happen. This is a serious problem, given that currently the degree of real convergence of the EU-15 economies remains unsatisfactory.

Tables 6.1 to 6.6 report data on real GDP, unemployment rates and structure of unemployment/employment, poverty levels and

Table 6.1 GDP per head in purchasing power standards, PPS (EU-15 = 100)

	Average 1993–97	1998	1999	2000	2001	2002	Average 1998–2002
Austria	111.1	109.5	110.9	111.0	111.5	111.1	110.6
Belgium	112.6	110.9	106.5	106.8	106.3	106.3	107.4
Denmark	117.7	118.0	119.4	120.9	120.9	120.8	120.0
Finland	95.1	101.2	101.0	103.0	101.6	101.2	101.6
France	103.2	99.0	99.9	100.0	100.6	100.5	100.0
Germany	108.8	106.1	106.2	105.3	104.2	103.9	105.1
Greece	65.5	66.9	68.3	69.0	68.6	70.1	68.6
Ireland	92.3	105.7	111.7	118.4	121.1	121.4	115.7
Italy	103.0	103.4	103.3	102.1	102.5	102.5	102.8
Luxembourg	171.7	178.4	185.2	195.5	191.7	191.9	188.5
Netherlands	106.7	115.3	114.3	115.2	114.0	113.0	114.4
Portugal	70.9	73.3	73.4	73.4	73.8	74.0	73.6
Spain	78.9	79.2	82.2	82.4	83.3	83.6	82.1
Sweden	101.5	101.5	101.3	101.8	101.0	100.8	101.3
UK	99.4	103.4	100.7	102.0	102.1	102.5	102.1
Standard Deviation	23.7						27.0

Source: Eurostat database, *Long-term Indicators*, Economy and Finance.

expenditure on social protection, real unit labour costs, capital formation and industrial production, namely variables that are crucial indicators of the degree of real convergence. Table 6.1 presents data on GDP per head in purchasing power standards (PPS) for two periods: 1993–1997, the period from the ratification of the Maastricht Treaty until just after the start of stage III of EMU; and 1998–2002 the period during stage III of EMU and until the first year of the circulation of the single currency. GDP in PPS is often used as a welfare measure since it makes possible cross-country comparisons of incomes per head by taking into account price-level differences and ignoring short-term exchange-rate movements. As can be seen form the table the 'less rich' European states Greece, Portugal and Spain experienced an improvement in their relative position between 1993–97 and 1998–2002 (by 3.1, 2.7 and 3.2 points respectively), but their real GDP per head remained well-below the mean welfare level of the EU-15 of 100 even after the start of stage III of EMU: in the 1998–2002 period GDP per head in PPS was on average 68.6 in Greece, 73.6 in Portugal and 82.1 in Spain, namely 31.4, 26.4 and 17.9 points below the EU-15 income. On the other hand, Belgium, Germany and France experienced in 1998–2002 a deterioration of their relative position (by 5.2, 3.7 and 3.2 points respectively on average compared with 1993–1997). Austria and Italy also experienced a slight deterioration of welfare (0.5 and 0.2 points respectively), while the UK improved its position on average in 1998–2002 compared with 1993–97 (by 2.7 points). At the same time, a significant improvement in relative position has occurred in the case of Ireland, Luxembourg, the Netherlands and Finland: GDP per head increased between 1993–97 and 1998–2002 by 23.4 points in Ireland, by 16.8 points in Luxembourg, by 7.7 points in the Netherlands and by 6.5 points in Finland. As a result of these developments, the degree of divergence of the EU-15 states in terms of real GDP per head actually increased since the start of stage III of EMU: the standard deviation is 23.7 for the period 1993–97 and 27.0 for the period 1998–2002, implying a rise in divergence among the EU-15 states in terms of welfare of 3.3 points. This pattern of income differences continued throughout the 2002–2004 period (see Figure 6.5).

An important aspect of convergence is the reduction of unemployment disparities among countries and more generally, of differences in labour market conditions. As can be seen from Table 6.2, the mean rate of unemployment in EU-15 was reduced between 1993–97 and 1998–2002 by 2.0 percentage points. Nevertheless, the employment experience of individual member states had varied considerably, and by 2002 one could still classify the EU-15 countries in three groups: the high-unemployment countries; the moderate-unemployment countries; and the low-unemployment countries.

Figure 6.5 GDP per head in PPS (euro), 2002–2004

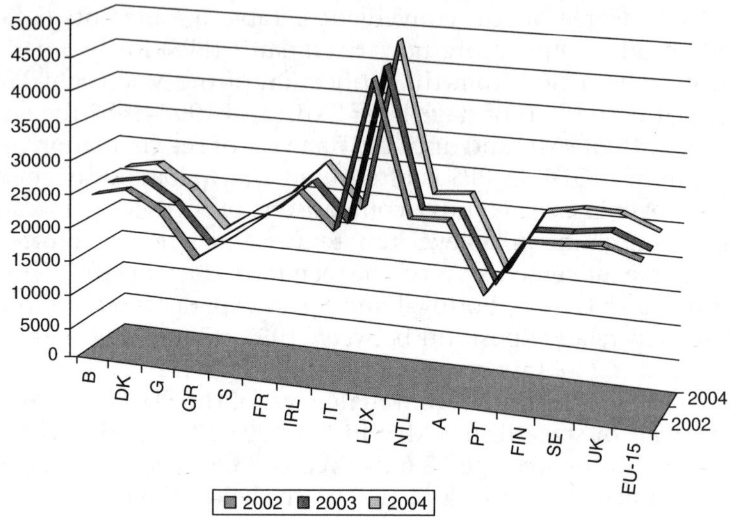

Source: based on data from Eurostat database, *Long-term Indicators*, Economy and Finance

Table 6.2 Total unemployment (% of labour force)

	Average 1993–97	1998	1999	2000	2001	2002	Average 1998–2002	Change between 1993–97 and 1998–2002
Austria	4.1	4.5	3.9	3.7	3.6	4.2	4.0	−0.1
Belgium	9.4	9.3	8.6	6.9	6.6	6.9	7.7	−1.7
Denmark	7.1	4.9	4.8	4.4	4.3	4.3	4.5	−2.6
Finland	15.1	11.4	10.2	9.8	9.1	9.3	10.0	−5.1
France	11.6	11.4	10.7	9.3	8.5	8.9	9.8	−1.8
Germany	8.5	9.1	8.4	7.8	7.7	8.3	8.3	−0.2
Greece	9.2	10.9	11.9	11.1	10.5	10.1	10.9	+1.7
Ireland	12.8	7.5	5.6	4.2	3.8	4.5	5.1	−7.7
Italy	11.1	11.7	11.3	10.4	9.4	9.0	10.4	−0.7
Luxembourg	2.9	2.7	2.4	2.3	2.0	2.4	2.4	−0.5
Netherlands	6.1	3.8	3.2	2.8	2.4	2.8	3.0	−3.1
Portugal	6.8	5.8	4.9	4.8	4.8	5.0	5.1	−1.7
Spain	18.5	15.2	12.8	11.3	10.6	11.3	12.2	−6.3
Sweden	9.4	8.3	7.1	5.8	4.9	4.9	6.2	−3.2
UK	8.6	6.2	5.8	5.4	5.0	5.1	5.5	−3.1
EU-15*	10.2	9.4	8.7	7.8	7.3	7.7	8.2	−2.0

* weighted average
Source: Eurostat database, *Long-term Indicators*, Population and Social Conditions.

Some of the core EU states belong to the first group: in Germany unemployment remained roughly unchanged throughout the period 1993–2002 at about 8 per cent; in France unemployment had fallen since 1993–97, but it continued to be high, at 8.9 per cent of the labour force in 2002; in Italy unemployment had on average exceeded 10 per cent during 1993–2002, showing little tendency for improvement. As for the non-core EU-15 countries belonging to the high-unemployment group, in Greece unemployment had risen since 1993–97, and stabilized at 10 per cent by 2002. And in Spain and Finland it amounted, respectively, to 11.3 per cent and 9.3 per cent of the labour force in 2002. In the moderate unemployment group in terms of the 1998–2002 performance we have Belgium with an average unemployment rate of 7.7 per cent of the labour force, Sweden with 6.2 per cent and Portugal with 5.1 per cent. In Ireland and also in the UK unemployment has been reduced considerably since 1997. Austria and Denmark belong to the low-unemployment group, having an unemployment rate in 2002 lower than 5 per cent. Also, Luxembourg has had over the years consistently low unemployment (around 2.5 per cent), while the Netherlands has managed to acheive unemployment around 3 per cent of the labour force after 1998.

Table 6.3 reveals the significant differences that exist between the EU-15 states in terms of structure of employment and unemployment. From column (iv) of the table, it follows that the low unemployment rate in the Netherlands during the period 1998–2002 had to a certain extent been achieved through part-time employment (43.8% of total employment in 2002). Higher than the EU-15 average part-time employment also exists in the UK, Sweden and Denmark (25%, 21.4% and 20.6% of total employment, respectively), namely countries that, like the Netherlands, had also experienced relatively low total unemployment in the 1998–2002 period. This does not apply to Germany: the high level of part-time employment, 20.8 per cent of total employment in 2002, did not help much in reducing total unemployment. The Mediterranean countries, that is Italy, Spain, Portugal and Greece, are showing much lower rates of part-time employment than the EU-15 mean: part-time employment in 2002 was 8.6 per cent in Italy, 8 per cent in Spain, 11.3 per cent in Portugal and 4.5 per cent in Greece. Columns (i)–(iii) of Table 6.3 present data on the structure of unemployment in the EU-15. Some member states, including Italy, Greece and Spain, have a large percentage of long-term unemployed, namely 5.4 per cent, 5 per cent and 3.8 per cent of their labour force or 59.2 per cent, 52.4 per cent and 34.3 per cent of total unemployment in 2002. Youth unemployment in these countries is also high (27.1 per cent of total unemployment in Italy, 25.1 in Greece and 21.5 per cent in Spain). Long-term unemployment is

Table 6.3 Labour-market conditions, 2002

	Long-term unemployment (% of labour force) (i)	Long-term unemployment (% of total unemployment) (ii)	Youth unemployment (% of total unemployment) (iii)	Part-time employment (% of total employment) (iv)	Early school leavers (% of total population)* (v)
Austria	1.0	20.3	7.2	18.9	9.5
Belgium	3.4	49.6	15.7	19.4	12.4
Denmark	0.8	19.7	7.1	20.6	8.4
Finland	2.2	21.2	28.2	12.4	9.9
France	2.8	32.7	18.9	16.2	13.4
Germany	4.1	47.9	9.3	20.8	12.6
Greece	5.0	52.4	25.7	4.5	16.1
Ireland	1.3	29.3	7.8	16.5	14.7
Italy	5.4	59.2	27.1	8.6	24.3
Luxembourg	0.7	27.4	8.1	11.7	17.0
Netherlands	0.7	26.7	4.6	43.8	15.0
Portugal	1.6	35.5	10.4	11.3	45.1
Spain	3.8	34.3	21.5	8.0	29.0
Sweden	1.0	20.1	12.9	21.4	10.4
UK	1.2	23.1	10.9	25.0	17.7
EU-15**	3.1	40.2	14.6	18.2	18.5

* Figures are for 2001 (latest available)

** Weighted average

Sources: (i)–(iv), Eurostat, *Labour Force Survey 2002*.
(v), Eurostat database, *Structural Indicators, Social Cohesion*.

a serious problem for Germany and Belgium, where about half of their unemployed are long-term unemployed. In Austria, Denmark, Sweden, the UK and Luxembourg long-term unemployment is below the EU-15 mean; Denmark and Austria also have relatively low youth unemployment (7.1% and 7.2% of total unemployment, respectively). In Ireland and the Netherlands, where aggregate unemployment is below the EU-15 average, a relatively large percentage of the unemployed workers are long-term unemployed (29.3% and 26.7% of total unemployment respectively) However, youth unemployment in these two countries is small (7.8% and 4.6% of total unemployment respectively). Youth unemployment is a problem for Finland, France and Belgium (28.2%, 18.9% and 15.7% of total unemployment respectively), and to a lesser extent for Sweden (12.9%) and the UK (10.9%). Column (v) of Table 6.3, 'early school leavers', shows the percentage of population aged 18–24 with at most secondary education and not in further training. Portugal has a very high rate of early school leavers (45.1%). Early school leavers above the EU-15 average exist in Spain (29%) and Italy (24.3%), while a relatively high rate can also be found in the UK (17.7%) and Luxembourg (17%). The Scandinavian countries and Austria have the lowest rates of early school leavers (10.4% in Sweden, 9.9% in Finland, 8.4% in Denmark and 9.5% in Austria).

The differences between the EU-15 states in terms of labour market conditions continued in 2002–2004 (see Figures 6.6(a)–6.6(d)). Thus, as far as total employment is concerned, the Netherlands, Luxemburg, Ireland and Austria (Spain, Greece and France) were the best (worst) performers throughout 2002–2004; above-average part-time employment continued to coexist with high (low) total unemployment in Germany and Belgium (the Netherlands, Sweden, Denmark and the UK); Greece, Italy, Spain and Finland continued to be confronted with large youth unemployment rates; and Portugal and Spain, and to a lesser extent Italy and the UK, continued throughout 2002–2004 to have high rates of early school leavers.

The data in Table 6.4 provide information about poverty rates within individual member states and about the level and funding of social protection. Household with incomes lower than 60 per cent of the national average are defined by the international organizations as being at the risk of poverty. As can be seen from the table, a significant percentage of the population in the Southern European states still lives below the poverty line: in Greece, Italy, Portugal and Spain about 20 per cent of the population lives below the poverty level. The same is true for Ireland, where 21 per cent of the population is receiving incomes lower that 60 per cent of national average. A smaller but still significant percentage of people living below poverty levels also

Figure 6.6(a)   Total unemployment EU-15, 2002–2004

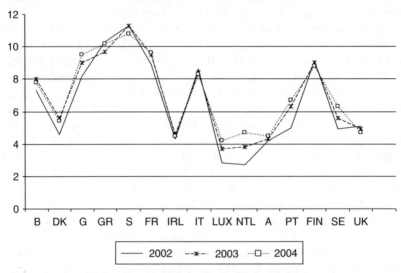

Source: based on data from Eurostat database, *Structural Indicators,* Employment

Figure 6.6(b)   Part-time employment EU-15, 2002–2004

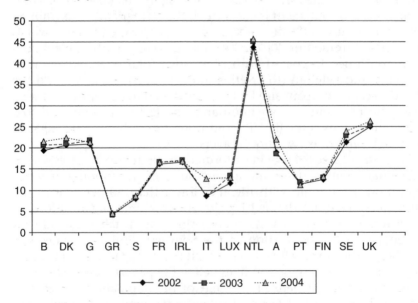

Source: based on data from Eurostat database, *Long-term Indicators,* Population and Labour Conditions

Figure 6.6(c)   Youth unemployment EU-15, 2002–2004

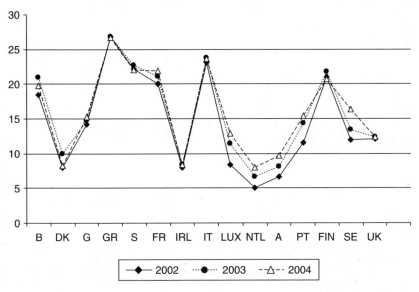

Source: based on data from Eurostat database, *Long-term Indicators,* Population and Labour Conditions

Figure 6.6(d)   Early school leavers EU-15, 2002–2004

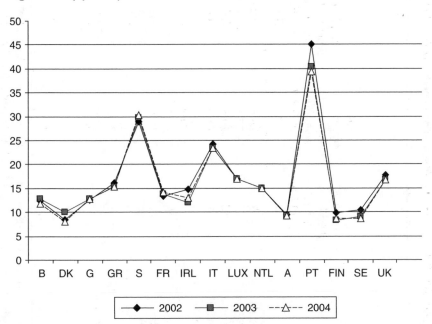

Source: based on data from Eurostat database, *Structural Indicators,* Social Cohesion

Table 6.4 Poverty, social protection and unemployment benefits, 2001

	At risk of poverty (% of total population) (i)	Total expenditure on social protection (% of GDP) (ii)	Unemployment benefits (% of total social benefits) (iii)	Funding of social protection (iv)				
				General government contributions (% of total funding)	Social security contributions (% of total funding)			Other (% of total funding)
					Total	Employers	Protected persons	
Austria	12	28.4	5.0	34.1	64.7	37.5	27.2	1.2
Belgium	13	27.5	11.7	23.0	74.4	51.4	23.0	2.6
Denmark	10	29.5	10.0	62.6	30.4	9.3	21.1	7.0
Finland	11	25.8	9.8	42.8	50.3	38.8	11.6	6.9
France	15	30.0	7.1	30.4	66.7	45.9	20.8	2.8
Germany	11	29.8	8.2	32.6	65.2	37.4	27.8	2.2
Greece	20	27.2	6.0	27.8	62.0	38.5	23.5	10.2
Ireland	21	14.6	8.3	58.3	39.4	24.8	14.5	2.3
Italy	19	25.6	1.6	41.1	57.0	42.4	14.6	1.8
Luxembourg	12	21.2	2.5	46.2	48.9	24.5	24.4	4.9
Netherlands	11	27.6	5.0	16.3	66.9	31.6	35.3	16.8
Portugal	20	23.9	3.6	37.8	54.4	36.4	18.0	7.8
Spain	19	20.1	12.9	26.7	69.2	52.9	16.3	4.1
Sweden	9	31.3	5.6	45.1	52.5	38.6	9.1	2.3
UK	17	27.2	2.9	48.2	50.0	30.5	19.5	1.7
EU-15	15	27.5	6.2	36.0	60.5	38.8	21.7	3.4

Source: (i) Eurostat database, *Structural Indicators*, Social Cohesion

(ii)–(iv) Eurostat, *Statistics in Focus*, Population and Social Conditions, 'Social Protection in Europe', 2004

exist in the UK (17%) and France (15%). Sweden and Denmark have a low percentage of people living in conditions of poverty (9 per cent and 10 per cent respectively). Disparities between member states also exist in terms of level and funding of social-protection spending. Sweden, France, Germany and Denmark spend about 30 per cent of their GDP on social protection; in Ireland, Spain, Luxembourg, Portugal, Italy and Finland social-protection expenditure is between about 15 and 25 per cent of their GDP (see column (ii) of Table 6.4). In Denmark and Ireland about 60 per cent of total social-protection spending is financed from general government contributions through taxes; in Belgium, Spain, the Netherlands, France and Germany more than 60% of total social-protection spending is funded from social security contributions (see column (iv)). Within the social-security contributions category there are marked differences across member states as regards the percentage funded by employers' and protected persons' contributions. The share of unemployment benefits in total social benefits also varies considerably across member states, reflecting differences in coverage, duration and value of benefits (see col. (iii)). For example, in Denmark, where unemployment was 4.3% in 2001, unemployment benefits amounted to 10% of total benefits; in Italy, where unemployment was 9.4% in 2001, unemployment benefits were 1.6% of total benefits.

Data on real unit labour costs (RULCs) are given in Table 6.5. This variable is considered by many as a key indicator of real convergence as it influences the profitability of capital and therefore the location of industry, something that is of particular importance in an internal market without frontiers like the EU. RULC is calculated as the ratio of compensation per employee to GDP per person employed. Thus a fall (rise) in RULC may reflect a fall (rise) in real wages, or an increase in (fall) labour productivity, or both. Whatever the source of the change in RULCs, the value of this variable can be taken to represent the degree of competitiveness of an economy: a fall in RULC indicates an improvement of competitiveness and a rise indicates a deterioration of competitiveness. As can be seen from the table, the degree of divergence between the EU-15 states in terms of real unit costs had been considerable in 1993–1997 and was widened in 1998–2002. In some EU states competitiveness deteriorated on average between 1993–1997 and 1998–2002. In Sweden RULCs increased from an average level of 95.8 points in 1993–97 to an average level of 97.7 in 1998–2002; in the UK it rose from 94.4 on average in 1993–97 to 94.9 in 1997–2002; and in Greece from 97.0 in 1993–97 to 97.2 in 1998–2002. By contrast, Ireland, Italy and Portugal managed to considerably improve their performance as far as competitiveness was concerned. In Ireland, RULC fell by 13.7 points, from an average level of 94.3 in 1993–97 to

Table 6.5 Real unit labour costs (1991 = 100)

	Average 1993–97	1998	1999	2000	2001	2002	Average 1998–2002	Change between 1993–97 and 1998–2002
Austria	96.9	93.4	93.2	91.9	91.3	90.2	92.0	–4.9
Belgium	98.8	96.2	96.1	95.7	94.8	94.0	95.4	–3.4
Denmark	95.7	94.8	94.7	93.0	92.7	92.0	93.4	–2.3
Finland	86.4	81.3	81.4	79.0	79.0	78.9	79.9	–6.5
France	97.0	97.0	97.0	96.9	97.0	97.2	97.0	0
Germany	99.3	96.1	95.8	96.0	95.4	95.2	95.7	–3.6
Greece	97.0	99.7	97.5	96.6	96.1	95.9	97.2	+0.2
Ireland	94.3	84.4	82.5	79.3	78.8	77.9	80.6	–13.7
Italy	93.4	86.9	86.9	86.3	85.5	84.5	86.0	–7.4
Luxembourg	–	–	–	–	–	–	–	–
Netherlands	98.8	97.2	97.5	96.9	95.6	95.9	96.6	–2.2
Portugal	92.6	84.3	83.8	84.9	84.8	84.5	84.5	–8.1
Spain	98.5	96.3	95.8	95.6	95.3	94.7	95.5	–3.0
Sweden	95.8	95.5	94.6	99.1	99.7	99.4	97.7	+1.9
UK	94.4	93.6	95.1	95.4	95.3	94.9	94.9	+0.5
EU-14*	96.9	94.0	94.0	93.9	93.5	93.1	93.7	–3.2
Standard Deviation	3.5						5.2	

* EU-15 excluding Luxembourg (export weighted).
Source: Eurostat, *European Economy 2003*, Statistical Annex.

an average level of 80.6 in 1998–2002. In Portugal it dropped by 8.1 points, from 92.6 on average in 1993–97 to 84.5 in 1997–2002; in Italy it was reduced by 7.4 points, from 93.4 on average in 1993–97 to 86.0 in 1997–2002. Austria and Finland also experienced an improvement in competitiveness between 1993–97 and 1998–2002 (an average of 4.9 and 6.5 points respectively). The other EU-15 states showed much smaller reductions in RULCs between these two sub-periods. As a result of the differing progress that the EU-15 countries made on the competitiveness front, their divergence between 1993–97 and 1998–2002 in terms of real unit labour costs was widened: the standard deviation is 3.5 for 1993–97 and 5.2 for 1998–2002, implying an increase in divergence during the third stage of EMU by 1.7 points. Progress towards reducing unit labour costs has not been uniform even after 2002 (see Figure 6.7).

Table 6.6 shows that significant differences within the EU-15 also exist as regards fixed capital formation and industrial production. Over the entire period 1993–2002 of stages II and III of EMU, Ireland had shown a very large increase in gross fixed-capital investment (10.4% on average). Greece, Denmark, Luxembourg and Portugal followed with a much lower but still high annual average rate of investment growth (equal to 6.3 per cent, 5.4 per cent, 5.2 per cent and 5.1 per cent respectively). The UK came next, with an average annual rate of 4.4 per cent. On the other hand, the average growth rate of gross fixed capital investment in France (1.3% per year), Germany (1.3% per year) and Austria (2.2% per year) had been rather unsatisfactory. As far as industrial production is concerned, Ireland is once again in the

Figure 6.7   Real unit labour costs growth in EU-15, 2003–2005

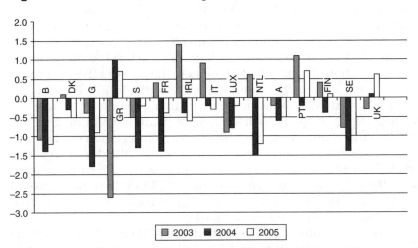

Source: based on data from Eurostat database, *Long-term Indicators*, Economy and Finance
*2005 forecasted value

Table 6.6 Gross fixed capital formation and industrial production

	Gross fixed capital formation 1993–2002 (annual average percentage change)	Industrial production 1993–2002 (annual average percentage change)
Austria	2.2	4.0
Belgium	3.1	2.4
Denmark	5.4	3.7
Finland	2.7	6.6
France	1.3	1.8
Germany	1.3	1.9
Greece	6.3	2.8
Ireland	10.4	13.6
Luxembourg	5.2	3.4
Netherlands	3.9	1.9
Portugal	5.1	2.8
Spain	3.9	3.1
Sweden	3.5	5.4
UK	4.4	1.7
EU-15	2.9	2.4

Source: Based on data from Eurostat, *European Economy 2003*, Statistical Annex.

first place (with an annual average rate of increase of 13.6 per cent) followed by Finland and Sweden in the second and third place, with average annual increases of 6.6 per cent and 5.4 per cent respectively. All the other EU-15 countries had shown less satisfactory industrial-growth performances during the entire 1993–2002 period.

Tables 6.7(a) and 6.7(b) present the findings of the *Lisbon Review 2002–2003* (see World Economic Forum (2003)) regarding the progress that the EU-15 countries have made towards achieving the goals set out at the Lisbon Summit of 2000, namely the goal of achieving social cohesion and sustainable development, of promoting information technology and R&D, of achieving a further opening up of markets and creating an adequate business environment, of promoting service networks and of improving the efficiency and integration of European financial markets. As can be seen from the tables, the degree to which the EU-15 member states have made progress in each of these areas varies: the EU-15 states are ranked from 1 to 14 in Table 6.6(a) (Luxembourg is excluded) according to the progress they have made in each field. Table 6.7(b) gives an overall ranking.

As far as social cohesion is concerned, the Netherlands occupies first place, followed by Belgium and Finland in second and third place respectively. The UK rates poorly on social cohesion (it is in 10th

Table 6.7(a) Ranking according to the achievement of the Lisbon Summit targets

	Social cohesion (1)	Sustainable development (2)	Information technology (3)	R&D (4)	Opening up of markets (5)	Service networks (6)	Efficiency of financial services (7)	Business environment (8)
Austria	5	5	5	7	4	8	9	8
Belgium	2	7	9	5	7	5	7	10
Denmark	4	3	4	9	5	4	3	5
Finland	3	1	1	1	1	1	2	1
France	6	9	10	6	11	7	10	12
Germany	9	2	8	2	9	2	8	11
Greece	14	14	14	14	14	14	14	14
Ireland	12	13	11	10	8	13	6	3
Italy	11	11	13	13	13	12	13	13
Luxembourg	–	–	–	–	–	–	–	–
Netherlands	1	8	7	8	3	6	4	4
Portugal	13	10	8	12	10	10	11	7
Spain	8	12	12	11	12	11	12	9
Sweden	7	4	2	3	6	3	5	6
UK	10	6	3	4	2	9	1	2

Source: World Economic Forum (2003).

Table 6.7(b) Overall ranking

Finland	1.4
Sweden	4.5
Denmark	4.6
UK	4.6
Netherlands	5.1
Germany	6.1
Austria	6.4
Belgium	6.5
France	8.9
Ireland	9.5
Portugal	10.1
Spain	10.9
Italy	12.4
Greece	14.0

Source: World Economic Forum (2003).

place), followed by Italy (in 11th place), Ireland (12th place), Portugal (13th place), and Greece (14th place). Germany's performance as far as social cohesion is concerned is also not satisfactory (it occupies 9th place). However, Germany has made good progress towards achieving the target of sustainable development: it occupies second place on this criterion. Finland occupies first place as far as sustainable-development is concerned, with Denmark and Sweden in third and fourth place respectively. The UK has shown a better performance in terms of sustainable development (it occupies 6th place) as compared to social cohesion. The opposite is true for the Netherlands, which in terms of sustainable development comes eighth. The Mediterranean countries, as well as Ireland, show a poor performance on both social cohesion and sustainable development.

In terms of information technology, R&D, opening up of markets, service networks and efficiency of financial services, Finland shows on average the best performance. Germany and Sweden are in second and third place respectively as far R&D and service networks are concerned. Sweden also shows a very good performance in terms of information technology (2nd place), and it has an above average performance in the field of financial-services efficiency, business environment and opening up of markets. Germany has shown much less progress in the field of information technology, opening up of markets, efficiency of financial services and business environment. France rates particularly poorly as far as information technology is concerned, opening up of markets, efficiency of financial services and business environment. The Netherlands occupies third place as far as opening up of markets and fourth place as far as efficiency of financial services and business environment are concerned, but rates less satisfactorily in terms of R&D and information technology (it occupies 8th and 7th place respectively). Ireland has shown satisfactory progress in terms of business environment (3rd place) and to a lesser extent in terms of efficiency of financial services (6th place). Denmark occupies, respectively, third and fourth place in terms of efficiency of financial markets and of information technology and service networks, and also occupies fifth place as far opening up of markets and the business environment are concerned. Greece, Italy and Spain show a poor performance in terms of all these criteria. Austria and Belgium show a 'mixed' performance in terms of criteria(3)–(8), with Belgium having the best result in the field of R&D and service networks and Austria having the best performance in the field of opening up of markets and information technology. As a result of this mixed performance, Austria and Belgium occupy seventh and eighth place in terms of the overall ranking.

In terms of overall performance, Finland occupies first place. Sweden and Denmark, which have shown a relatively good performance

Figure 6.8(a) Real GDP growth EU-15, 2003–2006

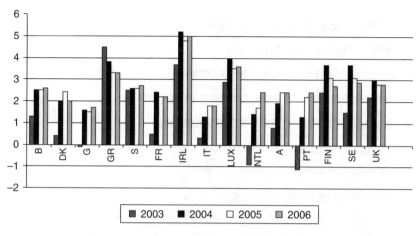

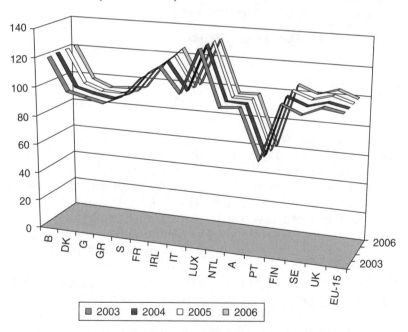

Source: based on data from Eurostat database, *Long-term Indicators*, Economy and Finance
*2005, 2006 forecasts

Figure 6.8(b) Labour productivity per person employment, 2003–2006
(EU-15 = 100)

Source: based on data from Eurostat database, *Long-term Indicators*, Economy and Finance
*2005, 2006 forecasts

Figure 6.8(c)   Gross fixed capital formation EU-15, 2003–2006

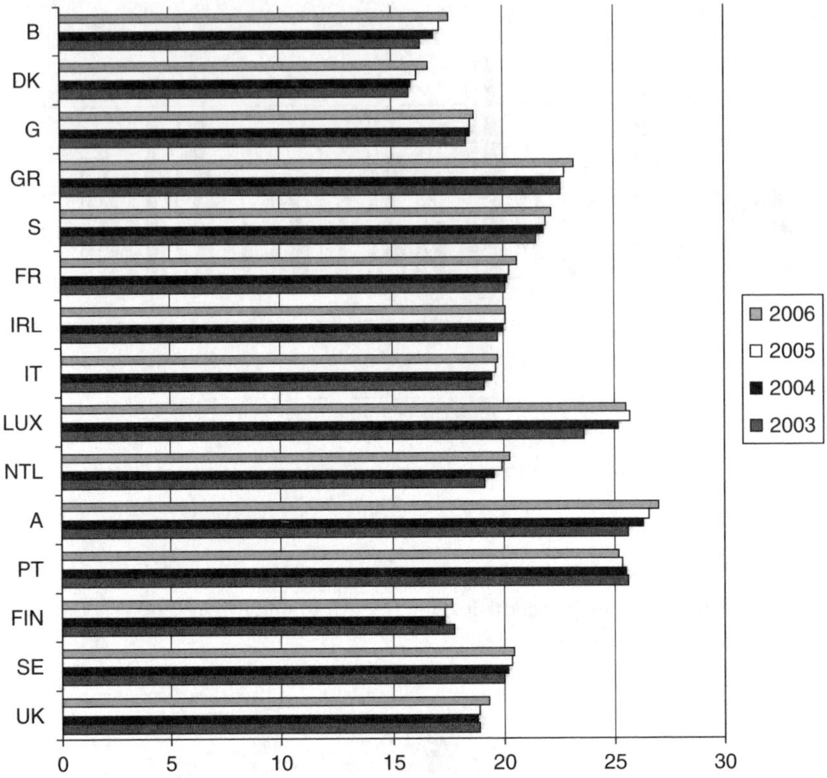

Source: based on data from Eurostat database, *Long-term Indicators*, Economy and Finance
*2005, 2006 forecasts

in all fields, occupy second and third place respectively. The UK occupies fourth place, due to its satisfactory performance in terms of financial services, opening up of markets, business environment and information technology, despite its poor performance in terms of social cohesion and service networks. The Netherlands is in fifth place, followed by Germany in sixth place. France and Ireland occupy ninth and tenth place respectively. The Mediterranean countries have the worst overall performance: Portugal is in eleventh place, Spain in twelfth place, Italy in thirteenth place and Greece in fourteenth place. Indeed, Tables 6.7(a) and 6.7(b) reveal that the progress towards achieving the Lisbon Summit targets has not been uniform, which is worrying since it implies that common policies will have different impacts in different places. This will further delay real convergence within the EU-15, something that is evident from figures 6.8(a)–6.8(c), which show forecasts for 2005 and 2006, together with actual values for 2003 and 2004, for real GDP growth, labour productivity and gross fixed capital formation.

Convergence is also an issue for the EU-25 given that the 10 new EU countries, which formally became members in May 2004, have already declared their intention to adopt the single currency as quickly as possible. As members of the EU, the 10 newcomers are obliged to respect several provisions of the Maastricht Treaty, including the consideration of their economic policies as a matter of common interest and the avoidance of excessive government debt and deficits. As far as nominal convergence is concerned, progress in these countries has already been made, although further effort is needed before they can be in a position to satisfy all the Maastricht criteria and apply for EMU membership (see Table 6.8)[13]. As regards real convergence, the picture is less satisfactory: according to some estimates, it may take up to 25 years for the 10 new member states to achieve real convergence with the rest of Europe.[14] These estimates however do not take account of the expected positive impact of EU membership on growth in these countries which may imply an increase in the their GDP between 1.5 and 19 per cent (see Baldwin *et al.* (1997)). Some studies stress the existence of shock dissimilarities between the

Table 6.8 Nominal convergence EU-10, 2004

	Inflation rate (%) (i)	Long-term interest rates (%) (ii)	Short-term interest rates: three-month interbank rates (%) (iii)	Government deficit (−)/surplus(+) (% of GDP) (iv)	Government debt (% of GDP) (v)
Cyprus	1.9	6.1	4.7	−4.2	71.9
Czech Republic	2.6	4.1	2.4	−3.0	37.4
Estonia	3.0	–	2.5	1.8	4.9
Hungary	6.8	8.2	11.5	−4.5	57.6
Latvia	6.2	4.9	4.2	−0.8	14.4
Lithuania	1.1	4.4	2.7	−2.5	19.7
Malta	2.7	4.7	2.9	−5.2	75.0
Poland	3.6	6.9	6.2	−4.8	43.6
Slovakia	7.4	5.0	4.7	−3.3	43.6
Slovenia	3.2	6.4	4.6	−1.9	29.4
EU-15	2.0	4.1	2.6	−2.6	64.7

Sources: (i), (iv), (v) Eurostat database – *Structural Indicators.*
(ii), (iii) Eurostat database – *Long-term Indicators,* Economy and Finance.

EU-10 and the EU-15, arguing that even in some of the most advanced newcomers, including the Czech Republic and Slovenia, the shocks are still largely idiosyncratical asymmetric, something implying that it is not clear whether they would benefit from an early EMU membership (see Fidrmuc and Korhonen (2004), Frenkel *et al.* (1999), and Süppel (2003) Frenkel and Nickel (2005)).

Summary and Conclusions

The main advantage of moving towards full monetary union in Europe is related to international interdependence: when countries are economically interdependent, monetary-policy actions taken by individual governments in an uncoordinated manner can lead to Pareto-inefficient macroeconomic outcomes. This is particularly relevant for the European economies since the inefficiencies resulting from the lack of cooperation are greater the more integrated countries are.

On the other hand, in evaluating the benefits and costs of EMU relative to the pre-EMU monetary regime in Europe, the EMS, one should take into account that the EMU is a symmetric system of monetary control while the EMS, at least after 1985, operated as an asymmetric system of monetary control with Germany being the centre country. The problem with the asymmetric EMS was that Germany conducted monetary policy without paying attention to macroeconomic outcomes in the other member countries. The result was that in the presence of shocks affecting the non-German countries, those countries were forced to adopt inappropriate policies, namely to contract their money supply when there was a tendency for domestic economic activity to fall, and to expand the money supply when there was a tendency for domestic economic activity to rise. This intensified the overall impact of shocks on their economies. Such a problem would not arise in an EMU: the ECB would take a union-wide perspective regarding monetary policy.

However, as early as in 1991 it was argued that without securing the full independence of the ECB, average inflation in Europe would be higher in an EMU than under the EMS. This view was based on the consideration that at the time of signing the Maastricht Treaty, some of the member states' central banks did not have the inflation consciousness of the Bundesbank. Thus it was argued that the ECB, in whose board representatives from all national central banks would participate, would cause an inflationary bias. These considerations convinced member states that the ECB should be independent of national governments and that its declared aim should be to achieve low inflation. Central bank independence, however, can create problems in an environment where other policy-makers, like the national fiscal authorities in the case of the EMU, also make decisions in a strategic manner.

As far as the way of proceeding to monetary unification is concerned, the EU-15 member states adopted the road of a gradual process of convergence of macroeconomic performances, although it was decided that the euro would in any case circulate on 1 January 2002.

At the same time, criteria for participation and stay in EMU have been adopted, including rules for the size of public deficits and debt. This criterion has been heavily criticized. Also heavily criticized has been the Maastricht Treaty's insistence on nominal convergence: the Maastricht Treaty has neglected real convergence which, from a longer-term perspective, is more important than nominal convergence. Some claim that nominal convergence will necessarily lead to real convergence. Others, however, argue that this may not be the case and/or that little attention has been paid to the question of exactly when this may happen. This is a serious problem given that currently the degree of real convergence of the EU-15 economies remains unsatisfactory.

Real convergence is also an issue for the EU-25, given that the 10 new member states have declared a strong desire to adopt the euro as soon as possible despite the fact that their economies differ from those of the EU-15 in many respects. Indeed, the question of choosing a process towards monetary union has recently taken new relevance following the May 2004 EU enlargement: the 10 new member states are currently in search for the optimal strategy for achieving monetary unification with the other EU states. Some academics argue in favour of an immediate adoption of the euro by these countries, a 'euroization', rather than a process of gradual convergence. Others however claim that a better strategy for these countries would be to join the ERM-II and remain in it for some years before attempting EMU membership, arguing that the ERM-II would assist them to achieve convergence.

Notes

1 See European Commission (1989).
2 See European Commission (1992).
3 See Canzoneri and Henderson (1988, 1991), Cooper (1985) and Hamada (1985).
4 For a discussion of the benefits and costs of EMU see European Commission (1990), and Emerson *et al.* (1992), and also Cohen (1988), Gros and Thygesen (1990, 1992, 1998) and Artis (1992, 1994). See Eichengreen (1993) for a critical review of EMU.
5 For a discussion of these issues see Artis (1992), Cobham (1991), Thygesen (1993), Currie (1992), Currie *et al.* (1992, 1996), Begg *et al.* (1997), De Grauwe (1994) and Dornbusch *et al.* (1998). See also De Cecco and Giovannini (1989).

6 See for example ECB (1999).
7 See Wyplosz (1997) and also Artis (1994), Gros (1996a) and Gros and Thygesen (1998).
8 See EMI (1997a, b).
9 See Buiter (1999) and Svensson (1999) for a discussion.
10 For an analysis of the various strategies for achieving monetary unification see Salin (1984), Hitiris and Zervoyianni (1983), Vaubel (1978, 1990), Gros and Thygesen (1990, 1992, 1998), Cobham (1989, 1991), Gros (1989, 1996a) and Kenen (1995) and Artis (1996). See also Gavazzi and Spaventa (1990) and Currie (1995).
11 See HM Treasury (1989).
12 This type of analysis in the European-integration literature has been inspired by the influential paper of Backus and Driffill (1985) regarding the 'type' of policy-makers.
13 See Rossi (2004) for an alternative way to integrate these countries into EMU. See also De Grauwe and Schnabl (2004).
14 See Boeri and Brücker (2001) and Fisher *et al.* (1998a, b). See also Korhonen (2001), Kočenda (2001), Gros (2000), De Grauwe (2003b), Hellmann (2001), Eichengreen (2002) and Schweickert (2003).

References

Artis, M.J. (1992) 'The Maastricht Road to Monetary Union', *Journal of Common Market Studies*, vol. 30, pp. 299–309.

Artis, M.J. (1994) 'European Monetary Union', in M. Artis and N. Lee (eds), *The Economics of the European Union: Policy and Analysis* (Oxford: Oxford University Press).

Artis, M.J. (1996) 'Alternative Transitions to EMU', *Economic Journal*, vol. 106, pp. 1005–15.

Backus, D. and Driffill, J. (1985) 'Inflation and Reputation', *American Economic Review*, vol. 75, pp. 530–8.

Baldwin, R., Francois, J.F. and Porterts, R. (1997), 'The Costs and Benefits of Eastern Enlargement', *Economic Policy*, vol. 24, pp. 127–76.

Begg, D., Giavazzi, F., von Hagen, J. and Wyplosz, C. (1997) *Getting the End-Game Right*, Monitoring European Integration, 7 (London: Centre for Economic Policy Research).

Belke, A. and D. Gros (1998) 'Evidence on the Cost of Intra-European Exchange-Rate Variability', Discussion Paper no. 9814, Centre for Economic Policy Research, Tilburg University.

Bini-Smaghi, L., Padoa-Schioppa, T. and Papadia, F. (1994) 'The Transition to EMU in the Maastricht Treaty', *Essays in International Finance* no. 194, November, Princeton University.

Boeri, T. and Brücker, H. (2001) *The Impact of Eastern Enlargement on Employment and Labour Markets in the EU Member States – Final Report*, Directorate General for Economic and Social Affairs, European Integration Consortium, Berlin and Milan.

Buiter, W. (1995) 'Macroeconomic Policy during a Transition to Monetary Union', Working Paper no. 261, August, Centre for Economic Performance, London School of Economics and Political Science.

Buiter, W. (1999) 'Alice in Euroland', *Journal of Common Market Studies*, vol. 37, pp. 181–209.

Buiter, W. and Sibert, A. (1997) 'Transition Issues for the European Monetary Union', CEPR Discussion Paper no. 1728, Centre for Economic Policy Research, London.

Canzoneri, M. and Henderson, D. (1988) 'Is Sovereign Policy-Making Bad?', *Carnegie-Rochester Conference Series on Public Policy*, vol. 28, pp. 93–140.

Canzoneri, M. and Henderson, D. (1991) *Monetary Policy in Interdependent Economies: A Game Theoretic Approach* (Cambridge, Mass.: MIT Press).

Cobham, D. (1989) 'Strategies for Monetary Integration Revisited', *Journal of Common Market Studies*, vol. 28, pp. 203–18.

Cobham, D. (1991) 'European Monetary Integration: A Survey of the Recent Literature', *Journal of Common Market Studies*, vol. 29, pp. 363–83.

Cohen, D. (1988) 'The Costs and Benefits of a European Currency', in M. de Cecco and A. Giovannini (eds), *A European Central Bank?* (Cambridge: Cambridge University Press).

Collignon, S. (1997) 'European Monetary Union, Convergence and Sustainability', Working Paper, November, London School of Economics and Political Science.

Cooper, R.N. (1985) 'Economic Interdependence and Co-ordination of Economic Policies', in J. Jones and P. Kenen (eds), *Handbook of International Economics*, vol. II (Elserier: Amsterdam).

Currie, D. (1992) 'European Monetary Union: Institutional Structure and Macroeconomic Performance', *Economic Journal,* vol. 102, pp. 248–64.

Currie, D. (1995) 'The Path to EMU: Blocked or Open? in D. Currie and J. Whitley (eds), *EMU: The Problems in the Transition to a Single European Currency* (London: Lothian Foundation Press).

Currie, D. (1998) *Will the Euro Work? The Ins and Outs of EMU* (London: The Economist Intelligence Unit).

Currie, D., Levine, P. and J. Pearlman (1992) 'European Monetary Union or Hard EMS?', *European Economic Review,* vol. 6, pp. 1185–204.

Currie, D.A., Levine, P. and Perlman, J. (1996) 'The Choice of Conservative Bankers in Open Economies: Monetary Regime Options for Europe', *Economic Journal,* vol. 106, pp. 345–58.

De Cecco, M. and Giovannini, A. (eds) (1989) *A European Central Bank?* (Cambridge: Cambridge University Press).

De Grauwe, P. (1994) 'Towards EMU Without the EMS', *Economic Policy*, vol. 17, pp. 147–85.

De Grauwe, P. (1996) 'The Economics of Convergence Towards Monetary Union in Europe', in Torres, F. (ed.) *Monetary Reform in Europe* (Lisbon: Universidade Catolica Editoria)

De Grauwe, P. (2000), *Economics of Monetary Union,* 4th edition (Oxford: Oxford University Press).

De Grauwe, P. (2003a) *The Economics of Monetary Union,* 5th edition (Oxford: Oxford University Press).

De Grauwe, P. (2003b) 'The Challenge of the Enlargement of Euroland', in Prausello, F. (ed.) *The Economics of EU Enlargement* (Milan: Franco Angelli).

De Grauwe, P. and Skudelny, F. (2000) 'The Impact of EMU on Trade Flows', *Weltwirtschaftliches Archiv,* vol. 136, pp. 381–402.

De Grauwe, P. and Schnabl, G. (2004) 'EMU: Entry Strategies for the New Member States', *Intereconomics,* vol. 39, pp. 241–47.

Dornbusch, R., Favero, C. and Giavazzi, F. (1998) 'Immediate Challenges for the European Central Bank, *Economic Policy,* vol. 26, pp. 15–64.

ECB (1999) 'The Stability Oriented Monetary Policy of the Eurosystem', *ECB Monthly Bulletin,* January, pp. 39–50

Eichengreen, B. (1993) 'European Monetary Unification', *Journal of Economic Literature,* vol. 31, pp. 1321–57.

Eichengreen, B. (2002), 'The Enlargement Challenge: Can Monetary Union Be Made to Work in an EU of 25 Members?', *Australian Economic Review,* vol. 35, pp. 113–21.

EMI (1997a) *The Single Monetary Policy in Stage Three: Specification of the Operational Framework,* European Monetary Institute, Frankfurt am Main.

EMI (1997b) *Annual Report 1996,* European Monetary Institute, Frankfurt am Main.

Emerson, M., Gross, D., Italianer, A., Pisany-Ferry, J. and Reichenbach, H. (1992) *One Market, One Money* (Oxford: Oxford University Press).

European Commission (1989) *Report on Economic and Monetary Union in the European Community* (Delors Report), Office for Official Publications of the European Community, Luxembourg.

European Commission (1990) 'One Market, One Money: An Evaluation of the Potential Benefits and Costs of Forming an Economic and Monetary Union', *European Economy.*

European Commission (1992) *Treaty on European Union,* Office for Official Publications of the European Community, Luxembourg.

European Commission (1996) 'Currency Management Costs', *The Single Market Review Series* (Subseries III – Dismantling of Barriers), Office for Official Publication of the EU, Luxembourg.

Fidrmuc, J. and Korhonen, I. (2003), 'Similarity of Supply and Demand Shocks Between the Euro Area and the CEECs', *Economic Systems,* vol. 27, pp. 313–34.

Fidrmuc, J. and Korhonen, I. (2004) 'A Meta-Analysis of Business-Cycle Correlation Between the Euro Area and CEEs: What Do We Know and Who Cares', *Bofit Discussion Paper,* no. 20/2004, Bank of Finland, Institute for Economies in Transition.

Fisher, S., Sahay, R. and Vegh, C. (1998a), 'From Transition to Market: Evidence and Growth Prospects', IMF Working Paper no. 98/52, International Monetary Fund, Washington, D.C.

Fisher, S., Sahay, R. and Vegh, C. (1998b), 'How Far is Eastern Europe from Brussels?', IMF Working Paper no. 98/53, International Monetary Fund, Washington, D.C.

Frenkel, M. and Nickel, C. (2005) 'How Symmetric Are the Shocks and Shock Adjustment Dynamics Between the Euro Area and Central and Eastern European Countries?', *Journal of Common Market Studies,* vol. 43, pp. 53–74.

Frenkel, M., Nickel, C. and Schmidt, G. (1999) 'Some Shocking Aspects of EMU Enlargement', Research Note no. 99-4, Deutsche Bank, Frankfurt am Main.

Giavazzi, F. and Spaventa, L. (1990) 'The New EMS', in P. De Grauwe and L. Papademos (eds), *The European Monetary System in the 1990s* (London: Longman).

Gros, D. (1989) 'Paradigms for the Monetary Union of Europe', *Journal of Common Market Studies*, vol. 27, pp. 219–30.

Gros, D. and Thygesen, N. (1990) 'The Institutional Approach to Monetary Union in Europe', *Economic Journal*, vol. 10, pp. 925–35.

Gros, D. (1996a) 'Towards Economic and Monetary Union', CEPS Paper no. 65, Centre for European Policy Studies, Belgium.

Gros, D. (1996b) 'German Stake in Exchange-Rate Stability', CEPS Paper no. 70, Centre for European Policy Studies, Belgium.

Gros, D. and Thygesen, N. (1992) *European Monetary Integration: From the European Monetary System Towards Monetary Union* (London: Longman).

Gros, D. (2000) 'How Fit Are the Candidates for EMU?' *The World Economy*, vol. 23, pp. 1367–77.

Gros, D. and Thygesen, N. (1998) *European Monetary Integration* (Harlow: Addison-Wesley-Longman).

Hamada, C. (1985) The Politial Economy of Monetary Interdependence (Cambridge, Mass: MIT Press).

Hasse, R. (1995) 'Analysis of the Convergence Criteria of the Maastricht Treaty: Are They Able to Create Stability?' in D. Currie and J. Whitley (eds), *EMU: The Problems in the Transition to a Single European Currency* (London: Lothian Foundation Press).

Hellmann, H. (2001) 'The Challenge of Enlargement for Candidate Countries and EMU', in R. Caesar and H.S. Scharrer (eds), *European Economic and Monetary Union: Regional and Global Challenges* (Baden-Baden: Nomos Verlagsellschaft).

Hitiris, T. and Zervoyianni, A. (1983) 'Monetary Integration and the European Monetary System', in J. Lodge (ed.), *Policies and Institutions of the European Community* (London: Francis Pinter).

HM Treasury (1989) *The Hard ECU Proposal*, Document, London.

Kenen, P. (1995) *Economic and Monetary Union: Moving Beyond Maastricht* (Cambridge: Cambridge University Press).

Kočenda, E. (2001) 'Macroeconomic Convergence in Transition Economies, *Journal of Comparative Economics*, vol. 29, pp. 1–23.

Korhonen, I. (2001), 'Some Empirical Tests on the Integration of Economic Activity Between the Euro Area and the Accession Countries', Discussion Paper no. 9/2001, Bank of Finland, Institute for Economies in Transition.

Krugman, P. (1990) 'Policy Problems of a Monetary Union', in P. De Grauwe and L. Papademos (eds), *The European Monetary System in the 1990s* (London: Longman).

Molle, W. and Morsink, R. (1991a) 'Intra-European Direct Investment', in B. Bürgenmeier and J. Mucchielli (eds), *Multinationals and Europe 1992* (London: Routledge).

Molle, W. and Morsink, R. (1991b) 'Direct Investment and Monetary Integration', *European Economy*, Special Edition no. 1, European Commission.

Rossi, S. (2004) 'Monetary Integration Strategies and Perspectives of New EU Countries', *International Review of Applied Economics*, vol. 18, pp. 443–69.

Salin, P. (eds) (1984) *Currency Competition and Monetary Union* (The Hague: Martinug Nijhoff).

Schweickert, R. (2003), 'One Currency for All the Europes? Relative Advantage and Political Economy Problems of EMU Enlargement', Working Paper, Kiel Institute of World Economics.

Süppel, R. (2003) 'Comparing Economic Dynamics in the EU and in CEE Accession Countries', ECB Working Paper no. 267, European Central Bank, Frankfurt am Main.

Svensson, L. (1999) 'Monetary Policy Issues for the Eurosystem', *Carnegie-Rochester Conference Series on Public Policy*, vol. 51, pp. 79–136.

Thygesen, T. (1993) 'Towards Monetary Union in Europe: Reforms of the EMS in the Perspective of Monetary Union', *Journal of Common Market Studies*, vol. 31, pp. 447–72.

Vaubel, R. (1978) *Strategies for Currency Unification, Kieler Studien*, no. 156 (Tübingen: Mohr & Siebeck).

Vaubel, R. (1990) 'Currency Competition and European Monetary Integration', *Economic Journal*, vol. 100, pp. 936–46.

World Economic Forum (2003), *The Lisbon Review 2002–2003: An Assessment of Policies and Reforms in Europe*, available on website: www.weforum.org/lisbonreview

Wyplosz, C. (1997) 'EMU: Why and How it May Happen', *Journal of Economic Perspectives*, vol. 11, pp. 3–21.

7 Monetary Policy in the EMU: Theoretical Issues and Assessment

Athina Zervoyianni

Introduction

From January 1999 the European Central Bank (ECB) has taken over responsibility for the conduct of monetary policy in the euro zone from national monetary authorities. The Maastricht agreement for the European System of Central Banks (ESCBs) has set out some general principles with regard to the ECB's objectives and has also determined the institutional framework within which it will make decisions. In particular, the ECB's primary objective is to maintain price stability, and, without prejudice to the price-stability objective, it will support Europe's general economic policies. According to Article 107 of the Maastricht Treaty, in order to achieve its price-stability objective, the ECB will be politically independent: its members will be forbidden from taking instructions from national governments, or from other community institutions, such as the Council. Indeed, the achievement of the national CBs' legal and institutional independence was a prerequisite for their participation in the ESCBs. The operational expression of the price-stability objective was left by the Maastricht Treaty to the ECB to decide.

As early as in December 1997, the European Monetary Institute (EMI, 1997) commented on the ECB's likely monetary strategy. Emphasizing the unsuitability of both the EU's nominal GDP and the euro exchange rate as an intermediate target of monetary policy in an area as potentially large as the EU, it restricted the final choice of intermediate target between a broad monetary aggregate, namely M2 or M3, and forecasts of future inflation.

At a press conference on 3 October 1998, and also on 1 December, the ECB formally announced its choice of monetary strategy. A principal role would be given to M3, with announcement of a reference value for its rate of change. This reference value would be consistent with the objective of price stability. As for the operational

expression of the objective of price stability, the ECB adopted an inflation target of no more than 2 per cent for the Harmonized Index of
Consumer Prices (HICP). Deviations of the current rate of increase of
M3 from its reference value would signal dangers to price stability and
would lead to corrective actions by the ECB's board of governors. In
any case, the board of governors of the ECB declared that it would
analyse at regular intervals the relation between the current rate of
increase of M3 and its reference value, and the conclusions of this
analysis as well as its implication for the ECB's decisions would be
explained to the public. In addition to the rate of growth of M3, an
important role in the ECB's policy would also be given to forecasts of
future price developments (see ECB (1998, 1999, 2003)).[1]

In general, monetary policy in a monetary union can be taken to
consist of three main elements:

- the final targets of the union's central bank and its degree of
  independence from member states' governments;
- the degree of democratic control exercised on it by other common
  institutions; and
- the framework of monetary policy, that is the choice of intermediate monetary target, of means of external communication with
  the public and of monetary tool.

As was also mentioned in previous chapters, 'final' targets are
aggregate macroeconomic variables whose magnitude reflects the
general performance of the economy; they are usually expressed in
terms of 'reference values'. The aim of a MU's central monetary
authority is to minimize deviations of the current values of variables
that constitute its final targets from their reference values. Obviously,
an important (final) target of monetary policy is price stability (or
zero inflation), but variables like the rate of GDP growth, the level of
employment, the balance of payments and so on can also be regarded
as other possible (final) targets.

The priority a MU's central bank attaches to each of these final
targets varies according to its degree of independence. An independent
central monetary authority will tend to give greater priority to the
maintenance of price stability and lower priority to the other objectives. On the other hand, when the union's central bank is not
independent of the politically elected national governments, the
priority attached to the individual objectives will, to a large extent,
reflect the priorities of governments. Such priorities are usually broader
than price stability *per se* and always include, for example, the achievement of low unemployment, a high rate of GDP growth and so on.
Thus, at the level of a MU, the primary objectives of the central
monetary authority and the degree of its independence from the
member states' governments are related issues.

In the last few years a vast analytical and empirical literature has been developed, emphasizing the need for central bank independence both at the national level and at the level of a monetary union.[2] However, having an independent Central Bank also involves 'costs', and such costs have been the driving force behind recent attempts by some member states to achieve agreement on exercising democratic control on the ECB. Democratic control exists when a union's central bank is accountable to the public, either directly or indirectly through another common institution, not only for the achievement of its own targets, but also for the impact of its actions on the objectives of other economic-policy units in the union.

As regards the framework of monetary policy, this consists of the tools of monetary policy, the intermediate target of monetary policy, and the means by which the CB communicates with the public. At the theoretical level, the tools of monetary policy are variables with which the union's monetary authorities aim to influence the development of the variables adopted as final targets. In practice, a common tool of monetary policy is a short-term interest rate. However, between the tools of monetary policy and the final targets of monetary policy, a number of other variables interfere that are only indirectly controllable by the monetary authorities. For this reason, a common practice of CBs is to adopt one or more of these variables as an intermediate target of monetary policy. In particular, the central bank decides on a reference value for these variables in a way that ensures that the final targets are achieved in the long run and, utilizing the tools of monetary policy, in the short run tries to minimize the deviations of the current value of these intermediate variables from their reference values. The choice of variable to be adopted as intermediate target is not an easy task. This is because an intermediate variable must possess certain properties if it is to be useful as intermediate target. For example, it must be directly and quickly measurable; and it must be in a stable relation both with the tools of monetary policy and with the final targets of monetary policy. Thus, because it can considerably influence the degree of a CB's success as far as the achievement of final targets is concerned, the choice of intermediate target constitutes an important element of monetary policy. External communication with the public is also part of the framework of monetary policy and may take the form of announcements by the central bank about the achievement of final objectives, of intermediate targets, or both.

Accordingly, a number of issues regarding the conduct of monetary policy in a monetary union in general, and in the European Monetary Union in particular, arise. One of them is central bank independence: what are the costs and benefits of having an independent central bank in a MU? And what does the empirical evidence suggest about the performance of independent CBs? Another issue has to do with the interactions between an independent CB and other union policy-makers: to what extent may conflicts between them arise? What are the likely effects of such conflicts? And to what extent is there a need for exercising democratic control on a union's central bank actions? Yet another issue is the choice of an intermediate target of monetary policy and of a means of external communication with the public: which variable can be regarded as the most appropriate intermediate target of monetary policy in a MU? And to what extent should the intermediate target and the means of communication with the public differ? Finally, there is the issue of the exchange rate policy of a monetary union and its relation to monetary policy.

These issues are examined in what follows. The next section addresses the issue of CB independence, followed by a consideration of the case for an accountable ECB. We then examine the choice of monetary strategy in a monetary union in general, before focusing on the ECB's monetary strategy. Exchange-rate issues in a EMU are then considered, before a final a summary and conclusions.

An Independent Central Bank?

The argument for central bank independence in a MU follows from the Barro-Gordon framework and is based on the principle of 'dynamic inconsistency' of monetary policy. This principle, which is characterized by the hypothesis that monetary policy has no systematic effects on real macroeconomic variables, was initially presented by Kydland and Prescott (1977), and further developed by others.[3] In the models analysed in these studies, the assumption is made that monetary policy-makers either have been created by national governments, and therefore are directly dependent upon them, or are politically linked to national governments and thus are dependent on them indirectly. Accordingly, the targets of monetary policy-makers are effectively the targets of governments.

In particular, the argument is that monetary authorities wish to achieve price stability or zero inflation. Nevertheless, politically elected governments know that, because of the existence of nominal rigidities, monetary policy can also have real effects in the short run and can thus be used to raise employment above its natural-rate level. This natural level of employment may be lower than the level governments regard as 'socially optimal' because of imperfections in goods and/or labour markets resulting from monopolistic competition, the actions of insiders in labour unions, the disincentive effects of unemployment benefits, and so on. In fact, the first-best for governments is to have full employment and zero inflation, and they will

thus attempt to use monetary policy to achieve these two objectives. Accordingly, governments present to monetary authorities a loss
function to be minimized of the form:

$$L = (\pi - \pi^*)^2 + \beta(\eta - \eta^*)^2, \text{ with } \pi^* = 0 \text{ and } \eta^* > \eta_0 \qquad (1)$$

where π is current inflation, π^* denotes the target value for the
inflation rate, η is the current level of employment, η^* is the target
value for this variable and η_0 is the natural level of employment. The
constant β reflects the priority placed on the objective of maintaining
high employment. The monetary authorities will attempt to minimize
the divergence of current inflation from its desired value and of
current employment from its socially accepted level using the tools of
monetary policy, namely short-term interest rates.

On the other hand, the private sector's behaviour is determined by
a Phillips-curve-type equation with rational expectations of the form:

$$\eta = \eta_0 + \gamma(\pi - \pi^e) - v \qquad (2)$$

where π^e is the expected inflation rate when expectations are formed
on the basis of all available information at the beginning of each
period, $(\pi - \pi^e)$ is unexpected inflation and v is an exogenous
stochastic variable with zero mean and a constant variance that affects
adversely employment. Equation (2) can be interpreted on the usual
grounds that trade unions target real wages and, for this purpose, form
expectations about inflation. However, wage contracts that determine
nominal wages in each period are signed at the beginning of the period
and therefore incorporate expectations that have been formed at the
end of the previous period. Thus, if, during the current period, the
rate of inflation rises relative to the level expected when contracts
were signed, that is if it happens that $(\pi - \pi^e) > 0$, the result will be a
reduction in real wages. This will create an incentive for firms to boost
production and therefore employment. If, however, $\pi^e = \pi$ and $v = 0$,
the current level of employment will be at its natural level.

The Dynamic Inconsistency of Monetary Policy

The problem of 'dynamic inconsistency' arises from the fact that while
wage contracts are signed at the beginning of each period, and therefore incorporate all information available at the end of the previous
period, the central bank conducts monetary policy during that period.
In particular, starting from the beginning of the period, assume that
there is full adjustment of inflationary expectations, namely that
$\pi^e = \pi$, and also there are no stochastic shocks and so $v = 0$. As is

evident from equations (1) and (2), in such a case, the best choice for a monetary union's CB is simply to adopt a policy of zero inflation. Suppose that the CB announces at the beginning of the period that it will indeed follow such a policy both in the current period and in all subsequent periods. In this case, the private sector will set $\pi^e = 0$ and will sign wage contracts. The problem is that while the CB's commitment to a policy of zero inflation is the best choice *ex ante*, it stops being such *ex post* when the CB has to conduct monetary policy. In fact, if the union's CB were to minimize equation (1) after wage contracts had been signed, namely during the current period, its best choice would be to take the private sector's inflation expectations as given, assuming that $\pi^e = 0$, and try to raise employment above its natural-rate level. But with rational expectations, the private sector will anticipate the CB's actions: it will recognize that it is best for the monetary authorities not to keep their promise and that they will actually attempt to boost employment.

The result is that the CB's announcement of an *average* inflation rate of zero will not be credible. The only credible policy will be that which involves discretion by the monetary authorities, that is they will proceed to a period-by-period minimization of equation (1) and will not be tied up by previous decisions. But then, in equilibrium, there will be an 'inflation bias': even in the absence of stochastic disturbances, inflation will not be zero. The principle of the dynamic inconsistency of monetary policy in effect points to the existence of this inflation bias and the issue is how such bias can be reduced or eliminated.

Indeed, assuming for simplicity that the relationship between the tools of monetary policy and inflation is non-stochastic and that the monetary authorities 'set' π to minimize the loss function (1), we can find equilibrium inflation by considering the actions of the union's CB as seen by the private sector. The private sector knows that the union's central bank will minimize equation (1), taking inflation expectations as given. The minimization of (1) with respect to π, for a given π^e, yields:

$$\pi = \beta_1 [\gamma\pi^e + v + (\eta^* - \eta_0)], \text{ with } \beta_1 = \beta\gamma/(1+\beta\gamma^2) \tag{1a}$$

The private sector uses this function to form inflationary expectations. Given that v is a stochastic variable with mean zero, taking expectations we have $\pi^e = \beta\gamma(\eta^* - \eta_0)$. Substituting this expression for π^e into equation (1a), we find the equilibrium inflation rate, π^E, as:

$$\pi^E = \beta_1 v + \beta\gamma(\eta^* - \eta_0) \tag{3a}$$

At the same time, taking expectations in equation (3a), we have that $(\pi^E - \pi^e) = \beta_1 v$. Inserting this expression for $(\pi^E - \pi^e)$ into equation (2), we obtain the equilibrium level of employment, η^E, as:

$$\eta^E = \eta_0 - \beta_2 v, \text{ with } \beta_2 = 1/(1 + \beta\gamma^2) \tag{3b}$$

In equation (3a) π^E incorporates a non-zero average inflation rate, or an 'inflationary bias' of $\beta\gamma(\eta^* - \eta_0)$. In particular, the first term in the right-hand side of (3a) represents inflation resulting form stabilization policy, namely monetary policy aimed at reducing the adverse impact on employment of the non-systematic stochastic shock v. But there is also a second term, which is positive even when there are no stochastic shocks and so $v = 0$, and therefore represents an inflation bias. The magnitude of the inflation bias depends on the weight placed by the government on employment, on the responsiveness of employment to unanticipated inflation and on the divergence between the natural level of employment and the government's target for employment. In a first-best equilibrium, where the CB could be committed that it would not attempt to use monetary policy in order to exercise a systematic influence on employment, this inflation bias would be absent. Monetary policy in such a case would simply have a stabilization role: it would only respond to exogenous stochastic disturbances. In terms of equation (3a), we would have an equilibrium rate of inflation of $\pi^E = \beta_1 v$ that would simply compensate for the impact of the exogenous disturbance v on η. However, as mentioned above, such commitment would not be consistent with the period-by-period minimization of equation (1) and thus would not be credible.

Assigning Monetary Policy to an Independent Central Bank

Of the second-best solutions to the problem of dynamic inconsistency and inflationary bias proposed in the literature is that of having a conservative and independent central bank. This solution, which was originally developed by Rogoff (1985) and Persson and Tabellini (1993), proposes[4] the removal of the responsibility for deciding on monetary policy from national governments and its assignment to an inflation-conscious central banker: a person who is more concerned about inflation than elected governments. Indeed, the CB's inflation consciousness can be chosen optimally, so that the person put in charge of the union's CB will not be so conservative that he leaves the central bank no scope at all to respond to supply-oriented exogenous shocks, and will make the extent of the intervention dependent upon the variability of these shocks (see Alesina and Grilli (1992) and Currie et al. (1995, 1996)).[5]

Accordingly, the theoretical framework underlying the assignment principle can be summarized as follows. Both the member states' governments and the elected governing board of the union's central bank have objective functions like equation (1). However, bankers tend to give a greater weight to nominal variables than national governments, so the weight they will assign to employment, say β_{CB}, will in general be lower than that of governments (that is, $\beta_{CB} < \beta$), although they may differ in terms of how conservative they are, namely in terms of how close β_{CB} will be to β. In choosing among potential agents to head the CB, national governments could then ask the candidates how much more inflation they would be prepared to accept in exchange for a given increase in employment and so select a governor for the union's CB with a given degree of inflation consciousness.[6] As emphasized among others by Al-Nowaihi *et al.* (1997), from this point of view, the choice of how close β_{CB} would be to β could be regarded as a choice of institutional structure for the union's CB: a structure that permits a given degree of national interference in the union's monetary policy. In the case of a fully independent CB, there will be no national interference in the union's monetary policy and so, assuming that bankers are typically conservative, the result would be a choice of β_{CB} close to zero. By contrast, a large extent of national interference in the union's monetary policy would mean a choice of value for β_{CB} close to β.

The argument for CB independence follows from this framework. After national governments have selected a β_{CB}, and thus in the case of the European Union the degree of conservatism of the ECB's governor, and after the private sector has adjusted expectations accordingly, the independent ECB will choose π so as to minimize equation (1b):

$$L^{ECB} = (\pi - \pi^*)^2 + \beta_{ECB}(\eta - \eta^*)^2, \text{ with } \pi^* = 0 \text{ and } \eta^* > \eta_0 \qquad (1b)$$

where $\beta_{ECB} < \beta$, that is, the weight placed on employment is smaller than the weight which the EU elected governments would consider optimal. This implies that, in equilibrium, we will have inflation and unemployment in the EU as follows:

$$\pi^{ECB} = [\gamma\beta_{ECB}/(1+\gamma^2\beta_{ECB})]v + \gamma\beta_{ECB}(\eta^* - \eta_0) \qquad (3c)$$

$$\eta^{ECB} = \eta_0 - \{1/(1+\gamma^2\beta_{ECB})\}v \qquad (3d)$$

For $v = 0$ equations (3c) and (3d), compared with (3a) and (3b), imply an increase in the level of welfare: in a non-stochastic equilibrium, the inflationary bias would be smaller since $\beta_{ECB} < \beta$, while, at the same time, the degree of conservatism and independence of the ECB would exert no systematic influence on employment. However, as is evident from equation (3d), with $\beta_{ECB} < \beta$, the 'stabilization impact' (that is when $v \neq 0$) of monetary policy would be smaller with an independent and conservative ECB: with $v > 0$, employment will fall more the more conservative the CB is.[6]

The Empirical Literature on CB Independence

As regards the empirical literature, results about the effects of independence are mixed.[7] Part of it suggests that politically independent central banks have achieved lower inflation than CBs in which this independence is absent, and indeed at no cost in terms of employment and output. The findings of, for example, Bade and Parkin (1978) and of Demopoulos *et al.* (1987), and subsequently of Grilli *et al.* (1991) who have been the first to construct 'independence indices' for the CBs of 18 industrial countries, show that at least for certain periods there is a statistically significant negative relationship between independence and inflation. Alesina and Summers (1993), extending the analysis of Grilli *et al.* (1991) as far as the choice of independence indices is concerned, have also found a clear negative relationship between these two variables. In addition, contrary to what is implied by equation (3d), they have not been able to find any positive relationship between CB independence and the variance of employment. Bleany (1996), using a sample of 17 OECD countries, also arrives at the same conclusion as he finds that the degree of CB independence, while having a favourable impact on inflation, does not influence the level of unemployment. Eijffinger and Schaling (1993), De Haan and Sturm (1994) and Eijffinger, van Rooij and Schaling (1997), among others, also report similar findings: CB independence is not found to have any statistically significant negative effect on the mean rate of increase of the GDP of the countries examined. In an attempt to justify these findings, Alesina and Gatti (1995) argue that CB independence reduces the politically-motivated part of the business cycle and this compensates for the reduced 'stabilization' impact of monetary policy on output and employment.

Nevertheless, a set of other studies arrives at different conclusions thus questioning the arguments in favour of having an independent ECB. Eijffinger and De Haan (1996) mention a series of arguments against the independence of monetary authorities, while Blinder (1999), Mangano (1998) and McCallum (1995, 1997) point out that, in general, independence is a problematic concept both in theory and in practice and that it does not actually resolve the time inconsistency problem.[8] Moreover, the existence of a clear negative relationship between independence and inflation does not seem to be confirmed in the empirical papers of, for example, Eijffinger and van Keulen (1994),

Posen (1993) and Fuijki (1996), while other studies, including Debelle and Fischer (1994), Hall and Franzese (1998) and Fuhrer (1997), question the argument that the independence of CBs can reduce inflation without creating either lower employment or increasing the variance of employment. Debelle and Fischer (1994) find that there is a significant cost from CB independence in terms of the stabilization impact of monetary policy. The results of Hall and Franzese (1998) also imply that independent CBs while reducing the mean value of inflation, lead to increases in the total variability of real GDP. Fuhrer (1997), Fuijki (1996) and Demertzis (2004) arrive at similar conclusions.

In general, as stressed for example by Cukierman (1992), a major problem with the empirical studies dealing with the issue of CB independence is that of constructing reliable independence indices. In most of the empirical studies, the degree of CB independence is measured on the basis of legal independence while what is relevant is the degree of actual independence. By its nature, a central bank interacts with a number of market participants and this in many cases automatically leads to informal agreements. Thus, a CB *formally*, that is on the basis of the existing legislation, may be independent, but *effectively*, that is on the basis of its existing interactions with other groups in the economy, may not be independent.

Another problem with existing studies is that their findings do not necessarily show causality, namely a relationship from independence to inflation. This is an important issue because the satisfactory performance of some CBs as far as inflation is concerned may be due to wider reasons. In Japan the fact that wage bargaining is conducted at the national level together with the high rate of labour-productivity growth may have made it possible for the monetary authorities to reduce inflationary pressures even though Japan's CB is not particularly independent (see Lapavitsas (1998), Hayo (1998) and Forder (1998)). Similarly, the Bundesbank's satisfactory performance in the sphere of inflation may have been due to the fact that anti-inflation policy has always been more acceptable by the public in Germany than in other countries, due to, on the one hand, the system of wage bargaining and, on the other, the negative experience that Germany had accumulated during the hyperinflation of the 1930s (see Berger (1997) and Berger and De Haan (1999)). For this reason, Debelle and Fischer (1994) argue against mimicking the Bundesbank both by other countries and by the ECB itself. Forder (1996) and Posen (1995, 1997) also express scepticism in general about the power of 'institutional remedies' to the credibility problem, including mimicking the Bundesbank.

Another argument put forward is that while CB independence can indeed be accompanied by significant social costs in terms of an increased variability of the business cycle, this may not show in the empirical findings due to the activation of appropriate fiscal policy. For example, the findings of Campillo and Miron (1997) indicate that when one isolates fiscal deficits as well as other factors like political instability and openness, CB independence does not seem to have always produced lower inflation. Melitz (1997) arrives at the same conclusion indirectly, as he finds that monetary- and fiscal-policy expansions tend to be negatively correlated in almost all of the OECD countries, irrespective of how independent their CBs are.

On the other hand, other studies question the main hypothesis upon which the argument for CB independence is based, namely the hypothesis that, with rational expectations, any attempt by the monetary authorities to increase employment above its natural level is futile and simply leads to inflationary bias. Lippi (1999b), among others, stresses that the argument for a non-systematic influence on employment of the priority given by the ECB to maintaining low inflation arises from the indirect assumption, usually made in the literature, that those who bargain for wages are atomistic agents, that is trade unions so small in size that do not internalize the effects of their actions on aggregate variables. Several studies show that when trade unions are inflation-averse, the degree of CB independence can have a systematic impact on the level of equilibrium employment, even if the private sector forms expectations rationally and has perfect information.

The argument that the monetary authorities' priorities regarding inflation are not necessarily neutral as far as their effects on unemployment are concerned is also stressed in Cukierman and Lippi (1999), who use a model in which different trade unions compete for the determination of wages. More specifically, Cukierman and Lippi stress that the effects of the degree of CB independence on inflation and unemployment depend on the structure of labour markets, and in particular on the degree of centralization of wage bargaining. They find a relatively large favourable influence of CB independence on inflation in cases of an intermediate degree of centralization, but the direction of influence is not clear in the case of a low or a high degree of centralization. They also find that CB independence exerts a negative influence on employment in the case of a low degree of centralization, but has a postive influence in the case of an intermediate degree of centralization. Their results indicate that when the degree of centralization of wage bargaining is not explicitly taken into account, the negative relationship between CB independence and inflation always appears. In general, they find that there is close interdependence among the degree of centralization of wage bargaining, the degree of central bank independence and macroeconomic performance. Thus, an increase in the degree of CB independence reduces inflation especially at the intermediate level of centralization, and tends to increase unemployment especially in the case of a low degree of centralization.[9] These considerations have recently started to be utilized as arguments for a reexamination of the case for assigning EU's monetary policy to an independent ECB.[10]

The argument that assigning monetary policy to an independent CB reduces inflation with no systematic effect on real variables has also been questioned by Velasco and Guzzo (1999). These authors develop a model in which, due to the assumption that inflation in general annoys trade unions, the appointment of a populist central banker, namely a central banker who does not care at all about inflation, would lead to the first-best solution for both inflation and employment. However, as stressed by Lippi (1999a), this finding rests on the assumption that wage bargaining is conducted in terms of real wages, and not in terms of nominal wages as is usually the case in practice. Nevertheless, Lawler (2000) shows that even when wage bargaining is concluded in nominal terms, for certain values of some structural parameters the social-loss-minimizing choice of a central banker is to attach a relatively large weight to unemployment as long as unions are risk-averse. Cukierman and Lippi (2001), on the other hand, point to the importance of the formation of a MU for the behaviour of unions, arguing that the creation of a monetary union will change the nature of strategic interactions between unions and the CB. In particular, it is argued that with the formation of the MU, each union will perceive that it has become smaller relative to the monetary area, that is the MU has reduced its wage share. This will decrease the unions' perception of the inflationary consequences of their individual wages, inducing them to be in general more aggressive, irrespective of the degree of CB independence. From a different perspective, Dixit (2000), using a repeated-game framework, argues that the most important general property of an 'optimal' monetary-policy rule is its flexibility: the level of inflation allowed by a MU's CB should be a function of the shocks hitting the member states' economies.[11]

Conflicts Between Monetary and Fiscal Policymakers: Is There a Need for 'Democratically Accountable' CBs?

The theory of CB independence as presented in much of the literature has a major deficiency: it assumes that central banks act alone, ignoring the existence of other independent policy-makers. Recent studies of monetary- and fiscal-policy interaction show that when such other policy-makers are taken into account, the usefulness of having an independent CB takes a new perspective since conflicts of priorities between multiple independent agents may arise.[12]

Indeed, according to Debelle and Fischer (1994), Fischer (1995) and De Haan and Eijffinger (2000), the concept of CB independence consists of two elements: 'instrument independence' (or functional independence) and 'goal independence' (or target independence). A CB is instrument independent if it is free to choose its monetary tool, its intermediate target and its operating procedures. It is goal independent if it is free to decide exactly what its targets imply. As Bean (1998) and Begg and Green (1998) among others note, the ECB can be considered fully independent (that is, not only instrument independent but also goal independent) given its autonomy to determine what price stability means and how it will support the general economic policies of the Community, without jeopardizing the objective of price stability. Comparing the ECB with the CBs of Canada, Japan, the UK and the US, Eijffinger and De Haan (1996) and De Haan and Eijffinger (2000) find that the ECB is actually very independent.

Many argue against the overall independence of a CB in an environment of multiple policy-makers (see Stiglitz (1998), Eijffinger and Hoeberichts (2000), Randzio-Plath (2000) and Demertzis *et al.* (1998)). If a CB has overall independence it will be considered by the public responsible, and will be accountable to it, only for the achievement of the objectives that it has openly adopted. Thus when there are other policy-makers, it will act as a non-cooperative player: it will minimize its own loss function ignoring the effects that its actions may have on other policy-makers' targets. However, the targets or priorities of those other policy-makers may conflict with those of the CB. As shown initially by Hamada (1985) and subsequently by others, the result in this case will be a reduction in the ability of each policy-maker to achieve his own objectives. The benefit from having an independent CB will then be limited: the target of zero inflation may be impossible to achieve, or policies designed to reduce average inflation may increase real output variability. Dixit and Labertini (2001a, b), for example, in a game where the CB is independent and the fiscal authority is a strategic player, show that the equilibrium outcome is sub-optimal: output is lower and inflation higher than what either authority wants.

As far as the EU is concerned, this is an important issue. The member states' fiscal authorities, as they are directly related to governments, represent the mean voter and are also accountable to it. Since the mean voter usually takes a high level of employment as a signal of general economic-policy competence, national fiscal authorities, independently of the government's political orientation, will tend to assign a relatively heavy weight to, for example, output growth rates and the creation of jobs. But then, if there are considerable differences in priorities between the national governments and the ECB and an environment of non-cooperative behaviour, the effectiveness of the ECB's policy will tend to be reduced.[13]

Direct Cooperation between an Independent Central Bank and the Fiscal Authorities in a MU

From a theoretical viewpoint, an environment of economic policy conduct by independent policy-makers with different targets or priorities will lead to a Pareto-inefficient macroeconomic outcome: the result will not correspond to the highest possible level of social welfare and Pareto improvements can be achieved if appropriate mechanisms are adopted. What are these appropriate mechanisms is easy to point out at the theoretical level: cooperative behaviour by the independent policy-makers is the solution. In particular, as game theory suggests, the minimization of a joint social welfare function, which is a weighted sum of the welfare functions of the various independent policy-makers, will lead the system to a Pareto-optimal equilibrium and therefore to the highest possible level of social welfare.

To see this point consider an independent CB and a fiscal authority (FA) along the lines suggested, for example, by Demertzis *et al.* (2003), von Hagen and Mundschenk (2003), Levine and Pearlman (2002) and Andersen and Schreider (1986). The CB is assumed to be concerned with maintaining price stability, but also to a certain extent with reducing deviations of current output from potential output. Accordingly, it has a (log-linear) loss function of the form:

$$L_{CB} = (\pi - \pi^*)^2 + \kappa_1(y - y^*)^2, \text{ where } \kappa_1 < 1$$

π^* is the CB's inflation target and y^* is (the log of) potential output. Normalizing y^* and π^* to zero and assuming for simplicity a one-to-one relationship between inflation and money-supply growth, we can write the CB's loss function as:

$$L_{CB} = \dot{m}^2 + \kappa_1 y^2 \tag{4}$$

The fiscal authority is concerned mainly with maintaining output at its potential level and also with achieving a 'reasonable' primary deficit or a balanced budget (along the lines suggested by the Stability and Growth Pact). Thus, its objective function is of the form:

$$L_{FA} = (f - f^*)^2 + \kappa_2(y - y^*)^2$$

where $f(f^*)$ is (the log of) the current (target) primary deficit and $\kappa_2 > \kappa_1$. Normalizing y^* and f^* at zero and assuming for simplicity a one-to-one relationship between f and government spending g, we can write the FA's loss function as:

$$L_{FA} = g^2 + \kappa_2 y^2 \tag{5}$$

Finally, assume that, during the period under consideration, current output is positively related to both money-supply growth and government spending by a function of the form shown in equation (6):

$$y = \alpha_1 \dot{m} + \alpha_2 g - u, \alpha_1, \alpha_2 > 0 \tag{6}$$

where u represents a stochastic productivity shock, affecting adversely real output.

Consider equilibrium outcomes following the productivity shock. In Figure 7.1, point O represents initial equilibrium before the occurrence of the productivity shock. Points B_{FA} and B_{CB} represent, respectively, the bliss points of the FAs and the CB after the shock. Relative to point O, B_{FA} involves no change in fiscal policy but an expansionary monetary policy. This is the best of all worlds for the fiscal authorities. As g remains unchanged, there is no adverse impact on their objective function through the primary-deficit target. At the same time, the rise in $\dot{m}$ offsets the negative impact of the productivity shock on output. Similar considerations hold for B_{CB}. At point B_{CB}, since there is no change in money-supply growth, there is no adverse impact on the CB's objective function through inflation. And as g is increased relative to point O, the negative impact of the productivity shock on output is eliminated. One can draw indifference curves around the bliss points, like those represented by the curves II_{FA} and II_{CB}.

Figure 7.1

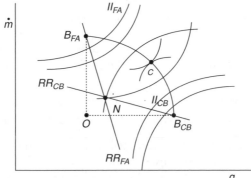

Under a cooperative regime, the CB and the FAs will operate along the contract curve $B_{CB}B_{FA}$, the locus of tangency between the two sets of indifference curves. Equilibrium will then be achieved at some point on this curve, for example at point C. At this Pareto-efficient point, the FA's and the CB's indifference curves are tangent to each other and so there is no room for welfare improvements.

Under a non-cooperative Nash regime, the CB and the FAs will act independently, ignoring any adverse effects that their actions will have on each other's targets. Accordingly, the CB will set $\dot{m}$ so as to minimize equation (4) taking g as given, and the FAs will set g so as to minimize equation (5) taking $\dot{m}$ as parametric. Thus we have equations (7a) and (7b):

$$\frac{\partial L_{CB}}{\partial \dot{m}} = 0 \tag{7a}$$

$$\frac{\partial L_{FA}}{\partial g} = 0 \tag{7b}$$

which give ordinary reaction functions in $(\dot{m}, g)$ space as:

$$\textit{Central Bank} \quad \dot{m} = -\frac{\kappa_1 \alpha_1 \alpha_2}{1 + \kappa_1 \alpha_1^2} g + \frac{\kappa_1 \alpha_1}{1 + \kappa_1 \alpha_1^2} u \tag{8a}$$

$$\textit{Fiscal Authority} \quad g = -\frac{\kappa_2 \alpha_1 \alpha_2}{(1 + \kappa_2 \alpha_2^2)} \dot{m} + \frac{\kappa_2 \alpha_2}{(1 + \kappa_2 \alpha_2^2)} u \tag{8b}$$

Equations (8a) and (8b) show each policy-maker's best response to changes in the other policy-maker's policy instrument and to the productivity shock u. The reaction functions (8a) and (8b) are shown in Figure 7.1 as the schedules RR_{CB} and RR_{FA} respectively.[14] In the absence of cooperation between the two policy-makers, equilibrium is at point N, where the two reaction curves intersect. Point N is not a Pareto-efficient point: the policy-makers' indifference curves corresponding to point N are not tangent to each other, implying that there is room for welfare improvements. Indeed, at N neither policy-maker manages to achieve his target (the bliss points in the figure), and for both policy-makers the outcome at N is inferior to that at C as it lies on a lower indifference curve.

Indirect Cooperation between the Union's Central Bank and the Fiscal Authorities: Democratic Accountability of the Central Bank in a MU

While in principle explicit cooperation between the union's CB and the national fiscal authorities would be the best option, in practice the union's central bank and the other policy-makers may find it impossible to cooperate directly, or may refuse to cooperate directly because of concerns that this will jeopardize their independence. In such a case, a solution recently advocated by many, including Buiter (1999), Demertzis *et al.* (1998), Svenson (1999) and De Haan and Eijffinger (2000), that could lead to Pareto improvements would be the democratic accountability of the union's CB. With democratic accountability, the CB of the monetary union continues to be independent. At the same time, either directly or indirectly through another common institution, for example the European Parliament in the case of the EU, it is fully accountable to the public not only for the achievement of its own objectives, but also for the impact of its choices on a relatively broad spectrum of macroeconomic variables (see Randzio-Plath (2000)). As Demertzis *et al.* (1998, 1999, 2003) note, something like this will guarantee a form of indirect cooperation: it will create an incentive for the union's CB to recognize the effects of its independently chosen targets on the targets of the other policy-makers when conducting monetary policy. This will reduce the extent of conflicts among the various policy-makers and will thus improve the performance of the union's monetary policy. At the same time, democratic control will create an incentive for the monetary authorities of the MU to learn to better evaluate their own policies. This would improve the reliability of monetary policy.

Along the lines suggested by Demertzis *et al.* (1998), one can represent this indirect cooperation as follows. Consider two independent agents, of which one is the CB of the union. The objective function of the union's CB can be taken to be of the general form given in equation (9a), while the objective function of the other policy-maker is represented by equation (10a):

$$W_1 = \sum_{i=1}^{n} c_i (Z_i - Z_i^*)^2 + \sum_{j=1}^{m} d_j (X_j - X_j^*)^2 \tag{9a}$$

$$W_2 = \sum_{i=1}^{n} f_i (Z_i - Z_i^*)^2 + \sum_{j=1}^{m} g_j (X_j - X_j^*)^2 \tag{10a}$$

$$c_i, f_i, d_j, g_j \geq 0$$

Z^* and X^* are, respectively, targets for final macroeconomic variables and for policy tools, Z_i and X_i are the current values of these variables, while the coefficients c_i and f_i (d_j and g_j) represent the relative importance that each of the policy-makers assigns to deviations of the current values of final targets (policy tools) from their target level. Thus $c_i, f_i, d_j, g_j \geq 0$ according to the priorities of each policy-maker. With democratic control, the CB of the union will replace equation (9a) with equation (9b):

$$V_1 = \left\{ \sum_{i=1}^{n} c_i(Z_i - Z_i^*)^2 + \sum_{j=1}^{m} d_j(X_j - X_j^*)^2 \right\} \tag{9b}$$

$$+\psi_1 \left\{ \sum_{i=1}^{n} f_i(Z_i - Z_i^*)^2 + \sum_{j=1}^{m} g_j(X_j - X_j^*)^2 \right\}, \ \psi_1 \begin{smallmatrix} > 0 \\ < 1 \end{smallmatrix}$$

and will then act as an independent, non-cooperative player; that is, it will choose values for the instruments of monetary policy so as to minimize V_1. The other policy-maker will do the same: he will set his own policy instrument so as to minimize V_2:

$$V_2 = \left\{ \sum_{i=1}^{n} f_i(Z_i - Z_i^*)^2 + \sum_{j=1}^{m} g_j(X_j - X_j^*)^2 \right\} \tag{10b}$$

$$+\psi_2 \left\{ \sum_{i=1}^{n} c_i(Z_i - Z_i^*)^2 + \sum_{j=1}^{m} d_j(X_j - X_j^*)^2 \right\}, \ \psi_2 \begin{smallmatrix} > 0 \\ < 1 \end{smallmatrix}$$

With ψ_1 and $\psi_2 > 0$, minimization of the loss functions (9a) and (10b) would correspond to making each policy-maker 'accountable': each policy-maker would take account of the spillover effects on other policy-makers when choosing his own policy.

The findings of several recent studies point to the necessity for a CB's democratic accountability. The results of Demertzis *et al.* (1999) indicate that taking into account fiscal policy, the ECB has poorer performance as far as the achievement of its own objectives is concerned when it has full independence and behaves like a non-cooperative player than when democratic control is imposed on it. Demertzis *et al.* (2003) find that full monetary independence creates an environment where liberal governments tend to be elected the more conservative the central bank is. This increases the likelihood of the development of conflicts between the instruments of monetary and fiscal policy, thus reducing the ability of each policy-maker to achieve his own targets. Other studies, including Power and Rowe (1998) and Levine and Pearlman (1996, 2002), also arrive at similar conclusions. Power and Rowe (1998) show that the independence of a CB may lead not only to problems of cooperation with the fiscal authorities, but also to excessive deficits. Levine and Pearlman (1996) show that if the interactions between an independent CB and the fiscal authorities, who conduct stabilization policy, are taken into account, the effectiveness of an independent CB's monetary policy deteriorates considerably and may, under certain circumstances, lead to a reduction in employment of up to 5 per cent. The results of Lenine and Pearlman (2002) also indicate that the choice of conservative bankers enhances the role for fiscal stabilization. All such findings seem to suggest that a fully independent ECB will tend to create the type of conflicts that lead to less effective monetary policy.

On the other hand, De Haan and Eijffinger (2000) explicitly analyse the concept of democratic accountability and then compare the legal accountability of the ECB with that of other CBs, the Banks of Canada, Japan and England and the Federal Reserve. Their results indicate that the ECB does have a low degree of democratic accountability. In certain aspects, such as reasoning behind decisions and monthly reports, the ECB exceeds the requirements of legal accountability (see Bini-Smaghi and Gros (2001) and Randzio-Plath (2000)). But even when this is allowed for, De Haan and Eijffinger (2000) conclude that the ECB is much less accountable than, the Bank of Canada, of Japan and of England, as well as the Federal Reserve.

The ECB's Monetary Framework: Is the ECB Transparent Enough?

Choice of Intermediate Monetary Target and Means of Communication with the Public

As mentioned earlier, because other macroeconomic variables often intervene between the tools of monetary policy and the final targets of monetary policy, a common practice of CBs is to have an intermediate monetary target. The variable selected as intermediate monetary target must posses certain characteristics that makes it useful as such. In particular, it must intervene in the transmission mechanism of economic fluctuations between the final targets and the monetary instruments, it must be easily predictable, it must be directly measurable, and so on. The idea then is that the CB selects a value for this intermediate variable which guarantees the achievement of the final target in the long run, and in the short run sets the instruments of monetary policy in such a way so as to reduce the divergence of the current value of the intermediate variable from its target value (see, for example, Bean (1998)).

On the other hand, communication is the way in which the CB of a monetary union reveals itself to the markets, the media and the general public. Several authors, including Svensson (1999), Buiter (1999) and Bini-Smaghi and Gros (2001), stress that external communication is a significant part of a CB's overall framework, since, through its impact on expectations, it affects its policy effectiveness.

It also influences the degree of transparency of monetary policy and thus the ability of others to evaluate it. External communication, at least in the short run, cannot be done in terms other than the CB's intermediate monetary target, namely with announcements about the extent to which this variable diverges from its reference value. Thus, at the theoretical level, 'communication' and 'intermediate monetary target' are, at least in the short run, interrelated.

In reality, however, the way the CB communicates with the general public may not be consistent with the true strategy of monetary policy. For example, the variable that has been formally adopted as intermediate target, and which therefore constitutes the key means of the CB's external communication may differ from the intermediate variable that the central bank actually uses in deciding about its actions. Thus a major issue in a CB's framework is the choice of intermediate target both as monetary strategy and as means of communication with the public, and also the extent to which 'strategy' and 'communication' should or should not differ.

As noted in EMI (1997) there are in principle five main alternatives as far as the choice of an intermediate monetary target is concerned:

- the exchange rate
- nominal GDP
- the real interest rate
- inflation forecasts
- a broad monetary aggregate, such as M2 or M3

Starting from the exchange rate, the reason it can be included in the set of possible alternatives is that in a world of high capital mobility, monetary policy and exchange-rate policy are inter-related. This is evident from the interest-rate parity condition $r = r^* + \Delta e^e$, where $r(r^*)$ is the local (foreign) interest rate and Δe^e is the expected rate of depreciation of the domestic currency. However, while the exchange rate may constitute a good intermediate variable in the case of a small open economy with a relatively large external sector, it cannot be regarded as the most appropriate intermediate target in the case of an area rather large, and therefore relatively closed, like a monetary union, as it may defy the objective of maintaining price stability in it.

By contrast, choosing nominal GDP as an intermediate target of monetary policy is a strategy that can be consistent with the objective of price stability in a MU. It also provides a monetary framework that is not particularly sensitive to fluctuations in variables affecting in the short run money demand, such as the velocity of circulation. Nevertheless, at the level of a monetary union, nominal GDP, to the extent that it is a weighted average of national GDPs, may be difficult to be managed by the monetary authorities. It may also be subject to considerable updates and amendments, arising from errors at the data-collection stage in individual member states. Moreover, because its precise division between volume and value is difficult to obtain in the short run, using nominal GDP as an intermediate monetary target may lead to uncertainties regarding the final objectives of the union's CB.

Similarly, adopting real interest rates as an intermediate target cannot be regarded as a particularly suitable monetary strategy in the case of a MU, due to difficulties in determining an equilibrium real interest rate for the union as a whole that will be also compatible with the target of achieving low inflation.

From this point of view, one could argue that at the level of a MU, the choice of monetary strategy is necessarily restricted between using forecasts of inflation and a money-supply measure. With this perspective in mind, the EMI made it clear in December 1997 that the choice of monetary strategy in the euro zone would be confined to these two alternative options. Of the most enthusiastic proponents of using monetary targets as a guide for setting nominal interest rates was the Bundesbank and several German academics, despite the fact that the Bundesbank's ability to stick to promised monetary-growth rates had not always been very impressive. On the other hand, the use of inflation forecasts as an intermediate monetary target was proposed by a number of academics and central bankers who either had bad experiences with money-supply targeting regimes in countries other than Germany, or were already familiar with inflation-targeting regimes.[15]

Consider the characteristics of each of these two regimes. Under an inflation-forecast regime, the union's CB announces to the public the inflation rate that will constitute the target of monetary policy in the long term. In the short term, it develops forecasts of inflation and then choose values for the tools of monetary policy (short-term interest rates) in such a way so as to ensure that eventually the forecast corresponds fully to its inflation target. As emphasized by several authors (see Svensson (1997, 1999), Alesina *et al.* (2001) Bernanke *et al.* (1998) and Bernanke and Mishkin (1997)), this regime has the advantage that the tools of monetary policy are functions of all the available relevant information. In particular, to the extent that the inflation forecast will be influenced not only by current inflation but also by the gap between current and potential output and to the extent that short-term interest rates will directly depend on the inflation forecast, the tools of monetary policy will indirectly take into account the divergence between current and potential real GDP. Thus, at any point in time, the real sector of the economy will be taken into account. As regards the CB's external communication, it cannot be done in a way other than announcing inflation forecasts and then publishing reports that explain, *ex post*, the choices of monetary policy.

From this point of view, it could be argued that under an inflation-forecast regime, monetary policy is characterized by a high degree of transparency. This makes its evaluation by the private sector relatively easy, something that enhances the CB's incentives to have a good performance. At the same time, since the settings for the monetary-policy tools will be based explicitly on forecasts of future inflation, which in turn are influenced by both current inflation and current and potential GDP, the CB becomes indirectly accountable to the public for the effects of its policy choices not only on nominal variables but also on real variables.[16]

Turning now to the money-supply targeting regime, a broad monetary aggregate like M2 or M3 is used as the intermediate target of monetary policy, with the union's CB announcing a reference value for its rate of change. This reference value for the rate of change of M2 or M3 is supposed to be chosen to be consistent in the long run with a low rate of inflation which is also the CB's final target for inflation. In the short and medium term, the CB sets short-term interest rates, the tools of monetary policy, in such a way that the divergence between the current value of the rate of change of M2 or M3 and its reference value is minimized.

This regime differs from the previous one in one major aspect: while in the long run it can produce an average inflation rate equal to the desired rate, in the short and medium term it may cause large fluctuations of current inflation around its reference value. This is because in the short and intermediate run, the rate of change of M2 or M3 is not the sole intermediate variable between the tools of monetary policy (short-term interest rates) and the final target of monetary policy (inflation). In the short run the rate of inflation is also influenced by other variables such as the velocity of circulation, the gap between actual and potential GDP, and so on, variables that in the short term can be subject to large fluctuations. Thus, using the money supply as an intermediate target of monetary policy is appropriate only if the relationship between movements in the monetary aggregates M2 or M3 and the final objectives of monetary policy is easy to predict, and if these movements in monetary aggregates cause the movements in final objectives. If this is not the case, the minimization of the divergence of the current rate of growth of M2 or M3 from its reference value will not necessarily imply the minimization of the divergence of the inflation rate from its target value.

Weale (1999), for example, stresses that a money-supply targeting regime is appropriate only when there is a stable relationship between the stock of money and spending. This may indeed be the case if money consists of cash and non-interest bearing deposits and the private sector holds money mainly in order to finance expenditure.

In broader measures of money, like M2 or M3, the link between the money stock and total spending is less close as it is influenced by the importance of portfolio demand for holding money. This in turn is influenced by elements like the term structure of interest rates and the efficiency and stability of the financial system. Thus, as Weale (1999) notes, when the financial system is unstable, the monetary authorities may be unable to set a sensible monetary target for M2 or M3; and, if they insist on setting a specific target, this may cause large fluctuations in the level of nominal spending.

This is a serious problem, especially in the case of a newly created monetary union, due to the structural changes in the money and credit markets that usually follow the establishment of a MU (see Randzio-Plath (2000)). Many empirical studies indicate that the information content of M2 and M3 as far as inflation is concerned can be very small if structural changes in the capital and/or the money markets are taking place.[17]

The fact that the adoption of M2 or M3 as intermediate target can lead in the short and medium term to considerable fluctuations in inflation is a major deficiency of money-supply targeting regimes, given that large fluctuations in the rate of inflation can adversely affect the CB's credibility. On the other hand, a money-supply targeting regime has the advantage that the CB's external communication is relatively easy: the union's CB is accountable to the public only as far as money-supply growth rates are concerned. That is, the CB is simply obliged to justify why the current rate of change of M2 or M3 diverges from its reference value, without having to explain whether and by how much it has missed its final target, namely inflation. This increases the CB's independence. At the same time, however, it reduces the public's ability to evaluate the CB's monetary policy and therefore the transparency of the policy. Since under this regime the CB's final target for inflation need not be fully specified, this regime also does not increase the CB's incentives to improve its performance (see Bini-Smaghi and Gros (2001) and Buiter (1999)).

As far as the European Central Bank is concerned, its governing board has declared on several occasions that the monetary policy of the ECB will consist of the following elements (see Duisenberg (1999) and ECB (1998, 1999)):

1 A key role will be given to money-supply growth inside the euro zone, with announcements of a reference value for the rate of change of a relatively broad monetary aggregate, in particular of M3. The reference value for this monetary aggregate will be chosen in such a way so as to ensure price stability. Price stability is defined as an inflation rate of under 2 per cent for the Harmonized Index of Consumer Prices (HICP), while the reference value for the rate

of growth of M3 is set at 4.5 per cent. Price stability is to be maintained over the medium term.

2 A divergence of the current rate of increase of M3 from its reference value will signal a danger to price stability.

3 The relationship between the current rate of change of M3 and its adopted reference value will be analysed regularly by the governoring board of the ECB and will not trigger mechanistic corrections.

4 The conclusions of the analysis regarding the divergence between the current rate of change of M3 and its reference value, as well as its impact on policy decisions, will be publicized and explained to the public.

5 In addition to the rate of growth of M3 in relation to its reference value, assessments of future price developments will play a major role in the strategy of the ECB. Such price assessments will be based on the behaviour of a broad spectrum of nominal and real macroeconomic variables.

Several authors, including Svensson (1999), Buiter (1999), De Haan and Eijffinger (2000), Allsopp and Artis (2003) and Surico (2003), interprete these elements as implying that the ECB has chosen a regime of inflation-forecast targeting as its guide for policy decisions and a regime of money-supply targeting as a means of external communication with the public. In particular, element 2 can be taken to imply that the reference value for M3 should not be considered strictly as an intermediate target for the growth rate of the money supply, but more generally as an indicator of problems with price stability. Also, elements 2 and 3, together with element 5, seem to imply that the ECB's monetary strategy will, to a large extent, be based on inflation forecasts. However, element 4 implies that the ECB's communication with the public will be done only on the basis of M3. That is, the true intermediate target of monetary policy and the means of external communication with the public will differ, and to that extent the ECB's policy could not be characterized as a policy of high transparency.

In Issing (1999, 2000) and ECB (2001) a number of arguments are put forward in defense of the transparency of the European Central Bank, while Bini-Smaghi and Gros (2001) comparing the transparency of the ECB with that of other central banks conclude that the ECB is on the basis of formal criteria the most transparent of all. They note however that the ECB's transparency is not apparent to the public because the ECB is not open enough about its choices. For example, before 2003, the ECB was not publishing inflation forecasts. And many commentators (see Demertzis *et al.* (1998, 1999), Eijffinger and Hoeberchts (2000) and Randzio-Plath (2000)) were pointing out at the time that the ECB's transparency would be enhanced if it were to explain the logic behind its decisions, something that effectively required publicizing its internal inflation forecasts. Issing (1999) was arguing against publication of internal forecasts on the grounds that the conditional nature of them might not be well understood by the public and that the ECB could be judged for the accuracy of the forecasts. A counter-argument however was that the ECB could set out clearly the risks attached to any forecasts before their publication (see De Haan and Eijffinger (2000)). Inflation forecasts are now published by the ECB. But the ECB is silent on how these forecasts are produced. This gives the impression that the ECB is still hiding relevant information. Also, its external communication with the public continues to be done exclusively in terms of M3.

Why has such a strategy been chosen by the ECB? One possible explanation is a desirability by EU politicians to ensure that the private sector regards the ECB as a continuation of the Bundesbank in the belief that this may contribute to its success (see Artis and Winkler (1998)).[18] Another possible explanation is a more general desire to maximize the ECB's independence, together with the view that this could only be achieved if the CB was not fully accountable for its general choices (see Lapavitsas (1998)). However, there are two counter-arguments to this approach. First, transparency is needed to secure predictability and credibility. Increased credibility will in turn help the ECB in the effective implementation of its policy: it would imply that the ECB could more directly and efficiently cooperate as an independent agent with other authorities (see Demertzis *et al.* (1998, 1999) and Buiter (1999)). This would reduce the likely adverse effects on the euro zone arising from the existence of many independent policy authorities with different targets or priorities who act non-cooperatively.

Debrun (2001) provides a third possible explanation as to why the ECB has adopted an operational strategy similar to that of the Bundesbank: the consideration that the EMU was negotiated against an alternative framework of implicit monetary cooperation based on fixed exchange rates to the deutchmark, the EMS. With the Bundesbank dominating the EMS when EMU was under discussion, Germany would have had an incentive not to allow the ECB to reflect the average European preferences and would have insisted that the common CB should adopt a similar policy stance. Thus Debrun's (2001) explanation is that the Germans managed to impose their will on the other EU countries.

In addition to the ECB's strategy, doubts have also been expressed by many commentators about the suitability of the operational expression of its price-stability objective. The fact that the ECB formally adopted an inflation objective of no more than 2 per cent for the

HICP made its inflation target asymmetric, in the sense that it set an upper limit for inflation but not a lower limit, implying that in principle negative inflation would be acceptable. However, subsequent press releases by the ECB have clarified that the term 'price stability' is to exclude persistently falling prices, thus implying a lower limit for the HICP inflation equal to zero. Nevertheless, several authors (see Buiter (1999) and De Haan and Eijffinger (2000)) have noted that this statement does not guarantee that the ECB's target will be symmetric, (that is centred at 1 per cent) and this does not help public opinion understand clearly the ECB's operational procedures and practices. Gali (2003) points out that the ECB's adopted reference value for M3 suggests an inflation target in the range of 1–2 per cent, and so a mid-point inflation target of 1.5 per cent. Yet the ECB's actions since 1999 have not shown that its inflation target is really symmetric (see Allsopp and Artis (2003)).

Misalignment and Exchange-Rate Policy in a Monetary Union

One could argue that the importance of the exchange rate for the performance of an economy depends on how open this economy is. 'Openness' can be taken to be determined by three parameters: the ratio of exports of final goods to GDP; the ratio of final imports to GDP; and the ratio of imported raw materials and intermediate goods to domestic value-added. In a relatively open economy these three parameters can be quite large (they may exceed 50%), so exchange-rate changes may significantly affect the general profile of the economy. In such cases, a strategy for coping with exchange-rate fluctuations is necessary, as is also necessary an explicit and comprehensive exchange-rate policy.

To the extent that a MU is a much more closed economy than the economies of the member states, it could be argued that the importance of the external value of the common currency *vis-a-vis* other currencies is relatively limited. In the case of the euro-zone area, exports to non-European states do not exceed 18 per cent of the EU's GDP, imports from non-European countries are about 16 per cent, and imported raw materials and intermediate products amount to only 12 per cent of the euro-zone value-added. Accordingly, one could rank the EU along with the 'closed' economies of the USA and Japan, which follow a policy of 'benign neglect' as regards the exchange rates of their currencies.

Nevertheless, both theoretical and empirical studies suggest that under high capital mobility, and especially when new monetary regimes are introduced, as is currently the case in Europe, the magnitude of short-run exchange-rate fluctuations may be much larger in relatively closed than in relatively open economies.[19] Large exchange-rate fluctuations can create problems even in rather closed economies: with wage/price rigidity they may cause changes in the terms of trade, the real exchange rate, and thus in the international competitiveness of domestic products and therefore in output and inflation. Accordingly, even in relatively closed economies, like the EU, some weight may need to be given by the monetary authorities to the real exchange rate, and this may not be inconsistent with the objective of maintaining price stability.

In the spirit of Svensson (1999), placing a weight on the common currency's real exchange rate would imply a minimization by the union's CB of a loss function of the form:

$$L = (\pi - \pi^*)^2 + \beta(z - z^*)^2 + \theta(e^R - e^{R^*})^2 \qquad (11b)$$

where e^R is the current value of the common currency's real exchange rate, e^{R^*} is the target value for this variable, and the variable z incorporates all the other final targets of the ECB besides inflation. The target value for the common currency's real exchange rate could be chosen to be consistent with the long-term prospects of Europe's economy. In such a case $(e^R - e^{R^*})$ would reflect the magnitude of the misalignment of the common currency, namely the extent to which the nominal exchange rate of the common currency deviates from fundamentals, including relative prices in Europe and abroad, differences in productivity potentials, and so on; in short, the extent to which the common currency's real exchange rate deviates from its long-run equilibrium level. Exchange-rate policy can then be taken to be reflected in the magnitude of θ, namely in the extent to which a misalignment of the union's common currency will trigger actions by the CB.

The Maastricht Treaty does not preclude such a policy. Under Article 109 of the Maastricht Treaty the Council of Finance Ministers, by special majority, can adopt 'general orientations' for the exchange-rate of the euro on the condition that they do not interfere with the ECB's price-stability objective. Such general orientations may be adopted under special situations, like in cases of misalignment of the euro, or when changes in its long-run equilibrium value take place, respecting at the same time the independence of the ECB.[20]

Summary and Conclusions

Of the main elements characterizing monetary policy in a MU is the degree of independence of its central monetary authority. If the union's CB is not independent of the politically elected national governments, the priorities attached to its various final targets will to a large extent reflect the priorities of the mean voter, which will be broader than price stability and will include the achievement of low unemployment, a high rate of GDP growth, and so on. On the other hand, an independent central bank will tend to give greater priority to the maintenance of price stability or zero inflation and lower priorities to other objectives. Recently, a growing analytical and empirical literature has been developed that emphasizes the need for CB independence both at the national level and at the level of a MU. Indeed, this literature has inspired the idea of creating an independent ECB. The claim is that an independent CB will guarantee low inflation, while at the same time it will have no systematic impact on employment levels.

Part of the existing empirical literature seems to confirm that politically independent CBs have achieved lower inflation than CBs in which this independence is absent. Other studies, however, arrive at a different conclusion, questioning the proposition that independence involves no cost in terms of higher short-run variability of output or employment. Indeed, some studies reveal that the degree of CB independence can have a systematic impact on the level of equilibrium employment, even if the private sector has perfect information and forms expectations rationally.

Much of the literature that stresses the need for CB independence also has the deficiency of assuming that CBs act alone, ignoring the existence of other independent policy-makers. The issue is that in an environment where there are other policy-makers, an independent CB will act as a non-cooperative player: it will seek to minimize its own objective function, ignoring the effects that its actions will have on other policy-makers' targets. The result will be a Pareto sub-optimal macroeconomic equilibrium.

What is the solution? A realistic solution, recently advocated by many, would be the democratic accountability of the ECB. With democratic accountability the ECB remains independent but, at the same time, either directly or indirectly through the European Parliament, it is made fully accountable to public opinion both for the achievement of its own objectives and for the impact of its choices on a relatively broader spectrum of macroeconomic variables.

As regards the framework of monetary policy in a MU, an important element is the choice of intermediate monetary target and of means of communication with the markets and the public in general. As far as the European Central Bank is concerned, its operational intermediate monetary target is the rate of growth of M3, although, as has been declared by its governoring board, price forecasts do play an important role in its overall monetary strategy. Inflation forecasts are now published by the ECB. However, the ECB still communicates with the public only in terms of M3, with analyses that explain the extent to which the current growth rate of M3 has deviated from its reference value and of why this has happened. Thus the ECB still remains silent on the logic behind its actions, namely on the extent to which it has missed its inflation target.

The operational suitability of the ECB's price-stability objective has also been questioned. In December 1998 the ECB formally adopted an inflation objective of no more than 2% for the Harmonized Index of Consumer Prices (HICP), with subsequent statements stressing that the term 'inflation' is to exclude persistently falling prices, implying a lower limit for HICP inflation equal to zero. This, however, does not mean that the ECB's price target is symmetric, something that would have helped the public understand more clearly the ECB's operational procedures and practices.

Notes

1   For an assessment of the ECB's actions and activities see Begg *et al.* (1997, 2002), De Haan (1997), Dornbusch *et al.* (1998), Bean (1998), Buiter (1999), Svensson (1999), Allsopp and Vines (1998, 2000), Alesina *et al.* (2001), Allsopp and Artis (2003) and Randzio-Plath (2000). See also Bayoumi *et al* (1997) and Eijffinger and De Haan (2000).
2   See Rogoff (1985), Persson and Tabellini (1993, 1996), Alesina and Grilli (1992), Alesina and Gatti (1995), Dolado *et al.* (1993), Jordan (1999) and Laubach and Posen (1997).
3   See Barro and Gordon (1983), Alesina and Tabellini (1987), Blackburn and Christensen (1989), Cukierman (1992, 1994), Cubitt (1992), Lohmann (1992), Al-Nowaihi and Levine (1994) and Guender and McCaw (2000).
4   The Rogoff solution has been studied by many: see for example Laskar (1989), Currie *et al.* (1995, 1996), Herrendorf and Lockwood (1997), Jensen (1997), Svensson (1997a), Al-Nowaihi *et al.*(1997), Debelle and Fischer (1995), Levine and Pearlman (1996, 2002) and Grüner and Hefeker (1998).
5   This would result from choosing the CB's degree of inflation-consciousness optimally by selecting a value for β that, for example, minimizes the median voter's loss function along the lines suggested by Alesina and Grilli (1992). The median voter has a loss function $L_M = (\pi - \pi^*)^2 + \beta_M(\eta - \eta^*)^2$, with fifty per cent of the population having a value of β greater than β_M and the other fifty per cent having a β smaller than β_M. The mean voter chooses β_M so as to minimize its objective function subject to the constraint imposed by equation (2). The value for β_M obtained from the minimization problem is then adopted as the 'desired' degree of inflation-consciousness that the government will have in mind in choosing a person to head the CB. This value for β_M obtained from the solution to the minimization problem is a positive function of the variance of the stochastic term v in equation (2).

6 Other solutions to the 'time inconsistency' problem have also been proposed: see for example Walsh (1995), Jensen (2000) and Lawler (2000). These studies show that an optimally-designed inflation contract for the CB can produce a superior outcome to Rogoff's conservative central banker.

7 See Debelle and Fischer (1994), Eijffinger and De Haan (1996), and Berger, De Haan and Eijffinger (2001) for a survey.

8 McCallum (1995, 1997) stresses that the problem of dynamic inconsistency remains when monetary policy is assigned to an independent CB: a government can always produce unexpected inflation by changing the terms of this assignment.

9 The importance of interactions between monetary policy and systems of collective wage bargaining has also been stressed by other authors, including Soskice and Iversen (1998), Iversen (1999) and Zervoyianni (1997).

10 See for example Demertzis (1998, 1999), Calmfors (1998) and De Haan and Eijffinger (2000).

11 For the issue of monetary-policy non-neutralities see Sockice and Iversen (2000), Berger, Hefeker and Schöb (2001), Coricelli et al. (2003) and Acocella and Di Bartolomeo (2004).

12 For monetary and fiscal policy interactions see Agell et al. (1996), Beetsma and Bovenberg (1998), Cooper and Kempf (2000), Dixit and Lambertini (2001), Levine and Pearlman (1996, 2002), Dixit (2001), Demertzis et al. (1998, 1999, 2003), Cobbillon and Sidiropoulos (2001) and Gatti and van Wijnbergen (2002).

13 In Dixit and Labertini (2001b), the value of precommitment in monetary policy, and thus the value of having an independent ECB, is completely negated if national fiscal authorities act like strategic players and have different output and inflation targets than those of the ECB. Their results indicate that the ideal goals for output and inflation can be attained only if the preferences of the ECB and the national fiscal authorities in the EMU can be made to coincide. Begg and Green (1998) also point out that with the ECB being both 'instrument' and 'goal' independent, there will be a big democratic deficit in the EU, which, if adverse economic circumstances arise, may, undermine the credibility of the EU Institutions. From a similar standpoint, Buiter (1999) also argues that the ECB, being an unelected institution, lacks political legitimacy. A number of other authors, including De Haan (1997), share the same concern.

14 The slopes of the reaction functions in the $(\dot{m}, g)$ plane are:

$$CB \quad \frac{d\dot{m}}{dg} = -\frac{\kappa_1 \alpha_1 \alpha_2}{(1 + \kappa_1 \alpha_1^2)} < 0 \text{ and } |\frac{\kappa_1 \alpha_1 \alpha_2}{(1 + \kappa_1 \alpha_1^2)}| < 1$$

$$FA \quad \frac{d\dot{m}}{dg} = -\frac{(1 + \kappa_2 \alpha_2^2)}{\kappa_2 \alpha_1 \alpha_2} < 0 \text{ and } |\frac{(1 + \kappa_2 \alpha_2^2)}{\kappa_2 \alpha_1 \alpha_2}| > 1$$

15 See Svensson (1997b) and Bean (1998). See also Rudebusch and Svensson (2002). The experience of money-supply targets in non-German EU countries, such as the UK and Sweden, was less happy than in Germany.

16   See also Herrendorf (1998) and Persson and Tabellini (1996). See, however, Bean (1998) and Artis and Kontolemis (1998) for some problems involved, including the choice of an appropriate price index.

17   Bean (1998) points out that euro monetary aggregates may not behave simply like the sum of the corresponding national monetary aggregates: their relationship with inflation may be difficult to predict, at least shortly after the adoption of the single currency. See also Svensson (1999) and Estrella and Mishkin (1998).

18   However, as argued by Bernanke and Mihov (1997) and Bean (1998), the Bundesbank was behaving as an inflation targeter despite its declared commitment to money-supply targets: it was willing to miss its monetary targets whenever its ultimate objective of low inflation was in danger. See also Von Hagen (1997).

19   See, for example, Zervoyianni (1996).

20   See Dornbusch *et al.* (1998) and Begg *et al.* (1997) for a discussion of these issues.

References

Acocella, N. and Di Bartolomeo, G. (2004) 'Non-Neutrality of Monetary Policy in Policy Games', *European Journal of Political Economy,* vol. 20, pp. 695–707.

Agell, J., Calmfors, L. and Jonsson, G. (1996) 'Fiscal Policy when Monetary Policy is Tied to the Mast', *European Economic Review,* vol. 40, pp. 1413–40.

Alesina, A., Blanchard, O., Gali, I., Giavazzi, F. and Uhlig, H. (2001) *Defining a Macroeconomic Framework for Europe,* Monitoring the European Central Bank 3 (London: Centre for Economic Policy Research).

Alesina, A. and Gatti, R. (1995) 'Independent Central Banks: Low Inflation at no Cost?', *American Economic Review,* vol. 85, pp. 196–206.

Alesina, A. and Grilli, V. (1992) 'The European Central Bank: Reshaping Monetary Policies in Europe', in M. Canzoneri, V. Grilli and P. Masson (eds), *Establishing a Central Bank: Issues in Europe and Lessons from the USA* (Cambridge: Cambridge University Press).

Alesina, A. and Summers, L.H. (1993) 'Central Bank Independence and Macroeconomic Performance: Some Comparative Evidence', *Journal of Money, Credit and Banking,* vol. 25, pp. 151–62.

Alesina, A. and Tabellini, G. (1987) 'Rules and Discretion with Non-Coordinated Monetary and Fiscal Policies', *Economic Inquiry,* vol. 25, pp. 619–30.

Allsopp, C. and Vines, D. (1998) 'Macroeconomic Policy After EMU', *Oxford Review of Economic Policy,* 14, pp. 1–23.

Allsopp, C. and Vines, D. (2000) 'Macroeconomic Policy', *Oxford Review of Economic Policy,* vol. 16, pp. 1–32.

Allsopp, C. and Artis, M. (2003) 'The Assessment: EMU – Four Years On', *Oxford Review of Economic Policy,* vol. 19, pp. 1–29.

Al-Nowaihi, Ali. and Levine, P. (1994) 'Can Reputation Resolve the Monetary Policy Credibility Problem?', *Journal of Monetary Economics,* vol. 33, pp. 55–80.

Al-Nowaihi, Ali., Levine, P. and Philp, D. (1997) 'Central Bank Independence: Gain Without Pain?', CEES Discussion Paper, Centre for European Economic Studies, University of Leicester, October.

Andersen, T. and Schneider, F. (1986) 'Co-ordination of Fiscal and Monetary Policy Under Different Institutional Arrangements', *European Journal of Political Economy*, vol. 2, pp. 169–91.

Artis, M.J. and Kontolemis, Z. (1998) 'The European Central Bank and Inflation Targeting', *International Journal of Finance and Economics*, vol. 3, pp. 27–37.

Artis, M.J. and Winkler, B. (1998) 'The Stability Pact: Safeguarding the Credibility of the European Central Bank', *National Institute Economic Review*, no. 16 pp. 87–98.

Bade, R. and Parkin, M. (1978) 'Central Bank Laws and Inflation: A Preliminary Investigation', in *The Australian Monetary System in the Seventies* (Clayton: Monash University).

Barro, R. and Gordon, D. (1983a), 'A Positive Theory of Monetary Policy in a Natural Rate Model', *Journal of Political Economy*, vol. 91, pp. 589–610.

Barro, R. and Gordon, D. (1983b) 'Rules, Discretion and Reputation in a Model of Monetary Policy', *Journal of Monetary Economics*, vol. 12, pp. 101–21.

Bayoumi, T., Eichengreen, B. and Von Hagen, J. (1997) 'European Monetary Unification: Implications of Research for Policy, Implications of Policy for Research', *Open Economics Review*, vol. 8, pp. 71–91.

Bean, C. (1998) 'Monetary Policy Under EMU', *Oxford Review of Economic Policy*, vol. 14, pp. 41–53.

Beetsma, R. and Bovenberg, A.L. (1998) 'Monetary Union Without Fiscal Policy Co-ordination May Discipline Policy-Making', *Journal of International Economics*, vol. 45, pp. 239–58.

Begg, I. and Green, D. (1998) The Political Economy of the European Central Bank', in P. Arestis and M.C. Sawyer (eds), *The Political Economy of Central Banking* (Cheltenham: Eldward Elgar).

Begg , D., Giavazzi, F., von Hagen, J. and Wyplosz, C. (1997) *EMU: Getting the End-Game Right*, Monitoring European Integration 7 (London: Centre for Economic Policy Research (CEPR)).

Begg, D., Canova, F., De Grauwe, P., Fatàs, A. and Lane, P. (2002) *An Update*, Monitoring the European Central Bank 4 (London: Centre for Economic Policy Research).

Berger, H. (1997) 'The Bundesbank's Path to Independence', *Public Choice*, vol. 93, pp. 427–53.

Berger, H. and De Haan, J. (1999) 'A State Within A State? An Event Study on the Bundesbank', *Scottish Journal of Political Economy*, vol. 46, pp. 17–39.

Berger, H., Hefeker, C. and Schöb, R. (2001) 'Optimal Central Bank Conservatism and Monopoly', CESifo Working Paper no. 407, Centre for Economic Studies and Ifo Institute of Economic Research, Munich, January.

Berger, H., De Haan, J. and Eijffinger, S. (2001) 'Central Bank Independence: An Update of Theory and Evidence', *Journal of Economic Surveys*, vol. 15, pp. 3–40.

Bernanke, B.S. and Mihov, I. (1997) 'What Does the Bundesbank Target?', *European Economic Review*, vol. 41, pp. 1025–53.

Bernanke, B.S. and Mishkin, F. (1997) 'Inflation Targeting: A New Framework for Monetary Policy?', *Journal of Economic Perspectives*, vol. 11, pp. 97–116.

Bernanke, B.S., Laubach, T., Mishkin, F. and Posen A. (1998) *Inflation Targeting: Lessons from the International Experience* (Princeton, NJ: Princeton University Press).

Bini-Smaghi, L. and Gros, D. (2001) 'Is the ECB Sufficiently Accountable and Transparent?', ENEPRI Working Paper no. 7/2001, European Network of Economic Policy Research Institutes, September.

Blackburn, K. and Christensen, M. (1989) 'Monetary Policy and Policy Credibility', *Journal of Economic Literature*, vol. 27, pp. 1–45.

Bleany, M. (1996) 'Central Bank Independence, Wage-Bargaining Structure and Macro-economic Performance in OECD Countries', *Oxford Economic Papers*, vol. 48, pp. 20–38.

Blinder, A.S. (1999) *Central Banking in Theory and Practice* (Cambridge, Mass.: MIT Press).

Buiter, W. (1999) 'Alice in Euroland', *Journal of Common Market Studies*, vol. 37, pp. 181–209.

Calmfors, L. (1998) 'Macroeconomic Policy, Wage Setting and Employment: What Difference Does EMU Make?', *Oxford Review of Economic Policy*, vol. 14, pp. 125–51.

Campillo, M. and Miron, J.A. (1997) 'Why Does Inflation Differ Across Countries?' , in C.D. Romer and D.H. Romer (eds), *Reducing Inflation: Motivation and Strategy* (Chicago: University of Chicago Press).

Cobbillon, B. and Sidiropoulos, M. (2001) 'Designing Fiscal Institutions in a Monetary Union', *Open Economies Review*, vol. 12, pp. 163–79.

Cooper, R.N. and Kempf, H. (2000) 'Designing Stabilisation Policy in a Monetary Union', NBER Discussion Paper no. 7607, National Bureau of Economic Research.

Coricelli, F., Cukierman, A. and Dalmazzo, A. (2003) 'Economic Performance and Stabilization Policy in a Monetary Union with Imperfect Labour and Goods Markets' in Sinn, H.W., Widgren, M. and Kothenburger, M. (eds), *Issues of Monetary Integration in Europe* (Cambridge, Mass.: MIT Press).

Cubitt, R.P. (1992) 'Monetary Policy Games and Private Sector Pre-Commitment', *Oxford Economic Papers*, 44, pp. 513–30.

Cukierman, A. (1992) *Central Bank Strategy, Credibility and Independence* (Cambridge, Mass.: MIT Press).

Cukierman, A. (1994) 'Central Bank Independence and Monetary Control', *Economic Journal*, vol. 104, pp. 437–48.

Cukierman, A. and Lippi, F. (1999) 'Central Bank Independence, Centralisation of Wage Bargaining, Inflation and Unemployment: Theory and Some Evidence', *European Economic Review*, vol. 43, pp. 1395–434.

Cukierman, A. and Lippi, F. (2001) 'Labour Markets and Monetary Union: A Strategic Analysis', *Economic Journal*, vol. 111, pp. 541–65.

Currie, D., Levine, P. and Pearlman, J. (1995) 'Can Delegation Be Counterproductive? The Choice of Conservative Bankers in Open Economies', CEPR Discussion Paper no. 1148, Center for Economic Policy Research, London.

Currie, D., Levine, P. and Pearlman, J. (1996) 'The Choice of Conservative Bankers in Open Economies: Regimes for Europe', *Economic Journal*, vol. 106, pp. 345–58.

Debelle, G. and Fischer, S. (1995) 'How Independent Should a Central Bank Be?' in J.C. Fuhrer (ed.), *Goals, Guidelines and Constraints Facing Monetary*

Policy-makers, Federal Reserve Bank of Boston, Conference Series no. 38, pp. 195–221.

Debrun, X. (2001) 'Bargaining Over EMU v. EMS: Why Might the ECB Be the Twin Sister of the Bundesbank', *Economic Journal*, vol. 111, pp. 566–90.

De Haan, J. (1997) 'The European Central Bank: Independence, Accountability and Strategy: A Review', *Public Choice*, vol. 93, pp. 395–426.

De Haan, J. and Eijffinger, S. (2000) 'The Democratic Accountability of the European Central Bank: A Comment on Two Fairly-Tales', *Journal of Common Market Studies*, vol. 38, pp. 393–407.

De Haan, J. and Sturm, J.E. (1994) 'The Case for Central Bank Independence', *Banca Nationale del Lavoro*, vol. 182, pp. 305–27.

Demertzis, M. (2004) 'Central Bank Independence: Low Inflation at No Cost? A Numerical Simulation Exercise', *Journal of Macroeconomics*, vol. 26, pp. 661–77.

Demertzis, M., Hughes-Hallet, A.J. and Viegi, N. (1998) 'Independently Blue? Accountability and Independence in the New European Central Bank', CEPR Discussion Paper no. 1842, Centre for Economic Policy Research, London.

Demertzis, M., Hughes-Hallet, A.J. and Viegi, N. (1999) 'Can the ECB be Truly Independent? Should it Be?' *Empirica*, vol. 26, pp. 217–40.

Demertzis, M., Hughes-Hallet, A.J. and Viegi, N. (2003) 'An Independent Central Bank Faced with Elected Governments', *European Journal of Political Economy*, vol. 20, pp. 907–22.

Demopoulos, G., Katsimbris, G. and Miller, S. (1987) 'Monetary Policy and Central Bank Financing of Government Deficits: A Cross-Country Comparison', *European Economic Review*, vol. 31, pp. 1023–50.

Dixit, A. (2000) 'A Repeated Game Model of Monetary Union', *Economic Journal*, vol. 110, pp. 759–80.

Dixit, A. (2001) 'Games of Monetary and Fiscal Interactions in the EMU', *European Economic Review*, vol. 45, pp. 589–613.

Dixit, A. and Lambertini, L. (2001a) 'Fiscal Discretion Destroys Monetary Commitment', Discussion Paper, UCLA and Princeton University, July.

Dixit, A. and Lambertini, L. (2001b) 'Monetary–Fiscal Policy Interactions and Commitment versus Discretion in a Monetary Union', *European Economic Review*, vol. 45, pp. 977–87.

Dolado, J.J., Griffiths, M. and Padilla, A.J. (1993) 'Delegation in International Monetary Policy Games, *European Economic Review*, vol. 38, pp. 1057–70.

Dornbusch, R., Favero, C. and Giavazzi, F. (1998) 'Immediate Challenges for the European Central Bank', *Economic Policy*, vol. 26, pp. 15–64.

Duisenberg, W.F. (1999a) 'Monetary Policy in the Euro Area', Speech given at the Chamber of Commerce and Industry, January, Frankfurt.

Duisenberg, W.F. (1999b) 'The Euro: The New European Currency', Speech given at the Council of Foreign Relations, February, Chicago.

ECB (1998a) 'A Stability-Oriented Monetary Policy Strategy of the ECB', Press Release, 13 October 1998, http:// www.ecb.int.press

ECB (1998b) 'The Quantitative Reference Value for Monetary Growth', Press Release, 1 Decembert 1998, http:// www.ecb.int.press

ECB (1999) 'The Stability-Oriented Monetary Policy Strategy of the Eurosystem', *ECB Monthly Bulletin*, January, pp. 39–50.

ECB (2001) 'The ECB's Monetary Policy – Accountability, Transparency and Communication', Press Release, 14 September 2001, http://www.ecb.int.press

ECB (2003) 'The ECB's Monetary Policy Strategy', Press Release, 8 May 2003, http://www.ecb.int.press

Eijffinger, S. and De Haan, J. (1996) 'The Political Economy of Central Bank Independence', *Princeton Special Papers in International Economics*, no. 19, Princeton University.

Eijffinger, S. and Hoeberichts, M. (2000) 'Central Bank Accountability and Trasparency', Discussion Paper no. 6/00, Economic Research Centre of the Deutsche Bundesbank, November.

Eijffinger, S. and De Haan, J. (eds) (2000) *European Monetary and Fiscal Policy* (Oxford: Oxford University Press).

Eijffinger, S. and van Keulen, M. (1994) 'Central Bank Independence in Another Eleven Countries', Discussion Paper no. 9494, Tilburg University, The Netherlands.

Eijffinger, S. and Schaling, E. (1993) 'Central Bank Independence in Twelve Industrial Countries', *Banca Nationale del Lavoro Quarterly Review*, vol. 184, pp. 1–41.

Eijffinger, S., van Rooij M. and Schaling, E. (1997) 'Central Bank Independence: A Panel Data Approach', *Public Choice*, vol. 89, pp. 163–82.

EMI (1997) The *Single Monetary Policy in Stage Three: Elements of the Monetary Strategy in the ESCB*, European Monetary Institute, Frankfurt.

Estrella, A. and Mishkin F. (1998) 'Is There a Role for Monetary Aggregates in the Conduct of Monetary Policy?', *Journal of Monetary Economics*, vol. 40, pp. 279–304.

Fischer, S. (1995) 'Central Bank Independence Revisited', *American Economic Review*, vol. 85, pp. 201–6.

Forder, J. (1996) 'On the Assessment and Implications of Institutional Remedies', *Oxford Economic Papers*, vol. 48, pp. 35–51.

Forder, J. (1998) 'Central Bank Independence: Conceptual Issues and an Interim Assessment', *Oxford Economic Papers*, vol. 50, pp. 307–34.

Fuhrer, J.C. (1997) 'Central Bank Independence and Inflation Targets: Monetary Policy Paradigms for the Next Millenium?', *New England Economic Review*, vol. 1/2, pp. 19–36.

Fuijki, H. (1996) 'Central Bank Independence Indices in Economic Analysis: A Re-appraisal', *Bank of Japan Monetary and Economic Studies*, vol. 14, pp. 79–99.

Gali, J. (2003) 'Monetary Policy in the Early Years of EMU' in M. Buti and A. Sapir (eds), *EMU and Economic Policy in Europe* (Cheltenham: Edward Elgar).

Gatti, D. and van Wijnbergen, C. (2002) 'Co-ordinating Fiscal Authorities in the Euro-zone: A Key Role for the ECB', *Oxford Economic Papers*, vol. 54, pp. 56–71.

Grilli, V., Masciandaro, D. and Tabellini, G. (1991) 'Political and Monetary Institutions and Public Financial Policies in Industrial Countries', *Economic Policy*, vol. 13, pp. 341–92.

Grüner, H.P. and Hefeker, C. (1998) 'How Will EMU Affect Inflation and Unemployment in Europe?', *Scandinavian Journal of Economics*, vol. 101, pp. 1–15.

Guender, A.V. and McCaw, S. (2000) 'The Inflationary Bias in a Model of the Open Economy: A Note', *Economics Letters*, vol. 68, pp. 173–8.

Hall, P.A. and Franzese, R.J. (1998) 'Mixed Signals: Central Bank Independence, Co-ordinated Wage Bargaining and European Monetary Union', *International Organization*, vol. 52, pp. 505–36.

Hamada, J. (1985) *The Political Economy of Monetary Interdependence* (Cambridge, Mass: MIT Press).

Hayo, B. (1998) 'Inflation Culture, Central Bank Independence and Price Stability', *European Journal of Political Economy*, vol. 14, pp. 241–63.

Herrendorf, B. (1998) 'Inflation Targeting as a Way of Pre-commitment', *Oxford Economic Papers*, vol. 50, pp. 431–48.

Herrendorf, B. and Lockwood, B. (1997) 'Rogoff's Conservative Central Banker Restored', *Journal of Money, Credit and Banking*, vol. 29, pp. 478–95.

Issing, O. (1999) 'The Eurosystem: Transparent and Accountable', or "Willem in Euroland"', *Journal of Common Market Studies*, vol. 37, pp. 503–19.

Issing, O. (2000) 'The ECB's Monetary Policy: Experience After the First Year', *Journal of Policy Modeling*, vol. 22, pp. 325–43.

Iversen, T. (1999) 'The Political Economy of Inflation: Bargaining Structure or Central Bank Independence?', *Public Choice*, vol. 99, pp. 237–58.

Jensen, H. (1997) 'Credibility of Optimal Monetary Delegation', *American Economic Review*, vol. 87, pp. 911–20.

Jensen, H. (2000) 'Optimal Monetary Policy Cooperation Through State-independent Contracts with Targets', *European Economic Review*, vol. 44, pp. 517–39.

Jordan, T. (1999) 'Central Bank Independence and the Sacrifice Ratio', *European Journal of Political Economy*, vol. 15, pp. 229–55.

Kydland, F. and Prescott, E.C. (1977) 'Rules Rather than Discretion: The Inconsistency of Optimal Plans', *Journal of Political Economy*, vol. 85, pp. 473–92.

Lapavitsas, C. (1998) 'Central Bank Independence: A Critical Perspective', Discussion Paper no. 147, University of London, Department of Economics, October.

Laskar, D. (1989) 'Conservative Central Bankers in a Two-Country World', *European Economic Review*, vol. 33, pp. 1575–95.

Laubach, T. and Posen, A. (1997) *Disciplined Discretion: Monetary Targeting in Germany and Switzerland*, Essays in International Finance, no. 206, Princeton University.

Lawler. P. (2000) 'Centralized Wage Setting, Inflation Contracts, and the Optimal Choice of Central Banker', *Economic Journal*, vol. 110, pp. 559–75.

Levine, P. and Pearlman, J. (1996) 'Central Bank Independence and Fiscal Policy: More Bad News for the Delegation Game', Paper presented to the Money-Macro-Finance Conference, September 1996, London Business School.

Levine, P. and Pearlman, J. (2002) 'Delegation and Fiscal Policy in the Open Economy: More Bad News for the Rogoff Delegation Game', *Open Economies Review*, vol. 13, pp. 153–74.

Lippi, F. (1999a) 'Revisiting the Case for a Populist Central Banker', CEPR Discussion Paper no. 2306, Centre for Economic Policy Research London December.

Lippi, F. (1999b) 'Strategic Monetary Policy with Non-Atomistic Wage-setters: A Case for Non-Neutrality', CEPR Discussion Paper no. 2218, Centre for Economic Policy Research, London.

Lohmann, S. (1992) 'Optimal Commitment in Monetary Policy: Credibility versus Flexibility', *American Economic Review*, vol. 82, pp. 273–86.

Mangano, G. (1998) 'Measuring Central Bank Independence: A Tale of Subjectivity and of its Consequences', *Oxford Economic Papers*, vol. 50, pp. 468–92.

McCallum, B. (1995) 'Two Fallacies Concerning Central-Bank Independence', *American Economic Review*, vol. 85, pp. 207–11.

McCallum, B. (1997) 'Crucial Issues Concerning Central-Bank Independence', *Journal of Monetary Economics*, vol. 39, pp. 99–112.

Melitz, J. (1997) 'Some Cross-country Evidence About Debt, Deficits and the Behaviour of Monetary and Fiscal Authorities', CEPR Discussion Paper no. 1653, Centre for Economic Policy Research.

Persson, T. and Tabellini, G. (1993) 'Designing Institutions for Monetary Stability', *Carnegie-Rochester Conference Series on Public Policy*, vol. 39, pp. 53–83 London.

Persson, T. and Tabellini, G. (1996) 'Monetary Cohabitation in Europe', *American Economic Review, Papers and Proceedings*, vol. 86, pp. 111–16.

Posen, A. (1993) 'Why Central Bank Independence Does Not Cause Low Inflation: There Is No Institutional Fix for Politics', in O'Brien, R. (ed.)., *Finance and the International Economy 7, The Amex Bank Review Prize Essays*, pp. 41–65 (Oxford: Oxford University Press).

Posen, A. (1995) 'Declarations Are Not Enough: Financial Sector Sources and Central Bank Independence', *NBER Macroeconomics Annual* (Cambridge, Mass.: MIT Press).

Posen, A. (1997) 'Lessons from the Bundesbank on the Occasion of its 40th Birthday', Discussion Paper no. 97–4, Institute for International Economics, Washington.

Power, S. and Rowe, N. (1998) 'Independent Central Banks: Co-ordination Problems and Budget Deficits', *Economic Issues*, vol. 3, pp. 69–77.

Randzio-Plath, C. (2000) 'A New Political Culture in the EU – Democratic Accounbtability of the ECB', ZEI Policy Paper no. B4/2000, Centre for European Integration Studies, Bonn University.

Rogoff, K. (1985) 'The Optimal Degree of Commitment to an Intermediate Monetary Target', *Quarterly Journal of Economics*, vol. 100, pp. 1169–1189.

Rudebusch, G. and Svensson, L. (2002) 'Eurosystem Monetary Targeting: Lessons from US Data', *European Economic Review*, vol. 46, pp. 417–42.

Soskice, D. and Iversen, T. (1998) 'Multiple Wage-Bargaining Systems in the Single European Currency Area', *Oxford Review of Economic Policy*, vol. 14, pp. 110–24.

Soskice, D. and Iversen, T. (2000) 'The Non-Neutrality of Monetary Policy With Large Wage Setters', *Quarterly Journal of Economics*, vol. 115, pp. 265–84.

Stiglitz, J. (1998) 'Central Banking in a Democratic Society', *De Economist*, vol. 146, pp. 199–226.

Surico, P. (2003) 'Asymmetric Reaction Function for the Euro Area', *Oxford Review of Economic Policy*, vol. 19, pp. 44–57.

Svensson, L. (1997a) 'Optimal Inflation Targets, Conservative Central Banks and Linear Inflation Contracts', *American Economic Review*, vol. 87, pp. 98–114.

Svensson, L. (1997b) 'Inflation Forecast Targeting: Implementing and Monitoring Inflation Targets', *European Economic Review*, vol. 41, pp. 1111–46.

Svensson, L. (1999) 'Monetary Policy Issues for the Eurosystem', *Carnegie-Rochester Conference Series on Public Policy*, vol. 51, pp. 79–136.

Velasco, A. and Guzzo, V. (1999) 'The Case for A Populist Central Banker', *European Economic Review*, vol. 43, pp. 1317–44.

Von Hagen, J. (1997) 'Monetary Policy and Institutions in the EMU', *Swedish Economic Policy Review*, vol. 4, pp. 51–116.

Von Hagen, J. and Mundschenk, S. (2003) 'Fiscal and Monetary Policy Coordination in EMU', *International Journal of Finance and Economics,* vol. 8, pp. 279–95.

Walsh, C.E. (1995) 'Optimal Contracts for independent Central Bankers', *American Economic Review*, vol. 85, pp. 150–67.

Weale, M. (1999) 'Monetary and Fiscal Policy in Euroland', *Journal of Common Market Studies*, vol. 37, pp. 153–62.

Zervoyianni, A. (1996) 'Product-Market Openness and Dynamic Responses to Unanticipated Shocks', *International Review of Economics and Finance*, vol. 5, pp. 269–90.

Zervoyianni, A. (1997) 'Monetary Policy Games and Coalitions in a Two-Country Model with Unionized Wage Setting', *Oxford Economic Papers*, vol. 49, pp. 57–76.

8 Fiscal Policy in the EMU: Analysis and Assessment

Athina Zervoyianni and George Argiros

Introduction

In addition to introducing the idea of EMU as a target to be achieved at the latest by January 1999, the Maastricht Treaty also established certain fiscal criteria for participation and continued membership. The Maastricht Treaty's provisions regarding the member states' fiscal policy can be summarized as follows:

- 'The member states should avoid having excessive public sector deficits' (Article 104c). This provision took the form of specific margins for the ratio of public debt to GDP and the ratio of deficit to GDP.
- 'Each member state alone will be responsible for the servicing of its own public debt, i.e. the payment of interest, dividends etc., even in the case of a fiscal crisis' (Article 104b). This provision is known as the 'no-bail-out clause': it forbids a government facing problems in financing its deficit or in rolling over its maturing debt from being 'bailed out' by other member states or by EU Institutions.
- 'The direct financing of public sector deficits by national central banks, as well as the indirect financing of such deficits on more favourable terms, is prohibited'.
- 'The margins for the deficit and the debt are set at 3 per cent and 60 per cent'. In particular, the general deficit of the government in market prices should not exceed 3 per cent of the GDP of the country concerned, while the gross public debt in market prices should not exceed 60 per cent of GDP.

With the Stability and Growth Pact (SGP), which was signed in Amsterdam in July 1997, these provisions were clarified and extended. Also, rules were established concerning the procedures to be followed in dealing with excessive deficits and with regard to the imposition of fines on member states.

Data for the ratio of deficit to GDP and for the ratio of debt to GDP in the EU-15 countries are presented in Table 8.1 for the period 1990–2003. As can be seen from the table, almost all the European economies had at times exceeded the percentages of 60 and/or 3. Especially during the period 1990–95, there had been frequent and relatively large fluctuations in both the ratio of debt to GDP and the ratio of deficit to GDP. Moreover, in 1991, the year when the Maastricht Treaty was signed and before the participation in the EU of Austria, Finland and Sweden, only four countries, namely France, Germany, Luxembourg and the UK, were in a position to satisfy both criteria. Of the other member states, Italy and Greece were facing serious problems with respect to both their debt to GDP and their deficit to GDP. Belgium had a relatively small deficit but a very large debt, while in the Netherlands the ratio of deficit to GDP was less than 3 per cent but the ratio of debt to GDP was above 60 per cent. In Portugal and Spain the ratio of deficit to GDP was higher than 3 per cent, but the ratio of debt to GDP was relatively small. In addition, while in certain countries, like Denmark and Ireland, the deficit as a percentage of GDP started to fall from 1995 onwards, other member states, like Spain, France and Germany, started in 1990 with a relatively small deficit and debt but during the process one or both of these two variables increased and exceeded the margins of 3 per cent or/and 60 per cent. And, while by 1999, the year when parities with the euro were locked, all the EU-15 states had managed to be below the Maastricht limits as far as their deficit to GDP was concerned, a number of member states, including Belgium, Italy, Greece, and Austria, were still unable to stay within the limit as far as their debt to GDP was concerned. Moreover, after 1999, budgetary positions deteriorated in several member states, making it impossible for some of them to maintain the deficit limits. Thus Portugal exceeded the 3 per cent limit in 2001 but met it again in 2002, following the enactment by the Commission of the excessive deficit procedure. Germany and France exceeded the deficit limit for two consecutive years, 2002 and 2003, leading the Commission to recommend the imposition of sanctions. But the Council did not adopt the Commission's recommendation: it simply asked Germany and France to reduce their deficits by 0.8 and 0.6 per cent respectively in 2004 and by 0.6 and 0.5 per cent respectively in 2005. There was no reference to sanctions for the previously observed violations of the deficit limits or for any future violation of the new arrangements. This development was seen by many as a serious challenge to the EU's fiscal framework; and it revealed the political difficulties of enforcing sanctions.

Indeed, the fiscal-policy restrictions of EMU have been a topic of discussion both among EU officials and in academic cycles ever since

Table 8.1 General government deficit/surplus and gross public debt

	1990	1991	1992	1993	1994	1995	1996	1997	1998	1999	2000	2001	2002	2003
Austria	-2.4	-3.0	-2.0	-4.2	-5.0	-5.1	-3.8	-1.9	-2.5	-2.3	-1.9	0.3	-0.6	-1.0
	56.8	57.0	56.9	61.4	64.2	68.0	68.3	63.9	63.5	67.5	66.8	67.3	68.7	66.4
Belgium	-5.5	-6.3	-6.9	-7.1	-4.9	-3.9	-3.7	-2.0	-1.0	-0.5	0.1	0.2	-0.1	0.2
	124.7	126.5	127.9	134.6	132.7	129.8	128.3	123.0	117.4	114.9	109.6	108.5	105.3	103.5
Denmark	-2.1	-3.1	-2.6	-3.2	-2.4	-3.3	-3.4	-2.7	1.7	3.3	2.4	2.9	2.0	0.9
	57.7	62.3	66.4	78.0	73.5	69.3	65.1	61.4	55.8	53.0	47.4	45.4	45.2	42.9
Finland	5.4	-1.5	-5.9	-8.0	-6.4	-5.0	-3.2	-1.5	1.3	2.0	6.9	5.1	4.7	2.4
	14.3	22.7	40.7	56.8	58.3	56.6	57.1	54.1	49.0	47.0	44.5	43.8	42.7	44.6
France	-1.6	-2.1	-3.9	-5.6	-5.8	-4.9	-4.2	-3.0	-2.7	-1.8	-1.4	-1.6	-3.1	-4.2
	34.9	35.2	39.0	44.3	47.6	51.9	57.1	59.0	59.3	58.5	57.2	56.8	59.1	62.6
Germany	-2.1	-3.3	-2.8	-3.5	-2.4	-3.6	-3.9	-3.2	-2.9	-1.5	-1.4	-2.8	-3.6	-4.4
	43.8	40.3	43.0	47.0	49.3	57.0	59.8	60.9	60.7	61.2	60.2	59.5	60.8	63.8
Greece	-16.1	-16.5	-12.3	-14.2	-12.1	-10.2	-7.4	-4.7	-3.1	-1.8	-1.9	-1.9	-1.2	-1.7
	89.0	91.2	97.5	110.2	107.9	108.7	111.3	108.5	105.4	105.1	106.2	107.0	104.9	100.6
Ireland	-2.3	-2.3	-2.5	-2.4	-1.7	-2.2	-0.6	0.8	2.1	2.3	4.3	1.1	-0.1	-0.9
	92.6	92.4	90.0	94.0	88.1	80.8	74.1	65.3	55.6	49.3	39.3	36.8	33.3	33.5
Italy	-11.1	-10.1	-9.6	-9.5	-9.2	-7.7	-7.1	-2.7	-2.8	-1.7	-1.8	-2.6	-2.3	-2.6
	93.7	100.6	107.7	118.1	123.8	123.2	122.2	119.8	116.3	114.9	110.6	109.5	106.7	106.4
Luxemburg	5.0	1.9	0.8	1.7	2.8	1.9	2.7	3.6	3.2	3.5	6.1	6.4	2.6	-0.6
	4.5	4.0	4.8	5.8	5.4	5.6	6.2	6.0	6.4	6.0	5.6	5.6	5.3	4.9
Netherlands	-5.1	-2.9	-3.9	-3.2	-3.8	-4.0	-1.8	-1.2	-0.8	0.7	1.5	0.1	-1.1	-2.6
	75.6	75.7	76.4	77.6	74.0	75.5	75.3	70.3	67.0	63.1	55.8	52.8	52.6	54.6

Table 8.1 (Continued)

	1990	1991	1992	1993	1994	1995	1996	1997	1998	1999	2000	2001	2002	2003
Portugal	-5.1	-6.0	-3.0	-6.1	-6.0	-5.7	-3.8	-2.6	-2.1	-2.8	-2.8	-4.2	-2.7	-2.9
	62.4	66.1	58.8	62.0	62.7	64.7	63.6	60.3	56.5	54.3	53.3	55.6	58.1	57.5
Spain	-4.3	-4.5	-4.1	-7.0	-6.3	-7.3	-5.0	-3.2	-2.6	-1.2	-0.9	-0.1	0.1	0.0
	43.2	43.9	46.3	57.9	60.4	63.2	68.1	66.7	64.9	63.1	60.5	56.9	54.0	51.3
Sweden	4.2	-1.1	-7.8	-12.3	-10.0	-7.7	-3.6	-0.8	-0.7	1.5	3.4	4.5	1.3	0.2
	42.1	51.2	64.8	75.1	77.7	76.6	76.0	75.0	72.4	62.7	52.8	54.4	52.6	51.7
UK	-1.2	-2.5	-6.3	-7.8	-6.8	-5.5	-4.8	-3.1	-2.3	1.1	1.5	0.8	-1.3	-2.8
	35.5	35.1	41.1	47.8	49.8	52.0	52.7	50.9	48.4	45.1	42.1	38.9	38.4	39.6
E.U.-15	-2.9	-4.1	-4.9	-6.2	-5.3	-4.9	-3.6	-1.5	-1.0	-0.7	-0.2	-0.9	-1.9	-2.7
	58.1	60.3	64.1	71.4	71.7	72.2	72.4	69.7	66.6	67.3	64.1	62.9	62.7	64.1

Source: Eurostat database, National Indicators, 2004

the signing of the Maastricht Treaty. And they have raised questions about the conduct of fiscal policy in a MU in general. A crucial question is whether the fiscal policy of a country participating in a monetary union should or should not be constrained. Another question is to what extent 'rules' need to be used to control member states' fiscal policies, if national fiscal policies should be controlled centrally. In addition, there is the issue of what form should these rules take. In the case of Europe, the particular fiscal-policy rules and criteria adopted need to be understood and evaluated. The provisions of the SGP, in particular the procedures for dealing with excessive deficits, and the possible effects of such provisions on member states, also need to be assessed.

In what follows we examine the theoretical arguments for and against the imposition of constraints on national fiscal policies in a MU, and we consider the shortcomings and merits of the fiscal-policy framework of the Maastricht Treaty and of the Stability and Growth Pact. The next section deals with the issue of whether or not fiscal policies in a MU should retain their independence. Following that we focus on the fiscal rules of the Maastricht Treaty, before moving onto analyse and assess the SGP's provisions. A summary and concluding comments are provided in the final section.

Should or Should Not National Fiscal Policies Retain their Independence in a Monetary Union?

There is currently a debate in the literature concerning the conduct of fiscal policy in a monetary union. Some authors argue that the fiscal authorities of member states need to maintain their flexibility and autonomy. Others argue that national fiscal policies in a monetary union should be constrained by explicit rules on the size of deficits and public debt. And there are those who take the view that national fiscal policies in a MU should be coordinated rather than being limited by arbitrary deficit and debt ceilings.[1] In particular, one can distinguish five different approaches/arguments:

- the approach based on the theory of optimum currency areas;
- the argument about the sustainability of deficits;
- the argument about the external effects of government deficits;
- the approach based on the effects of the creation of a MU on the member states' fiscal discipline; and
- the game-theoretic approach.

The Stabilizing Role of Fiscal Policy in a MU

The optimum-currency-areas (OCAs) literature is explicit on the conduct of fiscal policy in a MU. It stresses that individual members of a MU are subject to a common monetary policy and cannot devalue *vis-à-vis* other members. At the same time, their economies may experience asymmetric shocks. To offset such shocks, they should not be constrained by arbitrary rules on public borrowing and debt: countries participating in a MU should retain their flexibility and independence as far as fiscal policy is concerned.[2]

The basic argument can be presented as follows. Consider two countries, *A* and *B*, which are members of a monetary union. Assume that due to an exogenous unforeseen event, at each level of prices aggregate demand in country *A* falls while aggregate demand in country *B* rises. The result is that output in *A* drops and unemployment increases, while output in *B* rises and unemployment falls with the danger of creating inflationary pressures. As the two countries are in a monetary union, they are unable to use the exchange rate, or more generally monetary policy, to compensate for the impact of this asymmetric shock on their economies. At the same time, given the nature of the shock, an adjustment of the external value of the common currency cannot address the problem. However, if *A* and *B* have independent fiscal policies, the unfavourable effects of the shock on their economies will be softened through the operation of the automatic stabilizers of their budgets, which will operate like a counter-cyclical fiscal policy.

Automatic stabilizers are those items of the budget whose level depends on the private sector's real income and therefore on the phase of the business cycle. In particular, in country *A*, which is facing a fall in its real GDP and thus a drop in the private sector's real income, tax payments will decrease while at the same time transfer payments to the public, such as unemployment benefits and other social security expenditures, will tend to increase. Both the drop in tax payments and the rise in transfer payments will limit the extent to which the private sector's real disposable income will fall. This will operate as a counter-cyclical economic policy, reducing the adverse impact of the shock on aggregate domestic demand. The opposite effects will take place in country *B*: following the increase in demand and in the private sector's real income, tax payments will be higher and social security expenditures lower, thus reducing the tendency for the development of inflationary pressures.

However, in order to exercise such a counter-cyclical fiscal policy through the operation of automatic stabilizers, the government of country *A* must be in a position to leave its budget to be in deficit in the short and medium term, and thus it must be able to increase its borrowing. Provided that country *A*'s fiscal policy retains its independence and capital markets are efficient, this will not be a problem: to meet its borrowing needs, country *A* can draw from the increased

Figure 8.1

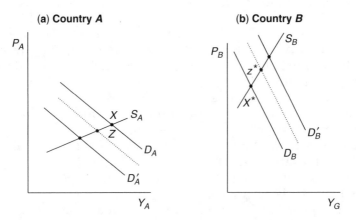

(a) Country *A*   (b) Country *B*

savings in country B that will result from the rise in the private sector's real disposable income.

Figure 8.1 illustrates this point. Two countries are assumed A and B. The D_A and D_B lines are aggregate demand schedules. S_A and S_B represent short-run aggregate supply. Initial equilibrium is at point $X(X^*)$ in A(B). Suppose that country A and country B have formed a monetary union and that, due to a stochastic shock to investment demand, aggregate demand falls in A and rises in B. As a result, D_A shifts to the left, for example to D'_A, and D_B to the right, for example to D'_B. With no binding rules on fiscal policies, the automatic fiscal stabilizers in country A (country B) will tend to shift the $D_A(D_B)$ schedule back to its initial position, establishing an equilibrium at $Z(Z^*)$. On the other hand, if country A's government was not in a position to exercise an independent fiscal policy or was facing constraints on the size of deficits or level of borrowing, it would be unable to leave the automatic stabilizers of the budget to work fully. Therefore it would not be in a position to limit the adverse effect of the asymmetric shock on its domestic economy. As far as the European Union is concerned, the implication is clear: given the assignment of the EU's monetary policy to price stability, fiscal policy may be the primary 'stabilization' tool in the presence of asymmetric shocks and should therefore retain its flexibility.

It should be noted that this approach to the need for independent fiscal policies in a MU is based on the implicit assumption of downward inflexibility of nominal wages, as well as on the assumption of labour immobility. With fully flexible wages, in our example, the fall in country A's domestic demand would have a relatively small impact on its output as money wages and prices would be adjusted accordingly. Thus there would be no significant change in country A's borrowing needs. Also, with labour mobility, in principle no serious problem would arise, as country A's residents, who were unable to find a job locally, could go and work in country B where excess demand for labour would exist. If this happened, the investment disturbance would have little impact on national budgets and thus on country A's borrowing needs. Nevertheless, downward flexibility of wages and labour mobility are assumptions that usually do not hold in practice, especially in the case of the EU.[3] From this point of view, the argument of the optimum-currency-areas theory remains valid. Indeed, the current reality is that of very little mobility of labour across Europe and so structural reforms to improve labour-market flexibility as a way of compensating for the absence of exchange-rate flexibility in the EMU has been advocated by many.[4]

On the other hand, a 'centralization' of national budgets would address the problem of asymmetric shocks even if nominal rigidities and labour immobility existed within the union. Centralization could take the form that income taxes in member states were imposed and collected by a central authority and that the same was true for social security expenditures. In such a case, the union's central budget would automatically re-allocate resources without country A encountering public-borrowing problems. More specifically, through the automatic stabilizers of the central budget, net public expenditures would increase in country A and would fall in country B, while the increased tax revenue from country B would be used to finance the increased social security expenditures in country A. The consequences of the asymmetric shock would therefore be neutralized.

In the case of the EU, a centralization of national budgets would correspond to a 'federalization' of Europe, namely the creation of a genuine Community budget with common targets in all sections of expenditure and revenue. In the last few years, considerable discussion has been going on about this matter,[5] with an increasing number of politicians and academics arguing in favour of a federal Europe. Proponents of federalization stress that a European fiscal union would ensure a more efficient allocation of the tax base, and of resources in general, and would also eliminate any adverse effects on member states resulting from the necessity of imposing fiscal-policy rules such as those of the Maastricht Treaty and the SGP. Others, however, argue that federalization could lead to a more inefficient outcome than in the current situation. Within the framework of Alesina and Perotti (1998), for example, a European fiscal union, while reducing inefficiencies regarding the tax base, could introduce uncertainty regarding tax rates. The reason is that the fiscal-board members' priorities could be so different that member states might find it difficult to agree on common tax rates, something that would create uncertainty about fiscal-policy matters in general in the euro area.

The Risk of Unstable Debt Dynamics

According to the deficit-sustainability approach, unconstrained flexibility in fiscal policy-making in a MU may lead to problems: it may give rise to an unstable process of debt accumulation that may leave the government of the country concerned no alternative than run primary surpluses for a series of years after the use of fiscal policy once.

Along the lines suggested by De Grauwe (2003a) the crucial point here is that outside a MU a government can finance its net expenditure either by borrowing from the central bank, and thus through an increase in the money supply, or by borrowing from the public, namely by issuing new public debt. In a MU, the first method of financing a deficit is no longer available as it is the central monetary authority that decides upon money-supply changes. Accordingly, outside a MU the government's budget constraint takes the well-known form of equation (1a), while inside the MU it takes the form of equation (1b):

$$\Delta m/m + \Delta b/b = g - t + (r - x)b \qquad (1a)$$

$$\Delta b/b = g - t + (r - x)b \qquad (1b)$$

where all variables, except for the nominal interest rate r, are defined as percentages of GDP. Thus $m(b)$ is the ratio of money supply (public debt) to GDP, $g(t)$ is the ratio of public expenditure (tax revenue) to GDP, $x = \Delta Y/Y$ is the rate of increase of nominal GDP, and $\Delta b/b(\Delta m/m)$ is the rate of increase over time in public debt (money supply) as percentage of GDP.

From equations (1a) and (1b) one can clearly see the argument about the sustainability of deficits in a MU. Starting from an initial equilibrium, where $\Delta b/b = 0$, an increase in net government expenditure would make the rate of change of the debt positive for any given nominal interest rate and rate of increase of nominal GDP. This would lead over time to increases in the existing debt as percentage of GDP. Such additional debt would have to be serviced: the government would have to pay interest to those who hold this additional debt. But if the rate of increase of GDP happened to be smaller than the nominal interest rate, new borrowing would be needed to finance the servicing of this additional debt. In particular, starting from an initial equilibrium with $\Delta b/b = 0$, an increase in $(g - t)$ will lead to $\Delta b/b > 0$ and this, in turn, will lead over time to an increase in b. However, if $(r - x) > 0$, there will be a secondary increase in $\Delta b/b$, and thus over time in b, because of the need to finance the increased debt-servicing payments. In such a case, an unstable process of debt accumulation will emerge: the debt-GDP ratio would explode rather than stabilize at a given level in the long run, something which at some stage would require corrective actions. Indeed, if the government is to eliminate the probability of seeing its debt to increase over time at an increasing rate, at some stage it will be forced to run tight fiscal policies, namely to proceed to large cuts in public expenditure or to tax increases, in order to start accumulating surpluses and thus achieve continual declines in the debt-to-GDP ratio. This, however, may not be desirable as it may drive the domestic economy into recession. On the other hand, if this country was not a member of a MU and so the government budget constraint of equation (1a) was valid, the process of debt accumulation could in principle be stopped for any given $(g - t)$ and $(r - x)$ through a drastic increase in the rate of growth of the money supply, namely through an increase in $\Delta m/m$.

The conclusion to be drawn from the above considerations is that when a country enters into a monetary union, its fiscal policy cannot always be used without problems in a discretionary manner to deal with shocks hitting its economy. From this point of view, binding rules on fiscal deficits can be considered a mechanism that limits irresponsibility in fiscal policy.

External Effects of Excessive Budgetary Positions

Excessive deficits, in addition to creating problems for the union countries that run them, may also have an adverse impact on the other member states and thus on the union as a whole. There are two main channels through which such 'external effects' may operate: through aggregate demand via market interest rates; and through debt-service burdens via the interest rate charged on public debt (see Wyplosz (1991), Masson (1996), Artis and Winkler (1999), Pisani-Ferry (2002b) and Allsopp and Artis (2003)).

Starting from the first channel, consider two countries, A and B, which are in a MU. Aggregate demand in A and B can be represented by equations (2a.1) and (2a.2) respectively:

$$y_A^d = -\delta r_A + \sigma e + \kappa(g_A - t_A) \tag{2a.1}$$

$$y_B^d = -\delta r_B + \sigma e + \kappa(g_B - t_B) \tag{2a.2}$$

$$\delta, \sigma, \kappa > 0$$

where r_i and $(g_i - t_i)$ for $i = A, B$ are market interest rates and net government spending (and therefore primary deficits), and e is the external value of the common currency *vis-à-vis* non-union countries (assumed to be given).[6] Suppose that country B has chosen to have a balanced primary budget, and thus $(g_B - t_B) = 0$. Country A, on the other hand, has chosen to have an increasing deficit and thus $(g_A - t_A) > 0$. Country A's deficit will affect r_A: an increasing deficit implies a high level of spending in the economy that eventually will cause interest rates to rise. But with perfect capital mobility and a common currency, the interest-rate-parity condition, equation (2a.3), will hold within the monetary union:

$$r_A = r_B = r_{MU} \tag{2a.3}$$

Accordingly the rise in the interest rate r_A in country A will be followed by a rise in union-wide interest rates and thus by a proportional rise in the interest rate r_B in country B, so a negative externality would result for this country. Moreover, faced with the higher market interest rate r_B, and therefore the prospect of a drop in investment demand and so aggregate demand, country B's government may have no other option but adopt an expansionary fiscal policy, namely it may decide to start running budget deficits $(g_B - t_B)$ despite its initial intention not to do so. But with country B start running primary deficits, there will be a further rise in union-wide market interest rates, something that will have an adverse impact on investment in country A and will thus induce its government to adopt an even more expansionary fiscal-policy stance. This process will lead to over-expansionary national fiscal policies, and so excessive deficits, throughout the union. Under such circumstances, rules that limit the size of national budget deficits would be regarded as an action in the right direction.

Adverse external effects through market interest rates may also arise from the fact that A and B share the same central bank[7]: the tendency for interest rates to rise in the MU, following an excessive fiscal position in country A, may have undesirable consequences for the MU's inflation rate. In particular, under the pressure from country B hit by the high interest rates, the union's CB may be forced to loosen up monetary policy and thus renege on its commitment to maintaining low inflation.[8] An excessive budget deficit in country A may thus lead to a higher union-wide inflation rate.

The second channel of external effects stressed in the literature is associated with the debt-service burden. Consider again country A and country B that are in a MU. Their government budget constraints as a percentage of GDP are:

$$\Delta b_A / b_A = (g_A - t_A) + (i_A - x_A) b_A \tag{3a.1}$$

$$\Delta b_B / b_B = (g_B - t_B) + (i_B - x_B) b_B \tag{3a.2}$$

where $i_A (i_B)$ is the interest rate charged on country $A's$ (country $B's$) public borrowing. However, the argument is that, with perfect capital mobility, we will have $i_A = i_B = i_{MU}$, so the same interest rate will be charged on all member states' public debt. Suppose then that, initially, country B has chosen to have a balanced budget, and thus $\Delta b_B / b_B = 0$, as well as a low debt-to-GDP ratio b_B. Country A has chosen to have a large debt and deficit, and thus $\Delta b_B / b_B > 0$. Country $A's$ deficit will eventually lead to an increase in the interest rate charged on its debt. But in the context of the interest-rate-parity condition $i_A = i_B = i_{MU}$, this will be followed by a proportional rise in union-wide borrowing rates, so (3b.1) and (3b.2) will hold with an increased i_{MU}:

$$\Delta b_A / b_A = (g_A - t_A) + (i_{MU} - x_A) b_A \tag{3b.1}$$

$$\Delta b_B / b_B = (g_B - t_B) + (i_{MU} - x_B) b_B \tag{3b.2}$$

Such an increase in i_{MU} will again create a negative externality for country B: as i_{MU} will rise, country $B's$ debt-service payments will increase, with the result that it will start running deficits, despite the fact that initially it has chosen to have a balanced budget and a low debt-to-GDP ratio. Moreover, if the rise in the union-wide borrowing rate i_{MU} happens to exceed the rate of growth of country $B's$ GDP, x_B, an unstable process of debt accumulation will start in country B, despite that fact that its debt has initially been small. And if country $B's$ debt is to stop increasing at an increasing rate, its government will be forced at some stage to increase its primary surplus $(t_B - g_B)$, namely tax receipts minus expenditure. This, however, may plunge country $B's$ economy into recession. It would then be optimal for country B to demand rules that impose ceilings on national budget deficits in the monetary union (see Artis and Winkler (1998) and De Grauwe (2003a)).

However, as many authors, including Eichengreen and Wyplosz (1998), have pointed out, spillovers through this channel will be very small if credit markets work efficiently. In general, the interest rate payable on the debt of a MU member state, i, can de expected to consist of two components: a given risk-free union-wide interest rate, $\tilde{i}_{MU}$, and a risk premium, ψ, which reflects risk of default, namely the probability that at some stage this country may stop servicing its debt. If we have two countries in a monetary union and one of them, say country A, has entered into a process of excessive deficits, the capital markets, realizing the increased likelihood of debt default, will start charging this country an increased premium on its borrowing. But, as the default risk associated with country B will remain unchanged, the risk premium, and so the interest rate charged, on its borrowing will remain the same. That is, we will have (3c.1) and (3c.2):

$$\Delta b_A / b_A = (g_A - t_A) + (\tilde{i}_{MU} + \psi_A - x_A) b_A \qquad (3c.1)$$

$$\Delta b_B / b_B = (g_B - t_B) + (\tilde{i}_{MU} + \psi_B - x_B) b_B \qquad (3c.2)$$

with $\psi_A > \psi_B$. Accordingly, there will be no negative externality for country B. In short, the argument is that provided capital markets function rationally and effectively, different borrowing rates will be charged to different member states according to their creditworthiness and the corresponding default risk. And if a MU country has an excessive deficit on a continuous basis, the risk-of-default component of its borrowing rate will be rising at an increasing rate: at a certain point in time the default risk premium will be so large that the cost of debt servicing will become sufficiently high to induce fiscal discipline. Experience with the developing countries seems to suggest that this is the case: financial markets seem to assess rather correctly the creditworthiness of different countries and charge appropriate risk premia.

There is, however, a counter-argument to this: excessive debt and deficit positions may create an externality through the financial system: by increasing the likelihood of debt default, they may cause instability in the union-wide financial markets.[9] Faced with the possibility of unstable financial markets, other union countries with smaller deficits and debts may then 'bail-out' the member state with the excessive deficit (that is, purchase part of its debt), something that may not have been desirable in the first place.

Effects of MU Membership on Fiscal Discipline

The need or not for binding fiscal-policy rules in a MU is not independent of the impact of the creation of the monetary union on the member states' fiscal discipline. As far as this impact is concerned, results in the literature are mixed. Some argue that participation in a MU reduces a country's fiscal discipline; others stress that participation in a monetary union increases this discipline.[10]

The idea behind the argument that participation in a monetary union reduces fiscal discipline is that when a country, say country B, does not participate in a MU, and thus the exchange rate of its currency fluctuates freely, the interest rate i_B charged on its debt is equal to a given risk-free market interest rate $\tilde{i}$ plus two risk premia, ψ_B and ξ_B, where the first reflects default risk and the second reflects exchange risk, namely the risk that the currency of country B may be devalued in the future relative to other currencies:

$$i_B = \tilde{i} + \psi_B + \xi_B, \text{ with } \xi_B = \Delta e_B^e \qquad (4)$$

where Δe_B^e is the expected rate of depreciation of the currency under consideration.[11] When country B becomes a MU member, the exchange-rate risk in equation (3a) is eliminated since there is a common currency whose stability against the currencies of non-union countries is supposed to be guaranteed by the union's central monetary authority. Accordingly, as this country becomes a union member, ξ_B tends to zero and the interest rate that its government has to pay on its outstanding debt is reduced. This increases its incentive to issue more debt since the unit cost of servicing the debt falls. Entry into a MU, in addition to the elimination of the exchange-rate risk and the fall in the borrowing rate, will also increase the size of capital markets for any individual member state. Thus national governments will be in a position to finance increased expenditures relatively easier, something that will also increase their incentives to run deficits (see Corsetti and Roubini (1997)). In general, these considerations reinforce the arguments in favour of imposing explicit rules that restrict a union country's budgetary policy: they imply that additional discipline has to be imposed on fiscal policy once countries have entered into a MU. The evidence reported in Agell *et al.* (1996) seems to provide support for this view. Agell *et al.* (1996) find that during the monetary cooperation period of the EMS, the ERM countries were running larger deficits than the non-ERM OECD countries.

The opposite view, stressed by De Grauwe (1992, 2003a) but also supported by many others, emphasizes the fact that, by participating in a monetary union, a country looses its ability to monetize public-sector deficits, namely to finance deficits through money creation. As De Grauwe (1992, 2003a) points out, the member states of a MU are faced with the stricter budget constraint of equation (1b) as opposed to countries that do not belong to a MU, which operate within the limits of the budget constraint of equation (1a). The argument then is that as the budget constraint of member states' governments becomes stricter with the establishment of the MU, their incentives to run excessive deficits weakens. Accordingly, there is no need for imposing additional fiscal discipline in the form of fiscal-policy rules following the creation of a MU.

Several studies have searched for evidence in support of this claim by considering currency unions that existed in the past, or still exist. Lamfalussy (1989), for example, has compared budget deficits in the USA, Australia, Germany, Canada and Switzerland with public-sector deficits in Europe. He has found that over the years budget deficits in these MUs have been smaller than the average of deficits of the EU countries. Other authors have attempted to answer the question of how the creation of a monetary union may affect the member states' fiscal discipline by relying on indirect evidence, from the relation between fiscal discipline and the degree of decentralization of the decision-making process in national public sectors. Their starting point is that because following the creation of the MU governments will no longer be able to monetize deficits and will thus face a harder budget constraint, the decision-making process in national public sectors will inevitably become more centralized. The crucial question then is to what extent greater centralization of the decision-making process in the public sector also implies smaller deficits. If this were the case, one could point to indirect evidence in favour of an expected positive impact of the establishment of a MU on member states' fiscal discipline.

Indeed, evidence that decentralized public sectors and dispersion of power within them tend to produce larger deficits than centralized public sectors and/or public sectors in which power is more concentrated can be found in a number of studies (see Poterba (1994), Roubini and Sachs (1989), Perotti and Kontopoulos (2002) and Poterba and von Hagen (1999)).[12] As the analysis, for example, in Persson and Tabellini (2000), Alesina and Drazen (1991) and Alesina and Perotti (1997) suggests, two main factors lead to such an outcome. First, in relatively decentralized public sectors, many parties are involved (ministers, local authorities, public enterprises, spending councils and so on) and each of these parties acts, taking no account of the impact of its spending claims on the claims of the other parties and thus on total public-sector spending. The result is that the cost of extra debt is not internalized and this leads to excessive spending. Second, the required fiscal adjustment to adverse shocks hitting the economy tends to be delayed in decentralized public-spending systems, as in such systems each party involved tries to avoid reducing its own spending and make the other parties adjust theirs. Delayed required adjustment then leads to greater debt accumulation and larger budget deficits. In general, these studies provide indirect support for the claim that the creation of a MU is most likely to increase fiscal discipline in member states, something implying no need for imposing strict deficit and debt rules. Indirect support for this claim can also be found in Moesen and Van Rompuy (1991) and Van Rompuy *et al.* (1991). As far as the eurozone countries are concerned, particularly the southern bloc, one could also argue that the reduction of revenues from seigniorage and their efforts towards price stabilization have further worked towards increasing, rather than reducing, their fiscal discipline.

The Game-Theoretic Approach

The game-theoretic approach stresses the need not for strict ceilings on deficits and debts, but for cooperation among member states of a MU in the fiscal-policy front. In particular, the argument is that cooperation in the field of fiscal policy among the member states of a MU

Figure 8.2

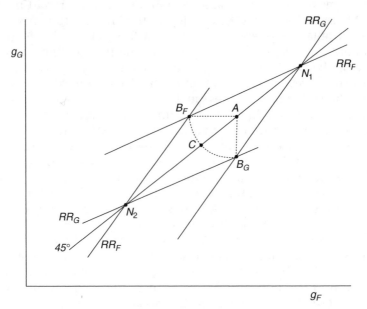

is required to limit the potential for atomistic behaviour and reduce the externalities arising from international macroeconomic interdependence, enhancing at the same time the stabilizing role of fiscal policy.[13]

Figures 8.2 and 8.3 can be used to illustrate the issues involved. Consider two countries, say 'France' and 'Germany'. In Figure 8.2 France and Germany have established a credible monetary union with a central monetary authority, but both want to promote exports. As exchange-rate changes between their currencies are not possible, national fiscal authorities in both therefore have an incentive to run tight fiscal policies: tight fiscal policy would reduce aggregate spending in the economy and so the prices of domestically-produced goods, thus leading to increased competitiveness and therefore exports. In terms of the figure, France has an incentive to reduce government spending so as to move from point A to point B_F, its bliss point. Germany also has an incentive to pursue a contractionary fiscal policy so as to move from point A to point B_G, its bliss point. However, competitiveness is a relative variable: an increase in competitiveness in Germany achieved through a reduction in g_G would imply a deterioration of competitiveness in France and so would induce France to respond by adopting a contractionary fiscal policy itself. France and Germany with Nash play will end up at a point like N_1 or N_2 depending on the steepness of the slope of their reaction curves RR_G and RR_F. If

Figure 8.3

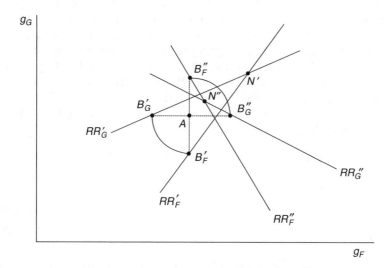

Germany and France decide to co-operate in the fiscal-policy front, they will end up at some point on the contract curve $B_G B_F$ which is the locus of points of tangency between the German and the French fiscal-policy makers indifference curves (not shown, but centred around the bliss points). Relative to points on the contract curve both point N_1 and point N_2 would represent Pareto-inefficient macroeconomic outcomes. Point N_1 implies overexpansionary fiscal policies while point N_2 implies overcontractionary fiscal policies. Through cooperation in the fiscal policy front, atomistic behaviour arising from the pursuit of own objectives without taking into account the impact of this behaviour on others would be eliminated. The result would be neither overexpansionary nor overcontractionary fiscal policies.

At the same time, cooperation would enhance the 'stabilizing role' of fiscal policy in a MU reducing externalities. Consider, for example, a stochastic supply-side shock that lowers output in both France and Germany. If the (net) international spillover effect of national fiscal policies is negative (positive), so that for example higher government spending in Germany on balance reduces (increases) output in France, Germany's bliss point following the shock would be at point B'_G (point B''_G) in Figure 8.3. Similarly the bliss point for France after the shock would be at point B'_F (point B''_F).

Relative to initial equilibrium at A, point B'_G (point B''_G) involves no change in Germany's fiscal policy and a contractionary (expansionary) fiscal policy in France. As g_G remains unchanged, Germany faces no budget-deficit problems; and, given the negative (positive) international spillover effects of national fiscal policies, as g_F drops (increases) the adverse impact of the supply shock on its output is reduced. Similar considerations apply in the case of France. At B'_F (B''_F), since g_F remains unchanged, there are no budget-deficit problems. At the same time, as g_G falls (increases) the adverse impact of the stochastic supply shock on output in France is neutralized.

Indeed, consider a set of loss functions for the fiscal authorities in Germany and France of the form shown in (5a.1) and (5a.2) and a set of reduced-form equations determining y_G and y_F of the form shown in (5b.1) and (5b.2):

$$L_G = g_G^2 + ky_G^2 \qquad\qquad (5a.1)$$

$$L_F = g_F^2 + ky_F^2 \qquad\qquad (5a.2)$$

$$y_G = a_1 g_G + a_2 g_F - u_G \qquad\qquad (5b.1)$$

$$y_F = a_1 g_F + a_2 g_G - u_F \qquad\qquad (5b.2)$$

where all variables are defined in terms of deviations from an initial equilibrium and $a_1 > 0$, $|a_1| > |a_2|$. Also $a_2 \gtrless 0$ depending on whether the international spillover effects of national fiscal policies are on balance positive or negative.

Non-cooperative minimization of the loss functions (5a.1) and (5a.2) with respect to g_G and g_F subject to (5b.1) and (5b.2) gives Nash reaction functions in (g_G, g_F) space with slopes as:

Germany $\quad dg_G/dg_F = -(ka_1 a_2)/(1 + ka_1^2) \quad \lessgtr 0$ for $a_2 \gtrless 0$

France $\quad dg_G/dg_F = -(1 + ka_1^2)/ka_1 a_2 \quad \lessgtr 0$ for $a_2 \gtrless 0$

Under Nash non-cooperative behaviour, equilibrium is therefore at N' or N'' in Figure 8.3. With cooperation in the fiscal-policy front, equilibrium will be at some point on the contract curve $B'_G B'_F$ or the contract curve $B''_G B''_F$. Points on the contract curve $B'_G B'_F$ ($B''_G B''_F$) are closer than point $N'(N'')$ to the bliss points, implying that cooperation will enhance the stabilizing role of fiscal policy.

While the above analysis is valid, it could be argued that in the EU context interactions with the ECB should be taken into account when examining the extent to which fiscal cooperation among the member states would be desirable. This issue has been the focus of attention of many studies in recent years (see, for example, Beetsma and Bovenberg (1997), Dixon and Santori (1997), Beetsma and Uhlig (1999), Dixit (2001), Gatti and Wijnbergen (2002), Beetsma et al. (2001), Demertzis et al. (2003) and von Hagen and Mundschenk (2003)).[15] Interactions with the ECB can be examined using equations (5a.1) and (5a.2) for

'Germany' and 'France' and also equation (5a.3) below, which can be taken to represent the ECB's objective function:

$$L_{ECB} = \pi^2 + \lambda y_{EU^2}, \lambda \geqslant 0, \lambda < k \qquad (5a.3)$$

$$\text{with } y_{EU} = \tfrac{1}{2}(y_G + y_F)$$

The ECB is assumed to be concerned with maintaining price stability in the EU (which for simplicity here is taken to imply a target for the common inflation rate π equal to zero), but it may also be concerned with stabilizing average EU output, $y_{EU} = \tfrac{1}{2}(y_G + y_F)$, with $\lambda < k$ implying that the ECB gives lower priority than the two national fiscal authorities to output stabilization. Taking aggregate demand in each country to respond in the short run positively to the common money-supply-growth rate $\dot{m}$ (determined by the ECB), one can write the reduced-form equations (5b.1) and (5b.2) as:

$$y_G = a_1 g_G + a_2 g_F + \omega_1 \dot{m} - u_G,$$

$$y_F = a_1 g_F + a_2 g_G + \omega_1 \dot{m} - u_F$$

$$\omega_1 > 0$$

which, assuming for simplicity a one-to-one relationship between π and $\dot{m}$, become:

$$y_G = a_1 g_G + a_2 g_F + \omega\pi - u_G \qquad (5c.1)$$

$$y_F = a_1 g_F + a_2 g_G + \omega\pi - u_F \qquad (5c.2)$$

$$\text{where } a_1, \omega > 0, |a_1| > |a_2|, a_2 \gtrless 0$$

With no fiscal cooperation between Germany and France, fiscal policy-makers in each country, treating π as given, will set their respective policy instruments, g_G and g_F, independently so as to minimize their own loss functions, subject to the constraints imposed by equations (5c.1) and (5c.2). With co-operative fiscal policies, policy-makers in France and Germany, taking π as given, will set g_G and g_F jointly to minimize the average of their loss functions, namely $L = \tfrac{1}{2}(L_G + L_F)$. Accordingly, one obtains trade-offs for the two fiscal authorities between budget deficits and output levels as:

Non-cooperative fiscal policies

$$g_G + ka_1 y_G = 0 \qquad (5d.1a)$$

$$g_F + ka_1 y_F = 0 \qquad (5d.1b)$$

Co-operative fiscal policies

$$g_G + ka_1 y_G + ka_2 y_F = 0 \qquad (5d.2a)$$

$$g_F + ka_1 y_F + ka_2 y_G = 0 \qquad (5d.2b)$$

Now as far as the ECB is concerned, if it behaves as a Nash player *vis-a-vis* the two national fiscal authorities, it will set π so as to minimize its loss function (5a.3) subject to (5c.1) and (5c.2), treating g_G and g_F as parametric. This implies a trade-off between the common inflation rate, π, and average EU output, y_{EU}, for the ECB as:

$$\pi + \lambda \omega y_{EU} = 0 \qquad (5d.3a)$$

Alternatively, the ECB may behave as a Stackelberg player: being aware of the desire of national governments to pursue counter-cyclical fiscal policies to stabilize output levels, avoiding at the same time large budget deficits, it may take the reaction functions of the two fiscal policy-makers explicitly into account when minimizing its own loss function. In such a case it will set π so as to minimize (5a.3) subject to not only (5c.1)-(5c.2) but also (5d.1a)-(5d.1b) or (5d.2a)-(5d.2b) depending on the fiscal regime in force. This leads, respectively, to trade-offs between π and y_{EU} for the ECB as shown in (5d.3b$_1$) and (5d.3b$_2$):

$$\pi + (1/a_3 \lambda) \omega y_{EU} = 0 \qquad (5d.3b_1)$$

$$\pi + (1/a_4) \lambda \omega y_{EU} = 0 \qquad (5d.3b_2)$$

where

$$a_3 = 1 + ka_1(a_1 + a_2) > 0, \, a_4 = 1 + k(a_1 + a_2)^2 > 0$$

Consider a common productivity shock (that is, $u = u_G = u_G$). Under Nash play by the ECB *vis-à-vis* the fiscal authorities, combining equations (5c.1), (5c.2) and (5d.3a) with (5d.1a)-(5d.1b) or with (5d.2a)-(5d.2b), depending on the fiscal regime in force, and substituting the resulting solutions for g_G, g_F, y_G and y_F into (5a.1) and (5a.2), the welfare loss of German and French policy-makers can be obtained as:

Non-cooperative fiscal policies

$$L_G^{nc} = L_F^{nc} = [(1 + ka_1^2)/(a_3 + \omega^2/\lambda)^2](k/4)u^2 \qquad (5e.1)$$

Cooperative fiscal policies

$$L_G^c = L_F^c = [a_4/(a_4 + \omega^2/\lambda)^2](k/4)u^2 \qquad (5e.2)$$

From (5e.1) and (5e.2) it follows that as far as governments in Germany and France are concerned, fiscal cooperation would pay (that is, $L_G{}^c = L_F{}^c < L_G{}^{nc} = L_F{}^{nc}$) so long as (5e.3) holds:

$$a_4 + (\omega^4/\lambda^2)\psi > 0 \tag{5e.3}$$

where

$$\psi = -(1/a_2)(\psi_1/\psi_2) \gtrless 0, \ \psi_1 = (2a_1 + a_2) > 0,$$
$$\psi_2 = [1 - (\omega^2/\lambda)(2a_1/a_2)](> 0)$$

This condition unambiguously holds when $a_2 < 0$ (the international spillover effects of national fiscal policies are on balance negative). It will also hold for $a_2 > 0$ (positive international spillover effects) provided that ω, the sensitivity of national output levels to changes in the common money-supply growth rate, and thus in π, is not particularly large. This can be understood as follows. With fiscal cooperation, by minimizing a joint welfare function, the two national fiscal authorities will 'internalize' the spillover effects of their policies. When such spillovers are positive, national fiscal policies under cooperation will be quite accommodating, something that will reduce to a large extent the tendency for national output levels to fall following the productivity shock. But as the tendency for y_G and y_F, and therefore average EU output y_{EU}, to drop will be relatively small in this case, the ECB's monetary policy will not be very expansionary, something that indirectly (through the impact of π on national output levels) will tend to increase in equilibrium the fall in y_G and y_F. This indirect effect, provided that ω is not particularly large, will be dominated by the direct effect on national outputs of the large 'stabilizing' cooperative fiscal-policy responses, in which case condition (5e.3) will hold even with positive spillover effects.[16]

On the other hand, under Stackelberg-leader play by the ECB, combining (5c.1)-(5c.2) with (5d.1a)-(5d.1b) and (5d.3b$_1$) or with (5d.2a)-(5d.2b) and (5d.3b$_2$), depending on the fiscal regime in force, and substituting the resulting solutions for g_G, g_F, y_G and y_F into (5a.1) and (5a.2), one obtains the welfare loss of the German and French governments as:

Non-cooperative fiscal policies

$$L_G'{}^{nc} = L_F'{}^{nc} = [(1 + ka_1^2)/(a_3 + \omega^2/\lambda a_3)^2](k/4)u^2 \tag{5f.1}$$

Cooperative fiscal policies

$$L_G'{}^c = L_F'{}^c = [a_4/(a_4 + \omega^2/\lambda a_4)^2](k/4)u^2 \tag{5f.2}$$

The welfare loss of the two national governments is larger here than in the case of Nash play by the ECB, irrespective of the fiscal regime in force (that is, $L_G'^{nc} = L_F'^{nc} > L_G^{nc} = L_F^{nc}$ and $L_G'^c = L_F'^c > L_G^c = L_F^c$).[17] An explanation for this is not difficult to find. When the ECB behaves as a Stackelberg leader, in minimizing its loss function, it takes explicitly into account the counter-cyclical policies of the two national governments. This improves its inflation-output trade off. In particular, by explicitly taking into account that national fiscal policies will attempt to partly offset the impact of the productivity shock on y_G and y_F, and so indirectly on average EU output y_{EU}, the ECB realizes that it need not have to play a major stabilizing role itself through monetary policy. Compared to the case of Nash play, it therefore adopts in general a less expansionary monetary-policy stance following the shock. This leads to a smaller increase in the common inflation rate π. But it also leads in equilibrium to a larger drop in y_{EU}, and also in national output levels y_G and y_F, something that implies a larger welfare loss for the two national fiscal authorities irrespective of whether they pursue cooperative or non-cooperative fiscal policies. Nevertheless, the outcome under fiscal cooperation will be superior to that under no cooperation from the point of view of the two national fiscal authorities provided that ω is not particularly large for the same reasons as in the case of equations (5e.1) and (5e.2). Indeed, from (5f.1) and (5f.2), one obtains that $L_G'^c = L_F'^c < L_G'^{nc} = L_F'^{nc}$ so long as

$$a_4 + (\omega^2/\lambda)\xi > 0 \qquad\qquad (5f.3)$$

where

$$\xi = -(1/a_2)\xi_1\xi_2 \gtrless 0,\ \xi_1 = (2a_1 + a_2) > 0,$$
$$\xi_2 = [2 + (\omega^2/\lambda)((2+a_4)/a_4 a_3^2)] > 0$$

(5f.3) unambiguously holds when $a_2 < 0$; it will also hold even if $a_2 > 0$ for a small enough ω.

Fiscal Policy in the Maastricht Treaty

The fiscal policy framework of the EU, namely the percentage limits on deficits and debts and the provisions of the Stability and Growth Pact, has been a subject of considerable disagreement among economists ever since the signing of the Maastricht Treaty. The disagreement has been intensified recently, following the May 2004 enlargement, which increased heterogeneity in EU, and also following the November 2003 ECOFIN Council's decision not to impose sanctions on Germany and

France, which had been running deficits above the 3 per cent limit for two consecutive years. Indeed, while between 1992 and 1999 the issue was whether or not the EU's fiscal framework needed reform, since 2000 the issue has been what else should be put in its place. The EU's fiscal framework has been criticized as having a number of weaknesses: the percentage limits for the deficit and the debt are arbitrary; they are too uniform disregarding important differences among member states; they do not focus on the true fiscal-policy stance of a country; they ignore differences in the structure of deficits; the SGP's provisions are too rigid, they do not allow for an efficient working of the automatic fiscal stabilizers, and have a deflationary bias.[18]

Maastricht's Fiscal-Policy Constraints: Evaluation

Starting from the 60 per cent ceiling for the ratio of debt to GDP, this was roughly the debt-to-GDP EU average when the Maastricht Treaty was about to be signed, namely in 1991 (see Table 8.1); and if the Maastricht Treaty had been under negotiation in another period, most probably a different ceiling for this ratio would have been adopted. On the other hand, the 3 per cent ceiling for the deficit was about one point below the community average for 1991. As many authors, including Buiter and Kletzer (1991b), Wickens (1993), Hughes-Hallett and McAdam (1996), Willett (1999) and Buiter (1995, 2003), have pointed out there is no reason to regard these two particular ratios as optimal in general for the EU. Nor is there any reason for these averages to be considered optimal for each individual EU state. The crucial issue is sustainability of deficits,[19] something that depends on a set of structural characteristics of the individual economies concerned and not on the level of the outstanding debt.

At the same time, assuming sustainability of deficits and, along the lines suggested by Buiter *et al.* (1993), using the Maastricht Treaty's definition of deficit $df_i = g_i - t_i + rb_i$, the budget constraint of member states' governments, say, country A and B, can be expressed as in equations (6a.1)-(6a.2) below:

$$\Delta b_A / b_A = df_A - x_A b_A \tag{6a.1}$$
$$\Delta b_B / b_B = df_B - x_B b_B \tag{6a.2}$$

from which, imposing debt sustainability $\Delta b_i / b_i = 0$, we obtain:

$$df_A = x_A b_A \tag{6b.1}$$
$$df_B = x_B b_B \tag{6b.2}$$

From (6b.1) and (6b.2) it follows that given debt sustainability, a rule for the deficit-to-GDP ratio will be consistent with a rule for the debt-to-GDP ratio only for a certain rate of nominal GDP growth. With $df = 3$ and $b = 60$ the two percentages will be consistent with each other and with $\Delta b_i/b_i = 0$ in both A and B only when $x_A = x_b = 0.05$ (that is, nominal GDP growth in the EU is on average 5 per cent). If average nominal GDP growth falls below 5 per cent, satisfying one criterion will necessarily contradict the other.

If we also assume that the ECB has an implicit mid-point target of 1.5 per cent for the rate of change of the Harmonized Consumer Price Index, a 5 per cent rate of nominal GDP growth requires real GDP growth of no lower than 3.5 per cent. An average annual rate of real GDP growth of 3.5 per cent is however an ambitious target. For example in 2002–03, while inflation in the EU was running at a rate of 1.9 per cent, real GDP growth was no more than 2.2 per cent on average, something that on average made the debt and deficit ceilings inconsistent with each other. Indeed, for some of the 'core' EU countries, meeting both fiscal criteria proved harder than many academics and EU officials had anticipated in the early 1990s: it required GDP real growth rates much higher than those of the recent past. In 2003, for example, real GDP growth was below 3 per cent for almost all the core EU countries, including France (2.2%), Germany (1.2%) and Italy (1.4%). This meant that France and Germany found themselves unable to satisfy the deficit criterion. On the other hand, member states like Greece, Spain, Finland and Ireland are most likely to continue in the future to have growth rates of real GDP higher than those of the other EU-15 states. These countries can therefore have a higher deficit to GDP ratio without violating the debt sustainability condition.[19] At the same time, achieving mutual consistency of the debt and deficit ceilings may require adjustments in the structure of primary deficits and spending. For example, if interest rates rise and df in equations (6.a.1) and (6.a.2) is to remain on target, total public expenditure will have to be reduced. Some categories of public expenditure, however, may not be flexible enough at least in the short run to achieve this, in which case a restructuring of expenditure will be needed. Also, meeting one criterion does not necessarily imply rapid progress towards the other: deficits and debts may move in different directions in the short and medium term and debt reductions may not be achieved quickly enough even if deficits are kept under control (see Hughes-Hallett and McAdams (1996)).[20]

Even if we assume that real GDP growth in the EU is on average 3.5 per cent and thus the values of 3 per cent and 60 per cent are consistent with each other in the long run, there is the issue of whether a theoretical rationale behind any of these two percentages exists.

There seems to be a theoretical justification (see European Commission (1990) and Buti and van den Noord (2004)), known as the 'golden rule' of public borrowing. According to this rule a country's fiscal authorities should finance current spending from current income, that is income from tax revenue, and borrow only to finance investment spending. In the period prior to the signing of the Maastricht Treaty, in particular during the period 1975–90, public investment in Community countries was on average 3 per cent of GDP. As many commentators, including Buifer *et al.* (1993), have pointed out this was taken as a basis by the Commission for proposing the deficit-to-GDP ceiling of 3 per cent. However, there is no reason why the particular percentage for the period 1975–90 should be considered optimal for all subsequent periods: as recent analyses show, the optimal ratio of investment to GDP may change over time with technological progress, labour productivity, and so on.

The appropriateness of the ratios taken by the Treaty as an indication of a country's fiscal stance, is also controversial. On the one hand, a deficit, when measured by the statistical office of a country, includes the interest payable on public debt in nominal terms. However, if one is to assess the burden of public debt, what is required is a measure of the interest-rate payments in purchasing power terms. Just after the signing of the Maastricht Treaty, a widespread view was that adopting a single currency would increase the credibility and solvency of the national fiscal authorities via lower debt burdens through a drop in interest rates. However, the 'debt burden' relates to interest payments in purchasing-power terms. Accordingly, experiencing a credibility and solvency gain would require a drop in real interest rates; if real interest rates were to rise there would be no such gains. Also, the deficit as defined by the Maastricht Treaty measures gross debt, while a more relevant measure would be governments' net liabilities. In particular, if one is to estimate the actual fiscal stance of countries, the governments' claims on foreign residents, including titles issued by other governments, should be subtracted from current obligations. This matter is important because using a country's gross liabilities as a criterion for its fiscal stance means that its government can achieve a superficial reduction in its declared debt by selling some of its holdings in titles issued by other governments and purchasing with the proceeds some of its debt held by the domestic private sector.

Another problem arises from the fact that several EU member states have public enterprises whose working-capital costs are financed party from the general budget. In such cases, in order to meet the EU's fiscal-policy targets the government of a country may proceed to large-scale privatization, which cannot be justified on grounds of economic efficiency, or may not be conducted under proper conditions, because of the pressure arising from satisfying the fiscal-policy ceilings. Moreover, the fiscal rules of the Maastricht Treaty do not take account of the existing differences among member states in terms of their basic economic structures: EU member states differ in terms of the level and type of social expenditures and more generally, in terms of the structure of their deficits. This implies that a given deficit in for example member state *A*, may not be directly comparable with a deficit in member state *B* of the same magnitude. For example, the deficit in *A* may include a relatively higher level of public expenditures that pay off in the future, such as expenditures in research, education, heath or environmental protection, than that of *B*.[21]

However, there are also arguments in favour of the fiscal rules of the Maastricht Treaty. For example, one can argue that the Maastricht Treaty left some margin for flexibility in the implementation of the rules, and therefore scope for exercising counter-cyclical fiscal policy. In particular, the Maastricht Treaty stated that:

- A deficit above 3 per cent may be regarded as acceptable if it is something unusual for the particular member state or something transitory.
- A deficit will not be considered excessive if it is showing a declining tendency and appears to be able to approach the reference value of 3 per cent in the longer run.
- Other factors relating to the particular country under consideration will also be taken into account in deciding whether its deficit is or is not excessive; like, for example, whether or not its government uses the deficit to finance public investment.
- A ratio of debt to GDP that exceeds the limit of 60 per cent will not be considered excessive if it is declining sufficiently over time, approaching the reference value of 60 per cent at a satisfactorily fast rate.

In general, what the Maastricht Treaty seemed to have established was that member states outside the margins of 3 per cent and/or 60 per cent might not be regarded as having excessive deficits if they had made stable and satisfactory progress towards these targets. Nevertheless, the Maastricht Treaty left open the issue of what could be regarded as stable and satisfactory progress, thus allowing for value judgements to influence the assessment of whether or not a country satisfied the fiscal-policy criteria. In particular, according to the original Maastricht-Treaty provisions, a member state had an 'excessive deficit' if the Council of Finance Ministers (ECOFIN) decided that this was the case after a 'general judgement' (Article 104(6) EC Treaty). There was no specific list of factors that had to be taken into account in identifying the existence of an excessive deficit. Neither the penalties were automatic, as the wording of the relevant provisions of the Maastricht Treaty was that 'the Council of Ministers may decide to implement one or more of the measures provided in the Treaty' (Article 104(11)). In general, the Maastricht Treaty gave the ECOFIN Council a considerable margin of discretion both in deciding whether an excessive deficit existed and with regard to the imposition of penalties. The acts of the Commission and of the Economic and Finance Committee also included elements of value judgement and interpretation and thus had a margin of discretion. The Maastricht Treaty in fact established the Commission as the guardian of the provisions for excessive deficits: the Commission was to observe the fiscal situation and the level of public debt of member states in order to identify possible large divergences, and prepare a report on which the Economic and Finance Committee had to express its view. Then, the Commission was to decide whether there existed, or might exist in the future, an excessive deficit, in which case it forwarded its view to the ECOFIN Council. Under the Maastricht Treaty's provisions, for a decision to be taken by the ECOFIN Council, a recommendation by the Commission was required, although this was not in principle binding, in the sense that the Council of Finance Ministers could, by special majority, decide whether an excessive deficit existed even if the Commission recommended to the contrary. One of the reasons for the signing of the Stability and Growth Pact was to provide a solution to these problems.

At the same time, it could be argued that restricting fiscal-policy intervention, particularly imposing debt ceilings, is necessary to secure the ECB's goal independence. As argued by, for example, Artis and Winkler (1999), despite the Maastricht Treaty's explicit provision that the ECB would be independent of national governments and its primary target would be price stability, fears that a fiscal crisis in one member state could spread into other member states might force the ECB to adjust interest rates. Debt ceilings, it may be argued, are necessary to make it less likely that the ECB will be exposed to such a dilemma. Some authors emphasize that fiscal discipline, in the form of deficit ceilings, is also necessary for the instrument independence of the ECB, as without it the European Central Bank would be unable to control the price level. This argument, advanced by Canzoneri *et al.* (2001), is based on a new theory of price-level determination, the 'fiscal theory' of the price level, according to which the equilibrium price level has to make the real value of current government liabilities equal to the expected present value of current and future surpluses.[22]

Fiscal deficits may also be instigated by institutional and/or political factors. For example, the findings of Roubini and Sachs (1989) imply that in Italy the existence of large deficits historically has, to a certain extent, been due to Italy's political instability arising from the frequent changes of governments and from the low degree of political cohesion of the governments in power. Another argument relates to the electoral business cycles theory:[23] governments sometimes manipulate their fiscal-policy instruments to stimulate aggregate demand in an attempt to improve their reelection prospects. According to Alogoskoufis and Christodoulakis (1991) and Alogoskoufis and Philipopoulos (1992), one of the reasons for the existence of historically large deficits in Greece has been the clientele-style relationships between various governments and certain parts of the private sector, including extended and often unjustifiable allowances to particular groups of people who have at times supported them. In such cases, where the institutional environment and the political situation influence fiscal policy, the adoption of debt and deficit ceilings, like those of the Maastricht Treaty, may be a viable solution to enforce fiscal discipline.[24,25]

The Stability and Growth Pact: In Need of Reform?

The Maastricht Treaty provided for a procedure for surveillance and correction of member states' budgetary-discipline infringements (Article 104 EC Treaty and Protocol no. 5 Annexed to the Treaty). However, this procedure was considered very lenient and ineffective, especially by Germany. In November 1995, to improve the situation, Theo Waigel, the then Federal Minister of Finance of Germany, presented a proposal for a stability pact that was to be complementary to the Maastricht Treaty's provisions for budget deficits. This proposal, also called the Waigel Plan, aimed at clarifying and making more precise the sanction mechanisms of the Maastricht Treaty insofar as they would take effect automatically once the deficit threshold had been reached.[26]

In December 1996 the Dublin European Council accepted the philosophy of the Waigel Plan and the Plan was adopted in July 1997 by the Amsterdam European Council under the name Stability and Growth Pact (SGP), after France's insistence to include the element of growth in it. In December 1997, the Luxembourg European Council adopted a Resolution regarding the coordination of the member states' economic policies in stage III of EMU, while a Declaration of Stability was annexed to the decision of May 1998 concerning those member states that were qualified to participate in the euro zone at its beginning, namely on 1 January 1999.

The SGP consisted of three components:

- The European Council Resolution on the Stability and Growth Pact.[27]

- The Council Regulation no. 1466/97 on the strengthening of the surveillance of budgetary positions and the review and coordination of national economic policies.[28]
- The Council Regulation no. 1467/97 on speeding up and clarifying the implementation of the excessive debt procedure.[29]

The European Council Resolution made an effort to take account of the effects of the business cycle and, more generally, of economic growth on member states' budgetary planning. In particular, the Resolution provided for almost balanced budgets or budget surpluses in the medium term so as to allow the automatic stabilizers of the budget to work in the short run. Indeed, the Resolution pointed out that 'the target of achieving a balanced budget or a budget surplus in the medium term will enable member states to cope with the normal effects of the business cycle and at the same time keep their deficits within the limit of 3 per cent'.[30] The Resolution also defined the actions of the Commission and the Council, with respect to the implementation of the SGP.

Regulation no. 1466/97 had as its main objective the formulation of a system of Community-wide surveillance of member states' budgetary and macroeconomic situations and of early warning so that excessive deficits was to be avoided. On the other hand, Council Regulation no. 1467/97 aimed at speeding up and clarifying the operation of the excessive deficit procedure provided for in Article 104 of the EC Treaty, so that an excessive deficit would be promptly corrected. This Regulation provided for an automatic mechanism of imposing sanctions on euro-zone member states that exceed the 3 per cent limit for the budget deficit, unless this excess was 'exceptional and temporary'.

The SGP actually reflects the dispute that was going on in July 1997 between those EU states that were advocates of restrictive implementation procedures, in which a strict timetable and a system of sanctions would be included, and states that were in favour of looser and more decentralized procedures with an element of discretion on the part of the national fiscal authorities. The 'excessive deficit procedure' was to satisfy the former countries, while the 'community-wide surveillance' of budgetary positions was closer to the latter countries.

The SGP also reallocated discretionary power, strengthening the role of the ECOFIN Council and weakening that of the Commission. As mentioned earlier, the Maastricht Treaty gave the Commission a gatekeeper role as regards the excessive deficit procedure: the Commission was to monitor the development of the deficits and stock of debt in member states with the view to identifying problems. It was also the competent institution to initiate the excessive deficit procedure by making a report. Unless the Commission made a report, the ECOFIN Council had no power to decide whether a member state had an excessive deficit. In making the decision that a member state had an excessive deficit, the ECOFIN Council was also to act on a recommendation from the Commission. The Council was not obliged to accept the substance of the Commission's recommendation, but, because a recommendation was an essential procedural step, the Commission could block an excessive deficit decision. This meant that the Commission could exercise informal pressure on the Council to agree with its judgement as to whether an excessive deficit existed or might occur, and thus could influence through the backdoor the Council's decision.

Now according to the SGP Resolution, the Commission is committed, following a request from the Council under Article 115 EC, to make 'as a rule' a recommendation in order for a decision regarding the existence of an excessive deficit to be adopted by the Council. The discretionary powers and the resulting blocking powers of the Commission are thus in practice reduced: under the SGP resolution, the assessment of whether or not there exists an excessive deficit is in effect in the hands of the Economic and Finance Committee and of the ECOFIN Council.

At the same time, under the Resolution of the European Council on the Stability and Growth Pact, the Commission is committed to always initiate the budgetary surveillance procedure and to prepare a formal report according to Article 104 whenever a planned or actual deficit exceeds the reference value of 3 per cent. From this point of view, the Stability and Growth Pact provides for an automatic initiation of the excessive deficit procedure, minimizing the Commission's discretion as to whether such an excess over the reference value of 3 per cent of GDP should be considered as excessive deficit. When an excess over the reference value of 3 per cent occurs, the Commission, even if it disagrees, is under an obligation to initiate the procedure provided in Article 104 EC, unless such excess is only 'exceptional and temporary'.

An excess over the reference value is defined as exceptional and temporary if it results from an unusual event, outside the control of the member state concerned, that has a major impact on its overall financial position, or if in the assessment year there is a fall in its real GDP of no less than 2 per cent resulting from a severe economic downturn.[31] A fall in GDP of less than 2 per cent in the assessment year may also be classified by the Council as exceptional in the light of further supporting evidence, such as the abruptness of the downturn or the accumulated loss of output relative to past developments.[32] In effect, a fall in real GDP of no less than 2 per cent in the assessment year provides for an automatic exception from the excessive deficit procedure, but a fall in real GDP of less than 2 per cent requires additional research by the Commission if the deficit is to qualify as exceptional. The member state concerned must make available the relevant documentation for such an assessment. At the same time, if an excess over the reference value is to be considered temporary, the budgetary forecasts provided by the Commission must show that this deficit will fall below the reference value when the unusual event or severe economic downturn has ended.[33]

If the excess over the reference value cannot be defined as exceptional and temporary, the Council takes a decision by qualified majority that an excessive deficit exists and makes recommendations to the member state concerned. In the case where the member state concerned fails to take effective action in response to these recommendations, the Council makes its recommendations public. If, after that, the member state concerned fails to reduce the deficit, because either it does not take any actions or its measures are ineffective, the Council takes a decision to impose sanctions. The Resolution requires the Council to always impose sanctions on member states failing, despite its recommendation, to take the necessary measures to bring the situation of the excessive deficit to an end.

Where the Council decides to impose sanctions on a member state, it requires, as a rule, a non-interest bearing deposit of an appropriate size to be opened at the ECB until the excessive deficit is corrected. In case of continued non-compliance with the reference value of 3 per cent, the amount of the first deposit consists of a fixed component equal to 0.2 per cent of GDP and a variable component equal to one-tenth of the difference between the reference value of 3 per cent and the actual deficit (expressed as a percentage of GDP) in the year that it was deemed excessive. An additional amount as deposit may also be asked as an intensification of the sanctions. In all cases, however, deposits cannot, on an annual basis, exceed 0.5 per cent of GDP. In addition, according to Article 14 of Regulation 1467/97, if, according to the Council's assessment, the member state concerned has not corrected the deficit within two years after the first deposit, the deposit is, as a rule, converted into a fine.

Another element of the SGP is the establishment of an early-warning system so that the occurrence of an excessive deficit is prevented at an early stage. Council Regulation 1466/97 provides the basis for establishing such a system. According to this Regulation, as from March 1999 every state participating in the euro zone is under an obligation to submit to the Council and the Commission stability programmes that are updated annually. The intention is to prevent at an early stage an excessive deficit and to promote the surveillance and the coordination of the member states' economic policies. The other EU countries that remain outside the euro zone must also submit convergence programmes of similar form and content to the stability programmes.

All stability programmes have to present information on how the corresponding government intends to meet the medium-term budgetary objective of an 'almost balanced budget'. Thus, there has to be an indication regarding the adjustment path towards this objective as well as a forecast of the expected development of the debt-to-GDP ratio. In addition, national governments must:

- Explain the main assumptions behind the expected behaviour of economic variables that are related to the realization of the stability programmes, such as the rate of real GDP growth, employment, public expenditure on investment, inflation, and so forth.
- Describe the fiscal and other economic policy measures that are adopted for the realization of the programmes and provide an assessment of the quantitative effects of the main fiscal measures on the budget.
- Analyse how changes in the main economic assumptions would affect the budgetary and debt positions of their respective domestic economies.

The ECOFIN Council, taking into account the assessments of the Commission and the Economic and Financial Committee, is to examine the stability programmes in order to determine:

- to what extent, on the basis of their content, an excessive deficit can be avoided;
- whether the main economic assumptions on which the programmes are based are realistic;
- whether the measures being proposed or being taken are sufficient to achieve the targeted adjustment path towards the medium-term objective of a balanced budget or a budget surplus; and
- whether the economic policies of the member state concerned are complying with the broader economic-policy guidelines of the EU.

The ECOFIN Council is to carry out this examination within two months of the submission of the programmes. It then has to issue its opinion on the programmes following a recommendation by the Commission and after consulting the Economic and Finance Committee. In the event that the Council identifies actual or expected significant divergence of the budgetary position from the medium-term budgetary objective, or from the corresponding adjustment path, it should, under Article 6(2) of Regulation 1466/97, make a timely recommendation to the member state concerned to take the necessary adjustment measures so that the occurrence of an excessive deficit is prevented. If the divergence persists or gets worse, under Article 6(3) of Regulation 1466/97 the Council can make a recommendation to the member state concerned to take prompt corrective measures. The Council may also make this recommendation public.

Since its adoption, a number of problems with the SGP have become apparent. The first two relate to enforceability and flexibility. Enforceability is an essential feature of all policy-coordination agreements; it is required to eliminate free-rider problems. Flexibility is also desirable: the precise mandate of the coordination agreement for policy should not be independent of the current state of the economies concerned. Yet these two elements do not characterize the SGP. As far as enforceability is concerned, ever since the signing of the SGP in 1997, concerns have been expressed that the sanctions mechanism will be difficult to be implemented in practice: a Council's proposal for imposing sanctions would be unlike to be easily adopted since a member state that would agree on adopting such a decision could next time be in the position of the member state against whom the sanctions are to be imposed. This concern was confirmed in November 2003, when the ECOFIN Council failed to reach agreement on imposing sanctions on Germany and France, despite the fact that they had been running deficits above 3 per cent for two consecutive years.[34] As far as flexibility is concerned, many regard the SGP in its present form as a rigid policy, which does not provide for enough automatic counter-cyclical fiscal stabilization and which fails to address current macroeconomic problems in Europe (see, for example, Hughes-Hallett and McAdam (1999), Hughes-Hallett and Warmedinger (1999), De Grauwe (1998, 1997, 2003a), Willett (1999), Crowley (2003), Eichengreen (1997, 2003), Von Hagen and Eichengreen (1996), Wylosz (1999), Allsopp and Artis (2003), Begg *et al.* (2003) and Begg and Schelkle (2004)). Indeed, automatic fiscal stabilization has not worked during recessionary episodes: many EU countries, especially those with deficits close to the 3 per cent limit, have been reluctant to leave the automatic counter-cyclical fiscal stabilizers to work fully because of fears that they will accumulate debts and will therefore face the SGP's sanctions. Thus several authors, including De Grauwe (1998) and Hughes-Hallett and McAdam (1999), have pointed to the danger of a deflationary bias under the SGP.

At the same time, the 'mechanistic' nature of the excessive deficit and sanctions procedures can work in a counter-productive way in the longer run: member states may be forced to focus all their efforts on how to avoid their deficits to be characterized as excessive and their stability/convergence programmes as insufficient and thus on how to avoid the SGP's sanctions, neglecting other important economic issues. For example, the high degree of automaticity regarding the conditions for imposing sanctions may have made member states' governments to proceed to rapid and not well organized structural changes, or proceed to privatizations that do not promote the supply-side of the economy and/or adopt policy measures that are incompatible with the notion of social justice which over the years has constituted one of the main characteristics of European nations. This could lead to a reduction of real GDP growth in the EU area and/or to conflicts among different groups of agents in the societies of the member states, something that would make the fiscal policy rules of the SGP even more burdensome.

There are also implementation problems with the SGP other than those relating to the issue of enforceability and flexibility. The original SPG provisions obliged EU member states to aim at an almost balanced budget or budget surplus in the 'medium- and long run', but gave no precise definition to these terms. The issue of how the 'medium- and long term' target would be achieved and what would be the margin for member states' fiscal policies in the short run was not properly dealt with.[35] At the same time, according to the original SGP provisions, the rules were to apply to nominal budget deficits, rather than cyclically adjusted deficits, something that in many cases resulted in pro-cyclical budgetary policies (that is, restrictive fiscal policy at times of declining economic activity and loose fiscal policy at times of increasing economic activity). This problem of the SGP was addressed by the 2001 ECOFIN Council's decision to incorporate in the SGP's provisions the requirement of a budget close-to-balance or in surplus 'over the cycle', something that can be taken to imply a balanced cyclically-adjusted deficit over the medium term. Yet a number of questions remain, including how cyclical factors are to be taken into account in computing cyclically-adjusted budgets.

The original SGP's provisions also relate to budget deficits: no weight has been given to the stock of debt. The decision to place a zero weight on the stock of debt was probably due to the fact that in 1997, when the Stability and Growth Pact was under negotiation, the debt-to-GDP ratio of a number of member states still exceeded the 60 per cent limit (see Table 8.1). However, exclusion of a debt-connected criterion from excessive deficit procedures like that of SGP can create inefficiencies.[36] On the one hand, it implies that countries with large and small debts are treated equally, as long as they have the same deficit, independently of their prospects for lowering debt levels. It also does not promote transparency in fiscal-policy matters, given that 'creative accounting' is easier to apply to budget-deficit data than to debt data. For this reason Calmfors and Corsetti (2002) have proposed to make the deficit ceilings dependent upon the stock of debt, that is apply the 3 per cent limit to countries with, for example, debt ratios of more than 50 per cent and set a lower than 3 per cent ceiling for countries with debt ratios less than 50 per cent.

As a result of the numerous problems associated with the SGP, many proposals for reforming the EU's fiscal framework have been put forward in the last few years.[37] A number of authors call for changes within the existing SGP framework, such as: a strengthening of cyclical smoothing through a more effective working of the automatic fiscal stabilizers; a re-definition of medium-term budgetary objectives; inclusion of debt levels or debt sustainability as well as deficits in the excessive deficit procedure; and improving quality in fiscal accounting (see Buti *et al.* (2003), De Grauwe (2003b), Artis and Winkler (1999), Calmfors (2001a), Calmfors and Corsetti (2002), Eijffinger (2003), Wyplosz (2002) and Buti and van den Noord (2004)). These proposals differ however in terms of who will have the overall responsibility for enforcing the new arrangements. The Commission's view is that its own role should be enhanced (Buti and van den Noord (2004)), but others stress the need for the creation of an independent fiscal-policy board, which will be fully accountable to the European Parliament (Wyplosz (2002) and Begg and Schelkle (2004)). At the same time, more radical approaches propose the replacement of the SGP with other rule-based schemes, such as: the 'golden rule' according to which deficits are allowed as long as they finance public-sector investment (Blanchard and Giavazzi (2003)); a 'permanent-balance rule', which will allow for larger deficits in fast-growing countries (Buiter and Grafe (2003)); an 'augmented-permanent-balance rule' that will also prevent the debt-GDP ratio from exceeding a given per cent in the long run (Buiter (2003)); and a 'debt sustainability pact' whose focus will be on safeguarding sustainability of deficits (Hughes-Hallett *et al.* (2003) and Pisani-Ferry (2002b)). Even more radical proposals call for changes in the philosophy of the EU's existing fiscal framework, proposing, on the one hand, market solutions, such as providing member states with tradable deficit permits while adopting EU average targets for deficit and debt (Casella (2002)), and, on the other, a federalization of Europe. And there are also some economists who argue against any rule-based new scheme. Instead they call for a coordination-based approach to fiscal policy, which could go hand in hand with coordination in other policy areas, including employment and wage policy, arguing that such an approach will significantly improve policy outcomes in Europe in general (see Von Hagen and Mundschenk (2001, 2002), Jacquet and Pisani-Ferry (2001), Collignon (1999, 2001, 2003), Breuss and Weber (1999), Korkman (2002), Allsopp *et al.* (1999) and Allsopp and Artis (2003)).

Summary and Conclusions

The fiscal policy restrictions of the Maastricht Treaty and the provisions of the Stability and Growth Pact have raised questions about the conduct of fiscal policy in a monetary union. A crucial question is whether the fiscal policy of a country participating in a MU should or should not be constrained. Another question is to what extent rules need to be used to control member states' fiscal policies, if national fiscal policies should be controlled centrally. There is also the issue of what form these rules should take; and in the case of Europe, the particular fiscal-policy rules adopted need to be evaluated.

One may argue that in general the need or not for adopting binding fiscal-policy rules in a MU depends on the impact of the creation of the monetary union on the fiscal discipline of member states. The findings of some recent empirical studies seem to imply that the creation of a monetary union on balance increases fiscal discipline, thus suggesting no need for imposing strict limits on deficits and debts in member states. The game-theoretic approach to fiscal-policy design in a MU also points against imposing strict fiscal-policy rules. It stresses the need not for strict ceilings on deficits and debt, but for cooperation among the member states of a MU in the fiscal-policy front to limit the externalities arising from international macroeconomic interdependence, enhancing at the same the stabilizing role of fiscal policy.

Indeed, the limits on deficits and debt in Europe and the provisions of the Stability and Growth Pact have been a subject of considerable disagreement among economists in recent years. Critics argue that the margins for deficits and debts are arbitrary and too uniform, thus disregarding important differences among the member states, and that they do not focus on the true fiscal stance of a country. Also, the SGP's provisions are too rigid, they have an asymmetric effect over the cycle, thus producing a deflationary bias, and they cause inefficiencies by not making the deficit ceilings dependent on the stock of debt. Defenders of the EU's existing fiscal framework argue that: the SGP's ceilings reduce the likelihood of excessive deficits; they eliminate the possibility of 'bail outs', safeguarding at the same time the ECB's credibility and its objective of maintaining low inflation; they limit the external effects of public deficits; and, most importantly, they work as an incentive for debt discipline.

Nevertheless, the SGP did not seem to be able to prevent excessive deficits from occurring. After 1999, budgetary positions have deteriorated in several EU countries; and sanctions have proved difficult to enforce. In November 2003, for example, the ECOFIN Council failed to agree on imposing sanctions on Germany and France, which violated the 3 per cent deficit constraint for two consecutive years without being able to justify this on the basis of factors consistent with the SGP.

Thus, unlike in the period 1992–2000 where the issue was whether or not the SGP needed reform, now the issue is what else should be put in its place. In the last few years a number of proposals have been put forward in this respect. All these proposals share the view that the SGP lacks flexibility; and that issues like a strengthening of cyclical smoothing, a more effective working of the automatic fiscal stabilizers and a re-definition of the medium-term budgetary objective need to be addressed in any new scheme. Where the proposals disagree is in terms of who will have the overall responsibility for enforcing the new fiscal-policy arrangements. Some authors propose market-based mechanisms; others are in favour of strengthening the role of the Commission in the enforcement mechanism, while several authors call for the creation of an independent fiscal-policy board that will be fully accountable to the European Parliament. And there are some who argue against any rule-based new schemes, proposing instead a coordination-based approach to fiscal policy in Europe or even a federalization of Europe. However, federalization is likely to prove a difficult task, given the recent EU enlargement, which has made the European Union an even more heterogeneous group than before.

Indeed, at the EU Summit of March 2005, only minor changes to the SGP were agreed. The main changes involve the following: a country experiencing prolonged period of low growth will not be automatically subject to the excessive deficit procedure; member states with temporary deficits or deficits close to 3 per cent may be able to avoid the excessive deficit procedure by referring to medium-term budgetary efforts or policies aiming at structural reforms or promotion of R&D; to correct an excessive deficit a member state will have 2 years rather than 1 year at its disposal; and in the definition of medium-term objectives in stability programmes country-specific elements will be taken into account, including their current debt level. [38]

Notes

1 For the various approaches towards fiscal policy see Masson and Melitz (1991), Masson and Taylor (1993), Buiter (1999), Driver and Wren-Lewis (2000), Buti and Suardi (2000), Buti and Sapir (1998), Sutherland (1997), Perotti (1999), Giavazzi *et al.*(1998), von Hagen and Lutz (1996), Alesina and Ardagna (1998), Barrell and Pina (2000), Canzoneri *et al.* (2001), Woodford (2001) and Taylor (2000).

2 See Melitz (1991), Hughes-Hallett and Vines (1991), Eichengreen and Wyplosz (1998), Eichengreen (1997) and Von Hagen and Hammond (1997). See also Eichengreen and Von Hagen (1995) and Bayoumi and Eichengreen (1995).

3 See Morrow (1996), Begg (1995), Bini-Smaghi and Vori (1993), Gros (1996b), Braunerhjelm *et al.* (2000) and Mauro *et al.* (1999).

4 See, for example, OECD (2000) and Calmfors (1998, 2001b).
5 See Von Hagen and Eichengreen (1996), Bayoumi and Masson (1996), Obstfeld and Peri (1998), McKay (1999) and Collignon (2004). See also Fatàs (1998).
6 A constant price level is assumed. To highlight the issues involved, interactions between *A* and *B* through income and relative price effects via the trade balance are also ignored.
7 See European Commission (1990), Beetsma (2002) and Fatàs and Mihov (2003).
8 See Artis and Winkler (1998, 1999) and Thygesen (1999) and also Eichengreen and Wyplosz (1998).
9 See Eichengreen and Wyplosz (1998) and Beetsma (2002) for a discussion.
10 See Wyplosz (1991) and Willett (1999) for a discussion of the various arguments.
11 For exchange-rate effects on fiscal discipline see Aizenman (1994), Allsopp and Vines (1996) and Beetsma and Bovenberg (1999).
12 See Fatàs and Mihov (2002) for a survey of the various studies.
13 See Allsopp *et al.* (1999), Korkman (2002), Hughes-Hallett and McAdam (1999), Collignon (2001, 2003), Pisani-Ferry (2002a,b), Begg *et al.* (2003) and von Hagen and Mundschenk (2001). See also Hamada (1986), Cooper (1985), Wyplosz (1991), Buiter and Kletzer (1991a), Levine and Brociner (1994), Andersen and Sorensen (1995) and Jensen (1996).
14 There is no consensus in the wider policy-coordination literature about the sign of the international spillover effects of fiscal policies. Some studies point to negative spillovers; other studies point to positive spillovers.
15 The results of these studies show that the extent to which fiscal cooperation in this context is beneficial depends on factors like the sign of the spillover effects of national fiscal policies and the decision structure of policy-making in the EU (that is, whether a Nash regime or a Stackelberg regime between national fiscal authorities and the ECB is assumed), as well as on the degree of differences in priorities between the ECB and national governments.
16 Note that within the framework assumed here, the case of no interactions with the ECB through output levels can be represented by setting $\lambda = 0$. In such a case, the condition for $L_G^c = L_F^c < L_G^{nc} = L_F^{nc}$ is a positive a_5. This unambiguously holds, independently of the sign of the international spillover effects of fiscal policy given that $a_5 > 0$.
17 Note that with $a_3, a_4 > 1$, $(\omega^2/\lambda a_3)$ and $(\omega^2/\lambda a_4)$ in (5f.1) and (5f.2) are smaller than (ω^2/λ) in (5e.1) and (5e.2).
18 See Hughes-Hallett *et al.* (2003), Beetsma (2002), Fatás and Mihov (2003), Allsopp and Artis (2003) and Begg and Schelkle (2004) for a analysis of the flaws and merits of the SGP. For an assessment of the Maastricht Treaty's fiscal-policy provisions see Bovenberg *et al.* (1991) and Masson (1996).
19 For the issue of debt sustainability see Collignon and Mundschenk (1999) and Hughes-Hallett *et al.* (2003).
20 See also Gros (1996a) and Buiter *et al.* (1993) for a discussion.
21 See Bovenberg *et al.* (1991) and Buiter and Kletzer (1991b).
22 See also Leith and Wren-Lewis (2000) and Woodford (1995, 2001).

23 For the political-business-cycle theory see Gärtner (1994), Persson and Tabellini (2000), Drazen (2000), Alesina and Perotti (1997), Alesina *et al.* (1993) and Rogoff and Sibert (1998).

24 However, according to the evidence provided in Andrikopoulos *et al.* (2004) EU governments have been primarily concerned with the pursuit of stabilization policies rather than policies creating electoral cycles.

25 For other arguments in favour of fiscal-policy rules in the EMU see Buti, Franco and Ongena (1998a), Iversen and Soskice (1999) and Beetsma and Uhlig (1999). See also European Commission (1999) and European Council (1997).

26 EU Bulletin 12, 1996.

27 EU C 236/1 1997.

28 EU L 209/1 1997.

29 See European Council (1997).

30 See Council Regulation No. 1467/97.

31 Regulation 1467/97, Article 2(3).

32 See Regulation 1467/97, Article 2.

33 For a discussion of the institutional and legal dimensions of the SGP see Hahn (1998) and Herdegen (1998).

34 See Begg and Schelkle (2004) for a discussion.

35 For an discussion of these issues and an attempt to resolve them see Begg *et al.* (1997), Eichengreen and Wylposz (1998), Buti *et al.* (1998b), Artis and Buti (2000), Dury and Pina (2000), Dalsgaard and DeSerres (1999) and European Commission (1999, 2000).

36 See Buti *et al.* (2003), Missale (2002) and Rostagno *et al.* (2002).

37 For a survey of the various proposals see Buti *et al.* (2003) and Begg and Schelkle (2004).

38 See http://www.euractiv.com,'Stability and Growth Pact Reform', 15 July 2005.

References

Agell, J., Calmfors, L. and Jonsson, G. (1996) 'Fiscal Policy When Monetary Policy is Tied to the Mast', *European Economic Review,* vol. 40, pp. 1413–40.

Aizenman, J. (1994) 'On the Need for Fiscal Discipline in a Union', NBER Working Paper 4656, National Bureau of Economic Research, Cambridge, Mass.

Alesina, A. and Ardagna, S. (1998) 'Tales of Fiscal Adjustment', *Economic Policy,* vol. 27, pp. 489–545.

Alesina, A., Cohen, G. and Roubini, N. (1993) 'Electoral Business Cycles in Industrial Democracies', *European Journal of Political Economy,* vol. 9, pp. 1–30.

Alesina, A. and Drazen, A. (1991) 'Why Are Stabilizations Delayed?', *American Economic Review,* vol. 81, pp. 1170–88.

Alesina, A. and Perotti, R. (1997) 'Fiscal Adjustments in OECD Countries: Composition and Macroeconomic Effects', *IMF Staff Papers,* vol. 44, pp. 210–48.

Alesina, A. and Perotti, R. (1998) 'Economic Risk and Political Risk in Fiscal Unions', *Economic Journal*, vol. 108, pp. 989–1008.

Allsopp, C.J. and Artis, M. (2003) 'The Assessment: EMU, Four Years On', *Oxford Review of Economic Policy*, vol. 19, pp. 1–29.

Allsopp, C.J., McKibbin, W. and Vines, D. (1999) 'Fiscal Consolidation in Europe: Some Empirical Issues', in A. Hughes-Hallett, M. Hutchison and S.E. Jensen (eds), *Fiscal Aspects of European Integration* (New York: Cambridge University Press).

Allsopp, C.J. and Vines, D. (1996) 'Fiscal Policy and EMU', *National Institute Economic Review*, vol. 158, pp. 91–107.

Alogoskoufis, G. and Christodoulakis, N. (1991) 'Fiscal Deficits, Seigniorage and External Debt: The Case of Greece', in Alogoskoufis, G. *et al.* (eds), *External Constraints on Macroeconomic Policy: The European Experience* (London: Centre for Economic Policy Research, Bank of Greece and Cambridge University Press).

Alogoskoufis, G. and Philippopoulos A. (1992) 'Inflationary Expectations, Political Parties and Exchange-Rate Regimes: Greece 1958–1989', *European Journal of Political Economy*, vol. 8, pp. 375–99.

Andersen, T. and Sorensen, J.R. (1995) 'Unemployment and Fiscal Policy in an Economic and Monetary Union', *European Journal of Political Economy*, vol. 11, pp. 27–43.

Andrikopoulos, A., Loizidis, I. and Prodromidis, K. (2004) 'Fiscal Policy and Political Business Cycles in the EU', *European Journal of Political Economy*, vol. 20, pp. 125–52.

Artis, M.J. and Buti, M. (2000) 'Close-to-Balance or in Surplus: A Policymaker's Guide to the Implementation of the Stability and Growth Pact', *Journal of Common Market Studies*, vol. 38, pp. 563–91.

Artis, M.J. and Winkler, B. (1998) 'The Stability Pact: Safeguarding the Credibility of the European Central Bank', *National Institute Economic Review*, vol. 163, pp. 87–98.

Artis, M., and Winkler, J.B. (1999) 'The Stability Pact: Trading Off Flexibility for Credibility?', in A. Hughes-Hallett, M. Hutchison and S.E. Jensen (eds), *Fiscal Aspects of European Integration* (New York: Cambridge University Press).

Barrell, R. and Pina, A. (2000) 'How Important are Automatic Stabilizers in Europe?', EUI Economics Working Paper no. 2000/2, European University Institut , Florens.

Bayoumi, T. and Eichengreen, B. (1995) 'Restraining Yourself: Fiscal Rules and Stabilization', *IMF Staff Papers*, vol. 42, pp. 32–48.

Bayoumi, T. and Masson, P.R. (1996) 'Fiscal Flows in the U.S. and Canada: Lessons for Monetary Union in Europe', *European Economic Review*, vol. 39, pp. 235–55.

Beetsma, R. (2002) 'Does EMU Need a Stability Pact?', in A. Brunila and D. Franco (eds), *The Stability and Growth Pact: The Architecture of Fiscal Policy in EMU* (New York: Palgrave).

Beetsma, R. and Bovenberg, A. (1997) 'Central Bank Independence and Public Debt Policy', *Journal of Economic Dynamics and Control*, vol. 21, pp. 873–94.

Beetsma, R. and Bovenberg, A. (1999) 'Balancing Credibility and Flexibility', in A. Razin and E. Sadka (eds), *The Economics of Globalization: Policy Perspectives for Public Economics* (Cambridge: Cambridge University Press).

Beetsma, R., Debrun, X. and Klaasen, F. (2001) 'Is Fiscal Policy Coordination in EMU Desirable?', *Swedish Economic Policy Review*, vol. 8, pp. 57–98.

Beetsma, R. and Uhlig, H. (1999) 'An Analysis of the Stability and Growth Pact', *Economic Journal*, vol. 109, pp. 547–71.

Begg, D. (1995) 'Factor Mobility and Regional Disparities in the European Union', *Oxford Review of Economic Policy*, vol. 11, pp. 96–112.

Begg , D., Giavazzi, F., von Hagen, J. and Wyplosz, C. (1997) *EMU: Getting the End-Game Right*, Monitoring European Integration 7 (London: Centre for Economic Policy Research).

Begg, I., Hodson, D. and Maher, I. (2003) 'Economic Policy Coordination in the European Union', *National Institute Economic Review*, vol. 183, pp. 70–81.

Begg, I. and Schelkle, W. (2004) 'The Pact is Dead: Long Live the Pact', *National Institute Economic Review*, vol. 189, pp. 86–98.

Bini-Smaghi, L. and Vori, S. (1993) 'Rating the EC as an Optimal Currency Area', *Temi di Discussioni*, no. 187, Banca d'Italia, Rome.

Blanchard, O. and Giavazzi, F. (2003) 'Reform that Can Be Done: Improving the SGP Through a Proper Accounting of Public Investment', MIT and Bocconi University, November.

Bovenberg, A.L., Kremers, J.J. and Masson, P.R. (1991) 'Economic and Monetary Union in Europe and Constraints on National Budgetary Policies', *IMF Staff Papers*, vol. 38, pp. 374–98.

Breuss, F. and Weber, A. (1999) 'Economic Policy Coordination in the EMU: Implications for the Stability and Growth Pact', EUI Economics Working Paper 99/26, European University Institute, Florence.

Braunerhjelm, P., Faini, R., Norman, V., Ruane, F. and Seabright, P. (2000) *Integration and the Regions of Europe* (London: Centre for Economic Policy Research).

Buiter, W. (1995) 'Macroeconomic Policy During a Transition to Monetary Union', Discussion Paper no. 261, Centre for Economic Performance, London School of Economics.

Buiter, W. (1999) 'Alice in Euroland', *Journal of Common Market Studies*, vol. 37, pp. 181–209.

Buiter, W. (2003) 'Ten Commandments for a Fiscal Rule in the EU', *Oxford Review of Public Policy*, vol. 19, pp. 84–99.

Buiter, W., Corsetti, G. and Roubini, N. (1993) 'Excessive Deficits: Sense and Non-Sense in the Treaty of Maastricht', *Economic Policy*, vol. 16, April, pp. 58–100.

Buiter, W. and Grafe, C. (2003) 'Reforming EMU's Fiscal Policy Rules: Some Suggestions for Enhancing Fiscal Sustainability and Macroeconomic Stability in an Enlarged European Union', in M. Buti (ed.), *Monetary and Fiscal Policies in the EMU: Interactions and Coordination* (Cambridge: Cambridge University Press).

Buiter, W. and Kletzer, K. (1991a) 'The Welfare Economics of Cooperative and Non-Cooperative Fiscal Policy', *Journal of Economic Dynamics and Control*, vol. 3, pp. 53–77.

Buiter, W. and Kletzer, K. (1991b) 'Reflections on the Fiscal Implications of a Common Currency', in A. Giovannini and C. Mayer (eds), *European Financial Integration* (Cambridge: Cambridge University Press).

Buti, M., Eijffinger, S. and Franco, D. (2003) 'Revisiting EMU's Stability Pact: A Pragmatic Way Forward', *Oxford Review of Economic Policy*, vol. 19, pp. 100–11.

Buti, M., Franco, D. and Ongena, H. (1998a) 'Fiscal Discipline and Flexibility in the EMU: The Implementation of the Stability and Growth Pact', *Oxford Review of Economic Policy*, vol. 14, pp. 81–97.

Buti, M., Franco, D. and Ongena, H. (1998b) 'Budgetary Policies During Recessions: Retrospective Applications of the Stability and Growth Pact to the Post-War Period', *Recherches Economiques de Louvain*, vol. 63, pp. 321–66.

Buti, M. and Sapir, A. (eds) (1998) *Economic Policy in EMU – A Study by the European Commission Services* (Oxford: Oxford University Press).

Buti, M. and Suardi, M. (2000) 'Cyclical Convergence or Differentiation? Insights from the First Year of EMU', *Revue de la Banque*, vols 2–3, pp. 164–72.

Buti, M. and Van den Noord, P. (2004) 'Fiscal Policy in EMU: Rules, Discretion and Political Incentives', *European Economy*, Economic Paper no. 206, July, European Commission.

Calmfors, L. (1998) 'Macroeconomic Policy, Wage Setting and Employment – What Difference Does the EMU Make?', *Oxford Review of Economic Policy*, vol. 14, pp. 125–51.

Calmfors, L. (2001a) 'Macroeconomic Policy Coordination in the EMU: How Far Should It Go?', *Swedish Economic Policy Review*, vol. 8, pp. 3–14.

Calmfors, L. (2001b) 'Unemployment, Labour Market Reform and Monetary Union', *Journal of Labour Economics*, vol. 19, pp. 265–89.

Calmfors, L., and Corsetti, G. (2002), 'How to Reform Europe's Fiscal Framework', *World Economics*, vol. 4, pp. 109–16.

Canzoneri, M., Cumby, R. and Diba, B. (2001) 'Discipline and Exchange Rate Systems', *Economic Journal*, vol. 111, pp. 667–90.

Casella, A. (2002) 'Achieving Fiscal Discipline Through Tradable Deficit Permits', in A. Brunila and D. Franco (eds), *The Stability and Growth Pact: The Architecture of Fiscal Policy in EMU* (New York: Palgrave).

Collignon, S. (1999) 'Unemployment, Wage Developments and the Economic Policy Mix in Europe', *Empirica*, vol. 26, pp. 259–69.

Collignon, S. (2001) 'Economic Policy Coordination in EMU: Institutions and Political Requirements', Working Paper no. 01/5, Centre for European Studies, Harvard University.

Collignon, S. (2003) 'Is Europe Going Far Enough? Reflections on the EU's Economic Governance', Working Paper, European Institute, London School of Economics and Political Science, November.

Collignon, S. (2004) 'The End of the Stability and Growth Pact?', *International Economics and Economic Policy*, vol. 1, pp. 15–9.

Collignon, S. and Mundschenk, S. (1999) 'The Sustainability of Public Debt in Europe', *Economia Internazionale*, vol. 52, pp. 101–59.

Cooper, R.N. (1985) 'Economic Interdependence and Co-ordination of Economic Policies' in J. Jones and P. Kenen (eds), *Handbook of International Economics*, Vol. I (Amsterdam: North Holland).

Corsetti, G. and Roubini, N. (1997), 'Politically Motivated Fiscal Deficits: Policy Issues in Open and Closed Economies', *Economics and Politics*, vol. 9, pp. 27–54.

Crowly, P. (2003) 'The Stability and Growth Pact: Review, Alternatives and Legal Aspects', *Current Politics and Economics of Europe,* vol. 11, pp. 225–44.

Dalsgaard, T. and DeSerres, A. (1999) 'Estimating Prudent Budgetary Margins for 11 EU Counties: A Simulated SVAR Model Approach', OECD Economics Working Paper no. 216.

De Grauwe, P. (1992) 'Fiscal Policy Discipline in Monetary Unions', *International Economic Journal,* vol. 6, pp. 101–13.

De Grauwe, P. (1997) 'Paradigms of Macroeconomic Policy for the Open Economy', in M. Fratianni, D. Salvatore and J. von Hagen (eds), *Macroeconomic Policy in Open Economies,* Handbook of Comparative Economic Policies, Vol. 5 (Westport Conn: Greenwood Press).

De Grauwe, P. (1998) 'The Risk of Deflation in the Future EMU: Lessons of the 1990's', in J. Arrowsmith (ed.), *Thinking the Unthinkable about EMU* (London: National Institute of Economic and Social Research).

De Grauwe, P. (2003a) *The Economics of Monetary Integration* (London: Oxford University Press).

De Grauwe, P. (2003b) 'The Stability and Growth Pact in Need of Reform', Working Paper, University of Leuven, Leuven.

Demertzis, M., Hughes-Hallett, A. and Viegi, N. (2003), 'An Independent Central Bank Faced With Elected Governments' *European Journal of Political Economy,* vol. 20, pp. 907–22.

Dixit, A. (2001) 'Games of Monetary and Fiscal Interactions in the EMU', *European Economic Review,* vol. 45, pp. 589–613.

Dixon, H. and Santori, M. (1997) 'Fiscal Policy Co-ordination with Demand Spill-overs and Unionised Labour Markets', *Economic Journal,* vol. 107, pp. 403–17.

Drazen, A. (2000) 'The Political Business Cycle After 25 Years', *NBER Macroeconomics Annual,* vol. 15, pp. 75–117.

Driver, L. and Wren-Lewis, S. (2000) 'European Monetary Union and Asymmetric Shocks in a New-Keynesian Model', *Oxford Economic Papers,* vol. 51, pp. 665–89.

Dury, K. and Pina, A. (2000) 'European Fiscal Policy after EMU: Simulating the Operation of the Stability Pact', EUI Economics Working Paper no. 2000/3, European University Institute, Florens.

Eichengreen, B. (1997) 'Saving Europe's Automatic Stabilizers', *National Institute Economic Review,* vol. 28, pp. 80–105.

Eichengreen, B. (2003) 'What to Do with the Stability Pact?', *Intereconomics,* vol. 38, pp. 7–10.

Eichengreen, B. and von Hagen, J. (1995) 'Fiscal Policy and Monetary Union: Federalism, Fiscal Restrictions and the No-Bail out Clause', CEPR Discussion Paper no. 1247, Centre for Economic Policy Research, London.

Eichengreen, B. and Wyplosz, C. (1998) 'The Stability Pact: More than a Minor Nuisance?', *Economic Policy,* vol. 27, April, pp. 65–113.

Eijffinger, S. (2003) 'How Can the Stability and Growth Pact be Improved to Achieve Both Stronger Discipline and Greater Flexibility', *Intereconomics,* vol. 38, pp. 10–5.

European Commission (1990) 'One Market, One Money: Evaluation of the Potential Benefits and Costs of Forming an Economic and Monetary Union', *European Economy.*

European Commission (1999) 'Budgetary Surveillance in EMU: The New Stability and Convergence Programs', *European Economy*, Supplement A, no. 2/3.

European Commission (2000) 'Public Finances in EMU 2000', *European Economy – Reports and Studies*, no. 3.

European Council (1997) *Resolution of the European Council on the Stability and Growth Pact*, Resolution 97/C.

Fatás, A. (1998) 'Does EMU Need a Fiscal Federation?', *Economic Policy*, vol. 26, pp. 163–203.

Fatás, A. and Mihov, I. (2003) 'On Constraining Fiscal Policy Discretion in EMU', *Oxford Review of Public Policy*, vol. 19, pp. 112–31.

Gärtner, M. (1994) 'Democracy, Elections and Macroeconomic Policy', *European Journal of Political Economy*, vol. 10, pp. 85–109.

Gatti, D. and von Wijnbergen, C. (2002) 'Coordinating Fiscal Authorities in the Euro-Zone: A Key Role for the ECB', *Oxford Economic Papers*, vol. 54, pp. 57–71.

Giavazzi, F., Jappelli, T. and Pagano, M. (1998) 'Searching for the New Keynesian Effects of Fiscal Policy', IGIER Working Paper no. 136, Innocenzo Gasparini Institute for Economic Research, Bocconi University, Milan.

Gros, D. (1996a) 'Towards Economic and Monetary Union: Monetary Problems and Prospects', CEPS Discussion Paper no. 65, Centre for European Policy Studies, Brussels.

Gros, D. (1996b) 'A Reconsideration of the Optimum Currency Area Approach', CEPS Working Document no. 101, Centre for European Policy Studies, Brussels.

Hahn, H.J. (1998) 'The Stability Pact for European Monetary Union: Compliance with Deficit Limit as a Constant Legal Duty', *Common Market Law Review*, vol. 35, pp. 77–100.

Hamada, K. (1986), 'Strategic Aspects of International Fiscal Interdependence', *Economic Studies Quarterly*, vol. 77, pp. 165–80.

Herdegen, M. (1998) 'Price Stability and Budgetary Restraints in the EMU: The Law as Guardian of Economic Wisdom', *Common Market Law Review*, vol. 35, pp. 9–32.

Hughes-Hallett, A. and McAdam, P. (1996) 'Four Essays and a Funeral: Budgetary Arithmetic Under the Maastricht Treaty', CEPR Discussion Paper no. 1505, Centre for Economic Policy Research, London.

Hughes-Hallett, A. and McAdam, P. (1999) 'Implications of the Stability and Growth Pact: Why the Growth Element is Important', in A. Hughes-Hallett, M. Hutchison and S.E. Jensen (eds), *Fiscal Aspects of European Integration* (New York: Cambridge University Press).

Hughes-Hallett, A., Fatás, A., Silbert, A., Strauch, R. and von Hagen, J. (2003) *Monitoring European Integration 13: Stability and Growth in Europe – Towards a Greater Pact* (London: Centre for Economic Policy Research).

Hughes-Hallett, A. and Vines, D. (1991) 'Adjustment Difficulties within a European Monetary Union: Can They Be Reduced?', in J. Driffill and M. Weber (eds), *A Currency for Europe* (London: Lothian Foundation Press).

Hughes-Hallett, A. and Warmedinger, T. (1999) 'On the Asymmetric Effect of a Common Monetary Policy', in J. Von Hagen and C. Waller (eds), *Common Money, Common Regions* (Bonn: Centre for Economic Integration Studies).

Iversen, T. and Soskice, D. (1999) 'Monetary Integration, Partisanship and Macroeconomic Policy', Paper presented at the 95th Meeting of the American Political Science Association (APSA), Atlanda, September.

Jacquet, P. and Pisani-Ferry, J. (2001) *Economic Policy Coordination in the Eurozone: What Has Been Achieved? What Should be Done?* (London: Centre for European Reform).

Jensen, H. (1996) 'The Advantages of International Fiscal Cooperation Under Alternative Monetary Regimes', *European Journal of Political Economy,* vol. 12, pp. 485–504.

Korkman, S. (2002) 'Should Fiscal Policy Coordination Go Beyond the SGP?', in A. Brunila and D. Franco (eds), *The Stability and Growth Pact: The Architecture of Fiscal Policy in EMU* (New York: Palgrave).

Lamfalussy, A. (1989) 'Macro-coordination of Fiscal Policies in an Economic and Monetary Union', in *Report on Economic and Monetary Union* (Delors Report), Office for Official Publications of the European Communities, Luxembourg.

Leith, C. and Wren-Lewis, S. (2000) 'Interactions Between Monetary and Fiscal Rules', *Economic Journal,* vol. 110, pp. 94–108.

Levine, D. and Brociner, A. (1994) 'Fiscal Policy Coordination Under EMU: A Dynamic Repeated Game Approach', *Journal of Economic Dynamics and Control,* vol. 18, pp. 699–729.

Masson, P. (1996) 'Fiscal Dimensions of EMU', *Economic Journal,* vol. 106, pp. 996–1004.

Masson, P. and Melitz, J. (1991) 'Fiscal Policy Independence in a European Monetary Union', *Open Economies Review,* vol. 2, pp. 113–36.

Masson, P. and Taylor, M. (1993) 'Fiscal Policy within Common Currency Areas', *Journal of Common Market Studies,* vol. 31, pp. 29–44.

Mauro, P., Prasad, E., and Spilimbergo, A. (1999) 'Perspectives on Regional Unemployment in Europe', IMF Occasional Paper no. 117, International Monetary Fund, Washington DC.

McKay, D.H. (1999) *Federation and European Union: A Political Economy Perspective* (Oxford: Oxford University Press).

Melitz, J. (1991) 'Brussels on a Single Money', *Open Economies Review,* vol. 2, pp. 323–36.

Missale, A. (2002) 'How Should the Debt Be Managed: Supporting the Stability Pact', in A. Brunila and D. Franco (eds), *The Stability and Growth Pact: The Architecture of Fiscal Policy in EMU* (New York: Palgrave).

Moesen, W. and van Rompuy, P. (1991) 'The Growth of Government Size and Fiscal Decentralisation', in R. Prud'homme (ed.), *The Hague/Koenigstein Foundation Journal of Public Finance,* pp. 113–24.

Morrow, K. (1996) 'The Wage Formation Process and Labour Market Flexibility in the Community, the US and Japan', *European Economy,* Economic Paper no. 118, October, European Commission.

Obstfeld, M. and Peri, P. (1998) 'Regional Non-Adjustment and Fiscal Policy', *Economic Policy,* vol. 26, pp. 207–59.

OECD (2000) *One Year On* (Paris: Organisation for Economic Co-operation and Development).

Perotti, R. (1999) 'Fiscal Policy in Good Times and Bad', *Quarterly Journal of Economics,* vol. 114, pp. 1399–436.

Perotti, R. and Kontopoulos, Y. (2002) 'Fragmented Fiscal Policy', *Journal of Public Economics,* vol. 86, pp. 191–222.

Persson, T. and Tabellini, G. (2000) 'Political Economics and Public Finance', in A. Auerbach and M. Feldstein (eds), *Handbook of Public Economics,* Vol. III (Amsterdam: North Holland).

Pisani-Ferry, J. (2002a) 'The EMU's Economic Policy Principles: Words and Facts', in M. Buti and A. Sapir (eds), *The Functioning of EMU: Challenges of the Early Years* (London: Edward Elgar).

Pisani-Ferry, J. (2002b) 'Fiscal Discipline and Policy Coordination in the Eurozone: Assessment and Proposals', Paper prepared for the 16 April 2002 Meeting of the Group of Economic Analysis of the European Union, European Commission, Brussels.

Poterba, J. (1994) 'State Responses to Fiscal Crises: The Effects of Budgetary Institutions and Politics', *Journal of Political Economy,* vol. 102, pp. 799–821.

Poterba, J. and Von Hagen, J. (1999) *Fiscal Institutions and Fiscal Performance* (Chicago: University of Chicago Press).

Rogoff, K. and Sibert, A. (1998) 'Elections and Macroeconomic Policy Cycles', *Review of Economic Studies,* vol. 55, pp. 1–16.

Rostagno, M., Hiebert, P. and Perez-Garcia, J. (2002) 'Optimal Debt Under a Deficit Constraint', in A. Brunila and D. Franco (eds), *The Stability and Growth Pact: The Architecture of Fiscal Policy in EMU* (New York: Palgrave).

Roubini, N. and Sachs, J. (1989) 'Government Spending and Budget Deficits in the Industrial Countries', *Economic Policy,* vol. 11, pp. 100–32.

Sutherland, A. (1997) 'Fiscal Crises and Aggregate Demand: Can High Public Debt Reverse the Effects of Fiscal Policy?', *Journal of Public Economics,* vol. 65, pp. 147–62.

Taylor, J.B. (2000) 'Reassessing Discretionary Fiscal Policy', *Journal of Economic Perspectives,* vol. 14, pp. 21–36.

Thygesen, N. (1999) 'Fiscal Institutions in EMU and the Stability Pact', in A. Hughes-Hallett, M. Hutchison and S.E. Jensen (eds), *Fiscal Aspects of European Integration* (New York: Cambridge University Press).

Van Rompuy, P., Abraham, F. and Heremans, D. (1991) 'Economic Federalism and the EMU', *European Economy,* Special Edition no. 1, European Commission, Brussels.

Von Hagen, J. and Eichengreen, B. (1996) 'Federalism, Fiscal Restraints and European Monetary Union', *American Economic Review,* vol. 86, pp. 134–38.

Von Hagen, J. and Hammond, G.W. (1997) 'Insurance Against Asymmetric Shocks in a European Monetary Union', in J.O. Hairault, P.Y. Henin and F. Porter (eds), *Business Cycles and Macroeconomic Stability* (London: Kluwer).

Von Hagen, J. and Mundschenk, S. (2001) 'The Political Economy of Policy Coordination in EMU', *Swedish Economic Policy Review,* vol. 8, pp. 107–37.

Von Hagen, J. and Mundschenk, S. (2002) 'The Functioning of Economic Policy Coordination', in M. Buti and A. Sapir (eds), *The Functioning of EMU: Challenges of the Early Years* (London: Edward Elgar).

Von Hagen, J. and Mundschenk, S. (2003) 'Fiscal and Monetary Policy Coordination in EMU', *International Journal of Finance and Economics,* vol. 8, pp. 279–95.

Von Hagen, J. and Lutz, S. (1996) 'Fiscal and Monetary Policy on the Way to EMU', *Open Economies Review,* vol. 7, pp. 299–325.

Wickens, M. (1993) 'The Sustainability of Fiscal Policies and the Maastricht Treaty, LBS Discussion Paper no. 10–93, London Business School.

Willett, T. (1999) 'A Political Economy Analysis of the Maastricht and Stability Pact Fiscal Criteria', in A. Hughes-Hallett, M. Hutchison and S.E. Jensen (eds), *Fiscal Aspects of European Integration* (New York: Cambridge University Press).

Woodford, M. (1995) 'Price level Determinacy Without Control of a Monetary Aggregate', *Carnegie-Rochester Conference Series on Public Policy*, vol. 43, pp. 1–46.

Woodford, M. (2001) 'Fiscal Requirements for Price Stability', NBER Working Paper no. 8072, National Bureau of Economic Research, Cambridge, Mass.

Wyplosz, C. (1991) 'Monetary Union and Fiscal Policy Discipline', CEPR Discussion Paper no. 488, Centre for Economic Policy Research, London.

Wyplosz, C. (1999) 'Economic Policy Coordination in EMU: Strategies and Institutions', CEPII Working Paper no. 99–04, Centre D' Etudes Prospectives et des Informations Internationales, Paris.

Wyplosz, C. (2002) 'Fiscal Policy Institutions Versus Rules', CEPR Discussion Paper no. 3238, Centre for Economic Policy Research, London.

9 Foreign Direct Investment and European Integration

George Agiomirgianakis

Introduction

In what follows we examine the growth, the determinants and the effects of foreign direct investment (FDI) in the EU. Foreign direct investment refers to the capital flows resulting from the behaviour of multinational corporations (MNCs). Thus, factors that affect the behaviour of MNCs will also affect the magnitude and direction of FDI flows. FDI facilitates the diffusion of knowledge among countries and contributes to general welfare of a country. This is the reason why governments in developing and developed countries alike try to attract FDI flows, by incorporating FDI-encouraging strategies in their industrial and competition policies. In the EU there has been an active promotion of FDI over the last two decades, not only for intra-EU FDI flows, but also, for US and Japanese FDI inflows into member states (Raines and Brown, 1999).

In the next section we consider the links between MNCs and FDI; we distinguish between *inward* and *outward* FDI, as well as between FDI and *portfolio investment*; we explain when FDI occurs and what are the alternatives to FDI, as well as the advantages and disadvantages of FDI compared to its alternatives. Moreover, with the use of graphs and tables we illustrate the growth of FDI worldwide and particularly in the EU. We then present several theories explaining the behaviour of MNCs and their choices in the process of internationalization, followed by an examination of the determinants of FDI. In our analysis we combine both the predictions of economic theory, as well as findings of empirical studies in identifying a number of factors that may affect the direction and size of FDI flows. The significance of FDI in the diffusion of knowledge, R&D, economic growth and unemployment for the EU is then examined, followed by a concluding section. Particular emphasis throughout is given to EU and UK practical experience documented by statistical data and empirical studies.

MNCs and FDI

Defining MNCs and FDI

A multinational corporation (MNC) is a company operating its businesses in more than one country. MNCs have a home base in one country and the whole or partial control of subsidiaries abroad. There are a number of reasons why a company may become multinational and there are several theories to explain the expansion of MNCs as we will see in the next section. However, a company that expands into foreign markets by setting up subsidiaries can exploit either economies of scale or scope arising from vertical or horizontal integration. By this expansion the MNC expects monopolistic or oligopolistic gains. Examples of multinationals are IBM and Ford (both from the USA); Glaxo and Shell (UK); Michelin (France); Mercedes-Benz and Volkswagen (Germany); Nestlé (Switzerland); and Toyota and Sony (Japan).

In order to achieve their goals – that is, to expand abroad by setting up subsidiaries – MNCs need to undertake investment that we call foreign direct investment (FDI), directed to the control of physical rather than financial assets. Thus, as a definition, we could say that FDI is the purchase of physical assets abroad over which the parent company retains control. These physical assets could be real estate, factories and businesses run by other firms or individuals.

Motives for Undertaking FDI

There are several motives for MNCs to undertake FDI as listed below:

- the parent company might decide to establish a new, *greenfield*, subsidiary abroad, that is the company constructs new plants and equipment in another country;
- the parent company could try, either by a *takeover* or a *merger* with a foreign firm, to acquire direct control over the assets of the foreign company;
- the parent firm might want to establish a *joint venture* with a foreign firm.
- the parent company might transfer capital abroad in order to finance an expansion of its subsidiary;
- profits of overseas subsidiaries are reinvested abroad.

FDI can be either inward when foreigners purchase assets into the home economy, or outward when home citizens purchase assets abroad. In the first case there are capital inflows into the home economy while in the second there are capital outflows.

FDI should be distinguished from *portfolio investment* with the latter being the acquisition of financial assets such as bonds, shares, treasury bills, bank accounts and other securities. Investment in financial assets is usually for a shorter-term than investment in physical assets. Moreover, an acquisition of bonds and shares in some company does not lead to direct control of this company,[1] which is the case with FDI.

Alternatives to FDI

Firms can internationalize, that is expand their activities into foreign markets, not only by following an FDI path, but also by adopting other strategies such as exporting, licensing or franchising.

Exporting. In the case that the foreign market is not heavily protected by tariffs, a home firm can expand into the foreign market by exporting its products. However, before the firm will embark in this sort of activity, it needs to know the characteristics of the foreign market: size, preferences, perspectives and the quality of other competing products. Although this information is costly, exporting is a lower risk activity relative to FDI, allowing the firm to exploit economies of scale and/or scope. However, as we have already mentioned, exporting could be prohibitive if there are high tariffs and transportation costs that effectively act as a protective wall for the foreign market. Non-tariff barriers to trade and exchange-rate volatility could also be very costly or prohibitive for exports.[2] However, the choice by the home firm between exporting and FDI is not always possible; for example, it has been better for Boeing to centralize its operations in Seattle in the USA and to export airplanes abroad rather than establish foreign subsidiaries that would require huge investment relative to the size of the foreign markets (Carbaugh (2000)).

Licensing. Licensing is when a home firm authorizes a foreign firm to manufacture and market its goods for the foreign market under the same or a different brand name. For example, coca-cola is manufactured in different countries with the same brand name. Under licensing the home firm gains either from royalties on sales or from a lump-sum fee. The advantage of this method is that the home firm does not need to know the characteristics of the foreign market, as in the case of exporting, since it uses the local market knowledge of foreign firms (the licensee); also this method does not require capital expenditure, and is less risky than FDI or exporting especially in the case of political uncertainty or social unrest in the foreign country (Harris *et al.*, 1999). However, the home firm does incur the cost of monitoring the quality of the product produced by the foreign form.[3]

Franchising. This is like licensing but for a longer period of time, with the home firm having complete control of the design of the product and standardization of its quality. Examples of franchising are Benetton, Pizza Hut, Kentucky Fried Chicken, The Body Shop and so on. The advantages and disadvantages of franchising are as in the case of licensing.

Advantages and Disadvantages of FDI Compared to its Alternative Forms

- FDI allows MNCs to overcome difficulties arising from high tariffs and non-tariff barriers to trade.
- MNCs, by undertaking FDI, can have tighter control over the production and marketing of their product abroad.
- MNCs can exploit economies of scale or scope by diversifying either horizontally or vertically.
- MNCs, by undertaking FDI, can spread their risk through market diversification, especially if there is exchange-rate volatility.
- FDI is the highest risk internationalization activity mainly due to lack of information about the foreign country arising from its different culture, language, consumer preferences and cost conditions.

The Growth of FDI in the EU

International capital flows have increased dramatically in the last 20 years, as is evident from Table 9.1. Indeed, outward FDI stocks increased from 4.9 per cent of world output in 1980 to about 10 per cent by 1995. OECD countries were responsible for, on average, about 95 per cent of the total outward FDI, while the EU-15 had a share of about 44 per cent in this period. On the other hand, about 75 per cent, on average, of world FDI was directed into OECD countries and about 37 per cent into the EU-15. Clearly, not only has there been a rapid increase in FDI worldwide, but the main bulk of FDI is among the developed countries (Barrell and Pain 1997).

The examination of FDI inflows rather than FDI stocks exhibits a similar pattern for the period 1989–97, as can be seen in Figure 9.1 for three groups of countries: developed, developing, and Central and Eastern European countries (CEEC). Developed countries are by far the main recipients of FDI inflows, with developing countries continuously increasing their share, with the same being true for the CEEC countries but to a much lesser degree. It is interesting, however, to note the cyclical behaviour of FDI inflows in developed countries during the recession of 1990–92 (Griffiths and Wall (1999)).

The geographical distribution of the cumulative FDI flows in the EU during the 1990s is shown in Table 9.2. The main recipients of

Table 9.1 Global foreign direct investment stocks

	Outward FDI				Inward FDI			
	1980	1985	1990	1995	1980	1985	1990	1995
World ($ bn)	513.7	685.5	1,6841	2,7301	481.9	734.9	1,7169	2,6579
GDP (% of)	4.9	5.9	8.1	9.7	4.6	6.3	8.3	9.4
OECD ($ bn)	501.9	657.4	1,6062	2,5032	356.4	526.3	1,3614	1,9220
GDP (% of)	6.8	6.1	10.6	13.2	4.8	4.9	9.0	10.1
Share of total	97.7	95.9	95.4	91.7	74.0	71.6	79.3	72.3
EU-15 ($ bn)	213.2	286.5	777.2	1,2088	185.0	226.5	712.2	1,0281
GDP (% of)	7.4	7.1	13.8	17.4	6.4	5.6	12.7	14.8
Share of total	41.5	41.8	46.1	44.3	38.4	30.8	41.5	38.7

Source: Barrell and Pain (1997).

Figure 9.1 Inflows of foreign direct investment

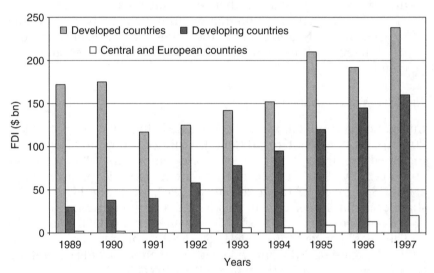

Source: UNCTAD (1998).

FDI are the UK, France and the Netherlands, while the countries that most heavily have undertaken FDI are the UK, Germany and France. These countries account for more than 50 per cent of the cumulative inflows and outflows of EU FDI. The EU also accounts for about half of the OECD FDI inflows during the 1990s.[4] The UK holds a dominant position in EU FDI flows by having a share of about 24 per cent in FDI inflows and 27 per cent in outflows. This is the result of an open-door policy towards FDI (Pass *et al.* (1995)). In the 1960s the focus of UK outward FDI shifted from Commonwealth countries towards

Table 9.2 Cumulative foreign direct investment flows in EU, 1990–99
(US $ millions)

Inflows		outflows		Net Outflows	
United Kingdom	319,726	United Kingdom	566,400	Germany	305,988
France	215,804	Germany	422,455	United Kingdom	246,674
Netherlands	159,523	France	347,839	France	132,035
Sweden	127,633	Netherlands	250,860	Netherlands	91,337
Belgium-Lux	123,206	Belgium-Lux	109,350	Italy	33,451
Germany	116,467	Sweden	102,114	Finland	17,919
Spain	97,780	Spain	93,236	Ireland	9,444
Italy	37,697	Italy	71,148	Denmark	782
Denmark	32,176	Finland	40,760	Austria	−2,929
Greece	26,942	Denmark	32,958	Spain	−4,544
Finland	22,841	Ireland	26,895	Portugal	−7,038
Austria	21,084	Austria	18,155	Belgium-Lux	−13,856
Portugal	17,501	Portugal	10,463	Sweden	−25,519
Ireland	17,451	Greece	573	Greece	−26,369
Total EU	1,335,831		2,093,206		757,375
Total OECD	2,709,512		3,552,013		842,501
% EU/OECD	49.30		58.93		89.90

Source: OECD, *Financial Market Trends*, no. 76, June (2000).

the EU and the USA,[5] while as a host country the UK is receiving FDI inflows from the USA, Japan and the EU. Indeed, the UK is the preferable location of US FDI outflows: as is evident from Table 9.3, about 17 per cent of the total US direct investment was directed to the UK in 1995. Also, about 40 per cent of the whole of Japanese investment in the EU for the period 1951–94 was located in the UK.[6]

Theories Explaining FDI

All theories of MNCs, in explaining their behaviour, make the assumption that markets are imperfect. If markets were perfect, then all firms and their products would be homogeneous and everybody would have perfect information. However, what we observe in examining the behaviour of MNCs is that they are very heterogeneous. Most of them are large companies, although there are also medium-sized MNCs. MNCs have considerable market power in well-differentiated products allowing them to be price-setters. It is exactly their oligopolistic nature that allows them to exploit economies of scale and/or scope. Here we briefly explain the main theories of why companies may become multinational, and refer the reader to several more detailed books such as Griffiths and Wall (1999), Harris *et al.* (1999), Harris (1999) and Sodersten and Reed (1994).

Table 9.3 US Direct investment abroad

	Value of investment, 1995		Employment, 1993	
	$ (billions)	Per cent of total	Thousands	Per cent of total
United Kingdom	120	17	866	13
Canada	81	11	875	13
Germany	43	6	569	8
Japan	39	6	411	6
France	33	5	403	6
Italy	17	2	164	2
All industrial*	509	72	4,379	65
Mexico	14	2	666	10
Total, all	712	100	6,731	100

*Includes W. Europe, Canada, Japan, Australia and New Zealand.
Source: Carbaugh (2000), p. 314.

The Specific Advantage

This theory (Hymer (1976)) says that a MNC should posses a specific advantage over competing local firms. This specific advantage could be technical knowledge, product innovations and managerial or financial expertise that the firm can better exploit and protect by setting-up foreign subsidiaries (Pass *et al.* (1995); and Pass (1996)). Examples are pharmaceutical products, intellectual property and production processes. Such specific advantages give the firm the edge over local firms that may have a better knowledge of the market than the MNC. So, the firm might become engaged in establishing a subsidiary abroad and in undertaking FDI if this advantage would give it benefits well-above the costs associated with the investment.

The Eclectic Approach

This theory (Dunning (1977)) encompasses several approaches. It is also known as the OLI approach, the initials standing for Owner-specific, Location-specific and Internalization factors. Ownership-specific factors give a specific advantage to a firm, such as innovation, the ability to diversify, and organizational or management skills.

Location-specific factors are associated with lower transport costs or proximity to markets and resources, while internalization is the process by which the MNC draws activities under centralized control rather than outsourcing them. Internalization allows the exploitation of economies of scale and/or scope, the minimization of risk and the maintenance of quality control (Harris *et al.* 1999).

Follow the Leader

The basic assumption of this theory (Knickerbocker (1973)) is an oligopolistic structure of the market with barriers to entry. In oligopolistic competition all firms are interdependent, that is they are engaged in a 'game' of actions and counteractions depending upon their competitors' positions and actions. So if one MNC undertakes FDI (the leader), then other MNCs should also follow in order to maintain their competitive edge. A characteristic example is the case of Japanese car manufacturers establishing subsidiaries in Europe in the 1980s and 1990s. Although this theory well-explains the behaviour of the follower, it does not explain the behaviour of the leader.

The Level of Development Theory

According to this theory (Dunning (1979)) a large and well-developed market will have all the resources, the technical infrastructure, human skills and a well-developed financial system to support FDI. Thus, this theory suggests that net outward investment is a positive function of the level of development in the foreign country, which in empirical studies is proxied by the level of output in the foreign country.

The Product Life-Cycle theory

This theory (Vernon (1966)) suggests that all products follow a life-cycle pattern. Initially a firm introduces its product into the home market and exports it overseas. At some point latter on, this product reaches a stage of *maturity*, that is fewer domestic buyers, the product is standardized and there is higher competition. During the phase of maturity, the firm's profitability is lower than at the beginning of the life-cycle and the firm will try either to expand into new markets or adopt a cost-reducing relocation. This implies that the home firm could establish a foreign subsidiary in one or several developed countries where the demand for the product could still be high and competition relatively low. Alternatively, the home firm could relocate its production to a less-developed country where unit labour costs might be lower.

Determinants of FDI in the EU

Labour Market Conditions

Labour cost. Labour cost is considered to be a major determinant of FDI since a lower labour cost abroad may induce MNCs to relocate some of their activities into a foreign country. Moreover, in an era of increasing globalization the barriers to FDI are falling continuously (FDI liberalization) thus reinforcing higher FDI flows worldwide. Indeed, empirical evidence in the UK and Germany suggests that high relative unit labour costs (ULC) in a country are associated with net FDI outflows from that country.[7,8] Tables 9.4 and 9.5 show that the UK (Table 9.4) has net inflows from Denmark and Sweden, both having higher relative unit labour costs; while in the case of Germany (Table 9.5) there is an even stronger association between net FDI outflows and high relative unit labour costs.

More specifically, according to Hatzius (2000), a 1 per cent increase in British unit labour costs could lead to a decrease in net UK FDI inflow by £139 million, or, equivalently, 1.7 per cent of UK 1993 manufacturing investment. Similarly, a 1 per cent increase in the German unit labour costs could lead to a reduction in net FDI inflow by between DM762 million and DM1,796 million, or between 0.3 per cent and 0.7 per cent of Germany's aggregate 1993 investment.

Table 9.4 FDI and relative unit labour costs (ULC): UK

	Outflows	*Inflows*	*ULC*
Australia	1.098	*n.a.*	+0.161
Belgium	0.348	0.135	+0.041
Canada	0.660	0.105	+0.001
Denmark	0.111	0.483	−0.284
France	0.148	0.190	+0.029
Germany	0.079	0.063	−0.088
Italy	0.127	*n.a.*	+0.337
Japan	0.007	0.025	+0.096
Netherlands	0.823	0.434	−0.033
New Zealand	0.582	*n.a.*	+0.335
Portugal	0.653	*n.a.*	+0.996
Spain	0.190	*n.a.*	+0.499
Sweden	0.077	0.637	−0.314
USA	0.458	0.200	+0.028

Notes:
The FDI data refer to manufacturing average real annual flows between 1979 and 1993 in volume terms, and scale the flows by the partner country's real value added in manufacturing. Outflows are from the UK. The unit labour cost (ULC) data refer to the UK's average logarithm manufacturing ULC in a common currency minus that of the partner country. Column figures are in percentages, except for ULC.

Source: Hatzius (2000).

Table 9.5 FDI and relative unit labour costs: (ULC) Germany

	Outflow	Inflow	Outward stock change	Inward stock change	ULC
Australia	0.037	0.002	0.110	0.004	+0.216
Austria	0.411	0.094	0.702	0.349	+0.029
Canada	0.062	0.008	0.074	0.029	+0.063
Denmark	0.053	0.042	0.099	0.157	−0.091
France	0.100	0.047	0.141	0.071	+0.128
Ireland	1.774	0.034	3.261	0.000	+0.143
Italy	0.074	0.010	0.168	0.021	+0.424
Japan	0.006	0.017	0.007	0.034	−0.153
Nethlands	0.369	0.108	0.345	0.868	+0.082
Portugal	0.183	0.000	1.089	0.002	+0.921
Spain	0.176	0.006	0.285	−0.003	+0.527
Sweden	0.062	0.075	0.142	0.248	−0.207
Switzland	0.292	0.007	0.297	0.669	−0.301
UK	0.149	0.029	0.232	0.058	+0.185
USA	0.063	−0.002	0.074	0.020	+0.009

Column percentage apart from ULC
Notes:
The FDI data refer to average real annual flows between 1982 (stock changes: 1984) and 1993 in volume terms, and scale the flows by the partner country's real GDP. Outflows and outward stock changes are from Germany. The unit labour costs (ULC) data refer to Germany's average logarithm total ULC in a common currency minus that of the partner country. Column figures are in percentages, except for ULC.

Source: Hatzius (2000).

A similar study by Barrell (1998), examining the determinants of US manufacturing FDI in the EU, finds that a 1 per cent increase in the relative unit labour cost in the USA could result in a 0.89 per cent increase in FDI inflow into the EU.

Strikes. Strikes could reduce the attractiveness of a country in hosting FDI inflows. To the extent that they might occur often, they would reduce the flexibility of the labour market in the host country. This reduction in labour-market flexibility could be seen by MNCs as a cost-increasing signal that would, potentially, threaten the expected (actual) profitability of their planned (existing) investment. This, of course, would deter MNCs from undertaking further risks by establishing (or expanding the scale of) a subsidiary abroad, resulting in a redirection to a new subsidiary (or the relocation of an existing one). Thus, strikes are expected to reduce FDI inflows into a country.

Indeed, empirical studies, suggest that strikes are negatively related to FDI flows (Barrell (1998) and Barrell and Pain (1998)).

The Real Exchange Rate and its Variability

The real exchange rate and FDI. The real exchange rate (RER) expresses the value of a currency in terms of its real purchasing power. Since RER can express the real value of goods and investment plans it is a measure of the real competitiveness of a country. Therefore, changes in RER will result in changes in that country's competitiveness, which in turn could either increase or decrease the level of FDI flows. Consider, for example, the case of an exchange-rate depreciation in the host country. The positive effects on FDI are:

- it will encourage import substitution[9] in the host country by increasing the value of imports;
- it will improve the international competitiveness of the host country hence the profitability of FDI; and
- facilities in the host country will become less expensive as the value of foreign financial flows increases.

The negative effects on FDI flows are:

- the expected profit repatriation will be less if profits are nominated in the currency of the host country;
- exchange-rate depreciation may cause inflation in the host country thus reducing international competitiveness in the longer run; and
- exchange-rate depreciation by reducing the value of the subsidiary in the host country will eventually reduce the total value of the parent MNE.[10]

Empirical evidence suggests that the negative effects dominate, and thus an exchange-rate depreciation in the host country will lead to lower inward FDI; see for example Apergis *et al.* (2000), De Menil (1999) and Clegg (1995).

Real exchange-rate variability. MNCs have the power to reduce the effects of exchange-rate changes on their profits. According to McCulloch (1993), large and unpredictable exchange-rate fluctuations as in the 1980s would induce MNCs to shift production and sales abroad for two main reasons: first, by having a foreign subsidiary a MNC can take advantage of unexpected declines in the variable costs abroad (De Menil, 1999); and, second, as real exchange-rate variability increases, the transaction costs involved in international trade will also rise inducing MNCs to undertake more FDI.[11] As a result of this shift of production abroad, FDI flows should increase.[12] Therefore, one should expect that greater exchange-rate volatility would increase FDI. Indeed, Goldberg and Kolstad (1995) and Cushman (1988) suggest the existence of a positive correlation between exchange-rate volatility and FDI in the EU. Moreover, De Menil (1999) quantifies that a 10 per cent increase in exchange-rate variability will raise FDI stocks by 10 per cent, suggesting further that cross-border FDI has increased in the EU in *spite of* rather than *because of* EMS and the progression to EMU.[13] On the other hand, Apergis *et al.* (2000) suggest that a 1 per cent decrease, rather than an increase, in the real exchange-rate volatility in Greece during the period 1987–97 led to a 4 per cent increase in FDI inflows.[14]

Output in the Country of Origin and the Host Country

According to the level of development theory, as we have seen, FDI volumes are affected by the level of output in both the host and origin countries. The reason for this is because the absorption capacity in each country depends on the size of its market, which in many empirical studies is approximated by the level of output (GDP) in each country. The size of the market in the host country is an important determinant of FDI since a large market will allow the MNC to capture the host-market demand by exploiting economies of scale. Furthermore, in a well-developed market an existing infrastructure will support the FDI. Empirical evidence supports the above theoretical considerations;[15] for example, De Menil (1999) suggests that a 10 per cent increase in the two GDPs (for the host and origin countries) will increase FDI stocks by 12 per cent. Moreover, Agiomirgianakis *et al.* (2003) using data from for the period 1975–97 have found that certain variables associated with the level of development in the host country, such as human capital, the density of infrastructure and the agglomeration factor,[16] are significant determinants of FDI inflows in OECD countries.

Distance between the Origin and Host Countries

Many empirical studies on the determinants of FDI use the distance between host and origin countries as a variable to capture the cost of coordination, communication and transportation between the subsidiary and the MNC. One should expect that the higher the distance between the two countries, the higher would be the above costs implying a negative relationship between distance and FDI. Indeed, empirical research suggests that a 10 per cent increase in the distance between the two countries will decrease the FDI stock by 6 per cent (De Menil (1999)).

Cultural and Language Differences

Cultural bonds and language similarities (CLS) between the two countries are important for the establishment of an efficient business network since they can facilitate a smooth flow of information from the MNC to the subsidiary, and the reverse. Empirical studies on OECD countries,[17] examining the relationship between FDI flows and CLS for three distinct language groupings, English, German and Latin, show that: (a) an English-language effect raises FDI stock by three times; (b) a Germanic-language effect raises FDI stocks by four times; and (c) there is no significant Latin language effect (De Menil (1999)).

European Integration

The European integration process and especially single-market policies have positively affected intra-EU FDI, either directly by the removal of capital controls, or indirectly by increasing the level and growth of overall economic activity. However, other aspects of the measures, such as the removal of non-tariff barriers to trade, have encouraged more intra-EU trade flows rather than FDI flows. Several empirical studies support the positive effect on FDI of the establishment of the internal market after 1987. It is estimated that the European internal market has increased intra-EU FDI stocks for the UK and Germany by 8–14 per cent or around 0.5 per cent of EU GDP at constant 1990 prices (EAG (1996) and Barrell and Pain (1997)). US FDI flows into the EU have also been higher due to the European integration process. Indeed, quoting Pain (1997): 'The SMP has raised the locational attractiveness of the European market for outsiders as well as insiders'. The launch of the euro in 2002 has been another incentive in attracting more FDI as it allows less transaction costs for MNCs.[18] The Japanese MNC Toyota, for example, asked its suppliers in Britain (a country that is not in euro-land) to use the euro to settle accounts in order to avoid currency exposure risks (*Financial Times*, 11 August 2000).

Government Policies

Many governments worldwide, including the EU states, try to incorporate policy measures in attracting FDI as part of their strategy for economic growth in their countries. There are several measures that a government can take in order to attract FDI, such as tariffs, taxes, subsidies, a regulatory regime and privatization policies.

Tariffs. The imposition of a high tariff on imported goods may effectively motivate foreign producers into establishing a subsidiary in that country in order to avoid the tariff wall. An example of this is the FDI flows in the EU in order to capture the gains from the internal market. Indeed, after 1987 the internal market resulted in a common external tariff to non-EU products and the elimination of barriers to trade among EU states. Thus, a foreign firm, from the USA or Japan for example, that would like to expand into the large EU market could only avoid this tariff wall by establishing a subsidiary in one EU state. An example of Japanese MNC is the car-maker Nissan with subsidiaries in England and Spain, and Toyota and Honda with subsidiaries in the UK. An example of an American MNC is General Motors with subsidiaries in the EU under the name Vauxhall in the UK, and Opel in several places in Europe (Barnes and Davison (1994) p. 13).

Corporate taxes. Higher corporate taxes in the host country, by increasing the cost of investment and thus its profitability, will deter a MNC from undertaking investment in that country and possibly motivate it to invest in another country. Empirical studies in the USA[19] have shown a negative relationship between tax rates and FDI (Dunn and Mutti (2000)). An implication of this is that governments in their efforts to attract FDI will be engaged, at some point, in a competition of low corporate tax rates. Indeed, Devereux *et al.* (2003), using data for the period 1983–99, find that OECD countries compete over corporate tax rates. Pain and Young (1996), examining FDI in the UK and Germany, suggest that 'there is a significant effect of tax competitiveness on the location of FDI'. This tax competition among EU governments, that some economists believe could be the result of the 1986 US fiscal reform (see for example, De Menil (1999), p. 19), is evident in Table 9.6. This table shows that although corporate taxes in EU started to fall after 1980, further reductions and some convergence was achieved in the period 1985–1991. In OECD countries the average corporate tax rate has fallen from nearly 50% in the early 1980s to under 35% by 2001 (see, for example, Devereux *et al.* 2003).

Subsidies. Most EU countries have used subsidies as part of their regional and industrial policies. Indeed, FDI has been seen as a key element in regional economic development and one of the areas of policy competition among EU countries (Raines and Brown (1999)). An example of this is the competitive offer by both the UK and the French governments of a £5 million subsidy to Hoover in 1994 to establish a subsidiary in their countries. Another example is an $80 million subsidy by the British government in 1995 to MNC Ford in order to attract it into an investment of £400 million for a new Jaguar car model (Pass (1996)). Subsidies, however, distort competition and are thus constrained by Article 92 of the Treaty of Rome.

Table 9.6 Overall corporate tax rates (%) in the EC[a]

	1980	1985	1991
Belgium	48	45	39
Denmark	37	50	38
Germany	61.7/44.3	61.7/44.3	57.5/45.6
Greece	–	49	46(40)[b]
Spain	33	33	35.5
France	50	50	34.2
Ireland	45	50(10)	43(10)[c]
Italy	36.3	47.8/36	47.8/36
Luxbourg	45.5	45.5	39.4
Nethlands	46	42	35
Portugal	51.2/44	51.2/44	39.6
UK	52	40	34
EC Average	46	46.9	40.1

Notes:
[a] Where two rates are given, the first is the rate for retentions and the second the rate for distributions. [b] The lower rate applies to firms quoted on the Athens Stock Exchange. [c] The lower rate applies to the manufacturing industry.
Source: Raines and Brown (1999), p. 116.

Regulatory regime and privatization policy. Although the above factors are very significant in attracting FDI, the successful experience of some EU countries shows the importance of other factors such as the regulatory regime concerning FDI, or the privatization policy of a government. The experience of the UK, the most successful country in attracting FDI inflows, shows three key factors: (a) the liberalization of foreign ownership regulation in the early 1980s; (b) the privatization programme of Mrs Thatcher in traditionally state-controlled activities (telecommunication, railways, electricity, water); and (c) financial deregulation, the 'Big Bang' in 1986 (Raines and Brown (1999)). Japanese firms have responded positively to these UK policies; for example about 80 Japanese MNC established affiliates in the UK in the period 1988–90 (Curwen (1997)).

The Size of the Parent Firm

The size of the parent firm is a crucial factor in determining the internationalization path that a firm will embark on and, consequently, the size of FDI flows. Large MNCs are primarily involved with wholly-owned subsidiaries; on the other hand, small and medium-sized enterprises (SMEs), that is firms with less than 500 employees, face much tighter managerial and financial constraints in their path to internationalization than do their competitors, the large firms. These constraints impose an adverse asymmetry, in terms of information cost,[20] against SMEs, forcing them to adopt other risk-minimization strategies such as joint ventures rather than wholly-owned subsidiaries. Consequently, the magnitude of FDI will depend of the size of the parent firms involved. Indeed, empirical evidence suggests that the size of the parent firm and the propensity for establishing a joint venture are inversely related (Mutinelli and Piscitello (1998)). This may explain why governments mainly target large firms in their effort to attract FDI.

The Importance of FDI for the EU

Capital Accumulation

Capital accumulation is the increase in the capital stock of a firm, which is created by investing over and above the depreciated capital of the firm. The accumulation of capital expands the productive potential of a firm and, consequently, the productive potential of a country. FDI inflows contribute to capital accumulation in the recipient country, and in this capacity FDI inflows are growth-enhancing (De Mello (1997)). In the period 1984–89, intra-EU FDI flows were on average 2 per cent of the gross domestic fixed capital formation in the EU, while in the period 1989–94 this increased to 4.5 per cent (Barrell (1998) p. 154).

Diffusion of Knowledge and Research and Development (R&D)

FDI is different from other forms of investment because not only transfers production know-how, but it also facilitates the diffusion of knowledge from one country to another and the assimilation of technologies or ideas across countries (Romer (1993)). FDI, by facilitating this diffusion of knowledge, effectively motivates research and development (R&D); that is, the research for and the adoption of new products, processes and techniques, as well as the introduction of new technical, managerial and marketing skills (Wu (2000), De Mello (1999)). This distinct characteristic of FDI has the potential to transform the host economy. Empirical studies indicate that FDI flows have indeed provided a channel for the diffusion of knowledge from other countries such as the USA and Japan into the EU, as well as for intra-EU FDI flows (Barrell (1999) and Barrell and Pain (1997)). Girma and Wakelin (2002), examining whether productivity spillovers from FDI activity occur in the UK economy, found that positive spillovers from MNCs occur to domestic firms in the same sector and region as foreign affiliates. Moreover, their findings suggest that domestic firms may gain more from these spillovers if the technology gap they have from foreign firms is low.

MNCs are fostering R&D not only at home but also in their subsidiaries abroad. The shares of R&D undertaken by foreign affiliates worldwide and particularly in Europe are large, as shown in Figure 9.2. Moreover, as will be evident shortly, R&D propensities of foreign affiliates are higher than those of domestic firms (see economic growth data below).

Economic Growth

Within endogenous growth theory, FDI flows may contribute directly or indirectly to economic growth in a country. While most of the empirical studies seem to focus on less-developed countries where FDI is considered to be the major source of economic growth (Balasubramanyam et al. (1996)), one might ask whether economic growth in the developed world and more specifically in the EU has also been affected by FDI.[21] According to Barrell and Pain (1997),

Figure 9.2 Share of foreign affiliates in manufacturing R&D (1997 or latest year available)

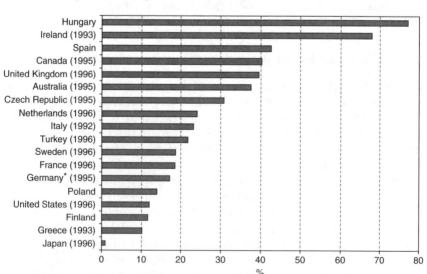

* Sample of the 500 most R&D-intensive firms.
Source: OECD database, *Activities of Foreign Affiliates*, 1999

FDI inflows in EU countries have indeed contributed to EU economic growth for a number of reasons:

- USA affiliates have a greater propensity to undertake R&D expenditures in all EU countries than domestic firms.[22]
- The labour productivity of US manufacturing affiliates in the UK is higher by one-third than domestic manufacturing productivity.
- The level of inward investment in many smaller EU states has been very significant; for example in Belgium and Ireland[23] 59 per cent of manufacturing output in 1989 was produced by foreign affiliates (Cassiers *et al.* (1996)). In the UK, FDI has transformed the production side of the economy (Eltis (1996)).

Barrell and Pain (1997), using a model of labour-augmenting technical progress, estimate that for the period 1972–95 around 30 per cent of UK manufacturing productivity growth was attributable to FDI inflows.

Unemployment

Large FDI flows, however, have led to concerns among the general public in several European countries as to whether they aggravate unemployment problems and thus lead to wage moderation. Public perceptions and attitudes regarding FDI liberalization differ from one country to another depending on the characteristics of the labour market. In continental European labour markets, characterized by labour market inflexibility such as in Germany and France, the public perception of FDI liberalization is that it may either lead domestic companies abroad (exporting jobs) or may reduce domestic wages (see Hatzius (2000)). On the other hand, with a flexible labour market, such as the British one, the public perception is that FDI liberalization will attract MNCs seeking access to the EU market. However, as is evident from Figures 9.3 and 9.4:

- A significant percentage of EU production is carried out by foreign affiliates. For example, about 28 per cent of French manufacturing production in 1996 was produced by foreign-owned firms; in Germany about 12 per cent of manufacturing output in 1996 was produced by foreign affiliates.
- A significant percentage of employees in less-flexible EU labour markets, such as France and Germany, is employed by foreign affiliates; for example 25 per cent of employees in French manufacturing worked in foreign affiliates in 1996, and about 8 per cent of German employees in the manufacturing sector worked in foreign-owned firms. These shares are also high for other countries, such as the UK, the Netherlands and Sweden.

Figure 9.3 Share of foreign affiliates in manufacturing production (or turnover) (1997 or latest year available)

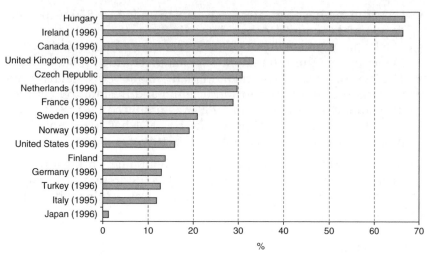

Source: OECD database, Activities of Foreign Affiliates, 1999

Figure 9.4 Share of foreign affiliates in manufacturing employment (1997 or latest year available)

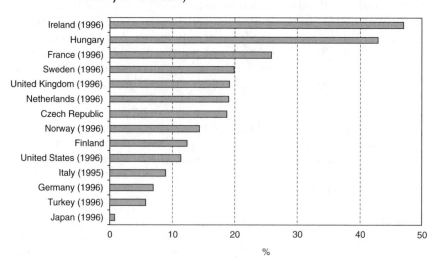

Source: OECD database, Activities of Foreign Affiliates, 1999

Also:

- Many EU citizens are employed in MNCs outside their country of origin. For example, 30 per cent of employees in French manufacturing worked in companies outside France (Barrell (1998)).
- High-wage EU states have been preferable locations for US affiliates. Table 9.7, for example, shows the geographical distribution of the activities of US manufacturing FDI affiliates, and it is evident that Germany is their preferable production location despite the fact that German wages are well-above the EU average[24] (see also Tables 9.3, 9.4 and 9.5).
- In the UK about 500,000 jobs were created by foreign affiliates in the period 1979–98. Also, 67 per cent of the intermediate inputs of Japanese-owned firms were from the UK (Griffiths and Wall (1999)).
- FDI outflows from the EU to the rest of the world either lead to an increase or no change in domestic employment in the EU (see, for example, Blomstrom *et al.* (1997)).
- Empirical evidence in the UK and Germany over the last twenty years shows that FDI has flattened the long-run labour demand curve (Hatzius (2000)), which, in turn, could lead to wage moderation and lower aggregate unemployment in the EU.

The above empirical evidence suggests that FDI inflows have resulted in a net output and job-creation effect in the EU.

Table 9.7 Geographical distribution of the activities of US (%)

	Gross product				Employment
	1977	1982	1989	1995	1995
Europe	56.5	54.9	57.8	60.0	45.1
UK	14.9	17.3	15.9	12.2	11.6
Germany	16.8	15.3	15.0	17.2	10.8
France	8.7	7.4	6.9	8.2	6.0
Italy	3.8	3.9	4.5	4.1	3.6
Netherlands	3.1	2.6	4.5	3.7	1.8
Belgium	3.6	2.4	2.9	3.3	1.7
Ireland	0.7	1.3	2.0	3.2	1.4
Spain	2.1	1.9	3.3	2.9	2.5
World total	$71.2 bn	$99.8 bn	$172.0 bn	$238.8 bn	3.66 million
Share of all industries	44.4	44.4	53.8	50.2	61.3

Source: Barrell and Pain (1999).

Conclusions

MNCs expand their activities abroad for a variety of reasons, including the exploitation of economies of scale/scope, the use of specific advantagess, due to a life-cycle pattern of their products, or simply because their competitors are engaged in similar activities. Other reasons such as the avoidance of tariffs and non-barriers to trade, relative labour costs, real exchange-rate volatility, cultural and language factors as well as human capital, the density of infrastructure and the agglomeration factor[25] could also induce FDI flows into and out of a country. In the EU, intra-FDI flows as well as FDI inflows from the USA and Japan have been greatly motivated by the European integration process. The EU encourages FDI inflows as they are considered welfare-improving for the host countries. FDI flows are associated with a number of positive effects, such as the diffusion of knowledge among countries by creating positive productivity spillovers to domestic firms, as well as with a positive contribution to economic growth, thus resulting in a reduction of unemployment in host countries.

Notes

1 However, in case a company buys a large amount of shares of another company it may take the form of acquisition and thus allow the first company to have direct control of the other.
2 See also Harris (1999) and Pass *et al.* (1995).
3 See Carbaugh (2000) for a diagrammatic comparison of FDI with exporting and licensing.
4 For a detailed analysis of recent trends in FDI in the 1990s see Miyake and Sass (2000).
5 See Kenwood and Lougheed (1999).
6 See for example Raines and Brown (1999) for a detailed analysis of the reasons, and also *EUROSTAT Statistics in Focus*, Economy and Finance, no. 28/2000.
7 See for example Barrell and Pain (1997).
8 Standard wage variables are quite often insignificant in some empirical studies; see Hatzius (2000) and Cheng and Kwan (2000).
9 A country following an import-substitution policy tries to become self-sufficient. The larger the country the more likely it is that such a policy will be successful; see Dunn and Mutti (2000) for a ranking of countries according to their openness in trade.
10 See Apergis *et al.* (2000) for a detailed explanation.
11 This is the case of substitutability between trade and FDI. See Alesina's point in De Menil (1999). However, the substitutability between trade and FDI is ambiguous in empirical studies; see for example Eaton's point in De Menil (1999) and also Barrell and Pain (1997) p. 1773.

12 See Firoozi (1997a) for a theoretical explanation.
13 See De Menil (1999) p. 175.
14 This result is not surprising since Apergis *et al.* (2000) takes into account the repatriation profits of the FDI.
15 See for example Barrell and Pain (1997) and Barrell (1999). See also De Mello (1997) for a summary of eight studies supporting these results in several countries including four EU countries.
16 That is, companies are located near to each other due to positive externalities created by this concentration. Agglomeration economies can arise from the presence of other firms and other industries, as well as from the availability of a skilled labour force.
17 EU countries are included in this group of countries.
18 Some MNCs had publicly voiced their preference in favour of the euro long before its adoption (see, for example, Raines and Brown (1999)).
19 For an empirical analysis with similar results in Mexico see Shah and Slemrod (1991).
20 For informational aspects of FDI decisions and the signalling game with domestic firms see Firoozi (1997b).
21 For the impact of FDI in OECD countries see De Mello (1999), while for the case of developing countries see Borensztein *et al.* (1998).
22 For a similar result see Blomstrom *et al.* (1999) where he suggests that technology spillovers are beneficial for domestic firms.
23 For a study on the significant role of FDI flows in transforming Irish traditional manufacturing sectors into high-tech ones see Ruane and Gorg (1998).
24 The fact that the largest four member states, namely Germany, France, the UK and Italy, also have the largest inflows may suggest an agglomeration effect.
25 See note 16 above.

References

Agiomirgianakis, G.M., Asteriou, D. and Papathoma, K. (2004) in G. Agiomirgianakis, T. Biswas, C. Tsoukis (eds), *Advances in International Economics and Finance* (London: Kluwer).

Apergis, N. Kyrkilis, D. and Rezitis, A. (2000) 'Exchange Rate Volatility and Inward Foreign Direct Investment in Greece: The Prospect of EMU Membership', Paper presented at the conference 'The Implications of the EMU for the Greek Economy', University of Ioannina.

Balasubramanyam, V.N. Salisu, M. and Sapsford, S. (1996) 'Foreign Direct Investment and Growth in EP and IS Countries', *Economic Journal*, vol. 106, pp. 92–105.

Barnes, I. and Davison, L. (1994) *European Business* (Oxford: Butterworth-Heinemann).

Barrell, R. and Pain, N. (1997) 'Foreign Direct Investment, Technological Change and Economic Growth within Europe', *Economic Journal*, vol. 107, pp. 1770–86.

—(1998) 'Real Exchange Rates, Agglomerations, and Irreversibilities: Macroeconomic Policy and FDI in EMU', *Oxford Review of Economic Policy*, vol. 14, no. 3, pp. 152–67.

—(1999) 'Domestic Institutions, Agglomerations and Foreign Direct Investment in Europe', *European Economic Review*, vol. 43, pp. 925–34.

Blomstrom, M., Fors, G. and Lipsey, R.E. (1997) 'Foreign Direct Investment and Employment: the Home Country Experience in the USA and Sweden', *Economic Journal*, vol. 107, pp. 1787–97.

—(1999) 'Technology Transfers and Spillover: Does Local Participation with Multinationals Matter?', *European Economic Review*, vol. 43, pp. 915–23.

Borensztein, E., De Gregorio, J. and Lee, J.W. (1998) 'How Does Foreign Direct Investment Affect Economic Growth?', *Journal of International Economics*, vol. 45, pp. 115–35.

Carbaugh, R. (2000) *International Economics* (Ohio: South-Western College Publishing).

Cassiers, I., De Ville, P. and Solar, P. (1996) 'Economic Growth in Postwar Belgium', in N. Crafts and G. Toniolo (eds), *Economic Growth in Europe since 1945* (Cambridge: Cambridge, University Press).

Cheng, L.K. and Kwan, Y.K. (2000) 'What are the Determinants of the Location of FDI? The Chinese Experience', *Journal of International Economics*, vol. 51, pp. 379–400.

Cushman, D.O. (1988) 'Exchange Rate Uncertainty and Foreign Direct Investment in the United States', *Weltwirtschaftliches Archive*, vol. 124, pp. 322–36.

Curwen, P. (1997) *Understanding the UK Economy* (London: Macmillan – Palgrave).

Clegg, J. (1995) 'The Determinants of United States Foreign Direct Investment in the European Community: A Critical Reappraisal', in R.Schiattarella (ed.), *New Challenges for European and International Business*, Proceedings of the 21st European International Business Association Conference, University of Urbino, Italy, 1995.

Devereux, M.P., Lockwood, B. and Redoano, M. (2003) 'Do Countries Compete over Corporate Tax Rates?' *New Economic Papers*, March.

De Mello, L.R. (1999) 'Foreign Direct Investment-led Growth: Evidence from Time Series and Panel Data', *Oxford Economic Papers*, vol. 51, pp. 133–51.

De Mello, L.R. (1997) 'Foreign Direct Investment in Developing Countries and Growth: A Selectivity Survey', University of Kent, Working Papers Series, UK.

De Menil, G. (1999) 'Real Capital Market Integration in the EU: How Far Has It Gone? What Will the Effect of the Euro Be?', *Economic Policy*, issue 28, pp. 166–201.

Dunn R. and Mutti, J.H. (2000) *International Economics* (London: Routledge).

Dunning, J.H. (1977) 'Trade Location of Economic Activity and the MNEs', in B. Ohlin (ed.), *The International Allocation of Economic Activity* (London: Macmillan – Palgrave).

Dunning, J.H. (1979) 'Explaining Changing Patterns of International Investment in Defence of the Eclectic Theory', *Oxford Bulletin of Economics and Statistics*, vol. 41, pp. 269–96.

EAG (1996) *The Development of Foreign Direct Investment Flows in the EU Due to the Internal Market Programme*, European Commission.

Eltis, W. (1996) 'How Low Profitability and Weak Innovation Undermines UK Industrial Growth', *Economic Journal*, vol. 106, pp. 184–95.

Firoozi, F. (1997a) 'Multinationals, FDI and Uncertainty: An Exposition', *Journal of Multinational Financial Management*, vol. 7, pp. 265–73.

Firoozi, F. (1997b) 'Informational Aspects of FDI', WEA (Westeren Economic Association)/IEFS (International Economic Finance Society), Congress Seattle.

Girma, S. and Wakelin, K. (2002) 'Are There Regional Spillovers from FDI in the UK?', in D. Greenaway, R. Upward and K. Wakelin (eds), *Trade, Investment, Migration and Labour Market Adjustment* (London: Palgrave-Macmillan)

Goldberg, L.S. and Kolstad, C.D. (1995) 'Foreign Direct Investment, Exchange Rate Variability and Demand Uncertainty', *International Economic Review*, vol. 36, pp. 855–73.

Griffiths, A. and Wall, S. (1999) *Applied Economics* (London: Longman).

Harris, N. (1999) *European Business* (London: Macmillan – Palgrave).

Harris, N. Mouatt, S. and Potts, N. (1999) *European Business Learning Pack* no. 32/00, Southampton Business School.

Hatzius, J. (2000) 'Foreign Direct Investment and Factor Demand Elasticities', *European Economic Review*, vol. 44, pp. 117–43.

Hymer, S.H. (1976) *The International Operations of National Firms: A Study of Direct Foreign Investment* (Cambridge, Mass: MIT Press).

Kenwood, A.G. and Lougheed, A. (1999) *The Growth of the International Economy* (London: Routledge).

Knickerbocker, F.T. (1973) *Oligopolistic Reaction and Multinational Enterprise* (Boston: Harvard University, Press).

McCulloch, R. (1993) 'New Perspectives of Foreign Direct Investment', in K. Foot (ed.), *Investment* (Chicago: University of Chicago Press).

Miyake, M. and Sass, M. (2000) 'Recent Trends in Foreign Direct Investment', *Financial Market Trends*, no. 76, June, OECD.

Mutinelli, M. and Piscitello, L. (1998) 'The Influence of a Firm's Size and International Experience on the Ownership Structure of Italian FDI in Manufacturing', *Small Business Economics*, vol. 11, pp. 43–56.

Pain, N. (1997) 'Continental Drift: European Integration and the Location of UK FDI', *The Manchester School*, Supplement, vol. 65, pp. 94–117.

Pain, N. and Young, G. (1996) 'Tax Competition and the Pattern of European Foreign Direct Investment', Prepared for the Institute for Fiscal Studies Conference on *Public Policy and the Location of Economic Activity*, November, London.

Pass, C.L. (1996) 'Multinational Companies and Foreign Investment', in G.B.J. Atkinson (ed.), *Developments in Economics*, vol. 12 (Ormskirk: Causeway Press).

Pass, C.L., Lowes, B. and Robinson, A. (1995) *Business and Macroeconomics* (London: Routledge).

Raines, P. and Brown, R. (1999) *Policy Competition and Foreign Direct Investment in Europe* (Aldershot: Ashgate Publishing).

Romer, P. (1993) 'Idea Gaps and Object Gaps in Economic Development', *Journal of Monetary Economics*, vol. 32, pp. 543–73.

Ruane, F. and Gorg, H. (1998) 'Irish FDI Policy and Investment from the EU', in R. Barrell and N. Pain (eds) *Investment, Innovation, and the Diffusion of the Technologies in Europe: German Foreign Direct Investment and its Role in European Growth* (Cambridge: Cambridge University Press).

Shah, A. and Slemrod, J. (1991) 'Do Taxes Matter for Foreign Direct Investment?' *World Bank Economic Review*, vol. 5, no. 3, pp. 473–91.

Sodersten, B. and Reed, G. (1994) *International Economics* (London: Macmillan – Palgrave).

Vernon, R. (1966) 'International Investment and International Trade in the Product Cycle' *Quarterly Journal Of Economics*, vol. 80, pp. 190–207.

Wu, J. (2000) 'Measuring the Performance of FDI: A Case Study of China', *Economics Letters*, vol. 66, pp. 143–50.

10 Internal and External European Migration: Theories and Empirical Evidence

George Agiomirgianakis

Introduction

International labour mobility is an issue of increasing interest and importance worldwide for many reasons. First, international labour flows affect the size, the age structure and the skills of the labour force in both the country of origin and the host country. Second, the magnitude of human flows across countries has become relatively large in recent years: in 1999 some 130 million people (2.2 per cent of the total world population) were residents outside their nations of citizenship.[1] In the United States the annual labour inflow as a percentage of population change was in 1999 about 30 per cent. Third, the scale of international labour flows might rise in the future as a result of widening economic differentials, of demographic pressures and differential labour-force growth rates, and as a result of the extension of transportation and communications.[2] Moreover, many governments of countries where labour is in abundance are currently following policies, which either explicitly or implicitly promote exports of labour. Given the high level of unemployment in many western countries, labour inflows generate concerns by both policy-makers and the general public about the possible adverse effects of immigration on the employment of native workers. Fourth, migration flows are volatile and unpredictable, with political as well as economic causes and consequences. Indeed, political and economic changes in Europe have resulted in millions of international migrants from Eastern European countries into EU countries. In Albania, for example, net emigration between 1991 and 1993 was estimated at between 6.2 and 9.2 per cent of the Albanian population, and that mass emigration brought about an 8 per cent fall in the Albanian labour force (see Cuka *et al.* (1999)). In Bulgaria, potential emigrants comprise up to 36 per cent of the population; in Poland, about 2–4 per cent of citizens would like to emigrate; and in the former USSR estimates of potential migrants, by the turn of the century, vary from 400,000 to 2 million emigrants per year (see Fassmann and Muntz (1994)). At the same time, countries of Central and Eastern Europe, such as Poland, are experiencing inflows of foreign workers from Russia, Lithuania and Ukraine. Also, traditional emigration countries such as Italy, Greece, Spain and Portugal have not only become net immigration countries, but along with Germany they are also the main destination countries in Europe. Fifth, the financial flows associated with international labour movements are substantial: official remittances were nearly US$70 billion in 1995, second in value only to trade in crude oil and larger than official development assistance.

In what follows we analyse international migration in Europe by presenting the empirical evidence, the relevant economic theory and the policies adopted by European countries. Throughout we emphasize European research, statistical evidence and policies, although where appropriate we have included non-European research and evidence. In the next section we present the types of European migration and discuss statistical data classifying the flows of people and describing the associated financial flows. We then present, briefly, the basic theoretical approaches in modelling international migration. Following on we consider the empirical evidence on the factors that may influence migration decisions and, consequently, migration flows, before examining the effects of international migration on European unemployment and wages, the effects of remittances, the consequences for economic growth in the sending country and, also, the brain drain hypothesis. European thinking on migration and migration policies is then presented, distinguishing between internal and external migration and raising the issue of the ageing EU population and consequently the case of replacement migration. The final section contains concluding comments.

Types of European Migration and Statistical data

International migration flows are categorized either from the point of view of the sending and receiving countries, or based upon the intensions and characteristics of the migrants. Both classifications, however, have problems and we will try here to include the classification adopted by the International Labour Organization and the World Bank.[3] First, we distinguish between immigration and emigration, regular and irregular migration, economic migrants and asylum-seekers. We shall then explain temporary and replacement migration, before finally analysing the role of remittances.

Immigration and Emigration

Immigration describes the case of migration flows into a country, often called the receiving or host country, while emigration describes migration outflows from a country, which is often called the sending or home country.

Regular Migration and Irregular or Illegal Migration

By regular migration we mean that migrants are authorized to enter the receiving country and to engage in activities under the laws and regulations of that country. Irregular or illegal migration, on the other hand, is when workers cross borders into foreign countries without the required authorization, or initially enter legally but then abuse their residence permit or visa to become illegal immigrants. From the economic point of view there is no basic difference between the causes of legal versus illegal migration other than the higher costs and uncertainty related to the illegal case.[4] Illegal immigration has recently become a topic of increasing interest worldwide, and in many OECD countries the quantitative importance of illegal migration is growing. In the European Union, for example, there were more than 3.0 million illegal migrants in 1996; and Lianos et al. (1996) report that Greece, a traditional emigration country, has become a net immigration country with illegal immigration from Albania equivalent to 9 per cent of the Greek labour force. In the USA the number of illegal workers is estimated to be between 3.5 and 4.0 million. Moreover, poor living standards and political unrest in many parts of the world are expected to raise the scale of migratory movements in the future.[5]

Economic Migrants versus Asylum-Seekers

Economic migrants are legal or illegal migrants that care about economic conditions both in the country of origin and the destination country. On the other hand, asylum-seekers are people pushed out of their country due to political persecution, civil war or violation of human rights.[6] Thus, the main difference between asylum-seekers and economic migrants is that asylum-seekers do not care about economic conditions in the country of origin. However, empirical evidence shows that they are sensitive to differences in economic conditions between potential destination countries (Zimmermann (1996)). As can be seen from Table 10.1, the total number of asylum-seekers in Europe was about 158,000 in 1980, 170,000 in 1985, 695,000 in 1992 and 344,000 in 1998. Clearly, Germany, the UK, the Netherlands, Switzerland, Belgium and France were the countries which attracted most of the asylum-seekers in the period 1980–98.

Table 10.1 Asylum-seekers in selected countries (000s)

	1980	1981	1982	1983	1984	1985	1986	1987	1988	1989	1990	1991	1992	1993	1994	1995	1996	1997	1998
Europe																			
Austria	9.3	34.6	6.3	5.9	7.2	6.7	8.6	11.4	15.8	21.9	22.8	27.3	16.2	4.7	5.1	5.9	7.0	6.7	13.8
Belgium[a]	2.7	2.4	3.1	2.9	3.7	5.3	7.6	6	4.5	8.1	13	15.4	17.7	26.5	14.7	11.7	12.4	11.8	22.0
Denmark[b]	0.2	0.3	0.3	0.3	4.3	8.7	9.3	2.7	4.7	4.6	5.3	4.6	13.9	14.3	6.7	5.1	5.9	5.1	5.7
Finland							0.1	0	0.1	0.2	2.7	2.1	3.6	2	0.8	0.8	0.7	1.0	1.3
France	18.8	19.8	22.5	22.3	21.6	28.8	26.2	27.6	34.3	61.4	54.8	47.4	28.9	27.6	26	20.4	17.4	21.4	21.8
Germany[c]	107.8	49.4	37.2	19.7	35.3	73.8	99.7	57.4	103.1	121.3	193.1	256.1	438.2	322.6	127.2	127.9	116.4	104.4	98.7
Greece[d]				0.5	0.8	1.4	4.3	6.3	9.3	6.5	4.1	2.7	2	0.8	1.3	1.4	1.6	4.4	2.6
Italy[a]				3.1	4.6	5.4	6.5	11	1.4	2.3	4.7	31.7	2.6	1.3	1.8	1.7	0.7	1.9	4.7
Luxemburg										0.1	0.1	0.2	0.1	0.2	0.2	0.2	0.3	0.4	1.6
Netherlands	1.3	0.8	1.2	2	2.6	5.6	5.9	13.5	7.5	13.9	21.2	21.6	20.3	35.4	52.6	29.3	22.9	34.4	45.2
Norway	0.1	0.1	0.1	0.2	0.3	0.8	2.7	8.6	6.6	4.4	4	4.6	5.2	12.9	3.4	1.5	1.8	2.3	8.3
Portugal	1.6	0.6	0.4	0.6	0.2	0.1	0.1	0.2	0.3	0.1	0.1	0.2	0.6	2.1	0.8	0.5	0.3	0.3	0.3
Spain[e]				1.4	1.1	2.3	2.8	3.7	4.5	4.1	8.6	8.1	11.7	12.6	12	5.7	4.7	5.0	6.5
Sweden				4	12	14.5	14.6	18.1	19.6	30	29.4	27.4	84	37.6	18.6	9	5.8	9.6	13.0
Switzerland	6.1	5.2	7.1	7.9	7.4	9.7	8.5	10.9	16.7	24.4	35.8	41.6	18	24.7	16.1	17	18.0	24.0	41.2
UK	9.9	2.4	4.2	4.3	4.2	6.2	5.7	5.9	5.7	16.8	38.2	73.4	32.3	28.5	42.2	55	37.0	41.5	57.7
EU total	157.8	115.6	82.4	75.1	105.3	169.3	202.6	183.3	234.1	320.1	437.9	564.4	695.3	553.8	329.5	293.1	252.9	274.2	344.4
Others																			
United States	26.5	61.6	33.3	26.1	24.3	16.6	18.9	26.1	60.7	101.7	73.6	56.3	104	144.2	146.5	154.5	128.2	79.8	50.8
Canada				5	7.2	8.4	23	35	45	19.9	36.7	32.3	37.7	21.1	21.7	25.6	25.7	22.6	22.6
Australia										0.5	3.8	17	4.1	4.6	4.2	5.1	6.0	9.3	7.8
Total	184.3	177.2	115.7	106.2	136.8	194.3	244.5	244.4	339.8	442.1	551.9	669.8	841	723.5	501.7	478.1	159.9	111.7	81.2

Notes:

[a] Excluding dependent children; [b] excluding application outside Denmark and rejected applications at the border; [c] including dependent children if parents requested asylum for them; [d] figures for 1989–92 are the sum of the applications registered with the Greek authorities and those registered with the United Nations High Commissioner for Refugees; [e] excluding dependents; [f] excluding children and some accompanying adults.

Source: Eurostat, Migration Statistics, *Yearbook* 1995; and Systeme d' Observation Permanente des Migration (SOPEMI), OECD database, International Migration Statistics, 1999.

The problem with asylum migration is that it causes certain costs to receiving countries such as administration, housing and maintenance expenses. In France the costs associated with asylum-seekers amounted to FF52.9 million in 1988, which increased to FF142.9 million in 1990; in Germany the figures were DM143.5 in 1992 and DM486 million in 1993. With the numbers of asylum-seekers and the associated costs increasing rapidly, most governments have had to impose higher restrictions. Due, however, to *asylum-shopping* behaviour[7] there is interdependence between countries in changing legislation since softer asylum laws in one country induce more asylum-seekers into that country. Thus, monetary costs and the asylum-shopping behaviour have induced many countries to take measures restricting asylum applications. To show the relative costs associated with an asylum-seeker it is better to express the number of asylum-seekers as a proportion of the foreign population. The countries with the highest proportions (relative costs) are the Netherlands, Sweden, Austria, Germany and Switzerland. As is evident from Figure 10.1 and Table 10.1, inflows of asylum-seekers have been lower since 1993 with the exception of the Netherlands, Switzerland, the UK and Belgium.

Temporary or Contract or Host-Worker Migration

This type of migration includes low-skilled and low-paid workers. A typical example is the European guest-worker programme and the resulting large-scale migration flows in the late 1950s and 1960s until 1973. This migration covered temporary gaps in the labour market of Western European countries such as Belgium, France and Germany, from the lesser-developed Mediterranean countries, with the intention that migrants would return to their countries after the period of invitation.[8] Indeed, Western European economies in their path to economic development pursued, from the 1950s up to the mid-1970s, relatively liberal migration policies. Given the large income differences between EU-host countries and non-EU sending countries,[9] these liberal policies of the EU resulted in large migration inflows that were self-perpetuated in subsequent years due to network migration (see below, on the modelling of international migration), and also due to the complementarity between domestic and foreign labour.[10] Moreover, as can be seen from Figure 10.2, migration flows increased dramatically during 1980–97. As a result of these human flows, by 1994 there were about 5 million people from the EU living in other member states, with the majority in Germany, France and the UK.[11]

Figure 10.1 Inflows of asylum-seekers, 1990–99 (per 100 foreigners at the beginning of each year)

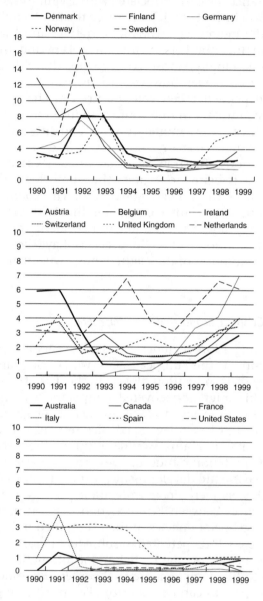

Note:

For Australia, Canada and the United States, the inflows of asylum-seekers are compared with the foreign-born population.

Source: 'Trends in International Migration', OECD, 2000

Figure 10.2 Inflows of foreigners in some OECD countries, 1980–98 (000s per 1,000 inhabitants and per 100 foreigners)

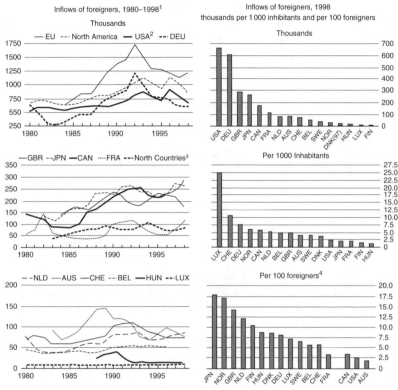

Note:
Data for the United Kingdom are from the International Passenger Survey; for Australia, Canada, France and the United States data are from permits of residence. For all other countries, data are based on Population Registers.
[1] The host countries have been split into 3 groups according to the volume of inflows in 1998.
[2] Excluding immigrants legalized under IRCA regularization programme.
[3] Excluding Finland and Iceland.
[4] For Australia, Canada and the United States, the inflows in 1998 are related to the stocks of foreign-born residents (last census data).

AUS	Australia
BEL	Belgium
CAN	Canada
CHE	Switzerland
DEU	Germany
DNK	Denmark
FIN	Finland
FRA	France
GBR	United Kingdom
HUN	Hungary
JPN	Japan
LUX	Luxembourg
NLD	Netherlands
NOR	Norway
SWE	Sweden
USA	United States

Source: 'Trends in International Migration', OECD, 2000

Replacement Migration

Replacement migration according to UN is the international migration that a country would need in order to offset population decline and population ageing resulting from low fertility and mortality rates. For example, according to a United Nations population report, in the period 1995–2050 countries like Italy will incur a reduction of between one-quarter and one-third of their 1995 populations. Such a future reduction in population and consequently in the workforce of Italy would raise doubts about the viability of the social welfare system of that country. It is suggested, therefore, that countries facing a decline in their population should allow replacement migration to be able to maintain their social welfare system intact (this topic is examined in more detail later).

Remittances

Remittances are the financial flows associated with the migration flows. They are the part of the migrant's income that is sent back to his country either for consumption or productive reasons. The total volume of global remittances was $2 billion in 1970 and increased to $66 billion in 1989 and about $70 billion in 1995.[12] Table 10.2 shows the remittances in several selected countries where a minus sign shows a net outflow from the country and a positive sign a net inflow into the country. Thus, we can see that the USA and Kuwait are countries that face net outflows, while in Europe the main source countries of remittances are Germany, France, the Netherlands and Norway to the benefit of recipient countries Turkey, Spain and, in the period before 1994, Greece, Italy and Portugal.

Modelling International Migration

In this section we present, briefly, the basic theoretical approaches to modelling international migration; we refer the reader to the references at the end for a more detailed analysis, and especially to Bauer and Zimmermann (1995a), Ghatak and Daly (1998) and Agiomirgianakis (1999) whom we follow quite closely here. However, it should be noted that most of the models and methodology adopted by the literature on international migration are based on the literature of internal migration,[13,14] allowing, of course, for country rather than region effects and also stressing the role of legal restrictions (Bauer and Zimmermann (1995a)).

Table 10.2 Workers' remittances, receipts (BoP, current US$) in selected countries, 1980–94

	1980	1981	1982	1983	1984	1985	1986	1987	1988	1989	1990	1991	1992	1993	1994
European															
Austria	-67	-55	-25	-2	6	28	82	178	202	179	307	240	74	44	33
France	-2,591	-2,375	-2,052	-1,854	-1,481	-1,652	-1,923	-2,053	-1,952	-1,687	-1,978	-1,788	-1,807	-1,530	-1,290
Germany	-4,437	-3,625	-3,393	-3,237	-3,161	-2,740	-3,447	-4,090	-4,250	-3,995	-4,379	-3,858	-4,385	-4,133	-4,634
Greece	1,066	1,057	1,016	912	898	775	942	1,334	1,675	1,350	1,775	2,115	2,366	2,360	0
Italy	1,609	1,486	1,510	1,465	1,418	1,346	1,560	1,600	1,480	1,460	1,236	814	531	432	242
Netherlands	-316	-296	-230	-200	-171	-172	-227	-298	-268	-250	-298	-317	-358	-353	-395
Norway	-23	-25	-29	-27	-20	-28	-42	-55	-51	-67	-114	-203	-257	-228	-236
Portugal	2,928	2,831	2,601	2,150	2,152	2,091	2,580	3,254	3,378	3,562	4,263	4,517	4,650	3,844	0
Spain	1,647	1,294	1,117	935	837	918	1,082	1,213	1,413	1,425	1,747	1,603	1,841	1,544	1,780
Sweden	0	0	-56	-60	-21	-20	-28	-16	-10	28	19	20	54	90	89
Switzerland	-603	-570	-805	-783	-726	-712	-1,064	-1,398	-1,534	-1,488	-1,980	-2,062	-2,141	-2,007	0
Turkey	2,071	2,490	2,140	1,513	1,807	1,714	1,634	2,021	1,776	3,040	3,246	2,819	3,008	2,919	2,627
Others															
Egypt	2,696	2,181	2,082	3,165	3,931	3,496	2,973	3,012	3,384	3,532	3,743	3,751	5,478	4,960	5,073
El Salvador	11	42	78	92	114	126	139	167	194	204	322	468	686	789	967
Ethiopia	22	27	47	90	109	147	211	150	122	189	174	201	316	248	0
India	2,786	2,333	2,525	2,568	2,509	2,219	2,339	2,724	2,225	2,186	1,947	2,540	2,086	3,050	3,200
Indonesia	0	0	0	10	53	61	71	86	99	167	166	130	229	346	480
Jamaica	51	63	73	37	20	88	47	54	74	114	131	130	150	181	0
Jordan	715	929	976	1,110	1,237	1,021	1,184	939	894	623	380	450	800	1,040	1,093
Kuwait	-6,92	-6,89	-8,75	-8,65	-9,63	-1,044	-1,084	-1,102	-1,179	-1,283	-7,70	-4,26	-8,29	-12,29	-1,445
Mexico	687	840	837	984	1,127	1,157	1,290	1,478	1,897	2,213	2,492	2,414	3,070	3,332	3,705
Morocco	989	967	812	882	845	950	1,383	1,571	1,289	1,325	1,995	1,973	2,148	1,945	2,072
New Zealand	143	138	164	167	204	166	166	192	263	266	246	247	266	256	0
Pakistan	1,748	2,097	2,227	2,888	2,738	2,456	2,597	2,280	2,013	1,897	1,942	1,848	1,468	1,562	1,446
Tunisia	304	342	361	351	306	260	351	479	539	482	591	562	563	589	675
United States	-810	-4,070	-4,420	-4,710	-5,170	-5,480	-5,890	-6,450	-6,700	-7,140	-7,410	-7,570	-7,540	-7,660	-7,680

Source: World Development Indicators, CD-Rom, World Bank, 1999.

Neoclassical Model

According to this model the decision to migrate abroad is based on a utility maximization of a potential migrant, under a budget constraint. Migrants face two alternative 'work regimes', either to work at home or to work abroad. Differences in labour market conditions between the home country and abroad result in a wage differential between them. For example, a large supply of labour relative to capital at home will create a low equilibrium wage at home. On the other hand, a low supply of labour relative to capital endowment in the foreign country will result in a high foreign wage. As a result of these different labour-market conditions between the home and foreign countries, there will be a wage differential in favour of the foreign country. Moreover, the utility of the potential migrant depends positively on the wage earned in each country, for example a higher wage abroad will most probably allow her/him a higher utility abroad than at home. Hence, a wage differential in favour of the foreign country will be the driving force in inducing workers to migrate and work abroad rather than staying and working at home. This approach can be traced back to Hicks (1932) who noted that 'differences in net economic advances, chiefly differences in wages, are the main causes of migration'. The neoclassical model assumes a market-clearing wage, which of course is in sharp contrast to the high unemployment in several western countries and especially in Europe. One, for example, could argue that the migration decision should depend not only on the wage differential, but also on the relative employment/unemployment rates since the migrant could not be certain of finding a job abroad. This has prompted an extension of the neoclassical model into the case of unemployment by the Harris–Todaro model,[15] thereafter called the HT model, where the utility of the migrant depends rather on the *expected* wage differential than the actual one. The expected wage differential depends on the probability of the potential migrant to find a job at his destination, which, in turn, depends on the unemployment rate in the destination country.[16] The predictions of the HT model are that: (a) an increase in the foreign wage or a decrease in the home wage will increase migration; (b) an increase in the migration cost will increase migration; and (c) an increase in employment abroad will increase migration (Ghatak *et al.* (1996)).

Human Capital Theory

The human capital model, hereafter called the HC model, assumes that migration is an investment in human capital.[17] Human capital is the set of skills, knowledge and experience that a worker can acquire by education and training, and an increase in the stock of capital embodied in an individual will improve his/her productivity and thus his/her capacity to earn more in the future. As in the case of physical capital, the stock of human capital can increase by undertaking an investment that implies certain financial costs, on the expectation of obtaining future higher earnings. Migration can be seen as an investment in human capital because the migrant incurs for a certain period of time some sacrifices, for example foregone earnings at home, psychic and transportation costs, in order to obtain higher expected earnings abroad. According to this view, if the present value of the expected earnings from migration exceeds the present value of the investment costs an individual will decide to migrate. Equation (1) formalizes these arguments:

$$U_p = \sum_{1}^{N} \frac{E_{ft} - E_{ht}}{(1+r)^t} - \sum_{1}^{N} \frac{C}{(1+r)^t} - P \tag{1}$$

where U_P is the present value of net benefits; E_{ft} is the earnings from work abroad in year t; E_{ht} is the earnings from the existing work in the home country in year t; r is the discount rate (interest rate); C is the direct and indirect cost of moving such as transportation, visas, and telecommunication costs; and P represents the psychic costs associated with the move.

If $U_p > 0$ then the expected earnings from migration are larger than the expected costs, and hence it will be worthwhile for the individual to migrate abroad.

The predictions of the HM model are:

- The likelihood of migrating abroad is a decreasing function of age, since older individuals have a shorter time horizon to gain higher future earnings by migrating abroad, and they also incur higher costs such as transportation and psychic costs.
- The higher the educational level of an individual the more likely it is that this individual will migrate abroad. This is so because there is a wider spectrum of salaries offered to higher-education graduates (thus, higher expected earnings) than to less-qualified workers, where we also often observe minimum wage legislation and national wage determination (McConnell and Brue (1995)). Also, a higher educational level is associated with a higher ability to collect, absorb and process information about the destination country, thus resulting in a lower migration cost (Bauer and Zimmermann (1995a)). Finally, education increases the adaptability of a person to adjust to different occupations and lifestyles (Ghatak and Daly (1998)).
- The probability of migrating abroad is a decreasing function of the distance between the origin and destination countries. A greater distance will not only increase the direct transportation costs, it will

also increase the cost of obtaining information about job opportunities abroad.

Family Migration

Instead of treating migration as an individual's decision, the recent literature on international migration treats it as a family or a household decision (see, for example, Stark (1991)). According to this model, the family is not only an income or utility maximizer; it also minimizes the risk associated with the labour market in the home country. Indeed, migration can be seen as a risk-sharing behaviour since by having some members of the family working abroad, the family can smooth out any worsening of economic conditions in the home labour market. Thus, the family, by diversifying its total work time into different labour markets in a way similar to portfolio diversification by an investor, manages to reduce the risk. This model is appropriate to explain migration flows even if there are no wage differentials between the home country and abroad. Also, some models following this approach, the *relative deprivation* models, by taking into account the income distribution in the home country suggest that international migration may also take place due to welfare competition between emigrating families. More specifically, these models suggest that there is a higher incentive for a family to migrate abroad, if it were among rich emigrating families than if it was among poor ones (see Stark (1991)). These family models of international migration are more appropriate to explain emigration from developing countries (Bauer and Zimmermann (1995a)).

Network Migration

This approach emphasizes the cost side of international migration and especially the cost of acquiring information about the foreign labour market and the cost of adjustment while abroad.[18] These models adopt the view that first migrants face higher costs in obtaining information about the host labour market than their relatives or friends that may follow their steps. Also the risks of finding a job abroad and establishing themselves abroad are lower for subsequent migrants compared to the first migrants due to better networking. In other words, the first migrants confer a positive externality on those who follow at a later stage.[19] As a result of this network effect, migration is expected to increase in the future provided that the first wave of migrants has been successfully established in the host country. This approach can explain the self-perpetuating character of migration since for every successful migration abroad there will be better economic and risk conditions for subsequent migrants.

Macroeconomic Models of International Migration

All the above models examine international migration within a microeconomic framework. Indeed, international migration has been relatively less-analysed in the context of a macroeconomic framework,[20] among the few exemptions being Agiomirgianakis (1999, 2000) and Agiomirgianakis and Zervoyianni (2001a, b). However, modelling international migration in a macroeconomic framework is important for several reasons. First, in the last two decades it has been generally recognized that the behaviour of the labour markets is crucial to macroeconomic performance. Thus, factors like international migration, which affects the stock, age structure and skills of a country's labour force, eventually affect the productive capacity of the economy and hence its overall performance. Second, because the micro-literature on international migration borrows assumptions and methodology from the literature on internal labour mobility, a key element of international migration is lost, namely that labour is moving away from countries with a relatively weaker currency towards countries with a relatively stronger currency. This implies that the real exchange rate is important in understanding international labour flows.[21] Yet, in the world of flexible exchange rates, real wage differentials vary according to the real-exchange-rate variability. The macroeconomic literature on international migration, by endogenizing migration flows, examines how governmental and trade-union policies will affect migration flows, as well as how migration flows may affect the macroeconomic variables, policies and wage-setting either within a single country or between countries.[22] More specifically, the predictions of the macroeconomic models of international migration are that:

- inflationary pressures associated with expansionary monetary policies will be lower
- the welfare of trade unions and policy-makers may improve
- the variability of the real exchange rate could be lower
- intergovernmental cooperation in the monetary field may be advantageous

Empirical Evidence on the Determinants of International Human Flows Into and Within Europe

Economic theory, as we have already seen in the modelling of international migration, suggests a number of factors that may influence migration decisions and the resulting migration flows. In this section we present the findings of several empirical studies[23] that have tried to identify and quantify the determinants of European migration. In general, factors associated with the sending (or home) country are identified as *push factors*, for example high home unemployment, low income or poverty, political instability and population growth; while factors associated with the host country are called *pull factors*, for example high wages abroad, availability of jobs, a social security system and political stability (Rotte and Volger (1998)).[24]

Wages or Incomes and Wage/Income Differentials

Most empirical findings confirm that migration flows are positively related to wages or income in the host country and negatively related to wages or income in the sending country.[25] The Harris–Todaro (HD) model suggests that *expected wages*, that is wages weighted by unemployment rates rather than actual ones, are inducing migration, and Straubhaar (1988) has confirmed this prediction of the HD model.

Other studies examining the *relative income*, that is the income differential between working at home and in a host country,[26] have also found that an increase in this differential results in an increase in international migration.[27] For example, Brücker (2000), in a study of migration from Central Eastern and European Countries (CEEC) towards Germany, finds that an increase of 1 per cent in the income differential will result in an increase of 1.3 per cent in the long-run stock of migrants. Zimmerman's (1996) findings suggest that not only economic migrants, but also asylum-seekers are sensitive to differences in relative wages, but in this case between potential host countries rather than between the host and sending country. Moreover, Faini (1993), examining the role of economic development in the sending countries, advocate that migrations from Southern to Northern Europe exhibit an *inverse-U pattern* suggesting that increases in the home country's income will result in more emigration, as more migrants will be able to afford the costs associated with the migration move. Rotte and Volger (1998) also confirm this inverse-U relationship between migration and income in the sending country by using data on immigration from 86 countries to Germany. This result, however, creates some doubts for the validity of policies that are designed to stem emigration from developing countries into the EU. Indeed, any measure undertaken by the EU that could improve welfare in the sending country would probably induce more migration inflows into the EU at least in an initial stage.

Unemployment Rates

Ghatak *et al.* (1996) suggest that unemployment may affect migrants in three different ways. First, individuals by being unemployed at home are more likely to migrate abroad, especially if they are heads of the family. This effect is, in turn, negatively affected by the size of the unemployment benefit and the duration of the unemployment. Second, for risk-averse migrants unemployment differentials are more important than wage differentials. Third, increases in national unemployment rates may deter first-time movers more than subsequent migrants. Consequently, one would expect that relative unemployment rates at home should be a push factor and high employment abroad a pull factor. While this may in principle be true, the empirical evidence on the importance of relative unemployment rates is inconclusive[28] (see, for example, Bauer and Zimmermann (1995a) and Ghatak et al., (1996)). Kau and Sirmans (1976), Fields (1991), Katseli and Glytsos (1989) and Hughes and McCormick (1994) find that migration flows are negatively correlated with employment opportunities in the host country, while employment opportunities at home have no clear effect on migration outflows. The findings of Lianos (2001) suggest that migrants' choice of place of residence is not affected by the unemployment rate. On the other hand, the findings of Faini (1993), Faini and Venturini (1994) and Brücker (2000) seem to suggest that high unemployment at home and/or high employment abroad encourages migration. Brücker (2000) claims that an increase in the employment rate of the host country by 1 per cent will increase the stock of migrants in Germany by 3.9 per cent to 4.4 per cent and, conversely, an increase in employment rates at home by 1 per cent, will decrease the stock of migrants by 3.6 per cent to 4.3 per cent. Furthermore, Ermisch's (1995) study of Irish migration to the UK confirms that for risk-averse migrants unemployment differentials are indeed more important than wage differentials. More specifically, he finds that the sensitivity of net migration to unemployment differential is 10 times higher than to the real wage differential.

Distance between the Origin and the Host Country and Education

The distance between the origin and the host country is a proxy of the direct costs and risks associated with the decision to migrate. Most empirical studies show that distance negatively influences migration flows. That is, a higher distance between origin and destination implies higher direct costs and risks resulting in lower migration flows.[29] However, more-educated migrants are less-influenced by the distance factor when taking their migration decision, which suggests that the distance factor has to do mainly with information costs of migration rather than the direct costs of migration such as flight tickets.[30] Also, education has a direct positive impact on migration flows[31] reflecting, as we have seen, a higher ability of educated migrants to collect, absorb and process information about the destination country, as well as a higher ability to adjust while abroad.

Networking

As we have already seen, networking allows migrants to acquire information about the foreign market and facilitates an easier adjustment while abroad. Thus networking has cost and risk-reducing effects that should encourage migration flows, and empirical evidence confirms that networking is a highly significant positive factor in migration flows.[32]

Political Factors

Political instability or social unrest in the home country can induce more emigration. Rotte and Volger's (1998) findings suggest that asylum migration is highly influenced by conditions of political terror in the home country, but is unaffected by the degree of political rights and liberties at home. However, overall immigration flows are positively influenced by the degree of political rights, and, moreover, Brücker (2000) reports that the civil war in Yugoslavia (1991–98) had a significant impact on immigration in Germany.

The Role of Governments

The positive effects that emigration has on the sending country (see next section) induced several net emigration countries to follow *emigration-promoting* policies in the past, as for example in Turkey, the Philippines, Portugal, South Korea, India, Pakistan, Bangladesh, Sri Lanka, Jamaica, Cuba, Barbados, Mexico, El Salvador and Nicaragua.[33] On the other hand, labour shortages induced many European governments to encourage, organize and actively promote immigration into their countries,[34] as for example in the invitation of foreign workers (guest worker agreements) to West Germany in the post-second World War period upto 1973. Indeed, Bohning (1970) shows that labour demand pressure in the host country was the main determinant of migration flows in West Germany for 1957–68, provided that there was large unemployment in the home country. This is a view also shared by Fischer and Straubhaar (1997) in examining German immigration during the period 1960 to 1992. Moreover, the guest worker agreements of Germany in the 1960s and 1970s had a much more significant impact on immigration into Germany than the free movement of labour established by the internal market in 1992, as suggested by Brücker (2000). Furthermore, econometric studies on the role of government policy in influencing migration flows also show that the inclusion of policy variables in explaining migration flows is significant.[35] For example, Rotte and Volger (1998) found that the tightening up of migration law in Germany had the expected negative effects. Finally, another example of government intervention is the invitation by the German government (summer 2000) to about 20,000 IT specialists from third-world countries and similar policies adopted by the Irish government (see the discussion on *Brain Drain*).

Age

Age affects the probability of someone migrating abroad. In general, older workers are less likely to migrate abroad than their younger fellow workers.[36] However, studies that allow for a non-linear relationship between age and migration have found an inverted U-pattern; the most likely age period for an individual to migrate abroad is between 20 and 33 years of age, as can be seen from Figure 10.3.

Common Language and Cultural Affinity

A common language can significantly reduce the costs faced by a potential migrant since it allows an easier acquisition of information before and after migration takes place and a less painful adjustment while abroad. Brücker (2000) finds that a common language is indeed a significant factor of migration flows into the EU, and Molle (1988) finds that cultural affinity is also a significant factor. Moreover, Bauer *et al.* (2002) find that migrants not speaking the language of the host country choose to migrate to destinations with large ethnic enclaves which are potential 'language traps'.

International Trade

According to the Heckscher–Ohlin (H–O) model, labour migration and international trade are substitutes. Thus a country where labour is abundant will export labour and import capital. Mundell (1957), extending the H–O model, suggested that an increase in international trade barriers induces migration flows while an increase in restrictions to factor movement stimulates international trade.[37] However, Markusen (1983) showed that Mundell's conclusions are not valid if the reasons for international trade are differences in technology or preferences; in that case, international trade and migration are complements. Quoting Molle (1988), 'factors will move to those countries where they are used intensively in the production of export goods'.[38] Indeed, several studies such as Kohli (1999) and Rotte and

Figure 10.3 Per cent distribution of immigrants by age in Australia, Canada and the United States, and model patterns

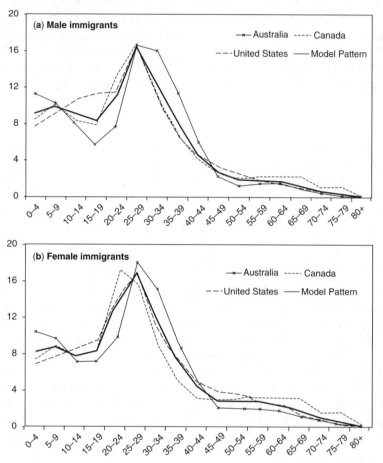

Note:
The model pattern is the average of the three countries.
Source: United Nations Populations Division, *Replacement Migration,* May 2001

Volger (1998) suggest that migration and international trade are complements, but this evidence is not conclusive yet as suggested by Faini *et al.* (1999) and Faini (1993).[39]

Population Growth

Population growth in the sending country has often been stressed as a rather important factor of migration; however, empirical evidence has not supported this prediction (Rotte and Volger (1998)).

European Migration: Effects on the Host and Receiving Countries

The existence of international migration has several policy implications, both at home and in the receiving country. In the home country it is expected to relieve unemployment pressures, to create an income from abroad and to contribute to economic development. In the receiving country it contributes to the flexibilization of the labour market, it changes the age structure of the population and it is often accused of depressing wages. In this section we examine these effects and present the appropriate empirical evidence in favour or against these predictions.

Unemployment

In examining the effect of migration on unemployment one has to distinguish between the asymmetric effects of *immigration* and *emigration*. Consider first the case of *immigration* into European markets. Empirical research finds no significant effect of immigration on aggregate domestic unemployment rates in member states. For example, Dolado *et al.* (1996), in their study on the effects of immigration in Spain suggests that labour-market outcomes for Spanish unskilled labour did not worsen due to immigration and that total employment increased. In Germany, empirical evidence shows that most of the immigrant groups are complements[40] to natives rather than substitutes (Bauer (1997)). In Italy, Venturini's (1997) study of illegal immigration shows that at the aggregate level there is a particularly small substitution effect on domestic labour while, at the same time, there is evidence of complementarity in certain sectors such as non-tradable services. In Greece, where illegal migration in 1994 was estimated to be about 9 per cent of the Greek labour force, Lianos *et al.* (1996) report a small substitution effect and an overall net contribution of illegal migration to Greek GDP of about 1 per cent. In France, Gros (2002) finds that there may exist temporary small adverse effects in the labour market, but that in the long run there is a negative relation between unemployment and immigration. In general, the empirical evidence indicates that either there have been very small negative or nil effects of immigration.[41]

We consider next the case of emigration and its effects on unemployment in sending countries. Several studies have qualified a positive effect of emigration on the unemployment of sending countries (see, for example, Hazari (1994) where in a framework of skilled and unskilled labour he finds that domestic unemployment is affected by the emigration of skilled workers).[42] Empirical research also suggests a significant effect of emigration on domestic unemployment. For example, Van den Broeck (1996, pp. 82–97) notes that reduced unemployment in the sending country is one consideration that has led many countries to encourage emigration (for a similar point, see Ghatak *et al.* (1996)). He also notes that Pakistan emigration has provided jobs equivalent to almost one-third of the incremental labour force during the period 1978–83, and that emigration from the Republic of Korea reduced unemployment in Korea from 6.6 to 5.5 per cent during 1978–81. Funkhouser (1992) provides similar evidence for El Salvador. Finally, Van den Broeck (1996) notes that this positive effect of migration on unemployment depends on a number of factors such as: (a) the size of the migration flows, (b) structural deficiencies of the domestic labour market, and (c) on whether demographic pressures continue.

Wages

We consider first the case of immigration and its effects on wages in receiving countries. Immigration does not necessarily cause a depression of domestic real wages. Dolado *et al.* (1996), for example, reports a positive effect of migration on the wages of unskilled domestic workers in Spain, and empirical studies on immigration in Germany[43] have shown that most of the native labour groups have experienced higher earnings following immigration and thus fears of wage depression due to immigration are unjustified (Bauer (1997)).

For the case of emigration and its effects on wages in sending countries we first examine the theoretical basis and then present the results of empirical studies. Hazari (1994) and Agiomirgianakis (1999) find that outmigration results in an increase in rewards for the remaining potential migrants. Empirical evidence, including Rourke (1996), Ghosh (1996), Ghatak *et al.* (1996), Boyer *et al.* (1993) and Carrington *et al.* (1996) is also supportive. Rourke (1996) notes that Irish emigration in the past allowed the convergence of Irish wages to British levels. Ghosh (1996) also records many instances of positive effects of emigration on real wages, in particular, the case of the Republic of Korea in 1975–80 where wages in the construction sector increased sharply. Similarly, in Pakistan, Thailand and Sri Lanka, since the mid-1970s, wages of workers in occupations affected by migration rose faster than in other sectors. Boyer *et al.* (1993) presents similar results for Ireland. Indeed, this positive effect of migration outflows on real wages has induced countries such as the Philippines, Portugal and Turkey to make the export of workers an integral part of their economic development strategies (see for example Carrington *et al.* (1996)).

Remittances and Growth

By remittances we mean the sums of money transferred by migrants back to their home countries. The general assumption about why migrants remit some of their earnings back to their home countries is that they care about their remaining family members. However, remittances may also be:[44]

- payments for services provided to the migrant by a remaining member of the family;
- reimbursement for education costs incurred by the migrant's family;
- part of a contract with his family;
- the migrant's overall saving strategy and plan to return home at some moment in the future; or
- an intertemporal transfer from parents to children.

Thus remittances can facilitate consumption needs, as well as productive purposes of migrants and their families. For the origin country, however, remittances constitute a substantial source of income. For example, in 1989 remittances as a share of a country's exports were about 46.4 per cent for Yugoslavia, 43.9 per cent for Morocco, 29.1 per cent for Portugal, 26 per cent for Turkey, 23.1 per cent for Greece and 16.6 per cent for Tunisia.[45] This income can be used to finance temporary deficits in the balance of payments in the home country, as well as to create positive conditions for employment and economic growth in the sending country (Ghatak *et al.* (1996)). Moreover, the existence of remittances will increase the demand for financial infrastructure in the home country, resulting in an expansion of the home financial system including banking, finance and insurance.[46] Remittances constitute another reason, besides the relief of unemployment pressures and the expected increase in domestic wages, that many governments of developing countries such as Turkey, Portugal, India, Pakistan and Mexico have actively promoted labour exports in the past and during their paths to economic development.[47]

Brain Drain

Emigration is not only an attractive option to members of the unskilled labour force, it is even more attractive to highly skilled professionals such as medical doctors, IT specialists, engineers, scientists and other professionals who can expect much higher returns abroad and at much lower risks than an unskilled worker could expect. As we have already seen, educated and skilled people have a much higher probability of migrating abroad because they face lower information costs and higher adaptability when abroad. Also, given that the spectrum of wages is wide and at a higher level than for unskilled labour, it is reasonable to assume that the migration option will be more attractive and much easier to qualified and skilled individuals. This emigration of highly skilled individuals from developing countries into advanced countries has been refered to as *brain drain*.[48] Skilled labour immigration is encouraged by governments of receiving countries simply because they may easily find the appropriate skills and qualifications (human capital) they need for the well-functioning of their economies without undertaking the costs of creating those skills. A typical example is the summer 2000 invitation by the German government to 20,000 IT specialists from India and CEEC countries (*Economist*, 6 May 2000). Another recent example is the Irish plan to invite 200,000 skilled workers for a period of seven years.[49] On the other hand, this emigration of skilled and qualified labour from the sending and often poor countries deprives those countries of the human capital that was created to serve their own needs. Moreover, brain drain also changes the composition of skills within sending countries, as well as resulting in costs for those countries, which has led to suggestions of imposing a brain drain tax to reimburse sending countries for their costs in creating human capital.[50]

European Union Thinking on Migration and Migration Policies

In this section we present EU thinking on migration and migration policies for both intra-European (internal) migration as well as immigration from non-member states (external migration). In general, one can say that policy-makers in European countries would prefer a high level of internal migration and a low external rate.[51] Also, EU migration policy is in favour of skilled and highly qualified migrants. However, these migration policies may change in the future due to changes in the population structure of the EU.

Intra-European Migration

In EU labour markets, European employees are not distinguished with regard to their countries of origin: the European treaties guarantee a 'common labour market'. Article 48 of the Treaty of Rome stipulates that

> the freedom of movement of workers shall entail the abolition of any discrimination based on nationality between workers of the

member states as regards employment, remuneration and other conditions of work and employment.

Furthermore, Article (8a) of the Single European Act requires the achievement of free movement of people, capital goods and services from 1 January 1993.

Intra-EU migration has been stressed as one factor that could contribute to further flexibilization of European markets and thus to the success of European Monetary Union (EMU). In particular, the establishment of EMU has motivated a revival of the literature on optimum-currency-areas theory (OCAs), originated by Mundell (1961), which aimed to identify the conditions under which a monetary union of different countries or regions would be successful. One of the key factors of the well-functioning of an OCA is labour mobility.[52] Indeed, a high level of intra-EU migration by reducing imbalances between countries could reduce the need for policy adjustment in individual member countries, thus contributing to the well-functioning of the monetary union. This, in turn, could further facilitate the process of European integration and cohesion.[53] However, as is evident from Figure 10.4, intra-EU migration rates both in the euro zone and the EU-15 have been low for the period 1990–98, varying

Figure 10.4 Net migration rate in the EU and the euro zone, 1990–98

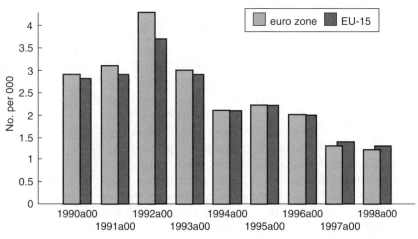

Note:

Net migration is estimated on the basis of the difference between population change and natural increase (corrected net migration); the figures are rates per thousand inhabitants.

Source: Eurostat database, Key Economic Indicators, March 2000.

from 1.5 to 4 per cent. The same picture emerges from Table 10.3 for selected countries, where the number of foreign employees has either remained about the same or has declined. For example, EU employees in Germany numbered 732,000 in 1980, but by 1993 they were reduced to 554,000; the same applies to France and the UK.

Migration rates are not only low between member countries, they are also low within each country. As Eichengreen (1997) notes, 'Americans move between US states about three times as frequently as Frenchmen move between *departments* and Germans move between *länder'*. Indeed, although wage differentials between members states are high,[54] European migration has been low and has not increased much following the establishment of the internal market in 1993. This low intra-migration is often attributed to cultural and linguistic barriers, as well as to similar employment situations among member states.[55] These factors may explain the low intra-migration rates in the EU compared to the much higher rates in the USA. Further prosperity and economic growth will make the prospect of an increase in internal migration in the future very unlikely. Although migration rates are low in the EU, the accumulated migration flows since the 1960s have created large shares of EU citizens in the total foreign population and the total foreign labour force as can be see from Figure 10.5.

External Migration

Political uncertainty in the Central Eastern and European countries (CEEC) and large differences in living standards between the EU and the CEEC have propelled migration flows into the EU, especially in the period 1985–95 with a peak in 1992, as can be seen from Figure 10.6 and Table 10.4. Contrary to the policies of encouraging internal migration, in the case of external migration the policies are designed to control it. The Schengen Accords' (I and II) objective is tighter external border controls and the elimination of internal border checks.[56] The Maastricht Treaty of 1992 set the framework for some harmonization of the visa policies and the policies for illegal migration and asylum laws, but these policies are far from being an explicit collective immigration policy of the EU since much is left to the discretion of individual states.[57] For example, the conditions or the duration of visa permission, as well as the mutual recognition of visa permissions among member states, have not been regulated. Thus each state, has to balance its own regulations with the general provisions of the EU.

Most EU countries have, however, adopted several measures such as tighter border controls, higher requirements for granting visa

Table 10.3 Foreign employees in EU countries (000s)

		Belgium	Denmark	Germany	Greece	Spain	France	Ireland	Italy	Luxemburg	Netherlands	Portugal	Finland	UK
Foreign employees total	1980	213	39	2,041	25	59	1,208	20	–	–	190	26	–	833
	1985	187	39	1,555	24	–	1,260	20	57	53	166	31	–	821
	1990	–	47	1,470	23	63	1,203	21	381	78	192	37	–	751
	1993	–	46	2,131	–	–	344	32	–	98	219	–	11	884
Of which: EU countries	1980	158	11	732	5	31	653	17	–	–	84	8	–	406
	1985	141	12	520	6	–	640	16	14	50	76	7	–	398
	1990	–	13	493	9	36	579	16	50	74	88	8	–	347
	1993	–	12	554	–	–	151	24	–	92	91	–	2	364
Of which: non-EU countries	1980	55	28[a]	1,309	19	28	555[a]	3	–	–	106	18	–	427
	1985	46	28	1,036	18	–	620	4	43	3	90	24	–	423
	1990	–	34	1,247	14	33	562	5	332	4	109	29	–	404
	1993	–	34	1,557	–	–	192	8	–	6	128	–	9	520

Notes:
[a] Data for 1981; Austria and Sweden are excluded because of non-availability of data.
Source: Eurostat database, Migration Statistics.

Figure 10.5 Foreigners in total population and labour force and European Union citizens in total foreign population and labour force; European OECD countries, 1997

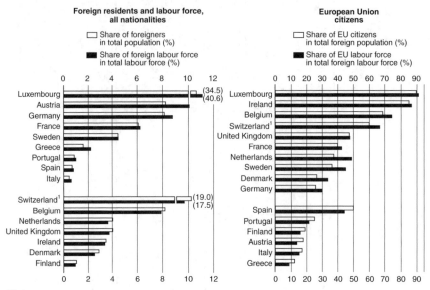

Note:

In both charts, the host countries have been split into two groups according to whether the proportion of foreigners (or Community citizens) in the labour force is higher or lower than their proportion in the total population (or in the total foreign population).[1] The data are from registers of foreigners. Figures for the labour force do not include seasonal and cross-border workers.

Sources: Eurostat, Labour Force Survey 1997; and Office Fédéral des Étrangers, Switzerland.

permissions, more frequent checks with employers, and new asylum laws that do not allow asylum-seekers from certain countries to apply for political asylum.[58] Also, EU countries are in favour of a more selective immigration policy, under an agreement with the sending country, for short-term employment of immigrants. Moreover, several policy-makers and researchers suggest the adoption of a more selective immigration policy that would be mainly targeted to highly qualified and skilled workers[59] as suggested by the endogenous growth literature that emphasizes the role of human capital. Highly qualified and skilled migrants by working in innovative sectors will contribute to a higher productivity and competitiveness of the host economy. Other researchers, however, have suggested several strategies in the past in order to stem unskilled external immigration, for example the

Figure 10.6 Gross inflows of foreign population i
Canada and Japan

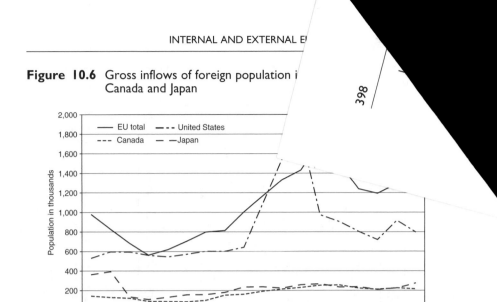

Source: SOPEMI, 1999, OECD database

promotion of trade with, and the increase of aid to sending counties. But from the empirical evidence presented earlier we know that these measures would require several years to work and would most probably lead to higher immigration in the short run.

EU policies on international migration may probably change in the future due to dramatic changes in the demographic profile of the EU population, particularly its ageing which we examine in the next subsection.

The Ageing EU Population and Replacement Migration

According to a United Nations population report,[60] the EU population is both declining and ageing due to the low fertility and longevity of Europeans. For example, in the period 1995–2050 countries like Italy will incur a reduction of between one-quarter and one-third of their 1995 populations. As a result of a smaller and older EU population, in the next 50 years there will be severe implications for healthcare and public-pensions systems in the EU. Consider, for example, the potential support ratio – that is the number of persons of working age (15–64) per old person. In Italy it will be reduced from 4 in 1995 to 2 in 2050; in Germany from 4.4 to 2.1; in the UK from 4.09 to 2.37; and for the EU-15 it will be reduced, on average, from 4.3 to 2. Clearly, this worsening of the support ratio raises doubts about the future

Table 10.4 Gross inflows of foreign population to selected countries, 1980–97 (000s)

	1980	1981	1982	1983	1984	1985	1986	1987	1988	1989	1990	1991	1992	1993	1994	1995	1996	1997
Europe																		
Belgium	46.8	41.3	36.2	34.3	37.2	37.5	39.3	40.1	38.2	43.5	50.5	54.1	55.1	53	56	53.1	51.9	49.2
Denmark				8.9	15.6	17.6	15.2	13.8	15.1	15.1	17.5	16.9	15.4	15.6	15.6	24.7		
Finland										4.2	6.5	12.4	10.4	10.9	7.6	7.3	7.5	8.1
France	59.4	75	144.4	64.2	51.4	43.4	38.3	39	44	53.2	102.4	109.9	116.6	99.2	69.3	56.7	75.5	102.4
Germany	631.4	501.1	312.7	273.2	331.1	398.2	478.3	473.3	648.5	770.8	842.4	920.5	1207.6	986.9	774	788.3	708.0	615.3
Luxembourg	7.4	6.9	6.4	6.2	6	6.6	7.4	7.2	8.2	8.4	9.3	10	9.8	9.2	9.2	9.6	9.2	9.7
Netherlands	79.8	50.4	40.9	36.4	37.3	46.2	52.8	60.9	58.3	65.4	81.3	84.3	83	87.6	68.4	67.0	77.2	76.7
Norway	11.8	13.1	14	13.1	12.8	15	16.8	23.8	23.2	18.5	15.7	16.1	17.2	22.3	17.9	16.5	17.2	22.0
Sweden				22.3	26.1	27.9	34	37.1	44.5	58.9	53.2	43.9	39.5	54.8	74.8	36.1	29.3	33.4
Switzerland	70.5	80.3	74.7	58.3	58.6	59.4	66.8	71.5	76.1	80.4	101.4	109.8	112.1	104	91.7	87.9	74.3	72.8
United Kingdom	69.8	59.1	53.9	53.5	51	55.4	47.8	46	49.3	49.7	53.2	53.9	52.6	55.6	55.1	55.5	216.4	236.9
EU total	976	827	683	561	620	705	799	814	1,004	1,168	1,331	1,432	1,720	1,498	1,239	1,193	1,291	1,226
North America																		
United States	530.6	596.6	594.1	559.8	543.9	570	601.7	601.5	643	1090.9	1536.5	1827.2	974	904.3	804.4	720.5	915.9	798.4
Canada	143.1	128.6	121.1	89.2	88.2	84.3	99.2	152.1	161.9	192	214.2	230.8	252.8	255.8	223.9	212.2	226.1	216.0
Others																		
Japan	362.5	393.1	134.3	108.1	131.1	156.5	157.5	180.3	234.8	237.4	223.8	258.4	267	234.5	237.5	209.9	225.4	274.8
Australia				93.2	69.8	78.1	92.4	113.3	143.5	145.3	121.2	121.7	107.4	76.3	69.8	87.4	99.1	85.8

Notes:

Includes holders of provisional work permits and foreigners admitted on family reunification grounds. Does not include residents of EEC countries who have not been brought in by the International Migration Office; entries of foreigners intending to stay longer than six months; some short-duration entries are not included; entries of foreigners with annual permits and those with permanent permits who return after a temporary stay abroad. Seasonal and frontier workers are excluded; entries correspond to permanent settlers within the meaning of the 1971 Immigration Act and subsequent amendments; permanent settlers only; asylum-seekers are excluded.

Sources: Systeme d' Observation Permanente des Migration (SOPEMI), OECD database, International Migration Statistics, 1999.

sustainability of social welfare systems and will force EU policy-makers to reassess their policies with respect to:

1   what is an appropriate age of retirement;
2   the level, type and nature of retirement and healthcare benefits for the elderly;
3   labour force participation; and
4   the contribution of workers and employees to support retirement and healthcare benefits for the increasing elderly population in the EU.

The above considerations imply a rethinking of EU policies[61] regarding *replacement migration*. More specifically, the UN report suggests that in order to maintain the same size of the working-age population, EU member states will need high annual inflows of migrants as illustrated in Figure 10.7. For example, both Italy and Germany will need about 6,000 annual immigrants per million inhabitants, and the EU will need on average about 4,100 per million domestic residents. Therefore, in the future the EU will probably need more migrants than it does now and so we may observe a sharp change in migration policies. It is also anticipated that this need for more migrants will raise further the issue of social inclusion and exclusion related to the integration of migrants and their descendants into the EU.

Figure 10.7   Average annual net number of migrants between 2000–50 to maintain size of working-age population per million inhabitants in 2000

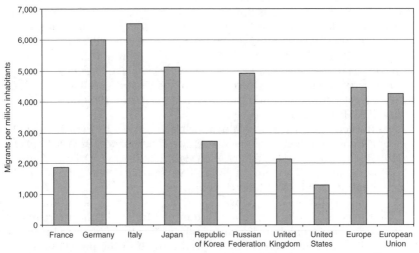

Source: United Nations, Department of Economics and Social Affairs – Population Division, *Replacement Migration*, 4 May 2000

Conclusions

European migration has been examined by considering both the empirical evidence and the economic theory that may explain this evidence. We presented the types of European migration and statistical data describing the flows of people and the associated financial flows. We also briefly discussed the basic theoretical approaches to modelling international migration, namely the neoclassical model, the human-capital theory, family migration, network migration and macroeconomic models. We then presented the empirical evidence on the determinants of the European migration, covering many European countries, which tries to identify and quantify the importance of each factor suggested by the theoretical models. The effects of international human flows were then examined, both in the sending country as well as the host European countries. More specifically, we considered the impact on unemployment and wages at home and in the host European countries. We also examined the significance of remittances and the issue of brain drain for sending countries, before finally considering European thinking and policies adopted so far, as well as future possibilities that may arise due to demographic reasons.

Notes

1 Opening Speech by Commissioner Antonio Vitorino for the conference on Migrations: Scenarios for the 21st Century, 21 July 2000 Rome. Also available on the website: *http://europa.eu.int/comm/comisioners/vitorio/ speeches/2000/julho/2000–12-jul-en_roma_conf _migrat _jubil.pdf*
2 See Russell and Teitelbaum (1992), whom we follow quite closely here.
3 See for example, *Migrants, Refugees and International Cooperation* (1994) by the International Labour Office. See also Russell and Teitelbaum (1992).
4 See 'Illegal Immigration and the Labour Market', July 1999 Bulletin of IZA, COMPACT, Germany.
5 See Zimmermann (1995) and Jahn and Straubhaar (1996) for a discussion of recent trends in migratory movements. See Espenshade (1995), School *et al.* (1996), Corry (1996), Dolado *et al.* (1996), Lianos *et al.* (1996), Venturini (1997), Bauer (1997), Goto (1998) and Straubhaar (1998) for a discussion of migratory trends in individual countries.
6 A formal definition of a refugee or asylum seeker is, according to the UN, a person who 'owing to a well-founded fear of being persecuted for reasons of race, religion, nationality. . . is outside the country of his nationality and is unable or unwilling to avail himself of the protection of that country'. See Russell and Teitelbaum (1992), whom we follow quite closely here.

7 That is, quoting Rotte *et al.* (1996) when 'asylum seekers are turned down in one country they use differentials in restrictiveness of law for reapplying in another country'.

8 See the paper by Russell and Teitelbaum (1992), from which we draw on the description of this migration type.

9 Income differences among the EU countries have decreased over time. Indeed, in 1960 the differences in GDP per capita between two groups of countries – the developed Western European countries (Denmark, Germany, France, Luxemburg and the UK) and the less-developed group of European countries (Greece, Spain, Italy, Portugal and Ireland) – were two and a quarter-fold. By 1970 they were reduced to less than two-fold; and by 1990 it was one and a half-fold.

10 See for example Werner (1996) and Fischer and Straubhaar (1997).

11 Bauer and Zimmerman (1995b)

12 See Stalker (2000).

13 See Mohlo (1986) for a review of the theories of migration.

14 See also the analysis of macroeconomic models of migration at the end of this section.

15 See Harris and Todaro (1970).

16 See Bauer and Zimmerman (1995a, b) for a detailed analysis and recent modifications of the neoclassical model.

17 See Sjaastad (1962) for measuring the costs and returns in a HC model.

18 See Massey (1990a, b) for more details.

19 See Carrington *et al.* (1996) for a theoretical treatment of this positive externality.

20 Withers (1994) notes that 'international economic analysis and policy have largely ignored the international flow of labour'.

21 See for example Bertola (1989).

22 For a two-country model with international migration, see Agiomirgianakis (1999, 2000) and Agiomirgianakis and Zervoyianni (2001a, b) where issues of interdependence and monetary-policy cooperation between policy-makers of different countries are examined.

23 Empirical studies on international migration are often restricted by poor quantity of data: missing information and incompatibilities of data from different sources. See Rotte and Volger (1998) and Brücker (2000).

24 See, however, Zimmermann (1996) for a different definition of pull and push factors according to the shifts in aggregate demand and supply in the host country.

25 See the studies for different EU countries: for example, Lundborg (1991) for Sweden, Hartog *et al.* (1989) for the Netherlands and Katseli *et al.* (1989) for Germany.

26 Bauer and Zimmermann (1995b) report that in 1993 the average worker's earnings in different CEEC countries as a percentage of German manufacturing earnings were: Hungary 14%, Poland 10.7%, the Czech Republic 9.7%, Slovakia 8.3%, Bulgaria 5.5% and Romania 3.5%.

27 See Bauer and Zimmermann (1995a) for a review. See Brücker (2000) for an analysis of migration determinants in Germany; Molle and Van Mourik (1989) in Europe; Geary and Ograda (1989) in the UK; Eriksson (1989)

in Sweden; Faini and Venturini (1994) in Europe; and Ermisch (1995) in the UK.

28 One explanation of these inconclusive results is the use of aggregate data of time-series studies. Aggregate unemployment rates may have a small effect, if at all, on those who are employed when they move compared to unemployed migrants.

29 Rotte and Volger (1998) find that distance is significant only for migrants from Asia.

30 Bauer and Zimmermann (1995a).

31 See O'Grada (1986).

32 See Rotte and Volger (1998) and Bauer and Zimmermann (1995a).

33 See Russell and Teitelbaum (1992) and Carrington et al. (1996), when referring to countries such as the Philippines, Portugal and Turkey that had made worker exports an integral part of their economic development strategy.

34 West Germany had set up offices in several sending countries in order to recruit emigrants for short contracts (Gastarbeiter). By 1973 the number of foreign workers was about 11 per cent of the German labour force (see Stalker (2000)).

35 See for example Molle (1988).

36 See for example Katseli et al. (1989).

37 In the case of satiability between migration and trade, one could raise the question as to what is the best policy – to have more trade or more migration. See Wellisch and Walz (1998) for a theoretical explanation of why rich countries may prefer trade rather than migration. There is a large area of research on the relation between trade and migration: see, for example, Faini et al. (1999) for a comprehensive coverage.

38 Molle et al. (1988) suggest a typical example: that migration of IT specialists accompanies trade flows in computers and software.

39 See Faini (1993) for findings suggesting a negative relationship between trade liberalization and migration. Also Faini et al. (1999) suggest that this relationship between trade and migration is much more complex than is often analysed, and stress the sensitivity of the relationship to financial and institutional constraints operating in the receiving country.

40 Foreign immigrants are complements to domestic workers if the presence of immigrants increases the employment or earnings of domestic workers; they are substitutes if they reduce either or both of these variables (earnings or employment). See Venturini (1997) for more details.

41 Ghatak et al. (1996) claim that there have been no adverse effects on the native labour market in terms of higher unemployment.

42 See also Agiomirgianakis (2000).

43 See Bauer (1997) for a review and also Haisken-De New and Zimmermann (1996) report that 'immigration has no effect on low-skilled workers, but a positive effect on the wages of the highly skilled'. They also find that trade (imports) has a worsening effect on German wages.

44 See, for example, Briere et al. (1996).

45 See Russell et al. (1992).

46 See also Russell and Teitelbaum (1992) and Ghatak et al. (1996).

47 See the role of governments described earlier.
48 The brain drain literature originated in the 1970s. See for example Bhagwati and Hamada (1974). It has been revived recently – see Miyagiwa (1991), Galor and Stark (1991) and Mountford (1997).
49 This example is cited in *The Economist*, 6 May 2000.
50 See for example Asheghian (1995).
51 See Faini and Venturini (1994).
52 The other factors are capital mobility, openness to international trade, wage and price flexibility, same objectives of member countries and the existence of asymmetric shocks.
53 See Faini *et al.* 1994.
54 Werner (1996) reports that wage ratios between the Northern and Southern European countries are about four to one and emigration from the southern countries is very limited despite the fact of the elimination of barriers to free movement of people according to the internal market.
55 See Eichengreen (1997).
56 See Bauer and Zimmermann (1995a, b) which we follow quite closely in this subsection.
57 See OECD (1999) for a detailed coverage of migration policies in several countries including the EU states.
58 These are the 'safe' countries, including the EU-states, Poland, the Czech Republic, Bulgaria, Romania, Hungary and others.
59 See Bauer and Zimmermann (1995b).
60 UN Population Report on Replacement Migration (17 March 2000). Available on web: *http://www.un.orgesa/population/unpop.htm.*
61 See Johnson and Zimmermann (1993) for the European dimension of ageing.

References

Agiomirgianakis, G.M. (1999) *The Macroeconomics of Open Economies under Labour Mobility* (Aldershot: Ashgate).
—(2000) 'Monetary Policy Games and International Migration in a Small Open Economy', *Review of International Economics*, vol. 8, pp. 698–711.
—and Zervoyianni, A. (2001a) 'Macroeconomic Equilibrium with Illegal Immigration', *Economic Modelling*, vol. 18, 181–201.
—and Zervoyianni, A. (2001b) 'Globalization of Labour Markets and Macroeconomic Equilibrium', *International Review of Economics and Finance*, vol. 10, pp. 109–13.
Asheghian, P. (1995) *International Economics* (Minneapolis: West Publishing).
Bauer, T. and Zimmermann, K.F. (1995a) 'Modelling International Migration: Economic and Econometric Issues', mimeo, Selapo, University of Munich, January.
—(1995b) 'Integrating the East: The Labour Market Effects of Immigration', CEPR Discussion Paper no. 1235, Centre for Economic Policy Research, London.
Bauer, T. (1997) 'Do Immigrants Reduce Native Wages? Evidence from Germany', Paper presented at the European Association of Population Economists, Essex University.

Bauer, T., Epstein, G. and Gang, I. (2002) 'Enclaves, Language and the Location of Migrants', CEPR Discussion Paper no. 527, Centre for Economic Policy Research, London.

Bhagwhati, J. and Hamada, K. (1974) 'The Brain Drain, International Integration of Markets for Professional and Unemployment', *Journal of Development Economics*, vol. 1, pp. 19–24.

Bertola, G. (1989) 'Factor Mobility, Uncertainty and Exchange Rate Regimes', in M. Cecco and A. Giovannini (eds), *A European Central Bank? Perspectives on Monetary Unification after 10 Years of the EMS* (Cambridge: Cambridge University Press).

Bohning, W.R. (1970) 'The Differential Strength of Demand and Wage Factors in Intra-European Labour Mobility: with Special Reference to West Germany', 1957–1968, *International Migration*, vol. 8, pp. 191–210.

Boyer, G.R., Hatton, T.J. and O'Rourke, K. (1993) 'The Impact of Emigration on Real Wages in Ireland 1850–1914', CEPR Discussion Paper no. 854, Centre for Economic Policy Research, London.

Briere, B. and Lambert, S. (1996) 'What Motivates Migrants to Remit? The Case of the Dominican Sierra', mimeo University of California, Berkeley.

Brücker, H. (2000) 'The Impact of Eastern Enlargement on Employment and Labour Markets in the EU Member', final report on Employment and Social Affairs – Key Documents, *http://europa.eu.int/comm/dgs/employment_social/parta.pdf*

Carrington, W., Detragiache, E. and Vishwanath, T. (1996) 'Migration with Endogenous Moving Costs', *American Economic Review*, vol. 86, no. 4, pp. 431–45.

Corry, D. (ed.) (1996) *Economics and European Union Migration Policy*, Institute for Public Policy Research, London.

Cuka, E., Papapanagos, H., Polo, N. and Sanfey, P. (1999) 'Labour Market Developments and Policy During Transition in Albania: An Analytical Overview', Paper presented at the IEFS Conference on Labour and Capital Markets in Europe, IEFS (Internal Economic and Finance Society), City University, London, April.

Dolado, J., Jimeno, J. and Duce, R. (1996) 'The Effects of Migration on the Relative Demand for Skilled versus Unskilled Labour: Evidence from Spain', CEPR Discussion Paper no. 1476, Centre for Economic Policy Research, London.

Eichengreen, B. (1997) *European Monetary Unification* (Cambridge, Mass.: MIT Press).

Ermisch, J. (1995) 'Demographic Developments and European Labour Markets', *Scottish Journal of Political Economy*, vol. 42, pp. 331–46.

Eriksson, T. (1989) 'International Migration and Regional Differentials in Unemployment and Wages: Some Empirical Evidence from Finland' in Gordon *et al.*, *European Factor Mobility* (New York: St Martin's Press).

Espenshade, T.J. (1995) 'Unauthorized Immigration to the United States', *Annual Review of Sociology*, 21, pp. 195–216.

Faini, R. (1993) 'Trade, Aid and Migrations: Some Basic Policy Issues', *European Economic Review*, vol. 37, pp. 35–442.

Faini, R., De Melo, J. and Zimmermann, K. (1999) *Migration: The Controversies and the Evidence* (Cambridge: Cambridge University Press).

Faini, R. and Venturini, A. (1994) 'Migration and Growth: The Experience of Southern Europe', CEPR Discussion Paper no. 964, Centre for Economic Policy Research, London.

Fassmann, H. and Muntz, R. (1994) 'Patterns and Trends of International Migration in Western Europe', in H. Fassmann and E. Munz, *European Migration in the Late Twentieth Century* (Aldershot: Edward Elgar).

Fields, G.S. (1991) 'Place to Place Migration: Some New Evidence', *Review of Economics and Statistics*, vol. 61, pp. 21–32.

Fischer, P. and Straubhaar, T. (1997) 'Is Migration into EU Countries Demand Based?', in D. Corry (ed.), *Economics and European Union Migration Policy*, Institute for Public Policy Research, London.

Funkhouser, E. (1992) 'Mass Emigration, Remittances, and Economic Adjustment: The Case of El Salvador In the 1980s', in G. Borjas and R. Freeman (eds), *Immigration and the Work Force* (Chicago: University of Chicago Press).

Galor, O. and Stark, O. (1991) 'The Probability of Return Migration. Migrants Work Efforts and Work Performance', *Journal of Development Economics*, 35, pp. 399–405.

Geary, P. and Ograda, C. (1989) 'Post-war Migration between Ireland and the United Kingdom: Models and Estimates', in L. Gordon *et al.*, *European Factor Mobility* (New York: St Martin's Press).

Ghatak, S.P., Levine and Price, S.W. (1996) 'Migration Theories: An Assessment', *Journal of Economic Surveys*, vol. 10, pp. 159–98.

Ghatak, S.P. and Daly, V. (1998) 'East–West European Migration: Questions and Some Answers', Paper presented at the IEFS-UK Conference, City University, April, London.

Ghosh, B. (1996) 'Economic Migration and the Sending Countries', in J. Van den Broeck (ed.), *The Economics of Labour Migration* (London: Edward Elgar).

Goto, J. (1998) 'The Impact of Migrant Workers on the Japanese Economy', *Japan and the World Economy*, 10, pp. 63–83.

Gross, D.M. (2002) 'Three Million Foreigners, Three Million Unemployed? Immigration Flows and The Labour Market in France', *Applied Economics*, pp. 1969–83.

Haisken-De New, J.P. and Zimmermann, K. (1996) 'Wage and Mobility Effects of Trade and Migration', CEPR Discussion Paper no. 1318, Centre for Economic Policy Research, London.

Harris, J.R. and Todaro, M.P. (1970) 'Migration Unemployment and Development: A Two-Sector Analysis, *American Economic Review*, 60, pp. 126–42.

Hartog, J. and Vriend, N. (1989) 'Post-War International Labour Mobility: The Netherlands', in Gordon *et al.*, *European Factor Mobility* (New York: St Martin's Press).

Hazari, B.R. (1994) 'An Analysis of the Impact of Outmigration on Unemployment, Income and Structural Change', *Journal of International Trade and Economic Development*, vol. 3, pp. 165–75.

Hicks, J.R. (1932) *The Theory of Wages* (London: Macmillan – Palgrave).

Hughes, G. and McCormick, B. (1994) 'Did Migration in the 1980s Narrow the North–South Divide?', *Economica*, 61, pp. 509–27.

Jahn, A. and Straubhaar, T. (1996) 'On the Political Economy of Illegal Immigration', Paper presented at the 1996 ESPE Conference, Uppsala, May, European Society for Population Economics.

Johnson, P. and Zimmermann, K. (1993) *Labour Markets in an Ageing Europe* (Cambridge: Cambridge University Press).

Katseli, L.T. and Glytsos, N.P. (1989) 'Theoretical and Empirical Determinants of International Labour Mobility: A Greek–German Perspective', in I. Gordon and A.P. Thirlwall (eds), *European Factor Mobility* (New York: St Martin's Press).

Kau, J.B. and Sirmans, C.F. (1976) 'New, Repeat, and Return Migration: A Study of Migrant Types', *Southern Economic Journal*, 43, pp. 1144–8.

Kohli, U. (1999) 'Trade and Migration: A Production-Theory Approach', in Faini *et al.* (eds), *Migration, the Controversies and the Evidence* (Cambridge: Cambridge University Press).

Lianos, T. (2001) 'Illegal Migrants to Greece and their Choice of Destination', *International Migration Quarterly Review*, vol. 39, pp. 3–28.

Lianos, T., Sarris, A. and Katseli, L. (1996) 'Illegal Immigration and Local Labor Markets: The Case of Northern Greece', *International Migration Review*, 34, pp. 449–83.

Lundborg, P. (1991) 'Determinants of Migration in the Nordic Labour Market', *Scandinavian Journal of Economics*, vol. 93, pp. 363–75.

Markusen, J.R. (1983) 'Factor Movements and Commodity Trade as Complements', *Journal of International Economics*, vol. 14, pp. 341–56.

Massey, D.S. (1990a) 'The Social and Economic Origins of Immigration', *Annals of the American Academy of Political and Social Sciences*, vol. 510, pp. 60–72.

Massey, D.S. (1990b) 'Social Structure, Household Strategies and the Cumulative Causation of Migration', *Population Index*, vol. 56, pp. 1–26.

McConnell, C.R. and Brue, S. (1995) *Contemporary Labor Economics* (New York: McGraw Hill).

Miyagiwa, K. (1991) 'Scale Economies in Education and the Brain Drain Problem', *International Economic Review*, vol. 32, pp. 743–59.

Mohlo, I. (1986) 'Theories of Migration: A Review', *Scottish Journal of Political Economy*, vol. 33, November.

Molle, W. and Van Mourik, F. (1989) 'A Static Explanatory Model of International Labour Migration to and in Western Europe' in I. Gordon *et al.*, *European Factor Mobility* (New York: St Martin's Press).

Molle, W. (1988) 'International Movements of Labour Under Conditions of Economic Integration: The Case of Western Europe', *Journal of Common Market Studies*, vol. 26, pp. 317–39.

Mountford, A. (1997) 'Can a Brain Drain be Good for Growth in the Source Economy?' *Journal of Development Economics*, vol. 53, pp. 287–303.

Mundell, R. (1961) 'A Theory of Optimum Currency Areas', *American Economic Review*, vol. 51, pp. 657–65.

Mundell, R. (1957) 'International Trade and Factor Mobility', *American Economic Review*, vol. 47, pp. 321–35.

O'Grada, C. (1986) 'Determinants of Irish Emigration: A Note', *International Migration Review*, vol. 20, pp. 651–6.

OECD (1999) *Trends in International Migration*, SOPEMI.

Rotte, R. and Volger, M. (1998) 'Determinants of International Migration: Empirical Evidence for Migration from Developing Countries to Germany', CEPR Discussion Paper no. 1920, Centre for Economic Policy Research, London.

—, Volger, M. and Zimmermann, K. (1996) 'Asylum Migration and Policy Coordination in Europe', Discussion Paper, SELAPO, University of Munich.

Rourke, K. (1996) 'Trade, Migration and Convergence: An Historical Perspective', CEPR Discussion Paper no. 1319, Centre for Economic Policy Reserach, London.

Russell, S. and Teitelbaum, M. (1992) 'International Migration and International Trade', World Bank Discussion Paper no. 160, World Bank, Washington DC.

Schoorl, J., De Bruijn, B., Kuiper, E. and Heering, L. (1996) 'Migration from African and East Mediterranean Countries to Western Europe', Paper presented at the Mediterranean Conference on Population, Migration and Development, Council of Europe, Strasbourg, June.

Sjaastad, L.A. (1962) 'The Costs and Returns of Human Migration', *Journal of Political Economy*, vol. 70, pp. 80–93.

Stark, O. (1991) *The Migration of Labor* (Cambridge, Mass.: Basil Blackwell).

Stalker, P. (2000) *Workers Without Frontiers*, International Labour Office, Geneva.

Straubhaar, T. (1988) *On the Economics of International Migration* (Bern and Stuttgart: Verlag Paul Haupt).

Van den Broeck, J. (1996) *The Economics of Labour Migration* (London: Edward Edgar).

Venturini, A. (1997) 'Competition or Complementarity of Illegal Immigrants: The Italian Case', Paper presented at the EALE Annual Conference 1997, Aarhus, Denmark.

Withers, G. (1994) 'Migration', in P. Kenen (ed.), *Managing the World Economy*, pp. 311–37.

Wellisch, D. and Walz, U. (1998) 'Why do Rich Countries Prefer Free Trade over Free Migration? The Role of the Modern Welfare State', *European Economic Review*, vol. 42, pp. 1595–1612.

Werner, H. (1996) 'Economic Integration and Migration: The European Case', in J. Van der Broeck (ed.), *The Economics of Labor Migration* (Brookfield, USA: Edward Elgar).

Zimmermann, K. (1995) 'Tackling the European Migration Problem', *Journal of Economic Perspectives*, 9, pp. 45–62.

Zimmermann, K. (1996) 'European Migration Push and Pull', *International Regional Science Review*, 19 (1–2), pp. 95–128.

Index